LABOUR IMMIGRATION IN SOUTHERN EUROPE

Research in Migration and Ethnic Relations Series

Series Editor: Dr John Wrench, *Senior Researcher,*
The University of Southern Denmark

Editorial Board:Danièle Joly CRER; Maykel Verkuyten ECOMER

The *Research in Migration and Ethnic Relations Series* is a joint series of the Danish Centre for Migration and Ethnic Studies, University of Southern Denmark; the Centre for Research in Ethnic Relations, University of Warwick; and the European Research Centre on Migration and Ethnic Relations, Utrecht University. Books in the series are intended to be of interest to students and scholars of migration, nationalism, racism and ethnic relations. The series aims in particular to publish volumes with a comparative European focus, or those nationally-based studies which have a broader relevance to international issues of migration and ethnic relations.

A mis padres, José y María, y a mi hermana Maite

Dansk Center for Migration
og Etniske Studier

EUROPEAN RESEARCH CENTRE
ON MIGRATION & ETHNIC RELATIONS

Labour Immigration in Southern Europe

African Employment in Iberian Labour Markets

CRISTÓBAL MENDOZA
Universidad de Guadalajara

ASHGATE

Published by
Ashgate Publishing Limited
Gower House
Croft Road
Aldershot
Hants GU11 3HR
England

Ashgate Publishing Company
Suite 420
101 Cherry Street
Burlington, VT 05401-4405
USA

Ashgate website: http://www.ashgate.com

British Library Cataloguing in Publication Data
Mendoza, Cristóbal
    Labour immigration in southern Europe : African employment
    in Iberian labour markets. - (Research in migration and
    ethnic relations series)
    1. Alien labor, African - Spain 2. Alien labor, African -
    Portugal
    I. Title
    331.6'26046

Library of Congress Cataloging-in-Publication Data
Mendoza, Cristóbal, 1967-
    Labour immigration in Southern Europe : African employment in Iberian labour
    markets / Cristóbal Mendoza.
        p. cm. -- (Research in migration and ethnic relations series)
    Originally presented as the author's thesis (doctoral)--King's College London.
    Includes bibliographical references and index.
    ISBN 0-7546-1898-6
        1. Alien labor, African--Spain. 2. Alien labor, African--Portugal. I. Title: African
    employment in Iberian labour markets. II. Title. III. Series.

    HD 8584 M46 2004
    331.6'26046--dc21

                                                                            2002032696

ISBN 0 7546 1898 6

Printed and bound by Athenaeum Press, Ltd.,
Gateshead, Tyne & Wear.

Contents

List of Figures

List of Tables

Acknowledgements

First of all I would like to express my gratitude to the European Commission which funded twice my projects on African employment in Iberia. Without this financial help, it would not have been possible to complete my PhD in the Department of Geography at King's College London.

My PhD supervisor, Keith Hoggart, knows this thesis as well as myself. He has been a supportive, patient, humorous supervisor in my years in the Geography Department at King's. Certainly he has taught me far more than the knowledge and skills for writing a PhD thesis. Thanks very much, Keith.

Ever since she guided me through my first steps in the research field of migration in the early 1990s, Àngels Pascual de Sans has been a supportive supervisor, collaborator and friend. *Moltes gràcies*, Àngels. The Migration Group at the Autonomous University of Barcelona reacted rapidly to my urgent need of data. Thanks very much. Jorge Malheiros at Lisbon University was also in the right place at the right time. *Obrigado*, Jorge. The Drawing Office at King's College made the maps in record time. Many thanks to Roma Beaumont and Caterine Megan. Finally many thanks to El Colegio de la Frontera Norte at Tijuana, México, for supporting three and half years of research in the field of migration in northern Mexico. Throughout these years I have been able to conduct my research on Southern Europe from a different perspective (and geography) in an encouraging environment.

This thesis would not have been possible without the collaboration of many people outside the academic world who helped me with my fieldwork. Indeed the list is too long and my memory too short. Those that spring to mind are: Raúl and Dolors (Palafrugell GRAMC Association, Girona), Gemma (La Pera, Girona), Conxa and El Gato (El Sugué, Torroella de Fluvià, Girona), Montse Canuda (social services of La Selva), Seta, Lluis and Conxa (Asdiga Association, La Bisbal, Girona, *quines festes*!), Chelo (Ministry of Labour and Social Security in Girona), Núria Ordoñez (social services of Sant Pere Pescador, Girona), Carme Noguera (Cáritas in Figueres, Girona), the social services of Blanes (Girona), Paco

Muñoz at the Social Science Library at the Universitat Autònoma de Barcelona (Bellaterra, Barcelona), Concha at the Dirección General de Migraciones Library (Madrid), Alcestina Tolentino (Cape Verdean Association, Lisbon), André Moreira (Cape Verdean Association, Seixal), Fernando Ká (Guinea-Bissau Association, Chelas, Lisbon), Maria de Lourdes (Obra Católica Portuguesa de Migrações, Lisbon), Maria de la Graça (social services of Olhão) and the social services of Albufeira, Portimão (Algarve) and Seixal (Península de Setúbal).

My interviewees showed much interest in my work (and displayed considerable patience). Unfortunately I cannot mention by name the 220 Africans who suffered from my hour-long questionnaire. I remember some interviewees with special *cariño* Boubou, Doudou and David in Sant Pere Pescador, Fatima in La Bisbal (lovely couscous), my interviewees in the Palafrugell *Casino*, Hammed in Palafrugell, Alpha in Figueres, 'el morito fino' in La Bisbal d'Empordà, my interviewees in the Bairro dos Pescadores (Quarteira), Matilde in Quarteria, Silvestre in Albufeira, Irene in Faro, Miguel in Olhão, José in Seixal and Zé in Setúbal.

Many thanks indeed to the employers willing to be interviewed. Their down-to-earth information on labour market dynamics proved invaluable. The agricultural employers awoke my interest in farming, and the construction employers at both sides of the border made me reassess the relevance of the state.

My friends have also been a very supportive group. My most sincere thanks must go to Mercedes Carbayo-Abengózar (Nottingham), Teresa Rosell (Castelló d'Empúries, Girona), Roser Cusó (Paris), Helena Vasques (Lisbon), María José González and Pau Miret (Barcelona), Raúl Lardiés (Zaragoza), Paula Pennnane, 'Georges', Fu, Fernando Gracia and Charles Wilson (London), Christian Zlolniski and Hugo Hurtado (Tijuana), and Maru de la O and Alejandro Canales (Guadalajara) who never doubted that I would complete this work.

Last but not least, my family (my *padres* and *hermana*) who have always been a solid reference point in my erratic life. I own them much of what I am (well, only the positive side).

1 Iberia in the New International Migration Map

The Iberian Peninsula currently receives a considerable number of immigrants from developing countries. This is new. The Peninsula has traditionally been a labour exporter; first to the Americas, then to Central and Northern Europe. The turnaround from emigration to immigration has been dated as 1975 for Spain and 1981 for Portugal (King and Rybaczuk, 1993). Even if this turnaround has been recent, this does not mean that Iberia did not attract immigrants before the mid-1970s. For Spain statistics record substantial growth in the number of foreign residents in the 1960s. To be specific, the 148,400 foreigners who lived in Spain in 1970 were more than twice the 1960 figure (Instituto Nacional de Estadística, 1962a; 1972a). This increase was mostly comprised of immigrants from Central and Northern Europe, who either took jobs associated with foreign direct investment in the country or came to retire in Spain (Mendoza, 1994; Solana and Pascual de Sans, 1994). A similar trend was observed in Portugal in the second half of the 1960s, after this country joined EFTA in 1960, reduced controls on foreign capital in 1965 (Hudson and Lewis, 1984; Lains, 1994), plus the increasing popularity of Algarve as a destination for tourists adding to the nation's appeal (Lewis and Williams, 1989).

More numerous than international immigration, internal migration and emigration were the two distinctive population movements in Iberia in the 1960s. In this decade, 4.5 million Spanish residents changed their municipality of residence within the country (Romero González and Albertos Puebla, 1996). As an illustration of the scale of internal migration in Spain, Cabré (1999) calculated that the population of Catalunya would be approximately three million (instead of six million in 1991), if it had received no in-migrants since 1900. As for international emigration, Nadal (1984) estimated that two million Spanish citizens left the country between 1960 and 1974. The bulk of both internal and international emigration in the 1960s originated in the same regions; namely, Andalucía, inland Spain and Galicia (García Barbancho, 1975; Nadal, 1984). By contrast, Portuguese emigration into Central and Northern Europe has considerably outnumbered internal movements since the 1960s (Cavaco, 1993; Peixoto, 1996). This huge emigration into Europe provoked labour shortages in construction and manufacturing in Portugal, which were filled by Cape Verdean workers in the late 1960s and at the beginning of the 1970s (Saint-Maurice and Pires, 1989; França, 1992).

Whether internally or internationally, migration is a key element in the recent development of the Iberian economies. Similarly for both countries, international emigration provided the Iberian economies with remittance foreign currency which contributed substantially to the balance of payments situation in the 1960s and 1970s (Payne, 1987; Pereira, 1992; Lieberman, 1995; Lopes, 1996a). Furthermore, emigration alleviated would-be social upheavals under both the Portuguese and the Spanish dictatorships, as it expelled 'redundant' workers (Fontana and Nadal, 1976; Leeds, 1980; Merigó, 1982; Poinard, 1994). Yet internal migration played a different role in both countries. Thus, the growth of Spanish manufacturing activity and of tourism centres was heavily dependent on inflows of unemployed agricultural labourers. In the 1960s, such flows were encouraged by the shared interests of the rural *latifundia* landlords and the urban industrial bourgeoisie (Giner and Sevilla, 1979; Martínez-Alier and Roca Jusmet, 1988). With Franco's strict control of the labour force through the regime's trade unions [*sindicatos verticales*], migration helped trigger mechanisation in agriculture, industrialisation and urban growth (Naredo, 1986). By contrast, there were weak connections between agriculture and manufacturing in Salazar's Portugal; the former stagnated as a result of high subsidy policies, while the latter developed through the importation of cheap raw materials and labour from Portugal's colonies (Sapelli, 1995).

From the late 1970s and into the 1980s, partly on account of return migration to regions of origin, migration balances changed between the Spanish Autonomous Communities. Thus, whereas Andalucía and Extremadura experienced positive migration balances with the rest of Spain in the 1980s, Catalunya and País Vasco recorded the opposite (Romero González and Albertos Puebla, 1996). Reasons for this turnaround lie in a reduction in income differentials across Spain,[1] alongside new economic dynamics in agriculture and tourism areas that previously suffered from out-migration (e.g. on the effects of intensive farming in Almería, see Tout, 1990). This has stimulated return migration, and has lessened out-migration. Yet, internal migration has been reduced enormously in Spain in the 1980s and 1990s (Olano, 1990; Blanco Gutiérrez, 1993; Bentolila, 1997). In the case of Portugal, Lisbon and Porto likewise attracted less immigrants over the 1980s and early 1990s, although the traditional movement from inland Portugal to coastal areas does persist (Peixoto, 1996). This is because substantial labour surpluses still exist in agricultural areas (García Lizana and Alcudia, 1990; André, 1991).

Contrary to this pattern of reduced internal migrant volumes, immigrants from developing countries have moved increasingly into Iberia. This is one reason why the international migration balance has turned from negative to positive in Southern Europe. Yet initially the shift to a positive international migration balance resulted mainly from a decrease in the volume of emigration[2] and the return movement by their own nationals, consequent upon the closure of Central and Northern European job openings during the 1970s economic recession (and, for Portugal, upon the African decolonisation process).[3] However, once return migration slowed, it was immigration that led to the current positive international migration balance in Iberia (as in other Southern European countries).

Iberia, a New Immigration Area

In 1996, more than half a million foreigners lived in Spain (Table 1.1 on next page). This constituted 1.4 per cent of the total population of the country. This percentage is slightly lower than for Portugal. Here, there were 172,912 non-Portuguese residents in 1996, which constituted 1.7 per cent of the population. Table 1.1 shows that there is a wide range of origin countries for these immigrants.

Behind these heterogeneous figures, some trends can be observed:

- A sizeable immigration inflow from Central and Northern Europe, and from the USA, which is composed of both professionals and business-owners (see, for instance, Mendoza, 1994, for Germans in transnational corporations in Catalunya, or Lardíes-Bosque, 1997, on European business-owners in the tourism industry in the same region), as well as retired people (see Williams et al., 1997, for an analysis of this group, or Warnes, 1991, for the specific case of retired immigration into Spain).

- A notable level of migration amongst the Iberian countries themselves. The number of Portuguese in Spain is substantial, with this group being the fourth largest non-Spanish nationality. The academic literature on the Portuguese in Spain has found common trends between immigrants from developing countries and those from Portugal (see Colectivo IOÉ, 1987; Galaz, 1993; López Trigal and Prieto Sarro, 1993; López Trigal, 1996). To a lesser extent, and probably for different reasons, the

Spanish constitute the sixth largest foreign nationality in Portugal. Yet the number of legally resident Spaniards in Portugal has diminished since 1960, passing from 60 per cent of foreigners in 1960 to 5 per cent in 1996 (Instituto Nacional de Estatística, annual a).

Table 1.1 Main legally resident foreign nationalities in Iberia, 1996*

Spain	n. residents	%	Portugal	n. residents	%
Morocco	77,189	14.3	Cape Verde	39,546	22.9
Britain	68,359	12.7	Brazil	20,082	11.6
Germany	45,898	8.5	Angola	16,282	9.4
Portugal	38,316	7.1	Guinea Bissau	12,639	7.3
France	33,134	6.1	Britain	11,939	6.9
Italy	21,362	4.0	Spain	9,314	5.4
Argentina	18,426	3.4	USA	8,503	4.9
Peru	18,023	3.3	Germany	7,887	4.6
Dominican Rep.	17,845	3.3	France	5,102	3.0
USA	15,661	2.9	Mozambique	4,413	2.6
Total	538,984	100.0	Total	172,912	100.0

* The ten countries listed above amount to 65.7 per cent of the total Spanish foreign population and 78.5 per cent of the Portuguese.

Sources: For Spain, Comisión Interministerial de Extranjería (1997); for Portugal, Instituto Nacional de Estatística (1997a).

- Significant volumes of immigration from former colonies, where socio-cultural and linguistic ties play a key role; e.g. from Argentina to Spain (see, for an overview of the characteristics of Latin Americans in Spain, Palazón Ferrando, 1996), or from Brazil to Portugal (see, for a characterisation of the different immigrant groups in Portugal, Machado, 1997).
- The emergence of substantial inflows from two African countries (Moroccans in Spain and Cape Verdeans in Portugal), which now constitute the main foreign nationalities in Iberia. These inflows are especially remarkable because nationals from Africa were scarcely recorded in official statistics in Spain in 1980 (Figure 1.1).

**Figure 1.1   Legal foreign residents in Iberia, by nationality group
1980-1996**

Portugal

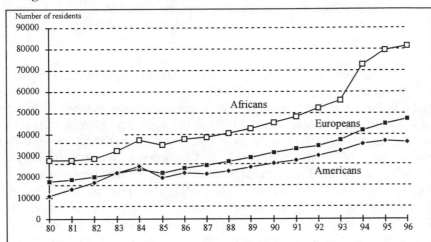

Spain

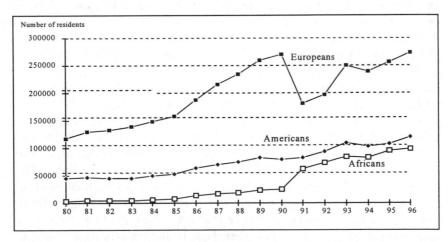

Notes:
a) Americans includes North, Central and South America.
b) The decrease in numbers in the Spanish figure in 1989 is due to a data file review which affected the numbers of EU nationals listed.

Source:
For Portugal, Instituto Nacional de Estatística (annual); for Spain, Dirección General de Migraciones (1996) and Comisión Interministerial de Extranjeria (1997).

Thus, there were only 4,067 legal Moroccan residents in Spain in 1980 compared with 77,189 in 1996 (Instituto Nacional de Estadística, 1985a; Comisión Interministerial de Extranjería, 1997). Even if relative growth in African nationals is not as remarkable as for Spain, Portuguese statistics record almost three times as many Africans in 1996 as in 1980 (Figure 1.1).

In addition to the legally resident African population, there is a sizeable component that is not officially registered. An indication of this is given in Figure 1.1, which shows sharp increases in the number of African nationals in 1991 in Spain and in 1994 in Portugal. These are not the result of large increases in inflows in these two years. Rather they are the direct consequence of legalisation processes that were undertaken in 1991 in Spain and in 1992-93 in Portugal; both of which brought previously illegal foreign residents into legality.[4] According to data provided by the Portuguese Foreigners and Borders' Service [*Serviço de Estrangeiros e Fronteiras*], three out of four of those who were 'legalised' in the 1992-93 campaign came from countries which have Portuguese as their official language (PALOP).[5] To be specific, out of the 39,166 foreigners who became a legal resident of Portugal at that time, 32.0 per cent were Angolans and a further 40.4 per cent were other PALOP nationals. Africans equally stood out in the 1991 legalisation process in Spain. Here Moroccans constituted 44.6 per cent, and other African nationals a further 12.3 per cent, of the 108,321 newly legalised residents (Dirección General de Migraciones, 1993). What is clear is that African nationals are increasingly living in Iberia. It is also clear that some of these nationals do not have a legal residence permit. Yet Izquierdo Escribano (1992) casts a word of warning here. By comparing legalisation data for previously illegal residents with estimations of the illegal population, he showed that researchers have tended to over-estimate the incidence of illegal residence.

The bulk of these new African residents are workers in Spain. Thus 75.6 per cent of legally-resident Africans were work permit holders (Table 1.2). This rate of paid economic activity is almost twice the figure for the total population in the country. For Portugal, even if the percentage of African residents who work is higher than for the country as a whole, the figure is not as significant as for Spain. This contrasting pattern points to differences in African communities in both countries. For Spain, it suggests that Africans are basically workers. By contrast, Table 1.2 suggests that Portuguese Africans are a more heterogeneous population, with a larger retired, housewife and child population than in Spain.

Table 1.2 Population and labour force by nationality in Iberia, 1996

	Portugal			Spain		
	Residents	Workers	%	Residents	Workers	%
Africans	81,176	43,365	53.4	98,820	74,693	75.6
Other non-EU	48,004	20,254	42.2	188,245	87,207	46.3
EU nationals *	43,732	23,191	53.0	251,919		
Population	9,831,000	4,780,000	48.6	38,848,000	15,872,000	40.9

* Spanish official statistics do not offer information about the labour market situation of EU nationals since 1992. In 1991, the percentage of the EU nationals who work in Spain was 29.4 per cent.

Sources: Data on population and labour force in both Portugal and Spain, Eurostat (1998). Data on foreigners: Portugal, Instituto Nacional de Estatística (1997a). Spain, Comisión Interministerial de Extranjería (1997).

So far it has been shown that international population inflows into Iberia in the 1980s and 1990s have seen significant increases in African workers. This has occurred in a context of increasing unemployment (for Spain at least) and changing labour markets (in both countries). As Figure 1.2 shows, Spanish unemployment rates have been almost twice the EU-15 average throughout the 1980s and 1990s. By contrast, Portuguese unemployment rates have always remained lower than the EU average. In fact, whereas Spanish unemployment has been the highest in the EU since 1981, the Portuguese economy has stood out as having one of the lowest unemployment rates in Europe.

The reasons for this contrasting picture have been explored by Blanchard and Jimeno (1995). After showing that differences in figures are not 'statistical artifacts',[6] these authors named the 'potential suspects' for the recorded divergence. Specifically, they investigated four economic indicators to see if they accounted for differences between the two countries:

• Fiscal policy. The ratio of general government receipts to GDP passed from 27 per cent in 1978 to 39 per cent in 1994 in Spain. Similarly, for Portugal, this percentage rose from 29 per cent to 46 per cent over the same period. Equal trends are observed with regard to the (high) fiscal deficit which both countries saw in the 1980s. Therefore, since government expenditure, deficits and debts are not higher in Spain than in Portugal, Blanchard and Jimeno (1995) did not consider them to contribute to higher interest rates, and consequently to higher unemployment.

Figure 1.2   Unemployment rates in Iberia, 1975-1997 (%)

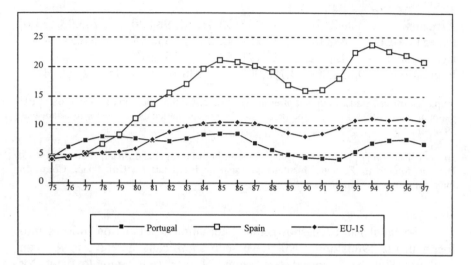

Source: Organisation for Economic Co-operation and Development (1997) and Eurostat (1998).

- Collective bargaining. Blanchard and Jimeno (1995) argued that labour market institutions are similar in the two countries. In both Portugal and Spain, sectoral collective bargaining dominates. However, sectoral bargaining in Portugal typically sets lower, less binding floors on firm-level wages than in Spain (for more information about the Spanish collective bargaining system, see Abellán et al., 1997; Portuguese collective bargaining is described in Ferreira, 1994a).
- Employment protection. These researchers argued that Portugal and Spain have the same level of employment protection, and have seen roughly similar changes to their employment protection systems, with a slow decrease in protection since the mid-1980s (for more information on the Spanish employment protection, see Toharia, 1997).
- Unemployment benefits. In this regard, Portugal and Spain are less similar. In Spain, workers are eligible for benefits if they have worked for one year in the last four years. This period was six months before the 1992 reform. By contrast, benefit is only payable if you have worked for one year and a half in the last two years in Portugal. This difference is reflected in the proportion of unemployed workers on

unemployment benefits; 59 per cent in Spain versus 41 per cent in Portugal.

With the exception of eligibility for unemployment benefit, Blanchard and Jimeno (1995) did not find substantial differences between Portugal and Spain. Contrary to their argument, other scholars believe that the peculiarities of the welfare state and of industrial relations in Spain cause rigidities in labour markets which in turn provoke high unemployment (e.g. Bentolila and Dolado, 1994; Salmon, 1995). The same lack of rigidity (or flexibility) in Portuguese labour markets is said to lie at the core of low unemployment here. In this regard, Modesto and associates (1992, p.171) have described the characteristics of Portuguese labour markets in the following terms:

> The main characteristic of the Portuguese labour market is its relative flexibility, when compared with other European states. The lack of rigidity in the wage determination process in the short run prevents workers from fully incorporating the productivity gain in their wage. This means that the adjustment in the market is made rather quickly which accounts for the low level of unemployment in Portugal.

The fact that gains in productivity are not incorporated into wages in the short run is easily demonstrated by comparing wages in Portugal with the rest of the EU. Thus, Branco and Melo (1992) have calculated that Portuguese wages were 60-65 per cent lower than Spanish ones. Indeed, labour costs are more comparable to those of Southeast Asia than to other European nations (e.g. in 1986, Portuguese labour costs were similar to Hong Kong ones and 10 per cent less than Taiwanese costs; Poinard, 1994). Thus Portuguese firms have faced less pressure than Spanish ones to mechanise their operations, which results in lower productivity per person in Portugal than in Spain (Brassloff, 1993). This model of labour-intensive firms in Portugal has been stimulated by the entry of foreign capital into industries such as electronic goods or food processing, which have been especially active since the 1980s (André, 1991; Branco and Melo, 1992). The Portuguese pattern of trade exhibits comparative advantage in industries that are intensive in unskilled labour, and comparative disadvantage in products that are intensive in either skilled labour or capital (Commission of the European Communities, 1991; Courakis and Roque, 1992; International Monetary Fund, 1995).

This model of labour-intensive firms is the reason for the country having high labour force participation rates (see Table 1.3). To be specific, the Portuguese economic activity rate of 72.6 per cent amongst those aged 15-64 (64.1 per cent for females in the same age group) is well above the

EU-15 average. Thus, not only has Portugal low unemployment, but its economy allows considerable shares of the Portuguese population to find a job.

Table 1.3   Labour force participation rates amongst the 15-64 aged population in the EU, 1996 (%)

	Total	Women
Austria	71.9	62.4
Belgium	62.5	52.3
Denmark	80.1	74.0
Finland	74.1	70.6
France	67.8	60.7
Germany	70.3	60.4
Greece *	62.0	45.3
Italy	58.5	43.7
Luxembourg	61.5	45.9
Netherlands	70.5	59.8
Portugal	72.6	64.1
Spain	61.8	47.6
Sweden	79.0	76.3
UK	77.3	68.4
EU-15	66.8	56.1

* Data for Greece, 1995

Source: Organisation for Economic Co-operation and Development (1997a).

By comparison, Spain, as with Italy, has the lowest activity rates in the EU (Table 1.3). For women, there is a 16.7 per cent difference between the activity rates of the two Iberian countries. Furthermore the Spanish economy not only provides jobs for a small percentage of its potential working population, but has the highest unemployment rate in the EU. The reason for extraordinarily high unemployment started in the last years of the Franco regime. Confronted with considerable social upheaval, oil prices were kept at artificially low levels to avoid the consequences of the international crisis that started in 1973 in the rest of Europe, but in 1975 in Spain. Maravall (1993, p.83) describes the hard times for the Spanish economy in the mid-1970s as follows:

Unions remained illegal, but the government was unable to control wage rises. From 1970 to 1979 wages grew forty percentage points ahead of productivity. Exports lost competitiveness, and the balance of trade deteriorated sharply. At the beginning of the transition, the Spanish economy was experiencing high inflation, an important trade deficit, growing unemployment, a collapse in profits, and an increasing public deficit as the government tried to compensate for the drop in external demand by expanding public expenditure.

As a consequence, in the 1975-1978 political transition, the crisis was more acute in Spain than in most of Europe (Tamames, 1985). Thus, 1,031,800 jobs were lost in the period 1975-1979, and a further 918,500 over 1980-1984 period (Espina, 1990), with unemployment rising from 4.3 per cent in 1975 to 11.1per cent in 1980 and reaching up to 21.1 per cent of the labour force in 1985 (see Figure 1.2). In this regard, Jimeno and Toharia (1994) have argued that the foremost cause of the massive employment loss of these years was the inefficiency and market weakness of most Spanish firms, whose viability was based on the existence of cheap labour and a lack of competition. Later periods of growth[7] have been unable to create enough jobs for the existing unemployed and new entrants into the labour market, so unemployment has never been below 15 per cent since 1982 (Figure 1.2). This is due to two factors. The first is related to growth in the labour force of more than one million over the period 1985-1990 (Salmon, 1995). These new entrants are primarily comprised of young people who were born in the Spain's 1960s baby boom, alongside females who have (re-) entered the labour market in the favourable economic context of the second half of the 1980s (Blanes, Gil and Pérez, 1996). Yet, even accounting for these new entrants, activity rates lie substantially behind other EU countries (see Table 1.3). The second reason for high unemployment is related to characteristics of Spanish labour markets. Contrary to what is observed for Portugal, Salmon (1995, p.30) is one of a number of researchers who have stressed that rigidity is a particular feature of Spanish labour markets. In his words:

A particular feature of the labour market has been its rigidity, maintaining uneconomic overstaffing and discouraging employment creation [...]. There has been a long tradition of job security dating back to legislation passed during the Franco era [...] and revised in the Basic Employment Law [...] and Workers Statute [...] in the early 1980s. Dismissals necessitated a lengthy redundancy procedure involving agreement from the government and trade unions [...] and large redundancy payments [...]. Inadequate training facilities, rent control and strong regional attachments further hindered labour mobility. Thus, rigidity was supported by the legal framework of employment and by labour market practices.

This might well be a faithful portrait of the Spanish labour market until the mid-1980s, but it should be noted that successive governments have implemented policies to increase labour market flexibility during the second half of the 1980s and 1990s. This turnaround in employment policies towards encouraging more 'flexibility' started in 1984, with the reform of the 1980 Workers' Statute [*Estatuto de los Trabajadores*], which introduced a variety of temporary contracts for different categories of workers (Palacio Morena, 1991).[8] Since then, new labour market regulations (e.g. on dismissal procedures, on collective bargaining, on strike action, on private employment agencies, on measures to encourage geographical mobility, and on new contracts) have been introduced with the same aim of increasing labour flexibility (Martín, 1997). In addition, regulations governing entitlement for unemployment benefits were hardened in 1992 (Toharia, 1997). None of these measures have reduced unemployment remarkably. Indeed, the ups-and-downs of Figure 1.2 suggest that the reduction of unemployment in Spain (and in Portugal) in the period 1986-1997 is related to a favourable international economic context (more than to the specific circumstances of these economies; see also Viñals and Jimeno, 1997). Furthermore, when new jobs have been created, these have commonly been temporary in nature. To be specific, temporary employment in Spain constituted 33.7 per cent of the employment in 1994, which was twice the 1987 figure (Organisation for Economic Co-operation and Development, 1996a). Especially notable here is the fact that the incidence of temporary employment is higher for the young (87.5 per cent for employees aged 16-19 and 70.6 per cent for those aged 20-24 in 1994) and for women (37.9 per cent for employed women, compared with 31.4 per cent for men; Organisation for Economic Co-operation and Development, 1996a). This throws doubt on the idea that the Spanish economy is not flexible. Indeed, if the indicator of flexibility is the number of fixed-term contracts, then Spain is the most flexible economy in the OECD. In this regard, Recio (1996) has argued that, more than job creation, policies aiming at increasing flexibility have stimulated casualisation.[9]

Despite contrasting differences over employment, there is one substantial similarity in the employment situation in Portugal and Spain. This is the role that the family plays in both economies, as well as in other Southern European countries (Mingione, 1995). For Portugal, family strategies complement relatively low wages with multiple activities, which often involve irregular engagements in manufacturing or service employment (Lewis and Williams, 1987). For Spain, even if this is changing fast, a large part of household strategies is still based on a relatively high wage for one working person (generally a male adult) which supports other non-working members of the family (Sanchís, 1992). It has even been suggested that the relatively high wages of mature male workers are at the expense of low participation rates for women, alongside particularly high unemployment rates for the youth (Castillo and Duce, 1997). The other side of the same coin is that, when living in family homes, young Spaniards may be not urged to take 'any' job, but one that matches their education and training. In this regard, jobs which carry negative social connotations can be rejected by increasingly more educated, young entrants to Spanish labour markets (Cabré, 1992).

When we place this picture for Spanish employment alongside continuing inflows of African labourers, it is not difficult to imagine why high unemployment has not stopped foreign immigration. Certainly, unemployment (or, at least, the national unemployment rate) does not look to be a key issue affecting immigration (given existing immigration rates). Furthermore, despite its low unemployment economy, Portugal is potentially the only net emigration country in the EU (Simon, 1991). For Simon, this is due to sociological (well-established immigrant networks in Europe) and economic reasons (labour surpluses in farming, plus high wage differentials between Portugal and other EU countries). As an illustration, the number of legal Portuguese nationals in Spain passed from 24,094 in 1980 to 38,316 in 1996 (Instituto Nacional de Estadística, 1985a; Comisión Interministerial de Extranjería, 1997), despite significant (adverse) unemployment differentials between the two countries.

Rather than unemployment, comparatively higher wages looks to be a key element for understanding why Portuguese (or African) workers move to Spain, although this does not explain why foreign labour is employed in a high unemployment context. However, higher wages in Central and Northern Europe (compared to Spanish ones) do not foster emigration from Spain (Poulain, 1996). Indeed, intra-European migration from Spain has decreased since the 1980s (Simon, 1991). The same is true for intra-Spanish migration, despite considerable unemployment differentials between the Autonomous Communities (Romero González and Albertos Puebla, 1996; Bentolila, 1997).[10] Indeed, not only do areas of high unemployment attract immigrants from other Spanish regions (some of whom are former emigrants), but certain areas in Andalucía and Extremadura are destinations for international immigrants. All this suggests that international migration does not arise from a simple adjustment process between EU regions, in which employment and wages tend to level through migration (as neo-classical approaches argue, see Chapter 2). There are other factors which need to be explored.

Opposite trends in wage rates and employment rates in the Portuguese and Spanish economies suggest that reasons for the employment of

Africans in these countries may differ. The objective of this book is to explore African employment patterns in these two rather contrasting economic settings. Inside each country, incorporation of immigrants into labour markets is examined in diverse local economic contexts and activity sectors. This is pursued through the analysis of two surveys on African employees[11] and a second on employers.[12] A four-type classification of the Girona municipalities in which immigrants were found to live, according to 1991 Census, was used as the base for the surveys (see the Methodological Appendix, for more details on how this classification was made). In all, 151 interviews were carried out with African immigrants in Spain. Out of the 151 Africans who were interviewed in Spain, 87 were Moroccans, 38 Gambians, 25 Senegalese and one person from Mali. In the particular case of Moroccans in Spain, the survey found immigrants from both rural and urban background, with considerable differences in formal education levels. For Portugal, the 69 interviewees were born in an ex-Portuguese colony in Africa (namely, Angola, Cape Verde, Guinea Bissau, Mozambique and São Tomé e Príncipe). Here the surveys on immigrants and employers were based on two types of municipalities. In all, 69 African-born immigrants were interviewed. At the time of interview, 31 of them had already obtained the Portuguese nationality either through family links or residence. Differences in labour market outcomes may arise depending on immigrants' origin or nationality. Finally, to provide a full picture of the reasons for African employment, this information is contrasted with insights from key informants (non-governmental organisations, key civil servants in municipal and state administrations, and trade unions), as well as observer participation in the studied areas; namely, Girona, Algarve and Setúbal.

Girona, Algarve and Setúbal

Situated in northeastern Iberia (see Figure 1.3), the Catalan province of Girona attracted an increasing number of non-Spanish nationals in the 1980s and 1990s, with foreigners passing from 0.8 per cent of Girona's population in 1981 to 3.3 per cent in 1995 (Table 1.4). This figure is almost twice the Spanish average. The growth of foreign residents in Girona should be placed in the context of the population dynamics of the province. Thus, Girona grew from 177,539 inhabitants in 1960 to 530,631 in 1996, which is almost a threefold increase (Valenzuela 1991, for the 1960 figure; Institut d'Estadística de Catalunya, 1997, for 1996 population register data). This growth was partly brought about by in-migration from the rest of Spain (Valenzuela, 1991). As well, Girona has always been a place of residence for a non-working, non-Spanish population, many of whom have come from Central and Northern Europe, because of the role of tourism in the area. Yet the share of Europeans in the total number of foreigners has fallen, as a consequence of the rise of African labour inflows over the 1980s and 1990s (Table 1.4; Figure 1.1).

Table 1.4 Demographic indicators for Girona, Catalunya and Spain

	Girona	Catalunya	Spain
1981 Census population	467,012	5,956,598	37,683,363
1991 Census population	509,628	6,059,494	38,872,268
1995 population	533,867	6,093,492	39,188,194
Growth 1981-91 (%)	9.1	1.7	3.2
Growth 1991-95 (%)	4.8	0.6	0.8
1981 foreign residents	3,912	39,640	198,042
1981 African residents	206	1,026	5,012
Foreigners/population (%)	0.8	0.7	0.5
Africans/foreigners (%)	5.3	2.6	2.5
1995 foreign residents	17,365	106,809	499,773
1995 African residents	8,650	36,408	95,725
Foreigners/population (%)	3.3	1.8	1.3
Africans/foreigners (%)	49.8	34.1	19.2

Sources:
　　For 1991 and 1981 population, Instituto Nacional de Estadística (1985, 1995).
　　For 1995 population estimates, Banco Bilbao Vizcaya (1997).
　　For 1981 foreign population, Instituto Nacional de Estadística (1982a).
　　For 1991 foreign population, Dirección General de Migraciones (1993).
　　For 1995 foreign population, Comisión Interministerial de Extranjería (1996).

Figure 1.3 The regional and provincial/*distrito* division of Iberia

Spain

Andalucía
1   Almería
2   Cádiz
3   Córdoba
4   Granada
5   Huelva
6   Jaén
7   Málaga
8   Sevilla

Aragón
9   Huesca
10   Teruel
11   Zaragoza

12   *Asturias*

13   *Balears*

Canarias
14   Las Palmas G. Canaria
15   Santa Cruz de Tenerife

16   *Cantabria*

Castilla-La Mancha
17   Albacete
18   Ciudad Real
19   Cuenca
20   Guadalajara
21   Toledo

Castilla y León
22   Ávila
23   Burgos
24   León
25   Palencia

26   Salamanca
27   Segovia
28   Soria
29   Valladolid
30   Zamora

Catalunya
31   Barcelona
32   Girona
33   Lleida
34   Tarragona

Extremadura
35   Badajoz
36   Cáceres

Galicia
37   A Coruña
38   Lugo
39   Ourense
40   Pontevedra

41   *Madrid*

42   *Murcia*

43   *Navarra*

País Vasco
44   Álava
45   Guipúzcoa
46   Vizcaya

47   *La Rioja*

Valencia
48   Alicante
49   Castellón
50   Valencia

Portugal

51   Aveiro
52   Beja
53   Braga
54   Bragança
55   Castelo Branco
56   Coimbra
57   Évora
58   Faro
59   Guarda
60   Leiria
61   Lisboa
62   Portalegre
63   Porto
64   Santarém
65   Setúbal
66   Viana do Castelo
67   Vila Real
68   Viseu

Autonomous Regions
69   Açores
70   Madeira

Figure 1.3   The regional and provincial/*distrito* division of Iberia

As Gozálvez Pérez (1995) has pointed out, Girona is possibly one of the Spanish areas where foreign workers will more easily increase in numbers in the future. This researcher has argued that the potential of the region as a future immigration area lies in its large tourism-oriented coast, which is associated with a large transient population, in the economic diversification of employment in the province (see Table 1.4), in the increasing importance of retired people in the demographic structure of inland towns, and on account of high provincial per capita incomes (in the Spanish context). As an illustration of this last point, the province passed from being the seventh highest in terms of per capita income in 1973 to be the second in the provincial ranking in 1995. Likewise, it has moved from eighth in 1971 to second in 1995 in terms of production levels per capita (Banco Bilbao Vizcaya, 1983; 1997). Valenzuela (1991) has held that tourism is centrally responsible for Girona's (good) economic performance.

Table 1.5 Economic indicators for Girona, Catalunya and Spain (%)

	Girona	Catalunya	Spain
Jobs by sector 1983			
Agriculture	12.4	6.2	16.9
Manufacturing	28.8	35.2	24.5
Construction	9.8	7.6	8.1
Accommodation and restaurants	9.0	4.3	4.9
Other services	39.9	46.6	45.7
Jobs by sector 1993			
Agriculture	6.5	3.3	9.5
Manufacturing	22.7	28.1	20.0
Construction	9.3	8.1	8.6
Accommodation and restaurants	16.6	6.2	6.8
Other services	44.9	54.3	55.1
Legal non-EU workers 1996			
Agriculture	17.6	12.2	15.2
Manufacturing	12.3	11.5	6.9
Construction	14.4	10.8	8.8
Services	36.5	56.7	64.4
Non-classified	19.2	8.8	4.7

Sources: For job data, Banco Bilbao Vizcaya (1985; 1997); for non-EU worker data, Comisión Interministerial de Extranjería (1997).

However, despite the number of jobs in accommodation services and restaurants, the share of services in provincial employment is similar to the Catalan and Spanish average (Table 1.5). What is not similar is the percentage of non-EU workers in service industries, with Girona having a more balanced distribution of non-EU workers across economic sectors (Table 1.5). This had implications for the survey undertaken for this book, as the 151 interviewed African workers lived in municipalities with contrasting economic characteristics.

Similarly to Girona, the percentage of foreigners in Algarve's population is the highest of the Portuguese regions (Table 1.6) and tourism plays a substantial role in providing jobs (Table 1.7).

Table 1.6 Demographic indicators for Algarve, the Setúbal *Distrito** and Portugal

	Algarve	Dist. Setúbal	Portugal
1981 Census population	323,534	658,326	9,833,014
1991 Census population	341,404	712,594	9,862,670
1994 estimated population	344,830	716,780	9,912,140
Growth 1981-91 (%)	5.5	8.2	0.3
Growth 1981-94 (%)	1.0	0.6	0.5
1981 foreign residents	3,895	7,258	62,692
1981 African residents	1,105	5,999	27,948
Foreigners in population (%)	1.2	1.1	0.6
Africans amongst foreigners (%)	28.4	82.7	44.6
1994 foreign residents	19,741	13,830	157,073
1994 African residents	6,215	10,621	72,630
Foreigners in population (%)	5.8	1.9	1.6
Africans amongst foreigners (%)	31.5	76.8	46.2

* Data on foreigners are only published at *distrito* level. The Setúbal *Distrito* includes the Peninsula of Setúbal and three Alentejo's coastal municipalities.

Sources:
  For 1991 and 1981 Portuguese population, Instituto Nacional de Estatística (1984; 1996c).
  For 1994 population estimates, Instituto Nacional de Estatística (1996d).
  For foreign population data, Instituto Nacional de Estatística (1982a; 1992a; 1995a).

Yet, there are considerable differences between the two regions:

- Even if the number of Africans rose from 1,105 in 1981 to 6,215 in 1994, the proportion of Africans amongst the foreign population has remained almost unchanged since 1981 (Table 1.6). In other words, growth in the number of non-Portuguese nationals in the region has been similar for Europeans and non-Europeans.
- Manufacturing does not have a key role in total employment in Algarve, unlike Girona. Furthermore, the few manufacturing industries in the region (like food processing firms) have been losing workers since the 1980s (see Table 1.7 which shows the declining trend in manufacturing employment in Algarve in the period 1981-1991).

Table 1.7 Employed labour force in Algarve, the Setúbal *Distrito* and Portugal, by economic sector (%)

	Algarve	Dist. Setúbal	Portugal [a]
1981			
Primary	25.0	9.8	19.7
Manufacturing	11.5	34.1	27.1
Construction	16.2	11.0	11.6
Accommodation and restaurants	9.8	3.0	2.7
Other services	37.5	42.1	38.9
1994 [b]			
Primary	10.6	5.7	11.5
Manufacturing	7.2	23.9	25.0
Construction	13.2	9.8	7.8
Accommodation and restaurants	20.1	5.0	4.4
Other services	59.2	55.6	51.3

Notes:
a) Only for continental Portugal. These data come from the Portuguese Employment Survey [*Estatísticas do Emprego*]. This survey does not cover the Autonomous Regions of Azores and Madeira.
b) The Setúbal *distrito* data are for 1991.

Sources: For 1981 data, and 1991 Setúbal data, Instituto Nacional de Estatística (1984; 1996c); for 1994, Instituto Nacional de Estatística (1995b).

- Agriculture is a more important employer in Algarve than in Girona. It gave jobs to 10.6 per cent of the labour force in Algarve in 1994; which is substantially above the Girona employment figure at 6.5 per cent in 1993 (yet, close to the Portuguese average; Table 1.7).

Given these differences, it is likely that African employment does not show as much inter-municipal dissimilarity in Algarve as in Girona. Hence, in order to broaden the employment base that was investigated in Portugal, two localities in the manufacturing-oriented Península de Setúbal were also examined (see Appendix 1). In absolute volume terms, the Península de Setúbal is the second area of concentration of African-born population in Portugal, after Lisbon. The first African inflows into the area occurred at the end of 1960s when Portuguese emigration left vacant numerous jobs in manufacturing and construction (Carreira, 1982; Saint-Maurice and Pires, 1989; França, 1992). The manufacturing base of Setúbal was largely based on heavy industries, but these suffered a remarkable re-structuring in the 1980s. Thus, in the period 1982-1984, 74 manufacturing firms closed down. For 1981-1985, 11,031 jobs were lost in the region (Torres, 1996). However, since 1986, new jobs have been created in light labour-intensive industries (Instituto de Apoio as Pequenas e Médias Empresas e ao Investimento, 1991). The manufacturing economic base of the Península of Setúbal offers a complementary view to Algarve's localities.

Structure of the Book

The aim of this book is the analysis of African employment patterns in two Southern European countries which are affected by similar overarching political-economic processes, as well as common immigration trends. Yet the economies of Portugal and Spain differ substantially one from another. African employment may also show contrasting patterns in both countries. To explore differences and similarities between Portugal and Spain, the surveys of African employees and employers cover the main economic sectors in which Africans are employed in both countries, as well as places with contrasting economic mixes (see Appendix 1 for more detail on the surveys). The results of these surveys are presented, discussed and contrasted with previous evidence from the literature throughout this book.

Before examining the survey results, Chapter 2 reviews the literature on labour migration in order to define the theoretical questions to be answered in this book. The theories which seek to explain international labour migration are largely based on principles of labour market economics and economic sociology. Here, the incorporation of immigrants into labour markets is viewed in terms of: (i) neo-classical and behavioural approaches; (ii) structural analysis; and (iii) ethnic entrepreneurship. These three groups of theories differ in their interpretation of immigrant incorporation into host labour markets. Yet they agree on the 'distorting' effect of both the state and social networks on labour markets. Thus, after reviewing these groups of theories, the chapter examines contrasting interpretations on the role of the state in managing immigration. In the current political situation of restricted immigration into Western Europe, social networks have been portrayed as playing a crucial role in channelling immigrants to jobs. The chapter therefore examines the extensive literature on immigrant networks. This literature distinguishes between those who argue that these networks are a hindrance to further job promotion and those who say that they are a great help in the incorporation and occupational progression of immigrants in host labour markets. A further consideration in this chapter is the literature on female migration. Effectively, this literature shows that changes in production practices in labour markets have smoothed the entry of immigrant female workers into more advanced economies. The review on the three main theories of immigrant labour market incorporation, as well as on the state, immigrant networks and gender, provides the book with questions to address from different (contrasting) ideological schools.

A first question revolves about the role of the state in managing international labour inflows. Chapter 3 places this role in the Portuguese and Spanish contexts. To explore the significance of the state in controlling, diverting and channelling immigrants in the Iberian economies, the legislative frameworks on immigration and naturalisation are presented and discussed. To illustrate the role of the state, the chapter uses data from both official statistics and my surveys. The relevance of this chapter lies in the fact that labour outcomes for non-EU immigrants may be highly conditioned by (restrictive) immigration policies. Indeed, partly as a result of their membership of the European Union and their geographical situation on the European mainland, the Iberian countries have been pushed to change their immigration legislation. As part of this re-structuring, processes of legalisation have been introduced for some illegally-resident foreigners. Despite attempts to harmonise policies across the EU, immigration remains a responsibility of each state. Therefore, the implications of the legislative framework on African employment are discussed separately for Portugal and Spain. In this regard, the chapter highlights the different approaches of the two Iberian states regarding immigration policies, as well as exploring its effect on African labour outcomes.

The next chapters contextualise African employment in specific settings by exploring work patterns in three economic sectors. Specifically, Chapter 4 focuses on farming, Chapter 5 on construction, and Chapter 6 on accommodation services and restaurants. Here the analysis is based on both African employees and employers surveys. To build up the picture of African employment in each sector, information from key informants is contrasted with views of employers and employees. Cross-border comparisons of the same economic sectors will highlight differences in both immigration policies and economic settings. Indeed, divergences across the border appear to be vital, for immigrants are employed in large numbers in, for example, farming in Spain, but not in Portugal. As well, within the same country, these three economic sectors show considerably different trends. This highlights how reasons for African employment differ by economic sector. As an illustration, Spanish farming (but not Spanish construction) has a large turnover in African employment. However, if Africans are found in the same unstable poorly-paid jobs at the bottom of Portuguese and Spanish labour markets, regardless of economic sector, then this conclusion has important theoretical implications. Underlying the analyses in these chapters then, there is an evaluation of the theoretical postulates outlined in Chapter 2.

Complementing the sectoral analysis, Chapter 7 focuses on localities. The underlying assumption of the chapter is that broader economic trends affect localities in different ways. In other words, local economic characteristics might shape economic activities, and, consequently, determine uneven (African) patterns of employment in the same industry. The point to explore here is if African employment varies due to local characteristics rather than simply economic sector or previous worker training and experience. In this regard, the Girona survey does cover African workers who live and work in municipalities with different economic bases. Specifically, four types of local economic structure were identified in Girona. For Portugal, the two regions of Algarve and Setúbal share few common economic trends. If African labour outcomes show no great differences between these regions, then this will mean that local employment characteristics hardly affect the involvement of Africans in labour markets. Assessing this question is the central focus of Chapter 7.

Chapter 8 complements the demand-side considerations of previous chapters with an examination of the characteristics of African workers. The first aim of the chapter is to evaluate whether the previous educational and occupational endowments of immigrants affect patterns of incorporation into Iberian labour markets. The 151 respondents to the Girona survey, as well as the 69 of the Portuguese one, incorporate varying experiences of immigrants who may (or may not) face relative common labour market positions, depending on their educational or job experience. The underlying questions asked here come from human capital theory. According to this theoretical position, workers attain and move between jobs depending on their skills or education. Thus, alongside immigrant characteristics, the issue of immigrant mobility patterns within Iberia (and further emigration out of Portugal and Spain) are examined.

Finally, Chapter 9 provides an overview evaluation of the validity of theories on immigrant incorporation in host labour markets for understanding African patterns of employment in Iberia.

Notes

1. With the Spanish average as 100, the difference in Gross Family Income between the Balearics and Badajoz (Extremadura), which are at the top and the bottom of the provincial league table, fell by 10 points over the period 1983-1995 (Banco Bilbao Vizcaya, 1985; 1997). For more information on the decline in inequalities in the Spanish provinces, see Villaverde Castro (1996) who supports the conclusion that this decline is due to changes in those provinces which initially had the lowest development levels.

2. Legal Spanish emigration changed from 834,100 for the period 1960-70 to 493,050 for 1970-81 and to 204,910 for 1981-91 (Dirección General de Migraciones, 1996). For Portugal, legal emigration dramatically fell from 66,300 in 1970 to 6,556 in 1984 (Commission of the European Communities, undated).

3. An annual average of 69,000 Spaniards returned to their home country in the period 1970-80 (King, 1984). For Portugal, the 1981 Census indicated that 505,087 residents lived in one of the nation's ex-colonies on 31 December 73. This constituted more than 5 per cent of the total population living in Portugal in 1981. The impact of return migration on Portuguese social and economic structures has been analysed extensively in the literature. Some examples are Pires et al. (1987) on *retornados* [return migration from ex-Portuguese Africa] and Brettell (1986), Reis and Nave (1986) and Cavaco (1993) on the impact of return migration from Central and Northern Europe on rural Portugal. For Spain, return migration has been studied by Rhoades (1978), Castillo (1980), Garmendía (1981), Solé (1988), Cazorla Pérez (1989), and Pascual de Sans and Cardelús (1990), amongst others. Pascual de Sans and Cardelús (1990) argued that, rather than return, this movement is a new migration, as the areas of origin at the point of emigration to Europe, and the destinations of 'return' migrants, are often different. In a high proportion of cases, rural-background emigrants prefer cities on their 'return'.

4. Two legalisation processes have been undertaken in Portugal (1992-93 and 1996) and three in Spain (1985-86; 1991-1992 and 1996).

5. PALOP refers to *Países Africanos de Lingua Oficial Portuguesa*. The PALOP countries are Angola, Cape Verde, Guinea-Bissau, Mozambique and São Tomé e Príncipe.

6. 'Official unemployment numbers in both countries are based on large labor-force surveys, using identical questions to assess whether somebody is unemployed. There is no obvious bias in the way the sample is designed or the way the survey is administrated' (Blanchard and Jimeno, 1995: 213-214).

7. The Spanish economy was the most dynamic in Europe in the late 1980s, with an annual growth rate at 4-5 per cent in the period 1987-1990 (Salmon, 1995). In the period 1985-1989, 1,950,900 new jobs were created (Espina, 1990).

8. Three types of temporary contracts were introduced: those for temporary jobs, those for fixed-term work (initially a minimun tenure of six months, which was raised to one year in 1992), and those for training and apprenticeships for young workers (Jimeno and Toharia, 1994).

9. Probably due to the percentage of employees on fixed-term contracts in Spain, the 1997 reform of labour market legislation introduced a new kind of permanent contract, with

incentives for employers to hire employees on a permanent basis (see Ministerio de Trabajo y Asuntos Sociales, 1998, for more information about current types of contracts).

10. Andalucía's unemployment rate (30.4 per cent) was three times that of Navarra (10.0 per cent) in 1997 (Instituto Nacional de Estadística, 1998c).

11. The survey on African employees was carried out between July and December 1995 in Girona and between January and June 1996 in Portugal. In particular, research attention was focused on the province of Girona in Spain and the region of Algarve and Peninsula of Setúbal in Portugal (to see the questionnaire see Appendix 2).

12. The survey on employers was carried out from July to October 1997 in the same regions as the previous survey of African employees. Thirty-two employers in farming, in construction, in accommodation and in two manufacturing industries (ceramics and metallurgical firms) were interviewed in Girona. For Portugal, 20 interviews with employers were concentrated on the construction, accommodation and metallurgical industries (the questionnaire on employers in on Appendix 3).

2 Theoretical Perspectives on Immigrant Labour Market Incorporation

As seen in Chapter 1, immigration into Iberia occurred in small numbers in the 1960s. By contrast, since the end of the Second World War, Central and Northern Europe have attracted a considerable number of immigrants from developing countries. This latter immigration experience has been illustrated extensively in the literature. Some of these studies are nowadays considered classics (see, for instance, Kindleberger, 1967; Böhning, 1972; Castles and Kosack, 1973). Although these studies differ on their theoretical approach, there is a general message that derives from this substantial research portfolio. This message can be summarised as:

> The overwhelming majority of immigrants in Western Europe have come since 1945, most of them in the late fifties and early sixties. The motivations of the movement have been primarily economic [...] The movements correspond both to the desire of the migrants themselves for higher incomes and to the need of Western European employers for additional labour to allow expansion. Typically, it is the workers who migrate first; non-working dependants are sent for only later, if at all. (Castles and Kosack, 1973, p.3)

Whether this literature is useful for the analysis of current international immigration into Iberia is another point. In this book, it is argued that this literature is of scarce interest for the study of African inflows into Iberia for four reasons:

- Even if international labour inflows into Southern Europe have increased in the 1980s and 1990s, they are smaller in volume than those to Central and Northern Europe in the 1950s, 1960s and early 1970s. In fact, legally-resident foreigners represent a small share of the total population in Southern Europe. To be specific, they constituted 1.7 per cent of the Italian population; 1.3 per cent for Portugal and 1.1 per cent for Spain in 1993 (SOPEMI, 1995). Although 1996 data show larger representations (1.4 per cent for Spain, Comisión Interministerial de Extranjería, 1997; 1.7 per cent for Portugal, Instituto Nacional de Estatística, 1997a), these stock figures are far below the representation of foreigners in Central and Northern Europe (e.g. for 1993, the figures were 8.5 per cent in Germany; 5.1 per cent in the Netherlands; and 3.5 per cent in the United Kingdom; SOPEMI, 1995). Whether this reflects the timing of inflows into Southern Europe or is a global trend in immigration is a moot point, for as Fielding (1993, p.14) has observed that '[...] the most important feature of mass migration under post-Fordist forms of production organization is its absence!'.

- Immigration into much of Southern Europe has occurred in a context of economic crisis and soaring unemployment. Even if European economies saw notable growth in the period 1986-1990, this expansion bore no comparison with the early post-war economic boom. Analysing the economic growth of Central and Northern Europe after 1945, Kindleberger (1967) has indicated that an essential factor in this growth was the substantial increase in non-agricultural employment. Some of the new job opportunities were filled by immigrants. According to this analyst, immigration played a key role in this growth, as it avoided wage inflation, which could have hampered the expansion of European economies. This picture does not correspond with the situation of limited job creation in the Iberian economies nowadays.

- Change in economic circumstances has seen counterpart shifts in political settings. Thus the political encouragement for immigration, as seen in the worker recruitment schemes that were implemented in several European countries in previous decades (e.g. the German *Gastarbeiter*), has now turned into openly hostile political concerns over the reception of foreign workers (Costa-Lascoux, 1989; Kastoryano, 1989; Convey and Kupiszewski, 1996; Marie, 1996).

- There is high diversity in the 'supply' countries involved in current international inflows into Southern Europe. There is no dominant country in the foreign inflows into Iberia '[...] to the extent that, say, Turks dominate in Germany, Maghrebins in France, or Afro-Caribbeans and south Asians in Britain' (King, 1993, p.286). Furthermore, unlike the relatively stable patterns of immigrant employment in Europe from the 1950s to mid-1970s, labour immigrants in Iberia (as in other Southern European countries) are characterised by high mobility, often informal sector economic activity and a tendency for ethnic groups to carve out 'niches' in host countries (King et al., 1997).

Aware of the partial relevance of previous research on inflows into Central and Northern Europe, several researchers have argued that

Southern European immigration need a different interpretive approach. In King and Rybaczuck's (1993, p.204) words: '[...] the waves of migration entering Southern Europe [...] have some historical parallels, but the search for historical analogy should not obscure the essentially new and specific context of the model of emigration into Southern Europe'. Early studies of immigration into Southern Europe explored the reasons for international migration turnaround in these countries, as they turned from places of international migration loss to gain. This was explained as being a result of a combination of push and pull factors, alongside other circumstances, such as geographical or cultural proximity (see, for instance, Montanari and Cortese, 1993; Pugliese, 1993). Amongst the push factors, scholars identify the importance of divergent standards of living, demographic differences and an inability of sender economies to absorb their existing labour force with a high level of education. For pull factors, the emergence of new labour market forms – segmentation and casualisation of labour demand and the consequent need for cheap, flexible immigrant labour – is considered a key factor in understanding current immigration.

Following this line of analysis, recent research has argued that there is demand for immigrant labour in Southern Europe owing to labour shortages which are not filled by home nationals (e.g. Cabré, 1992; King and Konjhodzic, 1995). This demand for immigrant labour is motivated by various processes. These include: modernisation, urbanisation and the tertiarisation of the Southern European economies and societies (for an overview of these processes, see Williams, 1984; Hudson and Lewis, 1985a; Hadjimichalis, 1987; Montanari, 1993); the dynamism of the informal economic sector (see, for Portugal, Lobo, 1985; Rodrigues, 1992; for Spain, Centro de Investigaciones Sociológicas, 1986; Recio, 1986; Martínez Veiga, 1989; Miguélez Lobo, 1989); the relevance of small-scale enterprises in the economy (for Portugal, see Vale, 1991; for Spain, Vázquez-Barquero, 1992); an enhanced level of education for most young people, which has led them to reject socially 'unacceptable' types of work (Cabré, 1992; Gabinet d'Estudis Socials, 1995; King et al., 1997; Huntoon, 1998).

For Iberia, there has been a noticeable increase in the amount of research on international immigration into both Portugal and Spain over the last decade. These studies tend to focus on quantitative aspects of immigration (i.e. recording the number of new residents and their characteristics, rather than processes of immigration), and are largely based on the analysis of official statistics (e.g. Muñoz Pérez and Izquierdo Escribano, 1989; Saint-Maurice and Pires, 1989; Gozálvez Pérez, 1990; Esteves, 1991; Izquierdo Escribano, 1992; Blanco Fernández de Valderrama, 1993; Solana and Pascual de Sans, 1994; Taller de Estudios

Internacionales Mediterráneos, 1996). More recently, some research has been undertaken using sample surveys of immigrants (e.g. Solé and Herrera, 1991; França, 1992; Colectivo IOÉ, 1994; Gozálvez Pérez, 1995; Ramírez Goicoechea, 1996; Mendoza, 1997). Even for this latter group of studies, most attention has been devoted to identify the characteristics of immigrants. Amongst the findings of these investigations, it is commonly agreed that new immigrants into Iberia are workers from developing countries, mainly from Africa, who usually do the least qualified jobs. Yet little consideration has been paid to the ways of incorporation of immigrants into Iberian labour markets and the impact these foreign-born workers have on local labour markets. Neither has much attention been given to the character of the labour markets that enable these workers to find a job in Iberia. Furthermore, there is a substantial lack of theoretical background to these studies, with few hypotheses tested using evidence from the surveys conducted.

This chapter reviews theories which are relevant for the study of patterns of incorporation of African workers in Iberian labour markets. These theories come from two main schools of thought; namely, labour market economics and economic sociology. The examination of different approaches that is offered here is accompanied by a review of empirical research on immigration experiences in developed countries. In parallel with this, the chapter questions the relevance of theoretical ideas in the existing literature for understanding patterns of Africans employment in Iberia, and explains hypotheses to be tested in this book.

The chapter first discusses theories of labour market economics. Here, there are two main groups of theories; those which are based on *neo-classical* assumptions; and the *Marxist-inspired structuralist* approaches. The main difference between these two is that, whereas the first depicts an homogeneous labour market in which workers' performances are related to their own personal endowments (e.g. education, job experience), the second portrays a segmented labour market. According to this second approach, workers' performances in labour markets depend on the segment in which they are, and not on workers' characteristics. That being stated, the stark differences that earlier manifestations of these groups of theories portrayed are now somehow blurred. Some neo-classical approaches now incorporate structural factors in their analysis (e.g. on the introduction of the role of the state in the neo-classical models, see Todaro, 1969; Harris and Todaro, 1970). Likewise some later developments in segmentation theory have included characteristics of the workforce in their understanding of labour markets (Morrison, 1990). All these theories deal with the incorporation of workers into labour markets. Yet, when examining immigrant inflows, it is clear that part of them is comprised of employers and self-employed workers. Even some analysts have held that small businesses and self-employed workers are proportionally more significant amongst immigrants than non-immigrants (Boissevain, 1984; Bailey, 1987; Light and Bonacich, 1988). Thus, to complement the analysis presented, the chapter reviews *ethnic entrepreneurship and ethnic enclave theories.*

The second part of the chapter examines two elements which may introduce 'distortions' to the assumptions of both neo-classical and structuralist approaches. These elements are the *state* and *social networks.* Unlike internal migration, international movements imply crossing a state border. This is not a superfluous element. For instance, for Germany and Switzerland in the 1950s and 1960s, state agencies recruited workers for their industries in the Mediterranean countries (see, for instance, Castles and Kosack, 1973; Castles et al., 1987; Hollifield, 1992). Even if the state does not directly recruit workers nowadays, it has a crucial role in deciding the number of immigrants that will be accepted inside their borders (and the purpose of their stay) (Costa-Lascoux, 1989; Kastoryano, 1989; Convey and Kupiszewski, 1996; Marie, 1996). The 'rationale' of the state is that these numbers should be conditioned by the economic conditions of the country of destination (especially, the unemployment rate). Set in this political (and economic) context, social networks play a crucial role in channelling information about jobs in destination countries (Grieco, 1987; Tilly, 1990; Portes and Sensenbrenner, 1993; Portes, 1994). Social network usage varies by the nationality of origin of immigrants in the same destination country (for Italy, see Campus and Perrone, 1990; for Spain, see Martínez Veiga, 1997) or by destination country for the same immigrant nationality (for the Turkish in several countries in Western Europe, see Böcker, 1995). Recent literature on immigrant networks also reveals that social networks are used in a different manner by men and women (Hanson and Pratt, 1991; Sassen, 1995). Differences by sex are not only restricted to networks, but affect other aspects of the process of incorporation of immigrants workers into labour markets (see, for instance, Phizacklea, 1983a; Morokvasic, 1984; Tienda et al., 1984; Harzing, 1995; Ortiz, 1996; Schoeni, 1998). Thus the final part of the chapter reviews literature on *female immigrant workers* in order to observe if there are 'peculiar' patterns of incorporation of immigrant women. These patterns will be contrasted with female immigrant experiences in Iberian labour markets.

Neo-Classical Approaches: The Human Capital Theories

The neo-classical approach to migration analysis can be traced back to Ravenstein (1889), Peterson (1958) and Lee (1966). Seen through this interpretative lens, migration basically takes places because of geographical differences in wages. Wages are in turn determined by the supply/demand of labour at a certain level of production. Put simply, if there are more workers than production requires, labour surplus makes wages descend. By contrast, labour shortages exert an inflationary influence on wages. Thus migration occurs from regions which have a large supply of labour (and low wages) to regions with a shortage of labour (and high wages), so bringing about positive effects in both regions.

Neo-classical approaches share some assumptions about the way labour markets function:

- The labour market is seen to fit people with different educational and occupational endowments efficiently into different jobs. If mismatches between the supply and demand for labour arise (and cause either unemployment or labour shortages),[1] they are occasioned by external elements to the labour market (e.g. the state or trade unions) that affect negatively the 'normal' functioning of markets (for a comprehensive review of the causes of labour market mismatches in developed economies, see Schioppa, 1991).
- Workers are assumed to be rational individuals in search of a maximum return on their human capital investment; namely, their years of schooling, on-the-job training and job experience (e.g. Hirshleifer, 1970; Gale, 1973; Greenwood, 1975).[2]
- Heterogeneity of the workforce arises from pre-market differences amongst people (i.e. their innate ability, upbringing and education) and not out of the operation of the labour market itself (e.g. Sjaastad, 1962; Becker, 1964).
- There is equilibrium in the operations of labour markets (e.g. Lee, 1966; Stark, 1991), so that an '[...] important contribution of economic theory is to describe the kind of equilibrium sorting that takes place in the market place' (Borjas, 1989, p.461).
- The economy responds more positively to higher profits than to higher wages (Gordon, 1989).[3]

If these assumptions correctly specify the reality of Iberian labour markets, immigrants should avoid the inflationary effects of labour shortages on wages. However, the idea that there are labour shortages is difficult to argue in a context of high unemployment, such as in Spain. More broadly, Coleman (1992) calculated that there was a hidden (non-employed) labour force of at least 30 million people in the EU. He has concluded that:

[...] increased immigration is not needed to satisfy quantitative work force deficiencies at least for the next ten or twenty years in Western Europe or the EC [...] Europe has very substantial reserves of employable manpower which greatly exceed any short-term demographic deficiencies. (Coleman, 1992, p.455)

These large 'reserves of employable manpower' tend to be disproportionately located on Southern Europe, with particularly high rates of un- and under-employment in Spain. Moreover, a logical result of the application of neo-classical assumptions is that greater migration occurs from regions with few employment opportunities into low-unemployment areas. However, intra-European migration has declined in the 1980s (Simon, 1991; Poulain, 1996), even though some nations saw substantial increases in employment, while maintaining relatively low unemployment levels (e.g. Germany, Britain), while others saw major increases in unemployment (e.g. Spain). It appears that intra-EU mobility is characterised by a rather specific kind of dynamics which disproportionately encompass certain categories of immigrant (namely, highly-skilled workers, youngsters and retired people; Simon, 1991; Kastoryano, 1994). But, while all this points to serious doubts over the appropriateness of neo-classical ideas to Spain's recent immigrant experiences, Portugal offers a quite different case. As stated in the previous chapter, the Portuguese economy is largely composed of labour-intensive industries which offer low wages in the EU context (Commission of the European Communities, 1991; International Monetary Fund, 1995). This is one reason for the country's low unemployment. Set in this context, the expansion of the Portuguese economy may need immigrant workers (as Western Europe did) to maintain its pace of growth. In this regard, labour shortages in construction have been reported extensively in the media (see, for instance, Expresso, 1996, which reported labour shortages in construction; Jolliffee, 1990, or Carvalho, 1997, who also denounced irregularities in the sector which mainly affected Africans).

Set in this context, this book explores if the characteristics of Portuguese labour markets are key reasons for increasing immigration into the country. The hypothesis to be tested is if a low unemployment, low wage economy makes it difficult for employers to find workers for the lowest-paid jobs. If this is so, immigrants could be playing a role in expanding the economy by avoiding the inflationary impact on wages that result from labour shortages. Information from employers, trade unions and employees are examined in order to investigate this point. Even if Spanish employers also face difficulties finding workers for the least-paid jobs, labour markets in Spain must function in a substantially different way.

Indeed, it is questionable whether it could be held that there are no workers available in such a high unemployment context.

Micro-Economics Issues in the Neo-Classical Literature: The Impact of Immigrants on Host Labour Markets

There are two main micro-economic issues on labour immigration literature: (i) the impact of immigration on a host labour market; and (ii) the performance of immigrants in the labour market of a destination country (Bauer and Zimmermann, 1994). Regarding the first of these, Borjas (1989) has argued that a natural starting point for analysing this type of question is a description of the interaction between immigrants, natives and capital in the production process, at a specific level of production. This interaction is commonly understood in the literature in terms of job competition between immigrant and non-immigrant workers; and in terms of the immigrant impact on general wages. Most of the existing evidence on labour market effects has been produced for the USA (Schmidt, 1994). Empirical research does not agree on the (positive or negative) interaction effects. On one side there is the view, as presented by DeFreitas (1991, p.229), that '[...] most prominent neo-classical writers on the subject long held that immigration was responsible for depressing the wages and increasing the unemployment of low-skilled labor'. Presenting the counter-argument is Borjas's (1989, p.481) conclusion about studies in the 1980s:

> [the] impact of immigrants on the earnings and employment opportunities of natives is very small [...] Immigrants, however, do have a significant impact on their own wage [...] The empirical evidence based on the neoclassical model of labor demand, therefore, does not support the claims that immigrants have been a major disruptive force in labor markets in the United States.

Some studies in Europe similarly report insignificant effects for immigration on unemployment (see for Germany, Winkelmann and Zimmermann, 1993 and Zimmermann, 1994; for France, Hunt, 1992). In this last country, Hunt (1992) argued that there is only weak evidence that the 1962 Algerian repatriates exerted downward pressure on wages. Likewise, for Germany, Zimmermann (1994) found that there is a small (yet significant) effect of foreigners on lowering the wages of blue-collar workers.

All these studies are based on retrospective analyses of either census or official survey data on wages, broken down by the nationality or origin of workers, and their occupation. This approach is not possible for Iberia, as information on wages are not disaggregated in this way in official sources. In this book, interaction between African and other workers is therefore studied through interviews with key informants, employers and African employees. Here, the key point is examination of competition (or substitution or complementary) between immigrant and non-immigrant workers. These processes are observed in two main settings; namely, in different economic sectors and in different types of locality.

Micro-Economic Issues in the Neo-Classical Literature: The Performance of Immigrants in Host Labour Markets

The second issue raised in neo-classical theories that concern us here is the performance of immigrants in labour markets. This question has been addressed by human capital theories such as Sjaastad (1962) or Becker (1964). In simple terms, these theories argue that there is a close connection between workers' investment in human capital (i.e. years of schooling, on-the-job training and job experience) and wages. In deciding investment in human capital, workers balance costs (e.g. time or money) and benefits (e.g. better career prospects) associated with any investment. From a human capital perspective, migration is an investment decision. The performance of immigrants in a host labour market is held to be a result of both the transferability of human capital between regions and the willingness of immigrants to invest in destination-specific human capital (Chiswick, 1978). The incentive to invest in destination-specific human capital depends on the socio-economic characteristics of immigrants (Bauer and Zimmermann, 1994). The underlining assumption of human capital theory is that immigrant prospects improve in labour markets as they 'adapt' to the new country. Here success is measured in terms of (high) wages.

Empirical studies of this issue are largely based on comparative research on the wages of immigrants with those of black and white local workers (e.g. Grossman, 1982; Borjas 1987), on the wages of different groups of foreign-born immigrants (e.g. Borjas, 1982) or on the wages of successive generations of immigrants (e.g. Carliner, 1980; Borjas, 1985). Chiswick (1978) was one of the first scholars to test human capital assumptions. His study of foreign-born men in the USA, as well as Long's (1980) research of foreign-born women in the same country, demonstrated the positive effect of 'Americanization' on earnings. Comparing Cuban refugees to other Hispanic groups, Borjas (1982) affirmed that Cuban refugees have been more successful in US labour markets than other Hispanic groups, because Cubans had '[...] accumulated significantly more human capital in the years *after* immigration' (Borjas, 1982, p.353). Cuban refugees are said to have a greater interest than 'economic immigrants' in adapting rapidly to the US labour market, since '[...] political refugees are likely to face higher costs of return migration' (Borjas, 1982, p.353). In short, these researchers argue that there is a correlation between wages and the degree of 'adaptation' of foreign-born workers in destination countries. This adaptation is measured in terms of investment in human capital after emigration. In all these examples, the focus is primarily on the newcomer and her/his ability to adjust (Schmitter Heisler, 1992).

The research literature on human capital theory is well developed in the USA. Yet it is arguable that this literature is valid for Europe. Schmidt (1994), for instance, on reviewing the literature on labour immigration into Germany concluded that evidence from the United States could not be translated directly to this European country. This is for two main reasons: First, because the process of wage and employment determination in Germany, with its institutionalised collective bargaining structure, is quite different from the United States. Secondly, because Germany has not experienced large-scale permanent immigration, as the United States has done (Schmidt, 1994). These two circumstances also apply to Iberia. For example, the immigration experience of Iberia is recent (see, for Portugal, Saint-Maurice and Pires, 1989; Esteves, 1991; França, 1992; for Spain, Izquierdo Escribano, 1992; Solana and Pascual de Sans, 1994; Taller de Estudios Internacionales Mediterráneos, 1996). Secondly, collective bargaining has a central role in determining wage and labour conditions in both Portugal (Costa, 1994; Ferreira, 1994a) and Spain (Roca Jusmet, 1993; Abellán et al., 1997).

Even if the circumstances in which immigration takes place in Western Europe are dissimilar from the US experience, job progression may occur as Africans stay longer periods in Iberia. In this book, job progression is taken to be synonymous with a move toward a more skilled, permanent type of employment. The key question is if this progression (if it exists) occurs as a consequence of immigrant 'adjustment' to Iberian labour markets. It is recognised here that the measurement of immigrant 'adjustment' in labour markets is a controversial point. For instance, some immigrant groups need to make greater efforts than others in order to 'adjust'. As an example, most immigrants from the former colonies of Portuguese Africa who move to Portugal did not need to learn new (oral) language skills. Taking this point into account, along with different educational and job experiences, this book examines the job evolution of African workers in Iberian labour markets. It asks if their patterns of job changes are a result of immigrant investments in human capital. This 'investment' is analysed in two particular contexts: that of improvement in formal education and that of developing job experience.

Structuralist Theories: Dual Labour Market and Labour Market Segmentation

As a response to neo-classical theories, and merging the 1950s structuralist tradition in labour market economics with 'core-periphery' models (e.g. Wallerstein, 1974; Petras, 1981), structuralist theories on international labour migration were born in the 1960s and 1970s (Gimble, 1991). Structuralist ideas locate international labour migration within an evolving economic and political world order (Castles and Kosack, 1973; Castells, 1979). Here immigration is viewed as an integral part of a world capitalist system, which is based on politico-economic inequality and domination. From this perspective, immigration helps support the capitalist system by providing cheap labour to developed countries and by relieving pressure for political and economic change in the less developed sending countries, thereby helping preserve the position of local elites in less developed countries, as well as ensuring the continued dependence of less developed areas on more developed places (Schmitter Heisler, 1992).

From the point of view of labour markets, the structuralist perspective challenges prevailing equilibrium models. Drawing on evidence which shows that there is no simple relationship between the distribution of wages and human capital endowments in the employed population, structuralist theories hold that there is no a single, unified labour market. With many workers not able to attain stable participation in labour markets, alternative interpretations that emphasised the discontinuity or segmentation of labour markets were developed. As expressed by Doeringer and Piore (1971) and Piore (1975), the labour market is conceptualised as being segmented into primary and secondary sectors. The former is characterised by high wages, relatively good working conditions, stability and opportunities for promotion. The latter is a segment of low wages, poor working conditions, high labour turnover and little chance of promotion. The main difference between the two sectors is the way in which labour is 'priced', for the rules and procedures in 'secondary' labour markets differ from those which govern the pricing of labour in the 'primary' market (Morrison, 1990). Mobility across these two segments is restricted, which makes it difficult for workers in secondary labour markets to compete with primary workers (Loveridge and Mok, 1979; Gordon, 1995).

Apart from labour market dualism, other relevant considerations in structuralist ideas have been summarised by Massey and associates (1993, p.440-444) as:

- Wages not only reflect conditions of supply and demand, but also status and prestige. As a result, the wages which are offered by employers are not entirely free to respond to changes in the demand for or the supply of workers. A variety of informal social expectations and institutional mechanisms (e.g. collective bargaining, bureaucratic regulations, company job classifications) ensure that wages correspond to the hierarchies of prestige and status that people perceive and expect.
- Linked with this, the maintenance of social status is seen to be critical for the continuing motivation of workers. Acute motivational problems arise at the bottom of the job hierarchy because there is little social status to be maintained and (especially in the secondary sector) few possibilities for upward mobility. The problem is structural, according to this theoretical tradition, because the bottom cannot be eliminated from the labour market.
- As a consequence of its mode of operations, the economy creates permanent demand for workers at the bottom of the hierarchy. The jobs that these workers do are unpleasant, low-paid, have unstable prospects, and there is a small chance that promotion is associated with them. In many economies, the traditional source of labour for these jobs were women often working part-time (Barron and Norris, 1976; Burchell and Rubery, 1994; Plantenga, 1995; Rubery et al., 1998) and teenagers (Ashton et al., 1990; Sanchís, 1992).
- An additional consequence is that the dual nature of employment may be associated with the nature of the firm. A first distinction between firms revolves around the use of capital-intensive or labour-intensive techniques, with the first commonly being associated with more regular production and more stable demand for their products than the second. This generally creates jobs for primary workers in the first group of firms, and (more commonly) employment in secondary labour markets in labour-intensive firms (Berger and Piore, 1980).

Immigrants in Secondary Labour Markets

Although these are general considerations on the functioning of labour markets, they have clear implications for immigrant employment. Thus, in contrast to the neo-classical image of foreigners entering a unified labour market, segmentation approaches place immigrants in jobs in secondary labour markets. Foreign-born workers are consequently seen to fill the most undesirable jobs in destination countries. In Piore's (1979, p.17) words:

> There is something in common among jobs held by migrants in widely diverse geographic areas and very different historical periods: the jobs tend

to be unskilled, generally but not always low paying, and to carry or connote inferior social status; they often involve hard or unpleasant working conditions and considerable insecurity; they seldom offer chances of advancement toward better paying, more attractive job opportunities.

Developing this idea, Portes (1981, pp.284-285) summarised the reasons why immigrants are directed into secondary labour markets under three main factors:

- Their *legal status* is commonly tenuous, ranging from illegal to temporary residence. Quantifying the significance of illegal immigration in Western Europe, Appleyard (1991) has estimated that there are between 1.3 and 1.5 million illegal resident immigrants in Europe, most of them located in Greece, Italy, Portugal and Spain. Illustrating this point, Lianos and associates (1996) have highlighted the entry of illegal workers into labour markets as a key trend for the Greek economy in the last decade. For Iberia, the successive legalisation campaigns of both the Portuguese and Spanish Governments in the period 1985-1996 stress the relevance of illegal residence in the Peninsula. In this regard, even if the level of illegal immigration has become a matter of controversy (for some estimates on Portuguese illegal residents, see Esteves, 1991; Eaton, 1996; for Spanish estimates, Colectivo IOÉ, 1987; Izquierdo Escribano, 1992), it is clear that part of the new immigrant inflow into Iberia did enter (and has stayed) illegally.

- Workers are not primarily hired according to their skills, but according to their *ethnicity or residential status*. A primary advantage of immigrants to employers is their vulnerability, owing to their legal position. But employers can also draw on characteristics such as ethnicity or national origin in order to discriminate between potential recruits, as well as using the varying social status and organisation of immigrant communities as elements of control over performance (Reich et al., 1973; Gordon, 1989). Thus immigrants are not simply workers who are endowed with different skills and familiarity with a language, but can be used in qualitatively different ways from 'native' employees (Piore, 1979). This point is illustrated by Castles and associates (1987). These analysts showed that 35 per cent of Turkish workers were engaged in unskilled work, and further 46 per cent did semi-skilled jobs in West Germany in 1980. They argued that the reason for this is discrimination, as many Turks had relatively high levels of education and training.

- Immigrants tend to be hired for *transient and short-term jobs* which are not part of a promotion ladder. This is one reason why these jobs are unattractive to non-immigrants. Illustrating this point, Odé (1996) found that the characteristics of the employed labour in Dutch horticulture (e.g. low wages, short-term contracts, lack of promotion and poor working conditions) rendered the sector scarcely attractive for Dutch workers, and caused labour shortages which are being filled by Polish immigrants. For similar reasons, workers from Eastern Europe are employed in seasonal jobs in farming and construction in Germany, through inter-governmental agreements (Cyrus, 1994).

A further point of interest in segmentation theories is competition between immigrant and non-immigrant workers. In Piore's (1979, p.3) words, immigrants '[...] appear to be coming to take a distinct set of jobs, jobs that the native labor force refuses to accept'. This might well be a faithful portrait of immigration into Central and Western Europe in the 1950s and 1960s. But it is arguable that this occurs today in Portugal, and especially in Spain, owing to substantial levels of unemployment and widespread labour market casualisation (see, for Portugal, Lobo, 1985; Rodrigues, 1992; for Spain, Centro de Investigaciones Sociológicas, 1986; Recio, 1986; Miguélez Lobo, 1989). In other words, even if African workers are mainly situated in secondary labour markets, groups of the non-immigrant population may be placed there as well. It follows that, even for secondary jobs, some competition can be expected. Supporting this idea, Pugliese (1993, p.514) has argued that:

> [...] it is evident that most immigrant are employed in secondary jobs (and this is more evident and true now than in the past). However, the lack of preference by the local and national labour forces for this type of job does not imply a rejection. This is to say that the presence of an immigrant labour force cannot be taken as an indicator of an unsatisfied labour demand, even in the secondary labour market.

Challenging the straightforward links that some segmentation theorists posit between groups of workers and segments in labour markets, Peck (1989) has argued that the composition of primary and secondary labour markets depends largely on local employment structures. This is because, even inside the same region, localities differ from each other in their employment structures, levels of market demand and the characteristics of local workforces (Massey, 1979; Morrison, 1990; Marsden et al., 1992; Haughton et al., 1993). Thus, the matching process between labour supply and demand (and consequently competition for jobs) is produced at the local level (Peck, 1989; Gordon, 1995). This could provoke labour shortages in an industry in one town, but not in another within the same region. Local labour shortages may be filled by either new local residents or commuters. In this regard, Sassen (1995) has concluded that local labour market variables, especially unemployment levels, did not seem to affect immigrants' propensity to settle in an area or, more generally, where they decided to settle. This is despite the fact that such variables help account for the decisions of 'native' workers (Sassen, 1995). The decision of a new arrival to settle in a locality may respond not only to labour market characteristics, but also to factors like local housing markets or personal contacts (Ballard and Ballard, 1977; Robinson, 1984; Byron, 1993; White, 1993). As an illustration, in their classical study of Irish, Caribbean and Pakistani minorities in Birmingham's Sparkbrook, Rex and Moore (1967) defined the position of immigrants and non-immigrants in housing markets and held that their respective positions are a key element for understanding conflict and residential segregation in the city.

Summarising the previous literature, there are four points of interest for this book:

- Segmentation theory analysts have argued that the reason for immigrants being hired does not lie in their skills, but in employers' preferences. The primary advantage of immigrants to employers is their vulnerability, owing to their legal position. A first point to examine in this book is the legal status of African workers in Iberia, as well as exploring its incidence on employment. The second point revolves around skills. They are seen as a less irrelevant element to understanding immigrant patterns of employment. This book analyses patterns of labour market outcomes in the light of immigrant formal education and job experience. The information that is provided in interview by employees is contrasted with information from key informants and employers.
- Segmentation-based research has found that immigrants tend to be hired for transient and short-term jobs which are not part of a promotion ladder. This book examines the characteristics of African employment in Iberian labour markets to assess this view. This is done in three particular sectors of activity (namely, farming, construction, and accommodation services and restaurants). These three sectors have specific sectoral dynamics and present different employment prospects in Portugal and Spain. As well, the number of employed Africans varies substantially across these sectors and, within the same sector, between Portugal and Spain. Despite these differences, if Africans are found in the same type of jobs, regardless of economic activity or host country, then support will be added to segmentation arguments.

- Segmentation theorists have argued that competition for jobs does not take place between immigrants and non-immigrants, since these two groups are in distinctive segments of labour markets. This is probably the most arguable question mark against the applicability of segmentation theory, owing to rising unemployment (in Spain) and widespread casualisation (in both Portugal and Spain). In other words, even if all Africans do secondary sector jobs, it is probable that non-immigrants are also found in this segment of labour markets. It follows that some sort of competition can be expected. Competition between African workers and other workers is examined with regard to two arenas; namely, different economic sectors and localities with dissimilar employment mixes.

- Not denying that residence may be conditioned by prior emigrant contacts or local housing markets, this book examines the significance of local employment structures in understanding residential patterns of African workers. As well, differences in African employment by sector are examined in the light of local employment structures. The point here is to explore if the characteristics of labour markets at the local level are a key element for understanding patterns of African employment. Alongside the role of local labour markets, the issues of mobility inside Iberia and further emigration out of Portugal or Spain are examined. This point is relevant because it has largely been demonstrated that people with a prior migration history are more likely to migrate again than other people (e.g. Morrison, 1971; Bailey, 1988). If this is demonstrated for African workers in Iberia, their greater propensity to change residence following job opportunities could raise a comparative advantage in labour markets.

Ethnic Enclaves and Ethnic Entrepreneurship

One of the risks of segmentation approaches is the reduction of the process of integration of foreign labour to a unique outcome in secondary labour markets. Yet not all foreign workers are found in secondary labour markets. Rather research emphasises a propensity for self-employment amongst foreign-born workers (Portes, 1994). For the USA, Bailey (1987, p.7) found that:

> [...] almost all foreign-born groups are over-represented among small business owners and the research in this area generally concludes that entrepreneurship has played an important role in the economic adjustment of many immigrants.

The important message is that the pattern of incorporation of immigrants in labour markets is far from homogeneous. Portes and Böröcz (1989, p.620) picked up this point when arguing that '[...] the diversity of contemporary immigration to the advanced countries contrasts with widely held images of a uniform working class origin and of a singular assimilation path'. These analysts established a typology of contemporary immigrants in advanced countries (Figure 2.1). Here the context of reception is defined as '[...] the stance of host governments, employers, the surrounding native population and the characteristics of the pre-existing ethnic community, if any' (Portes and Böröcz, 1989, p.618).

Figure 2.1   A typology of modes of incorporation into host labour markets

Context of reception	*Class of origin* Manual labour	Professional Technical	Entrepreneurial
Handicapped	Secondary Market Incorporation	Ghetto Service Providers	Middleman Minorities
Neutral	Mixed Labor Market Participation	Primary Market Incorporation	Mainstream Small Business
Advantaged	Upward Mobility to Small Entrepreneurship	Upward Mobility to Professional Possitions and Civic Leadership	Enclave Economies

Source: Portes and Böröcz (1989, p.620).

Figure 2.1 illustrates that ethnic entrepreneurship can take very different forms. Depending on the (hostile, neutral of favourable) context of reception, Portes and Böröcz (1989) delimit three main types of immigration incorporation into self-employment:

• Middleman minorities have been defined as groups that specialise in commercial and financial services amongst a numerically larger but impoverished hostile population (Bonacich, 1973; Portes, 1994). As examples of this kind of entrepreneurship, Bonacich (1973) mentioned, amongst others, the Chinese in Southeast Asia, the Japanese and Greeks in the United States and the Indians in West Africa. For Britain, Pakistani shopkeepers have been described as playing a similar role in low income inner city areas (Werbner, 1987).

- Mainstream small businesses are likely to be set up in neutral contexts of reception (Figure 2.1). Immigrants who enter neutral contexts of receptions face a situation where individual merit and skills are the most important determinants of successful incorporation (Portes and Böröcz, 1989). Yet these analysts neither give a definition nor an example of this kind of entrepreneurship. Following the general description of a neutral context of reception given by Portes and Böröcz (1989), the entry of immigrants into mainstream small business activity can be said to rely on immigrant skills and experience (rather than bounded solidarity between people from the same origin or nationality).

- Ethnic enclaves have been defined as '[...] spatially clustered networks of businesses owned by members of the same minority' (Portes, 1994, p.28). As one of the most influential works on ethnic enclaves, Wilson and Portes (1980) found that Cuban firms in Miami tended to concentrate in textiles, leather, furniture, cigar making, construction and finance. They argued that workers in the enclave economy have distinct characteristics, which include a significant return on past human capital investment. Other analysts have suggested that employment patterns in enclaves differ from incorporation into primary or secondary labour markets. For instance, Portes and Bach (1985) held that the enclave economy offers immigrant workers a protected niche of opportunities for career mobility and self-employment that is not available in secondary labour markets. Similarly, Bailey and Waldinger (1991) argued that the structure of (small, competitive) ethnic firms cannot reproduce the primary sector features that promote skill acquisition or upward mobility, although the characteristics of ethnic firms (as based on ties of a common community) do stimulate the sharing of information and skills.

However, more recently, Waldinger (1993) has suggested that the term ethnic enclave is perhaps not that appropriate, as it denotes a cluster of business under the control of the same ethnic minority group. Instead he proposes the use of *ethnic economies* as a more adequate means of describing the situation of the existing variety of ethnic entrepreneurship. This commentator has argued that this last concept eliminates reference to geographical concentration and economic links between different branches of activities under the same ethnic group management, and includes a myriad of small businesses which in many cases have no employees. For Western Europe, the term ethnic economies fits the immigration experience better than ethnic enclave, since entrepreneurs mainly concentrate in one or two branches of economic activity (see, for instance, Aldrich et al., 1984, or Cater, 1984, for Asian retailers in Britain; Ladbury, 1984, for Turkish Cypriots in the London clothing industry; Ma Mung and Simon, 1990, on Maghrebin and Asian traders in France; Tarrius, 1996, on Maghrebin businesses in the same sector in the Marseille region). In many cases, the links that entrepreneurs keep with their country of origin are a key element in the success of their businesses, as cheap products are guaranteed through these providers (see the example of Maghrebin businesses in the Marseille region, Tarrius, 1996; the Indian community in Portugal, Malheiros, 1997). Links are also built through the EU, as seen in the work of Beltrán Antolín (1997), who has found that a large part of Chinese restaurants in Spain are an extension of businesses elsewhere in Europe. Finally, a considerable part of these businesses are set up by men and women who used to be in business in their country of origin (see, for Indians who were expelled from Eastern Africa and settled in Britain, Aldrich et al., 1984; for the Indian community in Lisbon, Malheiros, 1997).

From evidence that immigrants are clustered in a limited number of occupations, recent research on ethnic entrepreneurship has argued that *occupational niches* constitute another type of immigrant experience. In Portes's words (1994, p.28),

> [another] form of ethnic entrepreneurship is the colonization of selected occupational niches [...]. Occupational niches are entrepreneurial only *latu sensu* since they do not involve independently owned firms. Instead they consist of the activities initiated by already-employed individuals to bring others of the same national origin to work with them and the gradual transformation of the workplace into an ethnic 'enterprise'.

Illustrating this point, Waldinger (1994) has showed the making of an immigrant niche in the New York City civil services. He found that the first immigrants were hired in New York City civil services in the mid-1960s due to labour shortages. These shortages were occasioned by jobs in New York City civil services being scarcely attractive for non-foreign workers at that time. This was because of wage stagnation and increasing job uncertainty, both occasioned by municipal budget restraints. When the economy of the city began to recover in 1977, the services offered by the municipality expanded. New workers were then recruited, largely through already employed immigrant workers (Waldinger, 1994).

One aspect of ethnic entrepreneurship which has not been mentioned so far is *casual self-employment*. In this regard, several analysts have outlined the diffuse border between ethnic businesses, self-employment and the informal economy in the light of increasing unemployment and casualisation in Western economies (Moulier Boutang, 1991; Palidda, 1992; Pugliese, 1993; King and Konjhodzic, 1995). In this regard, examples of street hawking activities have been reported in different European countries (see, for instance, Vicente, 1993, for Senegaleses in Madrid; King, 1993, for the same nationality in Italy; Costes, 1994, for immigrants on the Paris underground; Iosifides, 1997, for Egiptians in Athens; Knights, 1997, for Bangladeshis in Rome; and Martínez Veiga, 1997, for Moroccans in Madrid).

Previous empirical research produces few clear clear guidelines on immigrant entrepreneurhip. What it does show is that the experience of enterpreneurship varies with the destination country, nationality of origin, and the historic moment. This book examines which kind of immigrant entrepreneuship (if any) has been developed amongst the different nationalities of African-born immigrants in Portugal and Spain.

The Role of the State: Borders and Markets

So far this review of research has focused on two main theoretical schools on labour market economics; namely, neo-classical and segmentation approaches. To complement these theories, research on ethnic entrepreneurship has been discussed. What this treatment of immigrant workers has not included is consideration of the specific impact that states have on immigrants. It has noted state differences, but so far more as an empirical expression. Here the state's role is confronted directly.

Current immigration policies in Western Europe are characterised by being highly restrictive (Costa-Lascoux, 1989; Kastoryano, 1989; Convey and Kupiszewski, 1996; Marie, 1996). In this regard, O'Loughlin (1986) argued that initial differences in immigration policies between those countries which accepted permanent immigration (e.g. France or Britain) and those which only saw immigrants as temporary workers (e.g. Germany or Switzerland) blurred after the 1973 economic crisis. European governments have argued that restraining immigration is the normal consequence of increasing unemployment.[4] In the first part of this section, the implications of the changing political context of Western European immigration experiences will be explored. Later on, it is argued that the particular circumstances of each state, not only in terms of immigration policies, but also in terms of industrial relations and labour market policies, may determine patterns of African employment in Iberia.

Borders

Put simply, the only difference between internal and international migration is an international border. For international migration, neo-classical based studies parallel or extend the standard interpretation of inter-regional migration which sees prospective migrants making decisions based on a weighing of the costs and benefits of a change of residence (Gordon, 1989). In the light of growing global economic integration, Johnson and Salt (1990, p.12) argued that '[...] the nature and significance of the links between internal and international labour migration need elaboration, both at theoretical and practical levels'. An early attempt to bring together movements at both levels was offered by Pryor (1981), who tried a combined approach that identified several dimensions of continuity between internal and international movement (e.g. the rural/urban nature of communities of origin and destination; shared motivations, and a common reliance on personal networks). Nevertheless, the crossing of a national boundary does introduce peculiar legal conditions compared with internal migration. As Böhning (1981, p.31) claimed: 'The nation state draws a border line around it over which non-belongers may not step without explicit or tacit consent'.

   Crossing a border with the intention of staying in the destination country is regulated differently by each state. These regulations vary in form over time. In an attempt to find similarities over such varied political agendas, Freeman (1995) has distinguished three immigration settings which share common trends: the English-speaking settler societies (namely, Australia, Canada, New Zealand and the USA); the European states with post-colonial and guestworker migrations (Belgium, Britain, France, Germany, the Netherlands, Sweden and Switzerland); and Southern Europe (namely, Greece, Italy, Portugal and Spain). For this last group of countries, he argued that there are two significant circumstances in which political responses are fashioned. The first is the near complete absence of any institutional mechanisms or administrative experience for the planning or regulation of immigration. In fact, '[...] the dominant policy instrument thus far has been legalization' (Freeman, 1995, p.895). Secondly, for Southern Europe, the European Union has been notable in influencing immigration decisions.

   For Freeman (1995), then, Southern Europe is a specific political setting for immigration policy. Yet within this geographic space differences are notable. In Portugal, people from the ex-colonies constitute the bulk of

African immigrants (as well as a considerable percentage of the total number of foreigners), and, even if immigration legislation for this group is as restrictive as for others, the application of relevant rules is not as strict (Marie, 1995; Eaton, 1996; Guibentif, 1996). Perhaps the reason for this *'laissez-faire'* attitude lies in Portugal's colonial history, in its recent process of decolonisation and in strong current connections with ex-colonies. These links build bridges with the immigration experiences of Britain and France in the 1950s and 1960s (see, for Britain, Freeman, 1979; for France, Ogden, 1993), and the 'permissive' nature of immigration policies has parallels with the US experience (Hollifield, 1990). By contrast, even if northern Morocco was a Spanish protectorate until 1956, and the African cities of Ceuta and Melilla are still Spanish colonies, these nationals do not have the 'privileges' of Latin Americans, either when applying for nationality or renewing work permits. Yet, both entry and the awarding of first work permits are equally restrictive for all non-EU nationals (Santos, 1993a; Solé, 1997). The point to stress from this is that Portugal and Spain not only differ in economic conditions, but also in their political circumstances regarding immigration.

Markets

States also contribute to regulate labour markets. As Peck (1989, p.47) has claimed, the state '[...] ensures that some sort of 'balance' is maintained between labour supply and demand, and between the respective amounts of labour which can be supported within and outside the labour market'. As an illustration, even if there is no obvious link, the state may support their own nationals with unemployment benefits and at the same time accept foreign labour to meet specific labour shortages (e.g. through quota systems). This does occur in Spain. Whether currently unemployed workers could undertake the jobs that immigrants do is another question.

In the 1980s and 1990s, European states have strained to fight labour market rigidities which are thought to be a key reason for higher unemployment than in the USA (see, for instance, Organisation for Economic Co-operation and Development, 1995). The outcome of these changes in policy have been described by Atkinson (1987, p.102) in the following terms:

> Employers' current initiatives, under the same banner of flexibility, are moving towards higher levels of segmentation. As a result, the workforce is being ever more stratified by social class, sex, race, earning power, security and access to skills and training.

However, in his comparison of the USA with Italy, France and Spain, Piore (1986) has argued that US job security is more extensive, and employment relationships less flexible, than claims about European rigidities seem to recognise. Regarding these three European countries, Piore has held that flexibility is extensive due to the different official arrangements that apply for the primary and secondary segment of the economy, with the laying off workers being much easier in secondary labour markets.

For Spain, debate on labour market flexibility has been dominant in labour market economics and politics throughout the 1980s and 1990s. In this context, Recio (1996) has argued that the discourse on flexibility has been built up on segmentation concepts. For instance, Bentolila and Dolado (1994) blamed trade unions and the Spanish collective bargaining system for inefficiencies and unfairness in labour markets. They defended further de-regulatory policies in Spain (e.g. by reducing the cost of firing permanent employees) to gain both efficiency (as highly-protected workers in primary labour markets are considered to be resistent to innovation) and equity (as the existing extreme differences in protection and wages between the two sectors would diminish). Recio (1996) has replied to this by arguing that:

- The flexibility measures that successive governments of the centre-left PSOE have put forward have had a limited impact on job creation.
- The existence of a segment of protected primary workers is not occasioned by the state's (rigid) rules. Rather it is the result of decisions by firms to have a secure base of highly motivated workers. Yet, what seems clear is that current trends in Spanish labour markets tend to reduce the size of this segment.
- The Spanish model of industrial relations that is based on collective bargaining has little relevance for small-sized firms. Furthermore, firms with less than six workers do not participate in trade union elections, so the bargaining process is not likely to reflect the opinions of workers of this firm size, although they make up a third of the country's workforce (Abellán et al., 1997).
- The most transparent result of flexible measures has been an increase in casualisation in Spanish labour markets. As Miguélez Lobo (1989) has argued, there is a huge segment of young people, women and unskilled male workers who suffer from much worse working conditions that those in primary labour markets, irrespective of whether they are employed in the formal sector or not.

Probably because job losses were not as dramatic as in Spain, the debate on post-Caetano's Portugal has not focused extensively on flexibility, but on the role of the state in the economy. Until the first revision of the 1976 Constitution in 1982, the Council of the Revolution had powers to veto all laws which were considered against the socialist nature of the state (Lains, 1994). Since then, successive governments have converged in rejecting nationalisation, economic protectionism, isolationism and experiments beyond the market economy (Lopes, 1996a). Indeed, whereas other Southern European countries expanded public expenditure, Portugal reduced it in the late 1980s (Maravall, 1993). As for labour markets, only one reform was introduced after the Caetano regime (in 1989), which provides more scope for employers on dismissals, but also offers more restraints on fixed-term contracts (Lopes, 1996a). Obviously, economic priorities were different between the two Iberian countries. So were the attitudes of trade unions regarding employment. In Portugal, agreements on a reduction in real wages (if employment was guaranteed) have been accepted by trade unions (see, Costa, 1994; Lopes, 1996b) unlike in Spain (Bentolila and Dolado, 1994).

Yet how labour market flexibility affects immigration is not clear. In fact, the tendency toward more flexible modes of production has been accompanied by a reduction in the volume of international migration (Fielding, 1993; Odé, 1996). Yet even if immigration in the post-Fordist era is not as great as before, the increase in secondary labour markets (and in informality) which is one of the consequences of flexibility measures (as seen in Spain) has created openings for immigrants (Moulier Boutang, 1991; Palidda, 1992; Pugliese, 1993; King and Konjhodzic, 1995).

This book studies the impact of the state's policies on labour immigration by way of a comparison of the two Iberian states. Industrial relations and state regulations of labour markets are key elements in understanding the economic performance of individual states. The mixture of these policies with immigration rules may have a unique outcome in each state. Thus, differences in African employment may come purely from legislation, and its implementation. Yet it may be the case that, despite contrasting legislation on immigration and labour markets (which is the case for Portugal and Spain), African employment patterns do not vary significantly across political settings.

Immigrant Networks: Help or Hindrance?

As state-run agencies have done for some developed countries (e.g. Germany[5] or Switzerland in the 1950s and 1960s), social networks foster and channel immigration on a personal basis in the adverse political contexts of the 1980s and 1990s (Bach and Schraml, 1982; Fawcett, 1989; Gurack and Caces, 1992). Immigrant networks have been defined as '[...] a set of interpersonal ties that link migrants, former migrants, and non-migrants in origin and destination areas by ties of kinship, friendship, and shared community origin' (Massey, 1990, p.7). Research on links between emigrants and non-emigrants in sending and receiving areas, and how this stimulates further emigration, has received a great deal of attention in the literature (e.g. Portes and Walton, 1981; Massey and García-España, 1987; Massey et al., 1987; Boyd, 1989; Byron, 1994).

    In this book, the aspect of most concern is the role of social networks in channelling employers' demands for labour in Iberia. The relevance of social networks for immigrant job search has been outlined frequently in the literature (e.g. Grieco, 1987; Tilly, 1990; Portes and Sensenbrenner, 1993; Portes, 1994). For instance, Tilly (1990) has argued that immigrants cluster together in labour markets as a result of job specialisation which depends largely on the initial contact of an immigrant population with host labour markets. For the later nineteenth and earlier twentieth in the USA, he argued that the prevalence of subcontracting in manufacturing and construction was directly related to network action. In Tilly's (1990, p.86) words:

> In subcontracting, the owner of a business delegates to a second party (most often a foreman or a smaller entrepreneur) the responsibility both for hiring workers and for supervising production, and the second party delivers finished products to the owner. Migrant networks articulate neatly with subcontracting because they give the subcontractor access to flexible supplies of labor about which he or she can easily get information and over which she or he easily exert control outside the workplace.

This example reveals the direct action of social networks on labour market outcomes. In this regard, following Granovetter's (1985) ideas on embeddedness of economic action on social structures, Portes (1994, p.8) has argued that:

> [...] social networks are among the most important types of structures in which economic transactions are embedded [...] Networks are important in economic life because they are sources for the acquisition of scarce means, such as capital and information, and because they simultaneously impose effective constraints on the unrestricted pursuit of personal gain.

This double role for immigrant networks, as help (as sources for the acquisition of scarce means) and hindrance (in imposing constraints), is well reflected in the ethnic enclave literature. Ethnic enclaves have been described before in this chapter. The point to outline here is that enclaves are based on dense social networks between members of the same community, nationality or origin. Outlining the positive impact of these networks, some researchers have contended that workers in enclaves have more returns on past human capital investments, as well as more chances of promotion and skill acquisition than secondary labour market workers (Wilson and Portes, 1980; Portes and Bach, 1985; Bailey and Waldinger, 1991). However, other analysts have questioned this positive evaluation, which is largely based on the case of Cubans in the USA. Thus, for other US ethnic enclaves, Reimers (1985) in the case of Mexicans, Hirschman and Wong (1990) for the Chinese, and Chiswick (1991) for Hispanics, have agreed that ethnic enclaves make English language learning more difficult, and consequently reduce the chance of immigrants getting a job out of the enclave. By using data from the US census and from government surveys, these investigators found a negative correlation between the concentration of immigrants in particular geographical areas and wage rates. Maybe a crucial point to identify for the different roles that networks can have in progression within labour markets is the nationality or origin of immigrants, for Cuban experiences in the USA differ considerably from Mexicans in the same country.

Finally, a neglected issue in the literature is the differential use of networks by women and men, for the network literature has focused predominantly on male experiences (Boyd, 1989; Böcker, 1995; Sassen, 1995; Huang, 1997). From empirical research in the USA, Sassen (1995) has concluded that immigrant women's networks in general contain more relatives than men's, with men being more likely to have more co-workers. Along the same lines, Hanson and Pratt (1991) have found that ties are less workplace-based for women than for men. This leads to different job outcomes by sex. Indeed, even work contacts tend toward gendered outcomes (Sassen 1995). This is for two reasons. First, a significant percentage of women are in jobs where women are in the majority. Secondly, the locational distribution of female-dominated jobs is different from that of other jobs, as women are more location-sensitive in their journey to work (owing to commitments like child-minding). 'Women may lack access to information on non-female-dominated jobs insofar as these have a different locational distribution' (Sassen, 1995, p.103).

Strong reliance on social networks may limit labour market outcomes (as demonstrated by Jenkins, 1985, for the Black British). To examine if immigrant networks limit the labour market outcomes of Africans in Iberia, the usage of social networks for job searching is compared to other official channels (e.g. employment agencies) in the light of African patterns of employment. In undertaking this analysis, this focus is on the country of destination (Portugal or Spain), of origin (Moroccans, West Africans or Africans from ex-Portuguese colonies), and the sex of an immigrant. The key question is whether immigrant networks 'determine' work progression in Iberian labour markets.

The Gender Dimension

For sure, differences on immigrant involvement in labour markets by sex are not only restricted to their usage of networks, but are also observed in other aspects of the incorporation of immigrant workers in labour markets. For instance, the literature commonly agree on the divergent role of family ties for women and men when deciding a job change that involves a change of residence. Thus whereas family ties either stimulate or pose obstacles to women's changes of job when re-location is involved, these ties do not play such a significant role for men (see, for instance, Bielby and Bielby, 1992; Hendershott, 1995). Another example is the greater propensity of immigrant women to hold low-paid jobs than their male counterparts, as well as facing unemployment (see, for instance, the Harzing's, 1995, study on ethnic minorities in the Netherlands, Belgium, Germany and Britain).

Research has found that immigrant female workers from developing countries generally face a common disadvantageous position in host labour markets. These immigrant women are more likely to hold jobs which are characterised by being unskilled, low-paid, with little job security and with little (or no) chance of promotion. Illustrating this point, Ortiz (1996) concluded that Puerto Rican women were stuck in unskilled jobs in the US garment industry. This researcher also found that these female workers were the first to lose their jobs in the re-structuring of the industry that resulted from increased global competition after the 1960s. This vulnerability to unemployment has also been showed by Phizacklea (1983b) for France, Britain and West Germany. In the last of these countries, women constituted 31.6 per cent of the foreign labour force in 1979, but 49.3 per cent of unemployed foreign workers (Phizacklea, 1983). Likewise, using US census data, Tienda and associates (1984) found an increase in the proportion of immigrant women in the least-skilled, manual jobs over the the 1970s, alongside an upward occupational movement from these jobs for native-born white women.

All these studies on female immigration from developing countries into Western Europe or North America stress that they fill the least attractive, unskilled and unstable jobs in destination societies. These jobs have recently increased due to changes in the economies of the developed countries which have stimulated the entry of women in labour markets (Sassen-Koob, 1984; Beechey, 1988). Sassen-Koob (1984, p.1152-3) has identified three main structural economic changes which have helped in this:

- A shift to a service economy, which is generally recognised as resulting in a greater share of low-wage jobs than is the case if an economy dominated by a strong manufacturing sector (see also Marshall, 1988; Illeris, 1989).
- A process of job downgrading in the manufacturing sector. Major new industries, notably in high-technology, have a large share of low-wage jobs in production and assembly line work, while several older industries have undergone a reorganisation of their work process that is characterised by growth in non-union plants, sweatshops and homework (for Britain, see Borooah and Hart, 1995).
- A technological transformation of the work process which has helped polarise the workforce by either upgrading or downgrading a vast array of middle-income jobs (see also Castells, 1989).

Contextualising the first two points in an Iberian setting, service industries have passed from 45.8 per cent of total employment in 1980 to 61.7 per cent in 1997 in Spain (Instituto Nacional de Estadística, 1981b; 1998b). For Portugal, growth in services is even more spectacular, as the 36.3 per cent of employment that was recorded in 1981 had risen to 56.4 per cent by 1996 (Instituto Nacional de Estatística, 1983b; 1997b). This growth in services has been accompanied by an increase in female participation rates. These passed from 29.3 per cent of the workforce in 1980 to 38.9 per cent in 1997 for Spain (Instituto Nacional de Estadística, 1981b; 1998b) and, from 39.4 per cent in 1981 to 44.9 per cent in 1996 in Portugal (Instituto Nacional de Estatística, 1983b; 1997b). It has been argued that this increase in female participation (by 'native' residents) has created demand for workers in the domestic sector, which has come to be seen as suitable for female immigrants (Solé, 1994; Chell, 1997). Indeed, the domestic sector is the only activity which employs large number of female immigrants from developing countries in Iberia (França, 1992; Sánchez Martín, 1992; Berges, 1993; Solé, 1994; Ribas Mateos, 1996; Machado and Perista, 1997; Oso and Catarino, 1997).

A second point on job downgrading in manufacturing is illustrated by Portugal. Here a decrease in the number of workers in manufacturing industries has been accompanied by the entry of more female workers (from 35.3 per cent in 1981 to 42.0 per cent in 1993 for the workers in these firms), by a reduction in average firm size (manufacturing firms which had less that 10 employees constituted 54.3 per cent of the total in 1988 but 58.0 per cent in 1993) and a decrease in real manufacturing wages, with this reduction being more notable for women (Ministério de Emprego e da Segurança Social, 1994). Indeed, wages in the Portuguese manufacturing sector were just over one quarter of the EU average for the sector in 1996 (Chislett, 1997).

Whether these developments create openings for immigrant women in Iberia is another point. In this regard, women constituted 46.0 per cent of non-Portuguese EU nationals, 45.8 per cent of Brazilians and 38.1 per cent of legal PALOP residents in 1996 (Instituto Nacional de Estatística, 1997a). More significantly, from different official statistics, França (1992), for Cape Verdeans, and Machado and Perista (1997), for African nationals, showed that immigrant women have lower paid work participation rates than all the women in Portugal. For Spain, women constituted 35.1 per cent of non-EU legal workers in 1996. This percentage goes down to 16.3 per cent for Africans in the same year (Comisión Interministerial de Extranjería, 1997). Yet there are significant differences by nationality. Thus, amongst nationals from Cape Verde, Equatorial Guinea, Peru, the Dominican Republic and the Philippines, female workers in Spain were more numerous than their male counterparts (Comisión Interministerial de Extranjería, 1997). However, even if official data usually underestimate labour participation rates for immigrant women (Lebon, 1979), survey-based research for Iberia confirms that the majority of Africans in labour markets are men (Solé and Herrera, 1991; França, 1992; Gozálvez Pérez, 1995; Abril et al., 1998).

Summarising the main finding from different case studies on immigrant women, Chant (1992, p.197) has argued that '[...] even in situations where women are highly mobile [...], men seem to be more mobile still. In other words, [...] men are rarely 'left behind' by female migrants: it is usually the reverse which applies'.

With the notable exception of the domestic sector, research findings in the literature report that African women at paid work in Iberia are less numerous than their male counterparts. This book explores the employment of female workers in Iberia; and reasons for differences (if any) between Portugal and Spain. Complementing the interviews that were completed with female immigrant workers, information from male immigrants, as well as employers, trade unions and other key informants, will cast light on (the lack of) employment of female immigrants.

Conclusion

In this chapter the incorporation of immigrants into labour markets has been examined according to two main theoretical traditions; neo-classical approaches, structuralist analyses. The key question is whether patterns of African employment in Iberia primarily respond to immigrant educational and occupational endowments (as argued by neo-classical approaches) or to the structure of labour markets (as defended by structuralist analyses). These two theoretical positions posit (potentially) different outcomes for immigrant occupational attainment. Adding a further twist on the picture, ethnic entrepreneurship theories argue that patterns of incorporation largely depend on the origin of immigrants and the context of their reception in destination countries.

Elements which may introduce 'distortions' to these theoretical ideas have also been discussed. Amongst them, the state clearly stands out as an active agent in shaping immigrant labour outcomes. This is done by controlling borders and regulating markets. Quite feasibly, immigrant labour outcomes may be conditioned by political settings. Furthermore, in restrictive immigration contexts, the state may decide which jobs (if any) are available for non-nationals. If this is the case, immigrant patterns of employment may purely be a response to political decisions, which may be motivated by economic circumstances. Connections between political settings, economic contexts and African labour outcomes are discussed for Portugal and Spain in Chapter 3.

Notes

1. Keynesian ideas accept that labour market operations themselves produce unemployment. In contrast with early neo-classical theorists, Keynesian-based researchers have defended state action to avoid unemployment (Coleman, 1992).
2. One of the most important modifications of this neo-classical assumption was made by the behavioural models of Todaro (1969) and Harris and Todaro (1970). In their analysis of rural-urban migration in developing countries, they found that rural out-migration took place despite the inability of the urban economy to provide jobs for all the in-migrants. More than the immediate negative consequences of out-migration, for Harris and Todaro (1970), the 'rationale' of the move is explained by expected income in the future. Instead of rural-urban differentials, these researchers argued that neo-classical models should compare rural to expected urban wages.
3. Contrary to this Schumpeter-based assumption, and within the neo-classical tradition, Keynesian ideas argue that economies respond more positively to higher wages than to higher profits (for more information about this particular point, see Bilbao, 1990).
4. This can be (and is) over-stated. Thus, the UK first introduced more restrictive practices into its immigration policies in 1962, long before the major economic downturn that began in 1973 (Coleman, 1995). Likewise, for France and Germany,

Hollifield (1992) has argued that the decision to suspend worker immigration was motivated largely by political and social considerations, rather than unemployment.

5.   The German Government recruited foreign workers from the Mediterranean countries from the late 1950s up to the beginning of the 1970s. Workers were brought in groups to Germany, where employers had to provide initial accommodation. The number of foreign workers in the former Federal Republic of Germany rose from 95,000 in 1956 to 1.3 million in 1966 and 2.6 million in 1973 (Castles and Miller, 1993).

3 The Role of the State: The Iberian Peninsula in the EU Context

Control of borders, immigration, asylum seeker and naturalisation policies are matters for the state. These issues affect the very definition of the state in the sense that they define who is allowed to stay within its borders, either as a national or as a legal resident (or even as a visitor). Not surprisingly, the set of laws that relate to immigration, refugee status and naturalisation vary from state to state, even inside the European Union. Indeed, within the EU, efforts toward harmonising immigration regulations for third country nationals (let alone naturalisation) have so far been limited. Following a path that was initiated with the constitution of the 'Ad Hoc Immigration Group' and the signature of the Single European Act,[1] the Treaty on European Union was signed in Maastricht on 7 February 1992. The Treaty mainly focused on the right of free movement and residence of EU nationals and the internal cohesion of the Union.[2] Regarding immigration policies toward third country citizens, only Article 100c urges EU institutions to determine the third countries whose nationals must be in possession of a visa before crossing the external borders of member states (Schermers et al., 1993). By contrast, Article K.1 of the Treaty explicitly states that border control, as well asylum and immigration policies for non-EU citizens,[3] are the responsibility of each member state.

A further development in European immigration policy harmonisation is the Schengen Convention.[4] Even though not all EU countries have signed up to the Schengen Group, the Convention is subject to EU legislation (Article 134) (European Parliament, 1996b). The most immediate consequence of the Convention was the abolition of internal borders inside the Schengen space. As a result of this, greater external border controls and uniform visa requirements and formats for short stays (three months and less) were enforced across the Schengen countries. Yet issuing visas for longer stays comes under the criteria of each state. As well, according to the Convention (and the Treaty on European Union), legally-resident non-EU nationals are not allowed to work out of the country where they have been granted residence. Paradoxically, it has been argued that third nationals (alongside students and high-skilled workers) are more susceptible to changes in residence, which does result in them moving between nations within the EU (Simon, 1991; Kastoryano, 1994).

It follows that immigration, asylum seeking and naturalisation policies are mainly a matter for each state. However, even if the specifics of these policies largely depend on the peculiarities of states, there is a general trend in EU countries (as well as in other developed countries) to stop, control and channel new immigrant inflows (see, for instance, Castles and Miller, 1993, for an overview of immigration trends and changes in policy in this century). The time when immigrants were sought (and, even recruited, as in the German guestworker system) by European states is definitely over. Nowadays all EU countries have restrictive immigration laws, with southern European ones being the last to introduce such measures (e.g. 1985 Spanish Foreigners' Act; the 1986 Italian Law 943 and the 1990 Martelli Law; the 1993 Portuguese Decree-law 59). Alongside restraining immigration, some EU nations have endorsed restrictions on naturalisation (e.g. the French Law 93-933), as well as imposing restrictions on accepting asylum seekers and refugees (e.g. the 1992 revisions of German Asylum Procedures Act and the 1994 Dutch Aliens Act),[5] and establishing quota systems for non-EU workers (e.g. the Spanish quota system). As a general trend for the EU, visa requirements are now necessary for a common list of developing countries, in an attempt to stop illegal immigration.[6] Paradoxically, even if immigration, asylum seeking and naturalisation policies remain the responsibility of each state, responses to these issues are increasingly alike across the EU (O'Loughlin, 1986; Costa-Lascoux, 1989; Convey and Kupiszewski, 1996).

These developments have led some commentators to argue that there are different categories of citizens in the EU, with legally-resident third country nationals having restricted citizenship (Hammar, 1990). Indeed, political rights,[7] social security benefits,[8] access to public housing,[9] public health systems or state education[10] may apply differently to home nationals, other EU residents, non-EU legal residents and (non-EU) illegal residents. In other words, whereas legal residents may work (subjected to certain conditions, in several cases), other rights are more limited. These rights depend on the 'sensibility' of host countries toward their foreign-origin populations. The comparison between Portugal and Spain perfectly illustrates two different approaches to immigration. In this regard, the name of the bodies that both Portugal and Spain have created at the top of the state organisational hierarchy to deal with immigration denotes their dissimilar approaches. Thus, whereas the Spanish agency is called the

Foreigners' Inter-Ministerial Commission [*Comisión Interministerial de Extranjería*] and is under the Ministry of Interior rule,[11] the Portuguese High Commission for Immigration and Ethnic Minorities [*Alto Comissionado para a Imigração e as Minorias Étnicas*] is attached to the Presidency of the Government (Guibentif, 1996).[12] In other words, such immigrants are seen as foreigners in Spain, but as immigrants and ethnic minorities in Portugal.

The creation of the Portuguese High Commission was one of the demands of the Portuguese immigrant associations. These associations are heavily centralised in Lisbon and its metropolitan region, where the bulk of Africans live. As became clear in interviews with both the Cape-Verdean and the Guinean Associations, such organisations are actively involved in Portuguese politics (see also Machado, 1992). For instance, the immigrant associations signed an agreement with the Socialist Party for the 1991 elections. This pledged *Partido Socialista* support for the legalisation of illegal residents, the right to vote in local elections for legal immigrants, measures to fight poor school performance amongst ethnic minorities, the right to public housing for everybody, regardless of their nationality or origin, and measures on job equality (Carita and Rosendo, 1993). For Spain, probably because inflows are more recent, immigrant associations present a more scattered, less organised picture. Yet they have introduced a good range of local initiatives and are active in day-to-day work dealing with legal problems or other immigration matters, as became clear in my fieldwork.[13] At the state level, probably the most powerful Spanish organisation in terms of political bargaining power on immigrants' rights is Catholic Cáritas. This organisation published the pioneer research of Colectivo IOÉ (1987) on labour and living conditions of immigrants from developing countries in Spain. The proposals of Cáritas on a new work permit system (see Ballbé and Pich, 1994; Martínez, 1995a) are identical to the rules approved by the Spanish Government in 1996. Alongside Cáritas, certain politicians (mayors or MPs), as well as the left-wing political party Izquierda Unida-Iniciativa per Catalunya, have given public support for full citizenship for legal immigrants.[14]

All this is to say that immigration policies are not created in a political vacuum. The common political background for both Portugal and Spain is the same overarching EU legislation, with a shared national policy trend toward more restrictive policies. Yet these two countries have dissimilar political backgrounds which are reflected in their different approaches to citizens of third nations. The aim of Chapter 3 is to examine in more detail legal differences toward non-EU nationals between Portugal and Spain, and explore if these have any implication for African employment.[15]

Spain: Implications of Restrictive Immigration Policies on African Employment

As seen in Figure 1.1, official statistics show that there was a rising number of immigrants in Spain over the 1980s and 1990s, with Africans constituting the bulk of new entrants (see Figure 1.1). This new situation, alongside the impending incorporation of the country in the European Union in 1986, made the Spanish Parliament approve a new Foreigners' Act [*Ley de Extranjería*] in 1985.[16] This new *Ley* stated in its introduction that there had not been a similar immigration Act since 1852. To implement this Act, subsequent laws were approved by the Government in 1986,[17] which were modified for EU nationals in 1992[18] and then substituted by a new set of rules in 1996.[19] In parallel with this new legislative framework, in 1991 the Government created a Foreigners' Bureau [*Oficina de Extranjeros*] for each Spanish province. This was intended to simplify administrative procedures by concentrating in one body what had previously been scattered across units in the Ministry of Interior and the Ministry of Labour and Social Security.[20] In line with the Treaty on European Union and the Schengen Convention, new visa procedures for entry into Spain were introduced for nationals of several countries; amongst them, Maghreb nationals (Moroccans, Tunisians and Algerians), who needed a visa to enter Spain after 15 May 1991.[21] Finally, to deal with previously illegal residents, two legalisation processes were carried out in 1985-86[22] and 1991-92.[23] Likewise, after new regulations were approved in 1996, a period was opened which enabled illegal residents who had had residence permits in the past to legalise their residential situation.[24] These new regulations defined a permanent resident status, which came into being after six year of continuous legal residence, as well as simplifying the types and characteristics of work permits. This is just a brief description of immigration legislation changes over the period 1985-1996.[25]

This complex legislative framework is reflected in a great variety of identity cards that legal non-EU nationals may possess.[26] The main ID documents are the following:

- EU family cards, which are used for non-EU relatives (namely, husbands or wives, parents, sons or daughters of less than 21 years) of EU nationals or their partners. This card allows them to live and work in Spain. It is renewed automatically (provided kinship with the EU national still exists). This document is given for five years for relatives of Spanish nationals. For relatives of citizens of other EU countries, this document is for the same length as the EU resident card with which the person is attached.

- Residence permits (without work), which are divided into three types: initial, ordinary and special. The initial is valid for a period of between three months and two years. The ordinary is granted for a maximum of five years. The special is available for 10 years. For the concession of this permit, a visa for residence purpose is needed. When applying for a visa, non-EU nationals must justify their financial resources, as well as giving details on their housing. Amongst other groups, spouses and children of legal non-EU workers who come into the country through family reunion have the right to apply for these residence permits.
- A joint residence and work permit, which is issued as a single document. Unlike Portugal, the Spanish legislative framework clearly delimits residence permits which allow work and those which do not. There are six types of residence permit with work provisions.

Work and Residence Permit Procedures

Table 3.1 describes types of work and residence permits. With the exception of the 'A permit' which is not renewable, a main characteristic of work permit procedures is that there is a progression between the length of stay of the non-EU worker and the duration of a permit in Spain. Thus, in the case of employees, the initial 'b permit' is for a specific employer and cannot be longer than nine months. When renewed, the 'B permit' has a maximum duration of one year. According to the rules in operation during my fieldwork, African nationals, with the exception of Equatorial Guineans and legal foreign residents in the Spanish African enclaves of Ceuta and Melilla, could obtain a five-year permit after five years of legal work (i.e. hired job). Other nationalities could obtain a five-year permit after two years (see footnotes on Table 3.1).

There are three types of initial work permit (non-renewable A and renewable b and D; Table 3.1). Since the approval of the Foreigners' Act in 1985, there have been three ways of obtaining initial permits in Spain:

- Ordinary system. Non-EU workers need an entry visa to obtain an initial work and residence permit. For the visa, in the case of employees (permits A and b), the would-be worker must enter his application with a job offer made by a Spanish employer in the Spanish consulate of her/his origin country. Then this application is sent to the Ministry of Foreign Affairs in Madrid[27] which asks for a report from the Ministry of Labour and Social Security in the province in which the worker wants to work.[28] This report must spell out that there are no locally-registered unemployed Spaniards, EU nationals or other non-EU legal residents who can undertake the activity or profession in the application. The Girona office of the Ministry of Labour and Social Security informed me that certain provinces send applications to the local branch of the employment office to check if there are registered unemployed people who could take the job named in an application. In the case of Girona, due to the large number of applications, the decision is taken using figures that the National Employment Institute in the province send monthly.[29]

- In parallel with this ordinary system, the quota system is a second way of obtaining initial b permits (renewable, for employed activities). This was originally organised so as to channel new inflows into labour shortages in the country. Lack of success during the first (1993) campaign led to an opening of the quota to illegal residents in 1994.[30] Since the new procedures established that immigrants could be exempt from needing a visa for entry,[31] the number of accepted applications within the quota system went up from 5,220 in 1993 to 25,604 in 1994 (Table 3.2). But the quota system is not only about numbers. It also adjusts annually the allocation of new work permits by economic sector and province, depending on provincial labour market trends, as well as by nationality of origin[32] (Cachón Rodríguez, 1995). For instance, whereas the 1994 and the 1997 quotas foresaw the possibility of jobs in construction, the Spanish Government concluded that there were no labour shortages in the sector in 1993 and 1995. By contrast, since it started in 1993, the quota system has always had places for unskilled jobs in farming, the domestic sector, and other services (Table 3.2).

- A third way of obtaining an initial work permit (b for employed activities or D for self-employed workers) is through legalisation campaigns There were three campaigns through the period 1985-1996. Both the 1985-86 and the 1991-92 campaigns were open to all illegal workers and their relatives. The 1996 campaign was specifically aimed at those who had been lost their residential status or their relatives in Spain, as well as to relatives of legal workers. For all three, no visa of entry was necessary. The three campaigns were brought about by changes in immigration policies. Thus the 1985-86 was passed after the approval of the 1985 Foreigners' Act; the 1991-92 campaign preceded the implementation of the quota system which started in 1993; and the 1996 followed new residence and work permit procedures.

Table 3.1 Types of work permit in operation in Spain, 1986-1996

Type	Characteristics	Max. length
For employees		
A	For seasonal work or for fixed-term jobs. This type of permit is not renewable.	Nine months
b	For a specific employer. This type of permit is renewable.	Nine months
B	For those who renew a b work permit. For a specific profession, activity sector and province.	One year
C	For those who have had a B or b work permits for five years. For any profession, activity sector and province in Spain.	Five years
For self-employed workers and employers		
D	For a specific self-employed activity. Geographical restrictions may apply.	One year
E	For those who have renewed a D permit for five years. No geographical or job restrictions.	Five years

Notes:
a) There is also a special work permit for workers and self-employed people who commute on a regular basis into the Spanish territory. After 1992, it just applies to citizens of Gibraltar, Andorra and Morocco (if they work in the African enclaves of Ceuta and Melilla).
b) New rules have been in operation since 23 April 1996. The main difference with the above description is that C (employees) and E (self-employed) work permits are for three years. These can be obtained after three years of legal residence (two years for the special cases that are listed below). After six years (five years for the group listed in note 2), and this is a main difference with the old system, non-EU nationals can obtain a permanent joint residence and work permit.
c) B or D permits for one year were granted to the workers who were legalised in the 1991-92 campaign. These permits allowed them work in two types of job and sector in any Spanish province.
d) Ibero-americans, Filipinos, Andorrans, Equatorial Guinean nationals, as well as non-Spaniards who are legal residents in Gibraltar, Ceuta and Melilla or people of Sephardi or Spanish origin, enjoy a preferential treatment under the Spanish law. They need only two years of legal residence (with work) to obtain a five-year permit. This group of nationalities can apply for nationality after two years of legal residence.

Source: Civitas (1994).

Table 3.2   Accepted applications under the Spanish quota system, 1993-1997[a]

	1993	1994	1995	1997[c]
Farming	160	8,453	7,855	16,313
Construction		737		1,334
Domestic sector [b]	4,346	13,728	12,091	19,314
Other services	714	2,686		6,629
Non-classified				3,291
Total	5,220	25,604	19,946	46,881

Notes:
a)   There was no quota for 1996.
b)   For 1995, the 'domestic sector' figure includes 'other services'.
c)   For 1997, number of entered applications by June 1997.

Source: For 1993-1995, Dirección General de Migraciones (1997). For 1997, Dirección General de Migraciones (1997a).

Whatever the means used to obtain a first work permit (i.e. ordinary system, quota system or legalisation), in order to renew it, non-EU workers need both a hired contract and her/his social security contributions paid. This has to be done at least annually until the worker obtains a five-year permit, which is only obtainable after five years of legal work for Africans (see Table 3.1). In this regard, Cornelius (1994, p. 339) has argued that renewing (and obtaining) work permits is crammed with difficulties:

> The bureaucratic obstacles to obtaining or renewing work permits in Spain are formidable. Foreigners seeking to renew their work permits must present their social security cards, but only a minority of immigrants working in certain sectors (e.g. domestic sector) are able to obtain work contracts that include social security payments by the employer. Since Spanish immigration laws link work permits to residence permits, most illegal immigrants are unable to obtain legal work contracts.

Legalisation Campaigns in Spain

There were three campaigns over the period 1985-1996 in Spain. Under the 1985-86 campaign, 38,181 foreigners legalised their situation in Spain. There were 19,452 new legal residents (without work) and 18,729 legal residents who were allowed to work (Aragón Bombín and Chozas Pedrero, 1993). This campaign has been considered to be unsuccessful, since only

39 per cent of the almost 39,000 who were legalised were still legal permit holders in Spain in 1989 (Colectivo IOÉ, 1992; Izquierdo Escribano, 1992; Aragón Bombín and Chozas Pedrero, 1993). This low renewal rate was because 41 per cent of the permits issued during the legalisation process were for stays of three months at most (Izquierdo Escribano, 1992). Focusing on the 18,729 work and residence permits, almost half were for self-employed activities, with the other half for workers (Ministerio de Trabajo y Seguridad Social, 1989). The importance of self-employment in the 1985-86 legalisation was the result of this employment status being one of the acceptable entry points for unemployed Africans to obtain legalisation (Izquierdo Escribano, 1991).

Under the 1991-92 campaign, the number of accepted permits soared to 109,135 for work and residence, plus 5,889 for residence (Aragón Bombín and Chozas Pedrero, 1993). There are substantial differences between the two main legalisation campaigns. In 1991-92, the work permits were for one year and allowed work in two professions (and two economic sectors) in all Spain. The second point of difference is the number of accepted applications for self-employed work. In 1991-92, this constituted about 10 per cent of the 109,135 work (and residence) permits (Ministerio de Trabajo y Seguridad Social, 1993). This figure looks more realistic, as there is a real demand in Spain for street-hawking, gardeners and home care activities (the three main 'self-employed' jobs in this legalisation; Santos, 1993a). These three activities capture a precariously fluctuating pattern of self-employment. As for employees, 68.6 per cent of the total number of permits for hired work were allocated to four occupations. To be specific, 21,694 permits were granted for the domestic sector, 16,736 for agricultural labourers, 14,228 for construction workers, and 11,182 for unskilled work in accommodation industries and restaurants (Aragón Bombín and Chozas Pedrero, 1993).

The point to stress here is that legalisation has been a powerful tool in immigration policy. It has even been suggested that legalisation is the dominant policy instrument in Spain (Freeman, 1995). Indicating the significance of this point, three out of four of the 122 Africans who had residence and work permits of my Girona survey saw their status pass to legality in either the 1985-86 or 1991-92 legalisation campaigns. This high figure is confirmed in official statistics, with the number of legal Africans in Spain in 1991 being 297 per cent above the 1990 figure (Ministerio de Trabajo y Seguridad Social, 1992).

Those who passed their residential status from illegal to legal status in 1991-92 were granted a one-year permit. The difficulties of renewing these permits are recognised by trade unions and non-governmental organisations. These sources estimated that half of those who legalised their status in the 1991-92 campaign had not renewed their permit by 1995 (Pérez Oliva, 1995). Furthermore, after the 1996 campaign, which allowed around 25,000 to regain legality, there were 42,872 applications for the 1998 quota (against the 28,000 jobs that were offered by the Government for this year; Fuente, 1998). These figures suggest that illegality is still an issue in Spain. This is not surprising given the complexities and difficulties of permit renewal, alongside the short length of most permits issued in the legalisation processes.

Work without a Work Permit in the Girona Survey

My Girona survey found that 21 interviewed Africans (out of 151 interviewees; Table 3.3) worked without a valid work permit. This constitutes 13.9 per cent of the survey. Amongst these 21, 16 were illegal residents and five were legal residents whose permits did not allow them to work in Spain. This last group is comprised of spouses and children of legal non-EU residents who had entered the country through family reunion arrangements (or applied for family reunion requirements after an illegal entry).[33]

Table 3.3   Interviewed Africans by legal status in Spain

Legal residents	
EU nationals	3*
EU family card holders	5
Work and residence holders	122
Residence holders (no work permit)	5
Illegal residents	16
Total	151

* The three EU nationals were two Spanish nationals of Moroccan origin and a Swedish-Moroccan national. Spanish naturalisation laws allow only those from Andorra, Portugal, Iberoamerica, the Philippines and Equatorial Guinea to have double nationality (Álvarez Rodríguez, 1996).

Source: Girona interview survey.

Through four representative cases, this section highlights how the image of illegal workers being in a precarious position, as they are more open to 'abuses' by employers, presents only part of the picture. An additional consideration is jobs that are out of the control of the state (e.g. smuggling); and consequently operate illegally by definition. Clearly, illegal workers in these activities have no chance of legalising their present work status. Yet the border between legal and illegal activities is not clear.[34] In some circumstances, the state itself (or its rigid regulations) is directly responsible for placing some workers into illegality. Specifically, the first example given here indicates that legality is not single-track, as workers may pass from illegal to legal residence (and vice versa) on several occasions in their labour trajectories. Against existing prejudices (or perhaps suspicions is more appropriate), the second example shows that employers do not always enjoy advantages from illegality. By contrast, the third example reflects a common image of illegal immigration, with the employee engaged in precarious piece-paid work. The final case study analyses illegal work that was being undertaken by a legal resident.

Mr. Khalim, born in the Gambian province of Baje, entered Spain in 1981, when a visa was not needed for Gambian nationals. During his 15 year stay in Spain, he has done a variety of jobs (agricultural labourer, construction worker, shop assistant, unskilled manufacturing worker, cone picker) in many geographical regions (Girona, Lleida, Barcelona, Zaragoza). At the moment of his interview, he sold radios and radio-cassettes to African acquaintances on a informal basis and occasionally worked on construction sites. He had been an illegal resident for most of the time he had spent in Spain. Mr. Khalim was granted a residence and work permit in 1987, after the 1985-86 legalisation campaign, but he lost it in 1988. This was because he could not find a contracted job which would have let him renew his residence permit. Since he started dating a Spanish national in 1990, he did not apply for legalisation in the 1991-92 campaign. At the moment he was interviewed, he wanted to get married to his Spanish girlfriend, with whom he had been living.

The example of Mr. Khalim gives evidence of a relevant trend in illegality in Spain. He shows that it is possible to pass from legality to illegality (and vice versa) during a period of residence in the country. Likewise, 13 Africans out of the 122 who were on residence and work permits when they were interviewed declared that they had lost their legal status in the country at some time during their stay in Spain, and recovered it in one of the two legalisation processes. Furthermore, almost everybody in my survey had been employed without a residence and work permit at some moment of their life in Spain. To be specific, only nine out of the 122 who had a joint residence and work permit at the time they were interviewed had always been a legal resident who had been employed with a valid permit since they arrived in Spain.

The second example gives evidence of the rigidities of the current administrative procedures. Mr. Bushari is in his twenties and entered the country in 1994 with a false passport and visa. He first went to La Bisbal d'Empordà, a manufacturing town, where a relative had been living for the last 10 years. After doing several jobs in that town (gardener, agricultural labourer), each of which only lasted for a few days, he found a job in a small family business which specialised in restoring and then selling old furniture. Three people worked regularly for this firm; a carpenter (the owner), a vanisher (Mr. Bushari) and a shop assistant (the son of the owner). The interest of the employer to legalise the residential and work situation of this Moroccan national arises from the paucity of good artisans in the area.[35] In addition, Mr Bushari is reported to be a young enthusiastic worker. In fact, according to the interviewee, his employer has made enquiries to the Girona Foreigners' Bureau about how to legalise his residence. The response received was that the employer should write a pre-contract for this foreign worker and send it for approval. In the meantime, Mr. Bushari should leave the country, then apply for a visa to work in Spain. The Girona Ministry of Labour and Social Security could not guarantee a positive response to the employer's pre-contract, so Mr. Bushari's visa application could be denied. The provincial office of the Ministry of Labour and Social Security might argue that there are no labour shortages for this skilled work.[36] These are the procedures according to the ordinary system. However, Mr. Bushari is not able to apply for a work permit under the annual quota system because this system does not allow workers into manufacturing (Table 3.2). The bottom line is that non-EU workers are not allowed to do skilled (or professional) work in their first job in the country. Unless Mr. Bushari obtained an unskilled job in one of the sectors that the annual quota recognises, he will remain an illegal resident, and consequently could face expulsion at any time.

Despite being of the same age and having a similar career pattern in Morocco, Mr. Cassim's labour trajectory in Spain has followed a more precarious pattern than that of Mr. Bushari. He entered the country illegally in an engined *patera*[37] with a friend in November 1995. Mr Cassim went to Palafrugell (a tourist town with a significant presence of Moroccan nationals), where his friend's relative lived. He obtained a room in an unofficial Moroccan-run boarding house. Initially, Mr. Cassim picked cones in public forests with three other Moroccans. A Spanish national was in charge of driving them to the forests and selling the 'merchandise'. Discounting the costs of the petrol, profits were divided into four parts. Although he had been living in the country for only a month, Mr. Cassim explained that he was able to obtain this work because the cone season goes from October to February, with October and November as the months with most work.[38] Other interviewees confirmed that irregular work in forests, whether collecting cones, moss or broom, is mostly done by unemployed immigrants. The role of forests as occasional work source is of special relevance for seasonal agricultural labourers, as the off-peak farming season is winter (see Chapter 4). Yet the fringe characteristics of this job means that picking materials in forested areas is not open to the award (or renewal) of a work permit.

Ms. Farama is a completely different case from those recorded so far, as she is a legal resident (yet an illegal worker). She decided to follow her husband, who has now lived in Spain for 20 years, and moved to the country in 1988. Her husband has been working in the construction sector ever since he arrived in Spain. At the time of his entry, a visa was not required for Moroccan nationals entering the country. His wife stayed with him illegally until 1992. In this year, she and her two sons obtained a residence permit as part of the 1991-92 legalisation process, as they were the spouse and children of a legal non-EU worker. Her permit did not allow her to work.[39] Even so, Ms. Farama worked as a cleaner in a small hotel for four summer seasons without a contract. The rest of the year she used to take care of her children. In 1995, 'as my children were grown-up', she decided to work as a cleaner the whole year round. She was put in charge of cleaning her employer's businesses and home. This work was undertaken on an informal basis (viz. without a work permit). She earns 800 pts./hour, which is higher than the average wage for an agricultural labourer (which was 450-500 pts./hour in 1995). This irregular labour integration is not unusual in the domestic sector, with an official survey on the Spanish informal economy finding that a third of the jobs were irregular (Centro de Investigaciones Sociológicas, 1986).

These four examples show that reasons for illegality differ. Occasional irregular work as a seller of electrical devices (Mr. Khalim) or picking cones in public forests (Mr. Cassim) are clearly unregulated activities that occur on-the-fringe of the job market. By contrast, Mr. Bushari is employed in full-time skilled work, although, similarly, he has no possibility of obtaining a work permit. The case for Ms. Farama is perhaps more subtle, since her legal status in the country is guaranteed by her husband's work permit. She is still working illegally but this is in a sector were illegality is a major element of 'normal' practice (Centro de Investigaciones Sociológicas, 1986). The main difference between Ms. Farama and the other three cases is that Ms. Farama does not face expulsion. The threat of being caught and expelled is a real one. Although not exclusively aimed at identifying illegal immigrants, under the popularly known Corcuera Law (named after the Minister of Interior), since the early 1990s those who cannot provide a form of personal identification can be detained by police for up to six hours (Cornelius, 1994).[40] As well, through labour officials, the state has been active in controlling illegality at workplaces, as many agricultural employers made clear in interviews. All this depicts a picture of effective tools to expel illegal residents and explains the worries that many interviewed Africans expressed regarding their legal status. Set against this picture, official data for Catalunya show that only 1,030 persons per year (averaged for 1988 and 1991) were expelled out of 12,000-12,500 illegal residents who were apprehended each year (Cornelius, 1994). This is explained by the lengthy procedures that have to be followed between the moment of detention and the time of expulsion.[41] Amongst these, the illegal foreigner may be put in special centres until expulsion is determined. This preventive detention is decided by the courts. Yet, according to a report of the Ministry of Interior, judges are not keen to send immigrants to detention centres (Ministerio del Interior, 1994). Even so, expulsion is more than a possibility for illegal residents. For instance, in Girona alone, 512 illegal residents were expelled in 1995, which is 34 per cent higher than the 1994 figure (Costa-Pau, 1995).

Work with a Valid Permit in the Girona Survey

Unlike the previous examples, the majority of those interviewed had a valid residence permit which allowed work in Spain. Yet, there is a substantial difference between those whose residential status is not linked to their work status (i.e. naturalised immigrants and those married with a EU national), and those whose legal status is related to having a hired work. This last group had to renew their hired work to preserve their legal status in the country. According to the procedures in place during my fieldwork, his renewal has to be done at least once a year for those with work (and residence) permits of up to one year; and every five years for those on five-year work permits (Table 3.1) Two points of interest arise from this different permit duration; the first relates to the direct relation between length of stay and access to longer permits; and the second revolves around the more tenuous situation of those on work permits of one year and less.

For the direct relation between the length of stay and access to longer permits, Table 3.4 shows that 43 out of the 52 who arrived before 1986 had a five-year permit when they were interviewed.[42] By cor.trast, all those who arrived in 1992 or afterwards were on a one-year permit. These two trends are expected owing to the relationship between longer stays and permit length. Yet what is not expected is the fact that 61 out of the 63 workers who arrived between 1986-1991 (with more than five years of residence at their interview in 1995) were on one-year permits (or less). This high number of workers on short-length permits suggest that non-EU workers have difficulties securing five years of contracted work. As well, it points to illegality being a first step in the labour trajectory of these workers. To support this, 50 out of these 63 gained legality through the 1991-92 legalisation campaign.

Table 3.4   Interviewed Africans on work and residence permits, by length of work permit and year of arrival in Spain

Length of permit	*Year of arrival*			
	Before 1986	1986-91	1992 onwards	Total
Up-to-one-year	9	61	7	77
Five years	43	2		45
Total	52	63	7	122

Source: Girona interview survey.

Table 3.5   Interviewed Africans on work and residence permits, by length of work permit and hired status in Spain

Length of permit	*Hired status*			
	No contract	Temporary	Permanent	Self-employed	Total
Up-to-one-year	8	63	4	2	77
Five years	1	25	18	1	45
Total	9	88	22	3	122

Source: Girona interview survey.

The second point for consideration is the more tenuous legal situation of those on first year permits. This arises for two reasons. For one, with the exception of those who gain legality through the 1991-92 campaign, those on up-to-one-year b or B permits have geographical or occupational restrictions. Thus, initial b permits are exclusively for one employer. The rules clearly say that the up-to-one-year B permits were for one sector and province. Yet, the Girona office of the Ministry of Labour and Social Security gave permits for any profession, sector and province at the third renewal. An official at the office argued that the reason for this more 'flexible' application was caused by the (more favourable) criteria of the 1991-92 legalisation process. Through this legalisation, workers obtained one-year permits for two types of job or sector anywhere in Spain. The same official explained that this particular way of understanding the law may not be followed in other provinces. Second, as the maximum duration of the B permit is one year (and nine months for an initial b), workers must renew their permits at least once a year. In case they cannot obtain a contracted job, workers face illegality (and expulsion). In a context of high unemployment, obtaining or renewing a contract annually is not easy. Confirming the more stable situation of five-year permit holders in Girona labour markets, Table 3.5 shows that, even if temporary contracts are in the majority for those on one- and five-year permits, one out of every three on a five-year permit has a permanent contract. By contrast, the figure for those on a one-year contract is 5 per cent. It follows that there is a positive correlation between longer permits (and, due to the peculiarities of the work permit system, longer stays) and more stable patterns of employment.

To summarise, there are two main points to stress about Spanish immigration policy. First, legalisation has been a significant immigration policy in the period 1985-1996. Three out of four of those interviewed in Girona were brought into legality through the two campaigns which had taken place by the time of my fieldwork. Second, immigrants apply for residence either with or without work rights. For those on a joint work and residence permit, the legislative framework restrains their mobility both in geographical and in occupational terms in their first five years of legal residence. By law, these restrictions affect those on b or B work permits (up to one year, employees). Yet, those legalised in the 1991-92 campaign had no such restrictions. Similarly, for those in legal work through the ordinary system, restrictions were lifted after the third renewal of a permit in the province in Girona. There are two ideas to outline here:

• The ethos underlying legislation is that non-EU nationals are temporary (guest) workers for fixed-term jobs (Santos, 1993b; Cachón Rodríguez, 1995; Huntoon, 1998).
• The (less strict) application of the rules depends on individual provincial criteria.

These legal restrictions make obtaining (or renewing) work permits difficult. The four case studies show that illegal residence is partly caused by rigid work permit procedures. Furthermore, the considerable number of workers on up-to-one-year permits, who thereby have to renew their residential status annually, plus the fact that temporary contracts are the norm, points to the bulk of Africans being in a tenuous legal situation. As reported by non-governmental organisations, the return of illegality is not uncommon for up-to-one-year work permit holders in times of less favourable economic conjunctures.

Portugal: The *'Grande Confusão'*[43]

Like Spain, the recent democratic period in Portugal has been characterised by substantial changes in naturalisation and immigration policies. Thus, long before Spain, and occasioned by the end of the colonial empire in Africa, a new nationality law was passed in 1975.[44] This restricted Portuguese nationality to those who lived in the colonies of Portuguese ancestors.[45] By contrast, to obtain Portuguese nationality, those who were resident in the current territory of the Republic of Portugal when the independence of their country of origin was declared (and had no Portuguese-born parent or grandparent) needed a five-year period of residence in Portugal prior to 25 April 1974 (Ramos, 1976a). In 1981, a new nationality law was approved.[46] The main legislative change was the complete abandonment of the *jus soli* principle, with children of non-Portuguese nationals born in Portugal being considered foreigners from 1981. Finally, the 1994 amendment of the 1981 law hardly modified the legislative framework. The only remarkable change was that the new law established tougher criteria for nationals of non-Portuguese speaking countries to naturalise.[47]

For immigration policies, Portugal was a pioneer amongst Southern European countries, with a law package being passed in 1981.[48] This established a typology of residence permits which are still in place, as well as the administrative procedures to regulate entry, stay and expulsion of foreigners. As a consequence of the Treaty on European Union and the Schengen Convention, two new immigration laws were passed in 1993 in order to put the Portuguese legislative framework in tune with the country's international agreements. The first was aimed at non-EU nationals.[49] The second revolved about EU citizens.[50] Finally, to deal with previously illegal residents, two legalisation processes (1992-93 and 1996) were passed.[51]

Residence Permit Procedures

Portuguese legislation on non-EU immigration is less strict and less complicated than Spanish law (see Marie, 1996, who compares the procedures for the acceptance of entry and stay of non-EU workers across the EU countries). The following points capture the essence of its system:

- Similar to Spain, unless they are not in the country for a fixed-term job, EU nationals (and their families) are granted a five-year EU national card, which is renewable automatically.
- Unlike Spain, non-EU nationals apply for a residence (not for a work) permit. The three types of permits that exist are annual, temporary (which is for five years, but can only be applied for after five years of legal residence) and life (which can be applied for after twenty years of legal residence).[52]
- Similar to Spain, the two legalisation processes (1992-93 and 1996) denote that this practice has considerable importance in Portugal's immigration policy. For both, immigrants who wanted to legalise their residential status were not asked to produce a visa allowing them entry into the country. In these campaigns, immigrants were granted one-year permits. Procedures for renewing permits for those who obtained their legality through one of these processes are similar to those for the general system.
- The application for an initial (annual) residence permit needs a visa for residence purposes. For the concession of the visa, the would-be resident must make clear her/his financial situation and justify her/his accommodation in the country. These two last conditions also apply for renewals. In order to justify their financial situation, potential employees need a pre-work contract (or an employer's letter). For self-employed workers and employers, proof of the financial resources that are available to set up a business is required. Finally, professionals must obtain acceptance of their diplomas by the Portuguese administration to obtain a residence permit. There are three main differences with the Spanish system:

  a) There is no consideration of registered unemployment when deciding on acceptance.
  b) Residence permits allow workers to move freely within Portuguese labour markets both in geographical and occupational terms from the first permit.
  c) There are no distinctions between permits for self-employed activities and hired work.

Legalisation Campaigns and the Illegality Issue

Under the 1992-93 campaign,[53] 39,166 saw their residential status pass from illegal to legal (Table 3.6). This figure is similar to the 35,082 who legalised their status in the 1996 campaign (Table 3.6).[54] In both campaigns, PALOP nationals constituted more than half of those legalised (72.3 per cent in 1992 and 66.7 per cent in 1996), with Angolans being the main nationality in both processes.

Table 3.6 Legalisation campaigns in Portugal, by nationality of those 'legalised'*

1992/93	n.	%	1996	n.	%
Angola	12,525	32.0	Angola	9,255	26.4
Guinea Bissau	6,877	17.6	Cape Verde	6,872	19.6
Cape Verde	6,778	17.3	Guinea Bissau	5,308	15.1
Brazil	5,346	13.6	Brazil	2,330	6.6
São Tomé	1,408	3.6	Pakistan	1,754	5.0
Senegal	1,397	3.6	China	1,608	4.6
China	1,352	3.5	São Tomé	1,549	4.4
Mozambique	757	1.9	India	915	2.6
Pakistan	286	0.7	Bangladesh	752	2.1
India	261	0.7	Morocco	520	1.5
Total	39,166	100.0	Total	35,082	100.0

* The countries listed above amount to 94.4 per cent of the 'legalised' population in 1992/93; and 88.0 per cent of the 1996 campaign.

Source: Data provided by the Portuguese Foreigners and Borders' Service [*Serviço de Estrangeiros e Fronteiras*].

The weight of Angolans in these two processes reflects the ongoing consequences of decolonisation, as 61 per cent of *retornados* came from Angola (Dubois, 1994). In all, 12,525 Angolans (against 6,778 Cape Verdeans; Table 3.6) legalised their residence in 1992-93, although legal Cape Verdeans were five times more numerous than Angolans in 1992 (Instituto Nacional de Estatística, 1994a). This legalisation data suggest that there has been a notable incidence of long-term illegality, which is significantly constituted by Angolan nationals. Indeed, the 1992-93 legalisation process seems to have partly been introduced to address the long-term illegal population in Portugal, for one of the two requisites for legalised residence, which only applied to PALOP countries, was entry into Portugal before 1 June 1986 and proof of residence in the country since then.

Concerning long-term illegality, my Portuguese survey found that some illegal residents at the time of their interview had entered the country either before the independence of their home countries or in the aftermath of the decolonisation process. In this regard, Table 3.7 shows information on the past legal residential status in Portugal of those who were illegal residents when interviewed, as well as their year of arrival and current employment. Here it can be seen that four out of the seven illegal residents in my Portuguese survey arrived in Portugal in 1976 or before (interviews 159, 170, 209, 216). This long-term illegality points to the authorities being relatively less concerned at illegal employment than in Spain. Supporting this view, Marie (1995) has held that, despite a Decree as long ago as 26 November 1985 that laid down fines for the illegal employment of foreigners, few checks are made. Similarly, Eaton (1996) has argued that the Portuguese Government neither accepts nor prosecutes illegal immigrants. According to this analyst, the low number of expulsions confirm that this measure is used only as a last resort. Compared with Spain, low pressure on illegality became clear in my fieldwork. Interviewed Africans did not express fear over expulsion nor did they have a strong urge to legalise (or renew) their residential status. Furthermore, interviews with municipal officials showed that local authorities (and presumably the police) were well aware of where illegal residents lived.

Table 3.7 also shows that five out of seven who were illegal residents at their interview date had been legal in the country for a considerable number of years. As an example, Ms. Vasques (interview 209) who arrived in Portugal from Cape Verde in 1974 lost her residence permit in 1985. To renew permits, immigrants must produce proof of enough financial resources to live in Portugal. In the time she was living with her partner, the spouse's job was a sufficient guarantee of her financial resources. However, when their relationship finished in 1983, as they were not married, she could not renew her five-year permit in 1985. This was because she could not prove stable employment (she has always worked in the informal sector). In the 1992-93 legalisation campaign, she was granted a permit due to her length of stay in the country. But, as she could not find a hired job, she lost her legal residential status in 1995. Like Spain, this illustrates that the return of illegality is not uncommon for Africans.

Table 3.7 Interviewed illegal residents in Portugal

N.	Sex (*)	Country of nationality	Age	Year arrival	Periods of legality	Current job
159	F	Angola	33	1975	1975-83	Kitchen assistant
170	M	Cape Verde	30	1972	1972-95	Construction carpenter
185	M	Cape Verde	36	1984	1992-95	Construct. unskilled worker
196	M	Cape Verde	35	1995	None	Construct. unskilled worker
205	M	Cape Verde	30	1996	None	Construct. unskilled worker
209	F	Cape Verde	41	1974	1974-85 1992-95	Cleaner domestic sector
216	F	Cape Verde	46	1973	1973-94	Cleaner domestic sector

* F= female, M=male

Source: Portuguese interview survey.

Naturalised Immigrants

By contrast with the Spanish situation, where only three of 151 interviewed Africans had obtained any EU nationality (Table 3.3), 31 out of 69 interviewed workers in Portugal were African-origin Portuguese nationals (Table 3.8). Paradoxically, this is not because Portuguese naturalisation laws are less restrictive than Spanish ones. Thus, whereas the time of legal residence that is required before applying for Spanish nationality is two years for many countries (including all the nations of what is considered Iberoamerica),[55] Portuguese naturalisation laws establish a minimum of six years of legal residence for the six Portuguese-speaking overseas countries (PALOP). Nationals from these countries represented 77.3 per cent of legal non-EU immigration in 1996 (Instituto Nacional de Estatística, 1997a). For other countries, 10 years of legal residence is required. The same point can be made for the acquisition of nationality by marriage: one year of legal union is necessary to obtain Spanish nationality for those married to a Spaniard, whereas three years must pass for those who are married to a Portuguese citizen. Likewise, children of foreign parents who are born in Portugal need either six or 10 years of legal residence to naturalise, while just one year is sufficient in Spain. By contrast, the application of *jus sanguinis* is similar in both countries, with those born of a Portuguese or

Spanish father or mother, regardless of whether they are born in Iberia or not, being considered Portuguese and Spanish nationals, respectively.

Table 3.8 Interviewed Africans by legal status and year of arrival in Portugal

| | Year of arrival | | | | |
Legal status	Before 1974	1974-76	1977-85	1986 onwards	Total
Portuguese nationals	9	15	5	2	31
Residence permit holders	6	6	6	13	31
Illegal residents	2	2	1	2	7
Total	17	23	12	17	69

Source: Portuguese interview survey.

The reason for the high number of Portuguese African-born immigrants in the survey lies in the recent history of the country and its (chaotic) process of decolonisation in the mid-1970s (and not in the number of naturalisations over the 1980s and 1990s, which is extremely low). This is illustrated by Table 3.9 which shows the number of people achieving naturalisation in Portugal, Spain and the EU.

By contrast, census data show that 505,079 residents in Portugal in 1981 lived in one of the African ex-colonies in 1973. This constituted 5.1 per cent of the total Portuguese population in 1981 (Pires et al., 1987). As 60 per cent of these half million people had been born in Portugal (Pires et al., 1987) (plus the *jus sanguinis* rule which is dominant in Portuguese law), it is reasonable to argue that the bulk of these *retornados* never lost their Portuguese nationality. However, alongside this population of Portuguese origin, substantial (yet less numerous) inflows of Africans with no previous family link with Portugal came into the country (Dubois, 1994). This last group, as well as those who were already residents in Portugal but of non-Portuguese origin, were not automatically granted nationality.

All these characteristics are reflected in my Portuguese survey. First, one out of three of those interviewed had entered Portugal either in 1974 (the year of the Carnation Revolution), 1975 (the year of independence of the African colonies)[56] or 1976 (a reflection of the decolonisation process and of the civil wars in Angola and Mozambique; Table 3.8). Second, the bulk of those who arrived in the period 1974-76 were Portuguese nationals at the moment of their interview. In comparative terms, the percentage of Portuguese nationals in this 1974-76 group was greater than for those who arrived in earlier years (Table 3.8). This indicates the different origin of these two inflows; the pre-1974 group was largely comprised of immigrant workers, who filled jobs in construction and manufacturing that Portuguese emigration had left vacant (as reported by many researchers, see, for instance, Carreira, 1982; Saint Maurice and Pires, 1989; Esteves, 1991; França, 1992); the 1974-76 group was mainly composed of African-born refugees and their families, who mainly came from Angola and Mozambique (Lewis and Williams, 1985; Pires et al., 1987; Dubois, 1994; Saint-Maurice, 1995).

Table 3.9 Number of naturalisations in Portugal, Spain and the EU, 1986-1993

	EU-15	Portugal	Spain
1986	176,745	28	5,132
1987	187,809	48	9,086
1988	186,788	34	8,143
1989	263,865	210	5,919
1990	197,610	97	7,033
1991	238,115	43	3,752
1992	279,150	117	5,226
1993	290,658	2	8,348

Source: Eurostat (1995).

However, even if the majority of these were of Portuguese origin, my survey shows that naturalisation amongst those who arrived in 1974-76 was not exclusively through *jus sanguinis*. To be specific, out of the 15 who were Portuguese nationals at the moment of their interview and came into the country during these years, six declared that they had Portuguese ancestors of one or two generations, five naturalised through residence in Portugal, a further three obtained nationality after marrying a Portuguese national and one person said that Portuguese nationality was given to him because of his service in the Portuguese army in the Angolan independence war (see Table 3.10).

Table 3.10   Interviewed naturalised Africans by the way the Portuguese nationality was obtained

Year of arrival

	Before 1974	1974-76	1977-85	1986 onwards	Total
Jus sanguinis	3	6		1	10
Jus soli	6	5	4		15
Marriage		3	1	1	5
Others *		1			1
Total	9	15	5	2	31

* 'Others' refer to one interviewee who obtained the nationality because of service in the Portuguese army.

Source: Portuguese interview survey.

But whether of Portuguese origin or not, it is perhaps surprising that 16 out of the 40 who entered Portugal in 1976 and before (for whom use of the category 'immigrant' is questionable; Mendoza, 2000) were still foreign citizens in 1996. This suggests support for Hammar's (1990) evidence that rates of naturalisation in Europe are low. This analyst found that the number of foreign residents who had not acquired their host country's citizenship after 10 to 15 years of residence is surprisingly high in Western and Central Europe. Quoting a survey carried out on Turkish legal residents in Germany in 1985, Hammar (1990) reported that 78.7 per cent of those interviewed declared that they had no intention of naturalising, with 40 per cent of those who said 'no' to naturalisation arguing that they wanted to remain citizens of their origin country. Similarly, a survey on 150 young foreign people who were born in France (and, consequently, could naturalise at their adulthood) showed that more than half of all the national groups had no intention of applying for the French nationality (Catani and Palidda, 1989).

Access to the nationality of the host country secures legal residential status and full citizenship. In my survey, this stable legal situation is guaranteed for 31 of the 69 interviewed Africans in Portugal (Table 3.8). What we might expect is that this situation leads to more stable work contexts for Africans in Portugal compared with Spain. In this regard, Table 3.11 shows the hired situation of the interviewed Africans by legal status in the country. Here it is seen that, for the bulk of non-Portuguese nationals, not having a contract was common. By contrast, Portuguese nationals enjoyed a more stable employment situation, with half of them on permanent contracts. But we should note here that (Portuguese) nationality is compulsory for permanent employment in public administration (e.g. hospitals, municipality-owned firms, state-owned industries) or for public housing (Rocha-Trindade, 1995). In this context, it is pertinent to report that three of the Portuguese nationals said that they were 'pushed' into applying for nationality in order to secure a job. A further two declared that they opted for Portuguese nationality in order to obtain a municipal flat. These two facts, alongside a low number of naturalisations (Table 3.9) and the existence of long-term legal (and illegal) immigrants who have lived in the country long enough to obtain nationality, point to African-origin populations lacking conviction that their personal or their employment circumstances would change substantially if they naturalised.

Table 3.11   Interviewed legally-resident Africans in Portugal, by hired status and nationality

Nationality	Hired status				
	Permanent contract	Tempor. contract	No contract	Self-empl workers	Total
Portuguese nationals	16	8	4	3	31
Non-Portuguese nationals	4	8	16	1	31
Total	20	18	20	4	62

Source: Portuguese interview survey.

As a summary of the Portuguese section:

• Recent Portuguese history has conditioned the pace of African labour inflows into the country. It seems that the country has a limited capacity for the attraction of foreign nationalities, other than those from Portuguese ex-colonies. Linked to this, African-born workers in Portugal have entered the country in successive stages, with the first one dating from the late 1960s.

• A relatively high proportion of African immigrants have obtained Portuguese nationality. Surprisingly, many old immigrants (with more

than the necessary years required to take on Portuguese full citizenship)
still have an African nationality.

- Illegality is not restricted to recent immigrants, but is found in different
  immigrant inflows, some of them quite old. The overall impression
  from the fieldwork is that immigrants do not worry especially about
  their legal status. This is confirmed by official reports (Marie, 1995)
  and empirical research (Eaton, 1996). Yet, even for old immigrants,
  returning to illegal residential status is not uncommon. This is because
  many African immigrants cannot obtain hired work.

- Legalisation has been a relevant immigration policy in Portugal. The
  two processes have brought about 60,000 foreigners into legal
  residential status. The bulk of these were originally from the ex-
  colonies.

- Immigrants apply for residence, not for work (unless they are applying
  for work of a short duration). Once the immigrant is accepted as a
  resident, the law does not put any restriction on either occupational or
  geographical mobility within Portugal. The Portuguese
  (un)employment situation is not taken into account when deciding
  acceptance.

- More stable patterns of employment are observed amongst those who
  are naturalised. This is partially due to (Portuguese) nationality being a
  prior step to obtaining access to permanent employment in the public
  sector and public housing.

Conclusion

The state clearly affects immigrant patterns of employment. The
comparison between Portugal and Spain provides numerous examples of it.
For instance, the Spanish quota system only allows immigrants in certain
sectors (e.g. farming), but not in others (e.g. manufacturing). This can even
promote illegality (see the case of Mr. Bushari). For Portugal, non-
Portuguese nationals have no right to permanent employment in state-
owned firms or in public administration.

The state discriminates between those immigrants who are
considered to be more alike to the 'native' population, and other
immigrants who are thought culturally distant from the host country. The
cross-border Iberian comparison offers examples of both. For Portugal,
whereas nationals from Portuguese-speaking countries may obtain
nationality after six years of legal residence, citizens of other countries
must spend 10 years in the country. Spain treats differently Ibero-
Americans, as well as other nationalities with a prior colonial history with

the country, from Moroccans or Sene-Gambians. The first group may secure a five-year work permit after two years; the second, after five years. This discrimination affects employment, as immigrants with longer permits (Spain; Table 3.5) or naturalised immigrants (Portugal; Table 3.11) attain more stable patterns of employment.

These are common trends in both countries. Yet Portugal and Spain also have contrasting political answers to immigration and naturalisation. This occurs even if overarching EU rules have been enforced in both countries. For Portugal, once the visa (the main obstacle for immigration) is overcome, non-EU nationals enjoy rights both in labour markets (free occupational and geographical mobility) and in political settings (e.g. the right to vote in local elections for certain nationalities). The legislative framework considers immigrants as residents, not purely workers. Because of this philosophy, legally-resident children and spouses may join the labour force, without restriction. The Portuguese answer responds to both its longer tradition of immigration (especially from ex-colonies) and its links with the African sending countries (for an overview of the economic and commercial interests of Portugal in PALOP countries since 1973, see Ferreira, 1994b). In fact, many of those who are now living in Portugal came into the country when their home territories were part of the Portuguese 'empire'.

This picture contrasts with the Spanish answer to immigration. In general terms, this sees immigrants as temporary guest workers (Santos, 1993b; Cachón Rodríguez, 1995; Huntoon, 1998). Reflecting this philosophy, the Spanish residential permit system distinguishes between permits without or with work. As for those on a joint residence and work permit, considerable (geographical and occupational) constraints apply. Unlike Portugal, spouses and children of legal non-EU residents have no right to work, unless they change their residence permits. Spanish immigration policy is more restrictive than the Portuguese: whereas the Portuguese legislative framework puts constraints in entry (through visa), the Spanish puts constraints on both entry and stay.

Whether differences in legislative approaches impinge on African labour outcomes is another point. In this regard, Chapter 4 analyses patterns of African employment in farming. For Spain, it has been seen that the quota system accepts new foreign workers in agriculture, alongside other sectors. As the philosophy of the system is that annual quotas should channel immigrants into labour shortages, the state implicitly admits that new (foreign) workers are needed in farming. For Portugal, Chapter 4 will show that, even if non-EU immigrants have less legal constraints on obtaining jobs in Portugal, Africans are not found in great numbers in agriculture.

Notes

1. In October 1986, the Ministers of Home Affairs of the member states created the 'Ad Hoc Immigration' (AHI) Group in order to attempt to coordinate national asylum and immigration policies in the EU. This initiative was taken in anticipation of the Single European Act, which was signed in 1987, whose objective was the elimination of all barriers to the free circulation of goods, persons, services and capital before 1993 (European Parliament, 1996a).
2. An initiative toward further integration was the approval of the Spanish proposal of Union citizenship, which is described in Part Two of the Treaty on European Union. Apart from the right to move and reside freely in any country of the Union, EU nationals who reside in another member state of which he/she is not a national have the right to vote and stand as a candidate at municipal and EU elections (Article 8.b) (Schermers et al., 1993). For more information about Union citizenship, see Closa (1992).
3. Article K.1 (Point 3) specifies what is understood by 'immigration policy and policy regarding nationals of third countries'. This involves: (i) conditions of entry and movement of nationals of third countries in the territory of member states; (ii) conditions of residence by nationals of third countries in the territory of member states, including family reunion and access to employment; and, (iii) combating unauthorised immigration, residence and work by nationals of third countries in the territory of member states (Schermers et al., 1993).
4. This was initially signed by Belgium, France, Germany, Italy, Luxembourg and the Netherlands on 19 June 1990. Spain and Portugal joined the Schengen Group in 1991. It was not until 26 March 1995 that the Convention came into force (European Parliament, 1996b).
5. For more information, see the special issue on 'The decline of asylum: citizenship, migration and statelessness in contemporary Europe' in *Oxford International Review*, summer 1996.
6. Other measures have been brought forward across the EU to increase the authorities' powers of control over the entry, residence and employment of foreign nationals. They include more identity checks (Netherlands, France), more drastic conditions for entitlement to residence and work permits (Greece, France), cutting down the categories that are not liable to deportation (France), revising conditions for issuing visas (Belgium, Luxembourg), more severe penalties for helping immigrants enter a country illegally and employing foreign nationals without permits or stricter controls on accommodation for foreign visitors (France, Belgium, Portugal), restricting rights of appeal (Britain), and extending the possibilities for detaining foreigners who are liable to deportation (Netherlands) or raising the maximum duration of detention (Belgium) (Marie, 1995: 56-57).
7. In the EU, voting rights in local elections for foreign permanent residents have been recognised in Ireland since 1963 (the British have been able to vote in Irish national elections since 1984), in Sweden since 1976, in Denmark since 1981 and in the Netherlands since 1986 (Hammar, 1990). In Spain, non-EU residents have no voting rights at all. This would undoubtedly bring changes in power in some municipalities where Africans constitute considerable minorities (see Chapter 7). In September 1996, the Portuguese Parliament passed a law which enacts the European Union directive on the participation of nationals of other member states in local and European elections. For non-EU residents, voting in local elections was also approved, subject to reciprocity (SOPEMI, 1997). Since then, voting rights in Portuguese local elections

have been granted to nationals from Brazil, Cape Verde and Guinea Bissau (Geoideia Consulting, 1998).

8. For instance, the pensioners' minimum wage [*pensiones no retributivas*] (for those who had not paid enough national insurance contributions in their working live) is restricted to Spanish nationals.

9. The *Decreto-Lei 797/76 (6.11.1976)* restricts public housing to Portuguese nationals (Rocha-Trindade, 1995).

10. In the case of Spain, the state is de-centralised into 17 Autonomous Communities which have self-rule over many issues that concern immigrants (e.g. health, education). For Catalunya, the Autonomous Goverment [*Generalitat de Catalunya*] applies a particular *jus soli* policy which grants compulsory education to all the children, whatever their legal status or their parents' legal status. This policy is applied in education, but does not apply for the Catalan Health Service [*Servei Català de la Salut*], which is restricted to legal residents (Apap, 1997).

11. *Real decreto 511/1992 (14 .5.1992), por el que se crea la Comisión Interministerial de Extranjería.*

12. This was one of the points of the Socialist Party electoral programme. The High Commission was created in 1996, after the *Partido Socialista* won the elections in 1995 in Portugal (Marujo and Rocha, 1996).

13. One example of this is the organisation of Arabic lessons for children of immigrants in several municipalities (e.g. Sant Pere Pescador, Palafrugell), or food, clothing and music festivals which highlight African cultures to the local Catalan population.

14. In this regard, see Rodríguez and Torres (1994); El País (1995); Martínez (1995b); Soler (1995).

15. Taking into account the major changes in immigration policies in Iberia in the period 1997-2000, the discussion on the role of the state in channelling African inflows into certain type of jobs is developed in Mendoza (2001).

16. *Ley Orgánica 7/1985 (1.7.1985), sobre derechos y libertades de los extranjeros en España.*

17. *Real Decreto 1119/1986 (26.5.1986) por el que se aprueba el Reglamento de ejecución de la Ley Orgánica 7/1985.*

18. *Real Decreto 766/1992 (26.6.1992) sobre entrada y permanencia en España de nacionales de estados miembros de las Comunidades Europeas.*

19. *Real Decreto 155/1996 (2.2.1996) por el que se aprueba el Reglamento de ejecución de la Ley Orgánica 7/1985.*

20. *Real Decreto 1521/1991 (11.10.1991) sobre creación, competencias y funcionamiento de las oficinas de extranjeros.* This Ministry merged with the Ministry of Social Affairs after the Conservative *Partido Popular* took power in Spain in 1996. The current name is the Ministry of Labour and Social Affairs.

21. Visa requirements do not apply to travellers to the African enclaves of Ceuta and Melilla. These requirements also do not affect either the nationals of those countries who are living legally in another EU state or are in possession of a visa from another EU state, when travelling across Spain. Regarding Latin American countries, Cuba and the Dominican Republic have been affected by the visa requirements of the Schengen Convention (Lirola Delgado, 1993).

22. The process ran from 23 July 1985 to 31 March 1986.

23. The 1991 process ran from 10 June 1991 to 10 December 1991 for illegal workers. For relatives of legal non-EU workers (or relatives of those workers who applied for legalisation in 1991), who were illegal residents in the country, the process finished on 10 March 1992 (Aragón Bombín and Chozas Pedrero, 1993).

24. This process, which was restricted to previously legal residents, ran from 23 April 1996 to 22 August 1996.
25. Since the interest of this book is labour immigration, legislation on asylum-seekers and refugees has deliberately been put aside in this description.
26. For adult Spanish nationals, the national identity card [*Documento Nacional de Identidad, D.N.I.*] is compulsory. As well, EU nationals need an identity card [*Tarjeta de Residente Comunitario*].
27. Border control and immigration policies are the exclusive competence of the Spanish Government. The administration of these policies is undertaken at the provincial level, so implementation may vary from one province to another. In fact, the Girona administration was known, amongst immigrants and immigrant organisations, as being more 'flexible' than the Barcelona one, over procedures like issuing permits. At the time of my fieldwork (July-December 1995), the four Catalan provinces were implementing a policy of co-ordinating administrative procedures on work and residence permits.
28. The Ministry of Labour and Social Security may ask the employer to announce job vacancies in the local employment office.
29. The National Employment Institute [*Instituto Nacional de Empleo, INEM*] was transferred to the Catalan Autonomous Government in 1998.
30. In 1993, only 6,415 applications were received (and 5,220 were accepted; Table 3.2) for the whole of Spain (Dirección General de Migraciones, 1997). This contrasted with the 25,604 jobs that the Government finally accepted for 1994 (Table 3.2). The failure of the quota system to bring new workers into Spain resulted from the small number of job offers employers made. This is an essential pre-requisite for immigrant employees to obtain legal entry (residence and work). The reasons for this low number are said to be various: (i) employers must pay the return ticket of the employee; (ii) high unemployment in Spain; and (iii) the presence of illegal workers in Spain (Aprell Lasagabaster, 1994).
31. In the case of Girona, exemption of visa was granted to those with three years of (illegal) residence in the country in 1995. Many documents (e.g. a bank account) were accepted to prove residence.
32. The quota was not broken down by nationality in 1997 or 1998 (Fuente, 1998).
33. This does not mean that these legal residents cannot work legally in the country (provided they apply for a work permit). In fact, amongst the 122 interviewees who were on work and residence permits at the time of their interview, there were seven legal residents who could not work at the beginning of their stay, but afterwards successfully applied for a work permit.
34. Prostitution, for instance, is only an illegal activity in certain countries. In others, even it is not legal, it is tolerated. Finally, in certain countries it is prosecuted.
35. This point was made by several employers. Some skilled workers (e.g. carpenters, welders, vanishers) are in short supply in some localities in Girona. These are professions with a high craft component. See Chapter 7 for a deeper analysis of labour shortages in manufacturing localities.
36. In this context, two interviewed Moroccans complained that they had to change the (skilled) work category on their permit application in order to obtain clearance. These Moroccans were responsible for the surveillance and care of accommodation establishments. They were finally granted a work permit as a watch person.
37. A small precariously-built boat. While previously an unusual word, *patera* has become popular in the mass media and its usage has rapidly spread to general society.

38. Pines are quite appreciated as an expensive complement in Catalan cuisine. *Panellets*, a traditional Catalan dessert for the All Saints first of November celebration, is made of potatoes and pines.
39. If legally-resident relatives of non-EU legal workers want to work, they must apply for a work permit. This group has certain privileges when applying for a work permit. Spouses, sons and daughters of workers who have been living legally in the country for five years, as well as those born in Spain, have their work permit application considered without reference to the provincial employment situation. In other words, the Ministry of Labour and Social Security allows them to take any job, regardless of the number of registered unemployed Spaniards in a province (Escuin Palop, 1991).
40. This Law was aimed at drug dealers and terrorists, rather than illegal foreign workers. It also gave police the right to conduct warrant-less searches of private residences. This last clause of the Law was declared unconstitutional in December 1993 (Cornelius, 1994).
41. For instance, if a foreigner does not have an identity card, the authorities do not know where to extradite her or him to (Ministerio del Interior, 1994). In the media, it was reported that Moroccans or Tunisians pretend to be Algerians to avoid expulsion. This is because the Algerian Government does not accept immigrants who are expelled from Spain, unless the Spanish authorities can prove that they are Algerian nationals (Cia and Piñol, 1994).
42. However, nine workers who arrived in Spain before 1986 do not have a long-stay permit. An array of personal circumstances explain why this heterogeneous group has not secured five-year permits. The point is that personal circumstances (e.g. intention of stay, life cycle, personal choice) must be considered when dealing with immigration and permit possession. This point is further developed in Chapter 8.
43. African-born immigrants generally referred to the years prior to and after the independence of the ex-Portuguese colonies (1974-76) as '*a grande confusão*' [a big confusion].
44. *Decreto-Lei 308-A (24.6.1975).*
45. The Law extended Portuguese nationality to some special cases (e.g. those with a special link with Portugal).
46. *Lei 37/81 (3.10.1981). Lei da Nacionalidade.*
47. *Lei 25/94 (19.8.1995).* Until 1994, six years of legal residence were necessary to naturalise as a Portuguese citizen for all foreigners. From 1994, six years remained for those from Portuguese speaking countries (namely, Angola, Brazil, Cape Verde, Guinea Bissau, Mozambique, and São Tomé and Príncipe), but 10 years are necessary for nationals from other countries since then (Ministério de Administração Interna, 1995a).
48. *Decreto-Lei 264-B/81 (3.9.1981).*
49. *Decreto-Lei 59/93 (3.3.1993)* and *Decreto Regulamentar 43/93 (15.12.1993).*
50. *Decreto-Lei 60/93 (3.3.1993).*
51. *Decreto-Lei 212/92 (12.10.1992)* and *Lei 17/96 (24.5.1996).*
52. There are work permits in Portugal, but they are exclusively issued for temporary work. They are restricted to those who want to work to a maximum of 90 days (Article 18). Work permits may be extended by a further 60 days (Article 32) (Ministério da Administração Interna, 1995b).
53. The 1992-93 legalisation process ran from 12 October 1992 to 12 January 1993.
54. The 1996 legalisation process ran from 11 June 1996 to 11 December 1996.
55. Iberoamericans (plus Portuguese, Filipino, Equatorial Guinea nationals and Sephardies (Jews of Spanish origin) can obtain Spanish nationality after two years of legal residence. Five years are necessary for asylum seekers and refugees, 10 years in other

cases. The principle of favouring countries/people with historical links with Spain applies for the above-mentioned nationalities, but does not apply for the old Spanish protectorate of Morocco.

56. The Republic of Guinea Bissau and the Cape Verde Islands were the first African countries to get independence from Portugal. This occurred on 19 September 1974 (initially they were one country, but the Cape Verde Islands opted for self-rule from inland Guinea Bissau on 5 July 1975); Mozambique followed on 25 June 1975; São Tomé and Príncipe on 12 July 1975 and finally Angola on 11 November 1975 (Ramos, 1976b).

4 African Employment in Iberian Agriculture

Chapter 3 analysed the role of the state in managing the entry and stay of non-EU nationals. The state has also a decisive role in regulating the conditions in which labour markets operate. As an example, the Salazar and Caetano policies of high subsidies for agricultural products hampered technical change in Portuguese farming (Corkill, 1993; Sapelli, 1995). As well, as a result of the accession of Portugal and Spain into the EU in 1986, the Iberian farming sector suffered from increasing international competition, as well as acceded to new markets (e.g. Eisfeld, 1989; Etxezarreta and Viladomiu, 1989; Avillez, 1993; Pérez Yruela, 1995). Nowadays farming in the developed world is decided out of the fields, in an international forum (e.g. EU quotas, GATT agreements). In this context, this chapter draws insight on the characteristics and evolution of farming since the 1960s. More than examining these trends thoroughly, the point is to assess whether changes in farming (e.g. the introduction of new crops) are a key reason for the demand for African workers.

What will be clear from the analysis of trends in Iberian agriculture is that the sector exhibits contrasting characteristics in both countries. Within each country, regional differences are also notable on both sides of the border. For Spain, work permit data show that African employment is concentrated in several Autonomous Communities. The Communities where few immigrants are employed differ substantially one from another in terms of their agricultural specialisation. The same can be said for Portugal, as immigrants are not found in great numbers in either the Alentejo's extensive agriculture or Algarve's intensive fruit and vegetable production. This is to say that the reasons for the low African employment may differ regionally in Iberia.

A trend which seems to be associated with the entry of African workers in Spanish farming is the move toward more labour-intensive farming techniques. This change in production has produced a need for extra workers. However, if Africans constitute the bulk of these workers, the question that this prompts is why 'native' workers do not take new farm jobs. In fact, the considerable number of Africans who work (or have worked) in farming suggest that there is substitution of Spanish workers by Africans. Yet, this substitution may exist for certain jobs (and for certain farms), and not for others. Furthermore, the same move towards more intensive production in Portugal has not resulted in a substantial entry of Africans into farming. Presenting the results of the Girona and Algarve surveys, this chapter analyses the scope of substitution of 'native' workers by Africans and the reasons for it.

The chapter first examines differences in Spanish agriculture, with special reference to the places where immigrants find work. It explores relations between agricultural methods and products, and the increase in immigrant employment. After that, the chapter focuses on the Girona interview survey, which shows that Africans easily obtain employment in the agricultural sector. The processes of substitution, complementary and competition between local Catalan workers, seasonal in-migrants from other parts of Spain, and Africans, are placed in the specific context of the province's agriculture. The last part of the chapter compares the low African presence in Portuguese farming with the Spanish case.

Trends in Spanish Agriculture and Demand for African Workers[1]

Immigrant workers are over-represented in the Spanish agricultural sector. Farming employed 9.3 per cent of the working labour force in Spain in 1995 (Eurostat, 1996), but provided jobs for 14.1 per cent of legal non-EU workers in the same year (Ministerio de Trabajo y Seguridad Social, 1996). Immigrants, who are mainly from African countries, have worked in Spanish farming since the 1980s, as many studies have reported (e.g. Fuentes et al., 1988, and Balcells, 1991, on seasonal jobs in the Lleida picking season; Avellá Reus, 1991, and Moreno Torregrosa, 1993, on the Valencia orange sector; Jabardo Velasco, 1993, on Maghreb immigration into the Alicante vegetable sector; Ramírez, 1993, on African employment in Barcelona intensive farming; Checa, 1995, Cózar, 1996, and Roquero, 1996, on Almería's greenhouses; Sánchez et al, 1996, on fruit trees in Cáceres; Cruces Roldán and Martín Díaz, 1997, on immigrant employment in two Andalucía regions; see Figure 1.3 for the location of these provinces). Yet immigrants have been employed in farming long before in other countries. Thus, for the USA, studies dated as early as the 1970s outlined the significance of farm immigrant workers (see, for instance, Baker, 1976; Dunbar and Kravitz, 1976; or Goldfarb, 1981). Similarly, for Europe, Berlan (1986) has described the long French immigrant experience, with Iberians substituted by Maghrebins in the country's farming. Like

Spain, immigrants in the agricultural sector of Italy and Greece are more recent, as Venturini (1991) and King (1993) for Italy, and Black (1994) for Greece, have noticed.

Studies on immigrant workers in Spanish farming are based on empirical case studies. They are generally descriptive in tone and focus on the characteristics of workers (e.g. nationality, year of arrival, legal status in Spain). Some researchers have also outlined the relation between move toward labour-intensive farming and non-EU worker employment (Cózar, 1996; or Roquero, 1996, for Almería; Sánchez et al., 1996, for Cáceres), as well as Africans filling labour shortages in farming (Avellá Reus, 1991, for Valencia; or Balcells, 1991, for Lleida). However, these studies do not link evidence with broad theoretical questions. Specifically, they do not give reasons for the substitution of Spanish workers by immigrants; as Cyrus (1994) has shown for German agriculture or Odé (1996) for Dutch farming. These latter two analysts have agreed that the characteristics of employed labour in farming (e.g. low wages, short-term contracts, lack of promotion and poor working conditions) render the sector scarcely attractive for local workers, and caused labour shortages which are being filled by immigrants. In order to assess whether these trends also apply for Spain, this chapter first examines changes in agriculture in the last two decades, with special reference to the dramatic decline in Spanish farming population.

Spanish Agriculture on the Move?

Spanish agriculture has substantially changed in the last three decades. Whatever the indicator used (e.g. labour force, productivity, crop production, exports, mechanisation), agriculture at the end of the 1990s bears little similarity with the same sector at the beginning of the 1960s (for an overview of the trends in the sector since 1960, see Etxezarreta and Viladomiu, 1989; Pérez Yruela, 1995). Yet, whereas productivity per labour unit and production have grown incredibly over recent decades, farmers' incomes have suffered from relative systematic erosion (Etxezarreta, 1992; Pérez Yruela, 1995). Changes in Spanish agriculture have been produced by factors that are both external (e.g. joining the European Union; Mylokenko et al. 1987; San Juan de Mesonada, 1993) and internal to the country (e.g. the Spanish process of industrialisation in the 1960s; Naredo, 1986; Sapelli, 1995). Here the aim is not to examine these changes as such, but to give consideration to how these trends help explain African employment in farming.

One of the most dramatic changes in Spanish agriculture is the reduction of its labour force. Thus, whereas 33.7 per cent of the labour force was employed in agriculture in 1964 (Instituto Nacional de

Estadística, 1966a), by 1995 this figure was 9.3 per cent (Eurostat, 1996). In the 1960s, as manufacturing offered better-paid jobs, agricultural labourers fled from rural areas to Spanish cities (see, for instance, Nadal, 1984). Yet, in the 1970s, decline in the working agricultural population was more a response to natural decrease, caused by the sector taking on few new entrants and seeing an ageing of its labour force (Naredo, 1986). Alongside new job opportunities in manufacturing and service industries, decline was also occasioned by a crisis of confidence in the Spanish agricultural sector. This was recognised a long time ago in Greenwood's (1976) Basque study, in which he showed that young people were leaving farming in favour of urban jobs, even if this meant a reduction in their income. More recently, García-Ramon and colleagues (1995) have showed that women who were involved in agricultural activities held the view that it was not desirable for their sons to enter the sector. This finding applied in two contrasting agricultural areas: the booming strawberry sector in Huelva (Andalucía) and the inland area of Priorat (Catalunya), which has specialised in the hazelnut fruit sector and is suffering from competition from low-cost foreign producers, such as Turkey. According to García-Ramon and colleagues (1995), rural activities are associated with low social status in Andalucía, whereas, in the relatively wealthy Catalan area, low farm profits push would-be agricultural employers out of the sector. Both directly and through parental influence, then, farming is not appealing to younger generations. Indeed, Enciso Rodríguez and Sabaté Prats (1995), quoting data from Spanish agrarian censuses, demonstrate that the fall in the non-hired labour force in agriculture between 1982 and 1989 (130,710) was primarily due to a sharp reduction in the number of workers aged under 25 years or less (for this age group there were 139,949 less in 1989 than in 1982). By contrast, the 55-64 age group grew by 51,257 over the same period (and those of more than 65 years increased by 32,787).

The example of competition from Turkish hazelnut growers brings out two points: the internationalisation of agricultural markets and the capacity of Spanish agriculture to compete in international markets. It is commonly agreed that, as a result of accession to the EU and changes in the Common Agrarian Policy (CAP),[2] Spanish farmers are facing a more competitive productive environment (see, for instance, Mylokenko et al. 1987; Cruz, 1993; Pérez Yruela, 1995). Yet, as a general trend, Spanish agriculture looks poorly prepared to compete at an international level. An indication of how precarious operations are in agriculture is suggested by the fact that 67.9 per cent of farm employers worked part-time on their holdings, according to the 1989 Agrarian Census (Instituto Nacional de Estadística, 1991). As well as the magnitude of off-farm work, a characteristic of these units is their emphasis on family labour. Indicative of this, for Spain as a whole, while there were 1,405,190 employers' relatives working either full- or part-time on farm holdings in 1989, the number of permanent hired employees was just 135,646 (Instituto Nacional de Estadística, 1991).

However, the impact of joining the EU on agriculture (and the capacity of Spanish agriculture to compete internationally) largely varies by crop, region and type of farm. By crop, entry into the EU had a negative effect on cereals, milk[3] and products that were already produced in surplus within the Union. By contrast, EU membership offered an extra market for fruit and vegetable production (Etxezarreta and Viladomiu, 1989; San Juan de Mesonada, 1993). Yet the 'free' market for these products was not effective until 1992, and it has been argued that the market for fruit and vegetables is highly conditioned by agreements with third countries (Etxezarreta and Viladomiu, 1989). As well, accession to the EU has shown structural deficiencies in Spanish farming (e.g. inadequacy of marketing and distribution channels; Moreno Torregrosa, 1993; Salmon, 1995). By type of farm, large farms (just 3.1 per cent of farms had holdings of more than 100 ha. in 1993; Eurostat, 1996), for which productivity and output levels are above the average, are likely to compete better in world markets (Pérez Yruela, 1995). But small- and medium-sized firms (with 58.1 per cent of holdings having less than 5 ha in 1993; Eurostat, 1996) are in a more difficult position (Etxezarreta and Viladomiu, 1989; Cruz, 1993). By region, the impact of CAP reform (from price market policy to income policies) is thought to have been positive in assisting the more backward regions of the country (San Juan de Mesonada, 1993). Regional differences are also crucial to understanding unequal patterns of immigrant employment in Spain.

Immigrant Labourers in Farming: Differences by Autonomous Community

Work permit data by Autonomous Community show that few legal non-EU workers are found in the northern and central Autonomous Communities of Galicia, Asturias, Cantabria and Castilla y León (see Comisión Interministerial de Extranjería, annual). The crucial point to understand about the absence of immigrants in some of these Communities (namely, Galicia, Asturias and Cantabria) is their low productivity per labour unit, with values of less than half the Spanish average (Eurostat, 1997a). As one illustration, Romero (1993) calculated that for 1988 Galicia recorded only 25.7 per cent of the average EU Gross Value Added per agricultural labour unit. The low productivity in the region is occasioned by low levels of mechanisation, small holdings and a surplus of labour in agriculture (Colino Sueiras, 1984; Calcedo Ordóñez, 1996). By contrast, Castilla y

León, another Autonomous Community with a small number of non-EU workers in agriculture, records a labour productivity level above the Spanish average. The reason for the lack of immigrants in its agriculture lies in the specialisation of this region in cereal production, with Castilla y León having 32.2 per cent of the total cereal production of Spain in 1993 (Eurostat, 1997a). Cereals are less labour demanding than crops like fruit, vegetables or vineyards, and the cereal harvest can be mechanised more easily than fruit collection (Giles, 1964; Cook and Hill, 1994). Furthermore, when extra labour demand has been needed in the region, it has been seasonal in nature and has mainly been covered by temporary Portuguese immigration (López Trigal and Prieto Sarro, 1993; López Trigal, 1996).[4]

The kind of crop grown is also crucial to explaining the striking differences that exist in the number of non-EU workers within Andalucía. Thus, in Huelva, and especially Almería, which stand out as immigrant worker provinces (Figure 4.1), the utilised agricultural area has seen substantial expansion in fruit and vegetable cultivation. To be specific, whereas cereal production stagnated over the period 1982-89, land under fruit trees experienced an increase of 11.3 per cent in Almería and 90.0 per cent in Huelva (with figures for vegetables at 50.3 per cent in Almería and 122.1 per cent in Huelva; Instituto Nacional de Estadística, 1984; 1991). For these labour-intensive crops, research shows that it is immigrants who are mainly employed as hired workers (Moreno Torregrosa, 1993; Checa, 1995; Cózar, 1996; Roquero, 1996; Cruces Roldán and Martín Díaz, 1997). By contrast, few immigrants are recorded in the other provinces of Andalucía. These provinces specialise in cereals and olive trees, which are less labour demanding than vineyards, fruit or vegetables. Furthermore, the process of rural exodus in southern Spain, which started in the latifundia that are most prominent in inland Andalucía, Extremadura and La Mancha, forced large-scale farmers to undertake mechanisation (Sapelli, 1995). As a result of this, labour productivity in Andalucía is higher than the Spanish average (Eurostat, 1997a). In addition, large estates have a long-established rural proletariat (see, for instance, Martínez Alier, 1986), so openings for immigrant workers are limited. In this regard, despite the move toward more labour-intensive crops, Cruces Roldán and Martín Díaz (1997) have found that the existence of an abundant number of agricultural labourers in Cádiz are a key reason for the light African presence in the new developed intensive agriculture in the province.

The three examples of the northern Autonomous Communities, Castilla y León and Andalucía point to five different farm attributes that are associated with low levels of non-EU employment in agriculture. These are: (i) low productivity small holdings; (ii) crops that have low labour demands, such as cereals and olive trees; (iii) the existence of a long established rural proletariat; (iv) the hiring of seasonal Portuguese workers in Spanish areas neighbouring Portugal; and, (v) high levels of mechanisation. The Andalucía example also shows that the Autonomous Community level hides important geographical differences in immigrant employment, as indicated by figures at the provincial level. In the next section, this idea is extended through a provincial analysis which introduces new elements into our understanding of immigrant employment patterns in Spanish agriculture.

Immigrant Employment by Province

Focusing the discussion on the province level, Figure 4.1 shows those provinces in which non-EU nationals represented more than 0.7 per cent of the provincial farming population in 1995, with those having shares of 0.7 per cent or less being blank.[5] This Figure shows that foreign labour in agriculture is most notable in an array of provinces situated on the Mediterranean coast, along the Ebro Valley and in a few provinces in inland, southern Spain. In Figure 4.1, provinces have been divided into 'agricultural areas' (those with the percentage of their labour force in farming at above the Spanish average of 9.3 per cent in 1995; Instituto Nacional de Estadística, 1996b) and 'non-agricultural areas' (with percentages below the average). Taking a share of 5 per cent or more of non-EU nationals in the farming workforce as an indicator of high concentrations of immigrants in the sector (the average for Spain is 1.4 per cent), Figure 4.1 shows that non-EU nationals are clearly over-represented in farming in both 'agricultural provinces' (e.g. Murcia) and 'non-agricultural provinces' (e.g. Barcelona). In areas where agriculture accounts for a small percentage of the workforce, immigrant labour might be needed because non-immigrants can take alternative jobs. However, this explanation is not a complete one, for agriculture has varying shares of the local labour force in provinces in which the role of foreign workers in agriculture is high.

Adding a further twist to the analysis, provinces with a non-EU composition in their agricultural workforce above the Spanish average have contrasting crop specialisations. For instance, in 1993, cereals represented more than 50 per cent of the utilised agricultural area of the province of Zaragoza (Aragón), but this province had a marginal presence in fruit and vegetable production, which dominated farming in Murcia (Ministerio de Agricultura, Pesca y Alimentación, 1995). Yet provincial data on crop specialisation can be of limited interest when analysing immigrant employment, as foreigners are not necessarily employed to work on the dominant crop in a province. For instance, according to a 1994 survey that focused on seasonal workers in Mediterranean Spain (Metra-Seis, 1995), 96 per cent of seasonally employed agricultural workers in the Catalan

Figure 4.1 Non-EU employment in farming as percentage of the provincial agricultural workforce 1995

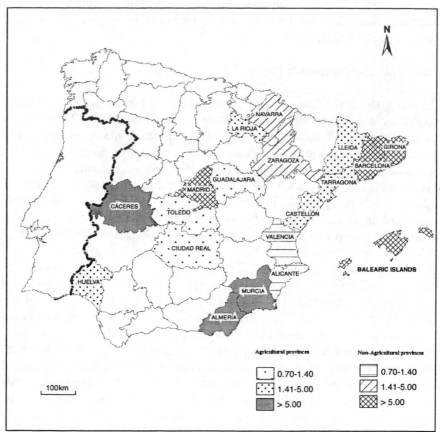

Notes: Blank provinces are those with shares of non-EU nationals in their agricultural labor force under 0.7 per cent.
The Canary Islands have shares below 7 per cent.
Agricultural provinces refer to those with shares of farming in total employment above the Spanish average.

Source: Comisión Interministerial de Extranjería (1996); Instituto Nacional de Estadística (1996b)

province of Lleida (in which the dominant crop, cereals, occupied one-third of the utilised land area; (Ministerio de Agricultura, Pesca y Alimentación, 1995) were engaged in the fruit tree sector. Adding further support to it, the literature on immigrant employment in Spanish agriculture indicates that non-EU nationals are most likely to be found in zones of intensive agriculture (Fuentes et al., 1988; Avellá Reus, 1991; Balcells, 1991; Jabardo Velasco, 1993; Moreno Torregrosa, 1993; Ramírez, 1993; Checa, 1995; Cózar, 1996; Roquero, 1996; Sánchez et al, 1996; Cruces Roldán and Martín Díaz, 1997). Yet, even if immigrant employment is not as remarkable as in intensive farming, Giménez Romero (1992) has noted that seasonal immigrant employment has been extended to areas of extensive dry farming (e.g. the vineyards of Castilla-La Mancha). Work permit data mapped in Figure 4.1 add support to this point, for levels of immigrant employment were above 0.7 per cent of the agricultural labour force (yet below the Spanish average) in the Castilla-La Mancha provinces of Ciudad Real, Toledo and Guadalajara. However, even if immigrant employment in extensive agriculture is noticeable (at least compared to the figures recorded in the northern and central Autonomous Communities of Asturias, Cantabria, Castilla-León and Galicia), numbers remain considerably lower than those recorded in the intensive agriculture of either Mediterranean provinces (e.g. Almería, Murcia or Girona) or the Ebro Valley (e.g. Zaragoza or Navarra) (Figure 4.1).

All the previous analysis has been based on statistical sources and existing literature. This partly offers insights on reasons for immigrant employment. For instance, the economic diversification of a province seems to be irrelevant in explaining the geography of immigrant farm employment in Spain, for provinces with divergent agricultural contributions employ both a few and substantial number of Africans in this sector. The kind of agriculture (intensive or extensive) is also not a sufficient explanation. The most remarkable example of this is the few non-EU workers who are found in the labour-intensive agriculture of the northern Autonomous Communities (e.g. Galicia). Here the key element to explain the lack of (immigrant) hired workers is the surplus of farming population, linked to low production (see, for instance, Colino Sueiras, 1984; Salmon, 1995; Calcedo Ordóñez, 1996). Only the kind of crops that are grown – particularly, fruit and vegetables – provide a convincing (yet partial) single-factor explanation for geographical patterns of immigrant employment.

Fruit and vegetables are agricultural products whose demand expanded long before entry into the EU. In this sense, García-Ramon (1985) has found that the 40 per cent irrigation increase in Baix Camp in the Catalan province of Tarragona between 1955 and 1971 was accompanied by the introduction of fruit and vegetable production and a reduction in the land area devoted to vineyards and olive trees. Yet Hudson and Lewis (1985b) have argued that changes in the pattern of agricultural production toward a more specialised export-oriented agriculture in Spain cannot be understood without reference to the operation of the EU, as Spain (along with Portugal and Turkey) had trade and association agreements with the EU before joining the Community. The move into intensive farming has continued after accession to the EU, as the data for Almería and Huelva in the 1980s showed previously. Significantly there has been a rise in demand for these labour-intensive crops at a time when farming activities were already not attractive for either farmers' relatives or local workers (as shown by Brandes, 1976; Greenwood, 1976). In the areas in which the move towards intensive farming dates from the 1960s and 1970s, this mismatch in demand was first met by either in-migrants, non-working local residents or both; and then by African workers (as shown by Avellá Reus, 1991; Balcells, 1991; Giménez Romero, 1992; Moreno Torregrosa, 1993). In the areas in which intensive farming is more recent, the expansion of labour-intensive crops has occurred in parallel with the entry of African workers into the sector (as found by Giménez Romero, 1992; Roquero, 1996; Sánchez et al., 1996). According to agricultural employers, farmers in the province of Girona started to substitute cereals by fruit trees at the 1960s. Nowadays, the employment of Africans in the sector is well-spread in the province. Based on the results of the surveys on African employees and employers, the next section explores the scope and reasons for the substitution of Spanish workers by Africans. The analysis does not only focus on the role of immigrants in agriculture, but also on the role of agriculture in immigrant labour market trajectories in Spain.

African Immigrants in Girona Agriculture

In Girona, Africans are mainly employed in intensive fruit production. Since 1960, land under trees has expanded at the expense of cereals and other crops in this province.[6] This expansion is even more remarkable given a reduction of almost 20 per cent in agricultural land use in the period 1960-1993 (Instituto Nacional de Estadística, annual[a]). The change toward more intensive production is illustrated by two employers' commentaries:

> Ten years ago, the majority of land in my holding was under cereals, either wheat, corn or barley. As well we had 2,000 calves and cows. Nowadays, the land under apple and peach trees is 15 ha., similar to those under cereals and the number of calves and cows have been reduced to 40.

My grandfather used to have alfalfa and cereals. Apple trees were introduced in 1961 on the farm. Nowadays we've got 3 ha. under peach trees, 1 ha. with pears trees and the rest of the 20 ha. are apple trees. Cereals are only for the time the trees are pulled up.

Linking change toward more intensive production with the evolution of those who are employed and the nature of tasks undertaken on the farm, another employer explained that more workers are needed as a result of the introduction of fruit trees:

Me and my wife work regularly on the farm. She's in charge of the administration, as well as cleaning the calves and milking the cows. In summer, she also picks fruit. I drive the tractor, sulphate lands, prune the trees and do the harvesting. So does the only permanent employee of the farm. He's been employed for many years with me. He's almost part of the family. My two daughters help us in summer with the fruit collection. They are students at Girona University. As livestock and cereals have been replaced by fruit trees, we had to hire temporary employees. Last year, for instance, we had seven workers on fixed-term contracts, one of them was Spanish and the rest were Africans. The Spanish worked permanently for the whole peak season (from June to September). The Africans were employed for one month or several weeks for specific tasks (like peach collection).

So far it looks clear that the entry of Africans into the agricultural labour force in the province is related to a move toward intensive fruit production. Further suggesting the strength of this link, as fruit production has expanded, African employment in the province has increased (Table 1.4), with farming being the main port of entry for Africans in Spanish labour markets. This was the sector that offered the first job in Spain to almost half the interviewees (Table 4.1). Furthermore, two thirds of the sample had at some time undertaken an agricultural job in Spain (99 out of 151).[7] To add further support for farming being a main African employer, the survey points out that there is a high concentration of African workers in farm holdings. Out of the 38 interviewees working in agricultural activities at the moment of their interview,[8] 20 declared that more than half of their co-workers were Africans; six said that all employees were Africans on their farm and five more held that he/she was the only employee. Just seven out of the 38 reported that Africans constituted less that 50 per cent of total employees. Furthermore, none of the interviewees said that he/she was the only African workers on the farm.

However, as they stay in Spain for a longer period of time (and so get to know channels through which to gain access to other jobs), foreign workers spill over into other economic sectors (as Table 4.1 shows). Significantly, only 24 out of the 67 who had entered the Spanish labour market through farming were in that sector at their interview. The reason for this net transfer lies in farming providing few permanent jobs for immigrants.

Table 4.1   Current and first jobs in Spain for interviewed Africans, by economic sector

Current *	First * Farming	Forestry	Manufact.	Construct.	Services	Total
Farming	24	2		5	7	38
Forestry	8				1	9
Manufacturing	9	2	6	3	5	25
Construction	11	2		8		21
Servicies	15	1		6	36	58
Total	67	7	6	22	49	151

* Those out of work at their interview have been classified in this table according to their last job.

Source: Girona interview survey.

Table 4.2   Type of job by hired status of interviewed workers in the primary sector in Girona

	No contract	Temporary	Permanent	Total
Farming, unskilled[a]	11	18	1	30
Farming, skilled[b]		4	4	8
Forestry, unskilled[c]	5	4		9
Total	16	26	5	47

Notes:
a)   Unskilled and semi-skilled farm tasks refer to spraying, picking-up, pruning, feeding livestock.
b)   Skilled farm jobs refer to foremen and workers in charge of using machinery (tractors).
c)   Unskilled forestry work refers to brushing or clearing forests.

Source: Girona interview survey.

Adding support to this, Table 4.2 shows that only five out of 38 were on permanent contracts. This contrasts with the higher number of non-contracted workers and workers on fixed-term contracts (Table 4.2). The low number in permanent employment is partly due to the seasonality of farm production. In the case of coastal Girona, the peak labour season goes from July to September. In this period, the different fruit in which coastal Girona specialises (peach, pears, nectarines, apples) are collected. After September, demand for farm labour is reduced to a few workers, who are charged with basic tasks concerned with maintaining fields and farm buildings. The production cycle conditions the employment of labourers. To illustrate this point, the tenant of a 40 ha holding (the average size for the province was 28.1 ha. in 1989; Instituto Nacional de Estadística, 1991) who had 30 ha. under fruit trees and the other 10 ha. under cereals, said that he had three permanent employees (the foreman, a Spanish national, and two skilled workers, one Spanish, the other from an African country). On temporary contracts (yet working the whole year), he said that there were three further African workers. These six people are employed on the farm for the whole year. In the low season which runs from October to April on this farm, they sulphate land and prune trees. At the end of April, five more workers are employed to do the *clareig* [eliminating blooms on trees so fruit can grow more]. They stay from April to the end of October, helping with successive harvests (first peach, then pear, and finally apple). On top of these eleven, seasonal workers are hired for these three harvests (between nine and 10 for the peach campaign, around 15 for the pear and between 25 and 27 for the apple). In the apple season, when more labourers are employed, there are about 35 hired employees in this farm. Regardless of their hired status, there are three types of workers: six who are employed the whole year round; a further five who are employed from April to October and seasonal workers for the successive harvests. For the picking season, which also runs from July to September in the neighbouring province of Lleida, Balcells (1991) has estimated that the need for extra labour was between 5,000 and 6,000 jobs. Significantly, this researcher has suggested that half of the extra demand for labour is met by the local population and by Spaniards from other provinces, leaving a need for 2,000 or so agricultural jobs to be filled by foreigners in Lleida. This 2,000 contrasts with the 300 work permits that were issued to non-EU nationals for agricultural tasks in the province in 1990.

Like Lleida, Girona farming has an extra demand for workers from July to September. Both interviews with employers and the immigrant survey in Girona clearly indicated that demand is now met by Africans. To illustrate this point, an interviewed young employer explained to me that:

In the holding all are Africans. They are temporary workers. This is a small-sized holding. We do not have permanent workers. When we started with the apple trees, we hired local women. But it is hard work. Later, Andalucians came over for the harvest, but they got drunk too often. There are still people who hire them [*els fa pujar*]. They've got room on their properties, so they provide accommodation for the Andalucians. These employers generally hire the same workers every season [*són de tota la vida*].

This young employer outlined the evolution of labour hiring practices in many farms in Girona. There has been a substitution of Girona women by temporary in-migrants from Andalucía, and then by Africans. This substitution is primarily due to local (female) residents opting for other jobs rather than farm work. Certainly, tourism activities offer higher wages on a regular basis than farming.[9] In this regard, wages in Spanish accommodation services and restaurants were 86.9 per cent higher than those in farming in 1993 (Banco Bilbao Vizcaya, 1997). It follows that Spanish workers are eager to accept jobs in tourism, but not in agriculture. If we add to the picture that the summer is the peak season for both activities, it is clear why labour shortages in farming arise as soon as intensive production was introduced in the 1970s. Initially, these shortages were covered by in-migrants from Andalucía. However, in the 1980s, internal inflows to cover seasonal jobs in Girona agriculture decreased. Employers shared the opinion that 'Andalucians are not coming any more'.

Many factors have affected the reduction of internal Spanish inflows oriented toward filling labour demands in the agricultural sector in Girona. But, first of all, it should be noted that agriculture has never played a leading role in channelling permanent in-migrant inflows into traditional in-migration areas in Spain (Cardelús and Pascual de Sans, 1979; Nadal, 1984). Secondly, a reduction in living standard differentials across Spain, alongside new economic dynamics in agricultural areas that traditionally suffered from out-migration, has lessened the availability of Spanish seasonal workers (for an overview on decreases in regional disparities, see Ferrer Regales and Calvo Miranda, 1987; or Villaverde Castro, 1996; for the specific example of greenhouse production in Almería, see Tout, 1990). Finally, the introduction in 1985 of unemployment schemes in agriculture in Andalucía and Extremadura [*Paro Obrero*][10] has contributed to reducing out-migration from these areas to other parts of Spain (Bentolila, 1992; Bentolila, 1997).[11]

However, there are few farmers in my area of study who hire Andalucians. Those that do are medium- to large-sized farms, by Girona standards, which have a stable demand for a considerable number of workers for the whole season. These farms provide accommodation to their temporary workers. As one illustration, an interviewed agricultural employer with a 55 ha. holding indicated that he regularly hired 40 workers for the picking season from Luque (a village in the Andalucian province of Córdoba). The Spanish Employment Agency [*Instituto Nacional de Empleo*] eases this temporary migration by paying travel expenses. By hiring for the season, the necessary labour force is guaranteed. Explaining the rationale for this action, the farmer stated that: 'This is a small town. There are no Africans, and locals are not prepared to take up seasonal tasks any more'. Contrasting with this view, another employer of a medium-sized holding had substituted Andalucians with Africans. In his words: 'Last year I hired 10 Andalucians. I gave accommodation for them. But they were not hard workers. Beside, Africans live in town, so I don't have to provide accommodation for them'. The holding of this last employer is situated in Castelló d'Empúries (see Figure 4.2), where a quite large African colony exists. It follows that, even if the trend is toward Africans constituting the bulk of seasonal workers in Girona, there is an uneven distribution of African employment owing to local characteristics and farm attributes.

Providing another example of substitution of local workers by immigrants, Avellá Reus (1991) has described the Valencia orange sector. Unlike Girona, there has been a traditional locally-resident workforce in this province's farming. This workforce is mainly constituted of small agrarian employers and their relatives, who work on larger holdings as employees in the peak season. Yet, in the 1980s, the number of agricultural labourers hardly covered the needs of the picking season which goes from November to December in this region. This was because the farming population has shrunk owing to few new entrants. This analyst reported that employers was 'pushed' into hiring groups of people who were not the traditional workforce in the region (namely, retired people and women). In this context, he concluded that since the mid-1980s immigrant workers have been a great help.

In Girona, Africans are not only employed in seasonal jobs, but also in more permanent types of work. In this regard, the survey identified five Africans (out of 38) who had attained a stable contractual position in Girona farming (Table 4.2). Yet demand for permanent employment is higher than the number of permanent contracts awarded. In this regard, Table 4.3 shows that those with temporary contracts are not simply those with seasonal work but include workers who have been on temporary contracts for many years. Specifically, 10 out of the 22 who were working with a temporary farm labourer contract had been employed for more than one year on the same farm, regardless of the length of their current contract. As an illustration of this point, one skilled agricultural worker had been

Figure 4.2   The Girona fieldwork area

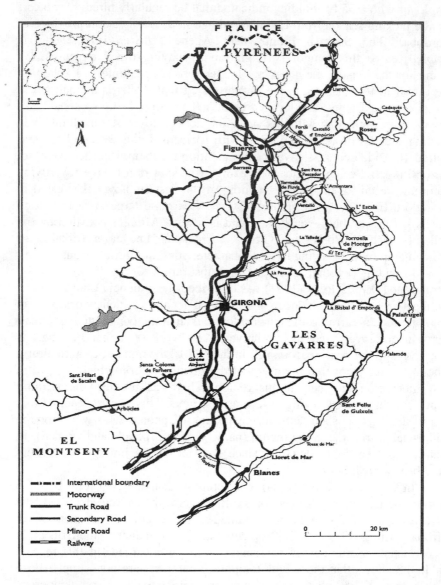

employed on the same farm for 14 years (yet he had a seasonal contract when interviewed). This denotes that more 'permanent' employees exist than the number of permanent contracts that are awarded.[12] For Almería greenhouses, Roquero (1996) found a similar pattern of African employment, with seasonal workers used for harvest time and temporary-hired Africans employed for nine or 10 months to undertake successive tasks throughout the year. Like Girona, more permanent types of employment are not synonymous with permanent hiring. Yet in many cases a rolling programme of temporary contracts is illegal, for Spanish law states that a worker has to be contracted on a permanent basis after the third year of employment with the same employer. To get around this provision, some employers sack employees and then contract them again after a short spell. On other occasions Africans work on the farm without a contract for a spell between two contracts. Either way, employers justify the claim that their workers have not been employed on a permanent basis for a three-year period. Out of these 10 who were employed for more than one year, five were not occupied on the farm in the low season (from October to February; interviews 6, 41, 51, 73 and 85; Table 4.3). Yet the same employer gave jobs to them from February to the end of September every year. This period covers the whole farm production cycle in Girona (i.e. pruning, spraying trees and picking fruit). The period of inactivity was sometimes referred as a 'holiday' by interviewees.

Logically, since some on temporary contracts work all year round, they do the same kind of work as permanent employees. To be specific, for four out of the five who were permanent employees (as well as for five workers out of 22 on temporary contracts who were employed for more than one year the whole year round on the same farm; interviews 1, 13, 15, 76 and 133; Table 4.3), it was common to do semi-skilled jobs (such as pruning) or skilled work (foremen, tractor drivers), alongside non-skilled tasks during the harvest season.[13] In this regard, only one worker on a permanent contract undertook unskilled tasks all the year round (Table 4.2).[14] Even if numbers are low, the figures indicate that permanent employment implies that workers possess certain skills. In other words, African workers are not just taking seasonal unskilled jobs, but are employed all the year round on both skilled and unskilled tasks. This is to say that they have replaced family and Spanish employees on some skilled tasks in farming production.

Unlike unskilled workers, for whom a move from farming to other sectors is accompanied by wage increases, sectoral mobility is less advantageous for skilled agricultural farmers. They can hardly apply their farm knowledges to jobs in another economic sector. It follows that, if they

Table 4.3   Temporary farm workers by time with current employer and length of contract in Girona

Interview number	Time with current employer	Continuous employment all year round	Length of current contract
1	Five years	Yes	One year
3	Seasonal	No	Seasonal
6	Four years	No[a]	One year
8	Season	No	Seasonal
10	Seven months	Yes	Seasonal
13	Six years	Yes	One year
15	Forteen years	Yes	Seasonal
21	Season	No	Seasonal
29	Season	No	Seasonal
32	One year	Yes	One year
41	Six years	No[b]	Seasonal
51	Three years	No[b]	Seasonal
71	Season	No	Seasonal
73	Three years	No[b]	Seasonal
74	Six months	No	Six months
76	Three years	Yes	One year
85	Five years	No[b]	Six months
90	One year	Yes	One year
93	Season	No	Seasonal
133	Nine years	Yes	Six months
144	One year	Yes	One year
146	Season	No	Seasonal

Notes:
a)   Brush forests at low season.
b)   Temporary return to Morocco.

Source: Girona interview survey.

want to move sectors, they suffer from a de-skilling process (and probably a decrease in wages). Thus, reasons for leaving agriculture are not purely based on wages, but also on social considerations. In this regard, researchers have found that Spanish farming is ascribed a low social status

(Brandes, 1976; Greenwood, 1976; García-Ramon et al., 1995). This is supported by key informants and employers in Girona. A social worker who was responsible for several small rural municipalities in Girona explained that: 'No one wants to work in farming. Middle-class urban values have quickly spread to the countryside. People want to be doctors, teachers, professionals, whatever – not *pagesos* [agricultural employers]'. Along the same lines, a farming couple, who had made an old second house [*masia*] suitable for visitors, saw no continuity in farming activities on their holding:

> We've got two children. The girl is working for the town social services. The boy is a butcher. There is no reason for us to make any major change in farming [e.g. they stick to cereal production]. Nobody is going to take on the farm after us. Yet rural tourism is a rock solid business in this area. Our children are happy with it.

If this view holds for would-be farming employers, it comes as no surprise that the agricultural sector is barely attractive for potential (unskilled or skilled; locally-resident or in-migrant) Spanish workers.

To sum up, this section on African employment in Girona farming:

- Africans are mainly employed in intensive fruit production. This was introduced in Girona in the 1960s. First, the extra demand for labourers were met by locally-resident women. But competition for labour from tourism-related activities quickly provoked labour shortages which were covered by Andalucian in-migrants. Nowadays Spanish temporary workers have been substituted by Africans to a great extent.
- Linked to this, farming is a main port of entry into Spanish labour markets for African workers. The sector offered the first job in the country for almost half of those interviewed (Table 4.1). Furthermore, two thirds of the Girona survey declared that they had had a farming job at some point in their labour market trajectory in Spain.
- High turnover of African workers in farming (plus the low number of Africans with permanent contracts; Table 4.2) suggest that immigrant employment is mainly for temporary tasks. Indeed, in Girona demand for labour changes throughout the year, peaking during fruit collection, from July to September, and reaching its lowest level from October to January.
- There is a permanent pattern of employment that is not captured by figures for the number of Africans with permanent contracts. In this regard, even if six of them are not employed in the low season, 10 out of 22 interviewed Africans on temporary contracts have been working

for the same employer for more than one year. The most striking example of this is an employee who had worked for the same farmer for 14 years (yet on a seasonal contract; interview 15, Table 4.3) This more permanent pattern of African employment is not translated into permanent work contracts. This is indicative of the high casualisation of the African labour force in Spanish farming.

- More permanent employment is associated with skilled tasks. Workers who are employed the whole year round do both unskilled and skilled tasks, depending on farm needs. In other words, African employment in Girona is not restricted to temporary harvest work, but also comprises skilled tasks (e.g. foremen). Even if this is on a lesser scale than unskilled work, Africans are substituting Spanish workers and members of the farm family even for supervisory tasks.
- The key element to understanding the scope of African employment in farming is the lack of attractiveness of the sector for Spanish workers. In this regard, even would-be employers prefer jobs in other sectors in Girona. A key reason for this is the low social status that is still attached to farming tasks in Spanish collective values.

No Need for Immigrants? Low-Productive Portuguese Agriculture in an Increasingly Competitive Environment

A characteristic of Spanish agriculture is its marked regional differences, with the dominance of large farms in the south (inland Andalucía, Extremadura and Castilla-La Mancha) and small- and medium-sized ones in the rest of the country. Similar regional disparities exist in Portugal, with small farms being prominent in the north and larger units in Alentejo. Yet, in contrast with Spain, few immigrants are employed in Portuguese agriculture. The 1,093 legal foreigners who worked as agricultural labourers in Portugal in 1996 constituted just 1.3 per cent of the legally-resident foreign population that was employed in the country (Instituto Nacional de Estatística, 1997a).[15] To put this figure in context, the number of foreigners in Portuguese farming is smaller than the 1,163 legal non-EU workers in Girona agriculture in 1996 (Comisión Interministerial de Extranjería, 1997). The low immigrant presence in Portuguese farming is confirmed by previous research. For instance, in her analysis of official statistics, Esteves (1991) reported that only 3 per cent of legally-resident foreign workers were employed in the Portuguese primary sector in 1988. This contrasts with the 15.2 per cent of legally-resident non-EU workers in Spain who worked in agriculture in 1996, with this ratio going up to 31.6 per cent for legal African workers (Comisión Interministerial de

Extranjería, 1997). The questions this prompts are why immigrants are not employed in this sector in Portugal and why agricultural labourers are demanded in Spain.

One of the reasons for this divergence is the different composition and evolution of farming in the two countries. Despite common geographical[16] and historical features,[17] differences in agricultural employment across the border are remarkable. The relation between agriculture and manufacturing in Portugal and Spain in this century is crucial to understand this divergence (Pérez Yruela, 1990; Sapelli, 1995). The two million, mainly landless, labourers who emigrated from rural Spain in the 1960s played the twofold function of forcing the mechanisation of agricultural tasks as well as fuelling manufacturing activities in industrial areas (Naredo, 1986). This mechanisation of agriculture started with the large landowners of southern Spain, who saw the biggest losses in their workforce, but the process soon spread to medium-sized land holders (Sapelli, 1995). By contrast, mechanisation did not take to the same extent in Portugal. The reasons for this vary between Alentejo and northern Portugal (as shown in the next section). Yet, taking the country as a whole, Portuguese agriculture is characterised by its low technological level, a fact well illustrated by appreciable differences in yield per ha. in Portugal and in other European Union countries (Avillez, 1993). In fact, in 1985, Portuguese production covered just 50.5 per cent of national demand. Home supply covered 100 per cent of demand for only four products - vegetables, fresh fruit, tomatoes for processing[18] and citrus fruits (Carrière, 1989).[19] Moreover, output grew at a slow pace over the 1970s and 1980s, and the ratio between agricultural and non-agricultural wages did not improve in these two decades (Graham, 1990). In line with this, farm household incomes were only 50 per cent of average household incomes at the beginning of the 1990s (Eurostat, 1997b). Not surprisingly, small farmers are inclined to seek jobs in other sectors (when they are available). Baptista (1994), for example, estimated that the main source of income for 61 per cent of family agricultural holders originated in another economic sector.

Even if Portuguese farming enjoyed special consideration as a result of the accession treaty,[20] entry into the European Union in 1986 does not seem to have had a positive impact on the sector. Like Spain, Portuguese agriculture has faced a more competitive environment under EU membership. As well, accession put Portuguese agriculture under pressure to modify both price levels for major commodities and policy instruments (Josling and Tangermann, 1987; Eisfeld, 1989; Corkill, 1993). Thus agricultural commodity prices have fallen since 1985. As an illustration, wheat prices moved down by 23 per cent between 1985 and 1989, with cash income per family unit going down by 16.1 per cent over this period (Avillez, 1993). Furthermore, some researchers have observed that EU funds were mainly channelled into the more competitive medium- to large-sized farms (and not into low production small- or medium-sized holdings; Avillez, 1993; Baptista, 1993b).

Regional Differences in Portuguese Agriculture

In continental Portugal, three main agricultural areas can be distinguished: the extensive agriculture of Alentejo which is largely comprised of cereals, the intensive farming of northern Portugal, mainly based on maize, potatoes and cattle raising, and the intensive fruit and vegetable agriculture of the Tagus Valley and Algarve (for a comprehensive description of these three main agrarian systems, see Pearson et al., 1987; Carrière, 1989).

Even if Alentejo presents similar traits and a comparable evolution to southern Spanish latifundia areas (namely, extensive agriculture, a long-established proletariat, emigration; see, for instance, Cutileiro, 1971; or, more recently, Fox, 1987; Baptista, 1993a), there are substantial differences between these regions:

- Unlike Spain, agrarian reform was a key political priority of the first democratic governments in Portugal. Thus, in 1975, 1,130,000 ha. were occupied and about 500 collective productive units were organised in Alentejo (Baptista, 1994). Yet changes in ownership did little to improve efficiency, as the new landowners lacked managerial skills and experience (Corkill, 1993; Baptista, 1995). In the 1980s, as the land question declined as an issue (Drain, 1994), land returned to their old owners in Alentejo. Specifically, 85 per cent of the area of the large estates that had been nationalised went back to their ex-landlords (Baptista, 1994). Especially compared with Portugal, the latifundia issue has remained marginal to new democratic Spain (Naredo, 1986; Salmon, 1995; Sapelli, 1995). For the whole of Spain, the only attempt to modify the land structure was the 1979 Law of Obviously Improvable Farms [*Ley de Fincas Manifiestamente Mejorables*], which turned out to be scarcely operative (Arnalte and Ceña, 1993). For Andalucía, the left-wing government passed a moderate reform of land property for non-productive estates. This was not an agrarian reform law, but was aimed at raising the productivity of low-yielding estates (Cruz-Villalón, 1987).
- Mechanisation did not take place to the same extent in Alentejo as in southern Spain. This was partly related to the policy of the Salazar and Caetano regimes to subsidise heavily cereal cultivation (Sapelli, 1995).

The consequence of this policy was a high level of specialisation in cereals in the region. As a matter of fact, Alentejo now produces most of the country's grains, whether wheat, oats or barley (Avillez et al., 1988). The adoption of new technologies and more efficient uses of either labour or land were 'discouraged' by the artificially high prices than resulted from this policy (Corkill, 1993). Effectively, these subsidies weakened pressures to innovate and become more efficient. As a result, the Portuguese average cereal yield per ha., excluding rice, was the lowest in the EU in 1993 (Eurostat, 1997a). When mechanisation has occurred, state intervention has been prominent in its promotion, acceptance and spread (Cavaco, 1981; Baptista, 1993b).

- As a consequence of lower levels of mechanisation than in Spain, agrarian workers were not released from the land to the same extent as in southern Spain. Thus, emigration from Alentejo into Europe was considerably less important than from northern Portugal (Peixoto, 1996) and, when it occurred, was mainly through organised fixed-term labour contracts (Leeds, 1980). Leeds has argued that this was because

> [...] the mobilization by and active support of the Communist Party [the *Partido Comunista* has been the main party in the region; Poinard, 1994] and other Left groups has permitted the possibility of articulating demands and the perception that life within Portugal is viable with struggle. (Leeds, 1980: 75)

Political reasons may have stopped emigration. But it is clear that there was a demand for workers in Alentejo in the years of great emigration to Europe. Indeed, Taborda, in a study which goes as far back as 1932 (quoted by Daveau, 1995), revealed labour shortages in the region which were met by temporary workers from northern Portugal. Labourers from northern Portugal were used for a different reason in the mid-1960s. They were 'imported' into Alentejo to press down agricultural wages, owing to strikes for wage rises of Alentejo's farm workers (Leeds, 1980). The political repression of strikes in the 1960s stimulated out-migration from the region to Lisbon and Algarve (Cutileiro, 1971). Since then, out-migration from Alentejo has been substantial (Baptista and Moniz, 1985; Ferrão, 1987; Cónim and Carrilho, 1989).

A key to understanding out-migration in Alentejo is the process of (late, partial) mechanisation which released a considerable number of agricultural labourers. As an illustration, Roseira (1977) found that redundant farm labourers from northern Alentejo (*Distrito* of Portalegre) moved for the vineyard season to Ribatejo in the Tagus Valley, and then to intensive production fields in Badajoz in Spanish Extremadura (see also Iríbar and Gil, 1998, who reported on child labour amongst Portuguese temporary workers in the tomato campaign in Badajoz). It seems that, more than labour shortages, there is now a surplus of agricultural workers in the region (see, also, García Lizana and Alcudia, 1990; André, 1991; Baptista, 1995). These redundant workers cannot be employed in other Alentejo industries because the region does not have many service or manufacturing jobs to offer (Carrière, 1989; Drain, 1994).

In short, extensive low-productive extensive farming, alongside a long-established proletariat, are the factors which explain the small number of permanent immigrants in Alentejo's agriculture. When workers have been needed in the harvest season, farm workers from northern Portugal have traditionally met this demand. Nowadays, with increasing mechanisation, the problem for redundant Alentejo agricultural workers is to find jobs in the region.

By contrast, northern Portuguese agriculture is composed of extremely small holdings, which mainly specialise in maize, potatoes and cattle raising (e.g. Peason and Monke, 1987; Carrière, 1989). To be specific, 75.9 per cent of holdings in northern Portugal – the administrative region of Norte – had less than 5 ha. in 1995, with a further 20.4 per cent having between 5 and 20 ha. (Instituto Nacional de Estatística, 1996e). This small size, plus adherence to traditional farming techniques and conservative attitudes amongst farmers, are thought to hamper any attempt to rationalise and modernise farming operations (Unwin, 1985; Pearson and Monke, 1987; Black, 1992). In this context, both Lewis and Williams's (1986) research on central Portugal and Drain's (1994) study of the north-western regions found that it was quite common for farmers to work part-time in textile or shoe manufacturing industries. This is to say that many farmers of northern Portugal cannot raise enough income to live off their holding (let alone pay for hired – immigrant – workers). The same reason explains the lack of immigrant workers in the northern Spanish Autonomous Communities of Galicia, Asturias and Cantabria, which have many common trends with northern Portugal (e.g. small holdings, weak market orientation in farming, maize production and cattle raising).

The land structure of northern Portugal has remained almost unchanged over the century, despite huge emigration from this area into Central and Northern Europe in the 1960s and 1970s (Anido and Freire, 1978; Cavaco, 1993).[21] Emigration affected both landless labourers and small farmers (see, for instance, Bentley's 1992 study of Pedralva, a parish in the Minho region of northwestern Portugal). Even if some scholars disagree (for instance, Bentley, 1992, has held that return migration fostered mechanisation in farming), emigrant remittances and savings have not altered significantly farming production techniques. To support this idea, it has been argued that remittances and savings were often spent on

Figure 4.3 The Algarve fieldwork area

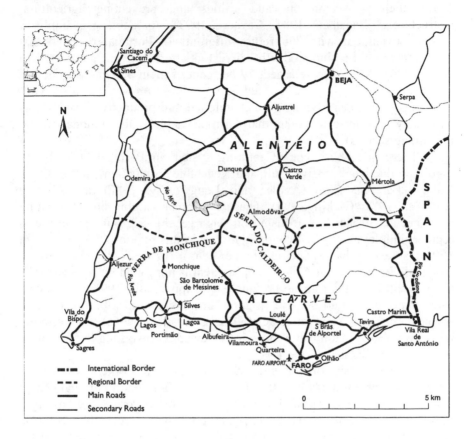

houses and expensive commodities associated with social prestige (King, 1996), thereby forcing up land values and preventing agricultural restructuring (Bacalhau, 1984; Cavaco, 1993). As another example, a survey carried out with 700 return migrants in Portugal revealed that emigrants rarely became productive investors after their time abroad (Silva et al., 1986). When they returned, 79 per cent of them purchased or built a house, but only 34 per cent invested in agriculture. As Mendonsa's (1982) work suggests, when savings were channelled into productive activity, this was likely to be in sectors other than farming (namely, accommodation and the fishing sectors).

There is a third type of farming system in Portugal. This is the highly-productive intensive fruit and vegetable production of the Tagus Valley [*Vale do Tejo*] (Avillez and Langworthy, 1987) and Algarve (Carrière, 1989; Corkill, 1993). These two areas exhibit similar farming attributes as Girona. Yet, focusing on Algarve, the share of agriculture in regional employment is substantially higher in this region (10.6 per cent in 1994; Table 1.7) than in Girona (6.5 per cent in 1993; Table 1.5). Another crucial difference is that African employment is not found in Algarve to the same extent as in the Catalan province. To support this, 1991 Census data show that Africans do not live in agrarian municipalities, but in tourism-oriented *concelhos* (Instituto Nacional de Estatística, 1996c). Furthermore, my survey found that none of those interviewed was working in farming in Algarve (or in Setúbal; Table 4.4).

However, six out of the 69 African-born workers who were interviewed for this study had their first work in farming in Portugal (Table 4.4). These six workers shared a common position in Portuguese farming - they were temporarily employed in Algarve's fruit and vegetable sector on an informal basis. According to one of these six, 'it is normal practice for employers to come over [she lives in one of the poorest bairros of Olhão, a municipality of Algarve which is mainly inhabited by Angolan immigrants, see Figure 4.3] to take women to the fields in the strawberry or in the onion picking season'. This practice denotes seasonal labour shortages in the agriculture of the region. This does not come as a surprise, since high competition for workers from tourism activities arises in Algarve, which has a low unemployment rate from April to September (6.6 per cent in 1994, Instituto Nacional de Estatística, 1995).[22]

Quite apart from these cases of temporary work, there is no evidence on Portuguese farming providing many jobs to African-origin workers on a permanent basis. It follows that, even for regions which specialise in intensive farm production, agriculture does not stimulate further African immigration into the country.

Table 4.4 Current and first jobs in Portugal for interviewed Africans, by economic sector

	First * Farming	Fisheries	Manufact.	Construct.	Services	Total
Current *						
Farming						
Fisheries		1				1
Manufacturing	1	1	2	4	3	11
Construction			1	14	3	18
Services	5		3	5	26	39
Total	6	2	6	23	32	69

* Those out of work at their interview have been classified in this table according to their last job.

Source: Portuguese interview survey.

Conclusion

Africans in Spanish farming are in 'secondary jobs'. The Girona survey showed that the bulk of Africans are found in fixed-term jobs which are not part of a promotion ladder. For other parts of Spain, the literature also records that Africans are mainly temporary workers (see Fuentes et al., 1988, and Balcells, 1991, for fruit production in Lleida; Avellá Reus, 1991, and Moreno Torregrosa, 1993, on the Valencia orange sector; Jabardo Velasco, 1993, on the Alicante vegetable sector; Ramírez, 1993, on Barcelona intensive farming; Checa, 1995, Cózar, 1996, and Roquero, 1996, on Almería's greenhouses; Sánchez et al, 1996, on fruit trees in Cáceres). A similar conclusion was reached by Cyrus (1994) for German agriculture and by Odé (1996) for Dutch farming. Yet, unlike these authors, a sizeable share of those on temporary contracts in Girona are employed on the farm for the whole year (in many cases, for several years). This adds support to segmentation theory postulates in the sense that, even for permanent jobs, Africans are mainly on insecure and fixed-term contracts.

African nationals have consolidated a niche for temporary work in intensive farm production in many parts of Spain. From the first enclaves of African employment in northern Catalunya and Almería in the early 1980s (Giménez Romero, 1992; Ramírez, 1993; Cózar, 1996), Africans are found to be the bulk of temporary workers in provinces situated as far apart as Lleida (Fuentes et al., 1988; Balcells, 1991) and Cáceres (Sánchez et al., 1996). Yet this niche does not seem to be based on immigrant skills, but in the abundance of unwanted unskilled work (especially in the harvest season). Even if the characteristics of the job are substantially different from farming, Waldinger (1994) has argued that the first reason for the creation of a niche in the New York administration services was the abandonment of these jobs by 'native' workers. This also looks to be the cause of the creation of an African niche in Spanish farming (for the 'urge' of the Spanish to leave agriculture, see the classical studies of Brandes, 1976; or Greenwood, 1976; or, more recently, Naredo, 1986; Enciso Rodríguez and Sabaté Prats, 1995; García-Ramon et al., 1995).

Linked to the abandonment of farming by the Spanish, there is little competition for jobs between Africans and other workers in Spanish agriculture. The survey on employers showed that if locally-resident non-immigrants are employed in Girona farming, they are generally permanent skilled workers. But the appeal of jobs in tourism-oriented activities did create shortages in Girona farming as soon as more intensive crops were introduced. These shortages were met by Andalucian in-migrants. The lack of competition between Spanish in-migrants and locally-resident Africans is more arguable. Yet interviews with employers made it clear that there were several factors which acted as a deterrent to the mobility of the Spanish workforce as temporary labourers (e.g. the possibility of applying for unemployment benefits for Andalucía and Extremadura agricultural labourers which are not available for labourers elsewhere in Spain). From a broader perspective, the decrease in internal migration in Spain since the mid-1970s has been extensively demonstrated (Olano, 1990; Blanco Gutiérrez, 1993; Romero González and Albertos Puebla, 1996; Bentolila, 1997). Not denying that in certain cases reasons for employing Africans go beyond the Andalucians-do-not-come-any-more argument, labour shortages in the sector look to be the key element in hiring Africans. The same was found for Lleida (Balcells, 1991) and for Valencia where Avellá Reus (1991) found that the traditional local workforce was not sufficient for the needs of the orange high season. Further supporting the importance of low competition between African and Spanish workers in accounting for substantial African employment, Cruces Roldán and Martín Díaz (1997) have found that the existence of an abundant number of locally-resident agricultural labourers in Cádiz is a key reason for the light African presence in the newly developed intensive agriculture in the province. As well the main reason for low African employment in Portuguese farming lies in substantial labour surpluses in the agricultural population (García Lizana and Alcudia, 1990; André, 1991). This evidence points to Africans essentially being employed in farming jobs and in agrarian geographical areas in which other sources of labour are not available.

In this chapter, two questions have remained unanswered:

- First of all, even if they are few in number, the survey found some Africans in skilled work. So far, it has been argued that rejection by the Spanish labour force of farming jobs has provoked labour shortages so there are few openings for skilled work for Africans. An alternative reason may be that Africans are a skilled labour force, with extensive experience in farming in their countries of origin, which suits employers' demands. This would confirm human capital postulates. This point is analysed in Chapter 8, where occupational and educational endowments of Africans are discussed in the light of their labour outcomes in Iberia.
- Secondly, the mechanisms through which a niche for temporary work has been secured require further attention. Immigrant networks could be the key link through which information on job availabity is channelled. The role of social networks in African labour outcomes is also a matter for Chapter 8.

In this chapter, farming has proved to be a main port of entry into Spanish labour markets. The next chapter will show that construction is the main port of entry for African males in Portuguese labour markets. Yet immigrant employment in Portuguese construction has a longer tradition than African work in Spanish farming. Hence, Africans in Portugal may have gained job promotion through experience inside construction. However, if segmentation analysts are right, Africans in Portuguese construction will be found in the same unstable position in secondary labour markets as Africans in Spanish farming. This is the question we now turn to.

Notes

1. Most of the ideas of the section on African employment in Spanish farming have been developed in Hoggart and Mendoza (1999).
2. Long before the Iberian countries joined the EU, reform of the CAP was under discussion (Naylon, 1981). From 1984, price support policies were progressively weakened in order to narrow the difference between world prices and internal EU prices. Price subsidies under the old CAP had helped northern farmers capitalise and consequently enabled them to become more competitive in world markets (Berlan, 1987). In this sense, the abandonment of price supports is likely to reveal flaws in the competitive position of Mediterranean

EU regions, because of their high costs compared with non-EU producers (Berlan, 1987).

3. The case of milk production requires special attention. Spain, a deficit producer of milk and dairy products, had to accept the milk quota system of the EU and, consequently, had to reduce its milk production (Etxezarreta and Viladomiu, 1989).

4. Since 1 January 1992, Portuguese workers, as with other EU nationals, have not needed a work permit (the exception for the EU is Luxembourg, whose nationals needed a permit until 1 January 1993 to work in Spain). Consequently, statistics do not record recent Portuguese worker involvement. In 1992, there were 11,609 Portuguese workers with a valid Spanish work permit. The neighbouring Autonomous Communities of Galicia (2,349 permits) and Castilla y León (1,831) had the most numerous Portuguese colonies (Ministerio de Trabajo y Seguridad Social, 1993). An indication that the movement toward Spain for seasonal work still persits comes from the media which have denounced child labour amongst the temporary Portuguese workers in the 1998 tomato campaign in Badajoz (e.g. Iríbar and Gil, 1998).

5. The average share of non-EU workers in Spanish farming was 1.4 per cent in 1995. The 0.7 per cent figure is half the average, so it is used here as a quantitative expression of scarce immigrant employment in farming. Provinces with non-EU workers constituting 0.7 per cent or less of their workforces in 1995 are blank in Figure 4.1.

6. As told by key informants, the growth of land under industrial crops (specifically, sunflowers) in the province is related to EU policy on subsidising such crops.

7. The questionnaire probed extensively on the employment of African workers in both their country of origin and in Spain (or Portugal).

8. For analytical purposes, unless the contrary is stated, unemployed people have been classified in the last sector of activity in which he/she worked.

9. Wages are paid per worked hour in agriculture in this area. For instance, when it is raining, labourers do not work and consequently do not earn any money.

10. Agricultural employees who are resident in Andalucía and Extremadura have the right to get unemployment benefit after 60 working days [*jornadas*] in any Spanish region or in a foreign country (provided the Spanish Emigration Institute [*Instituto Español de Emigración*] certifies their status; *Real Decreto* n. 2298/84, 26 December 1984). Agricultural labourers who are living in the rest of Spain are not eligible for these unemployment benefits. In terms of the supply of migrant Spanish workers for agriculture, Andalucía and Extremadura have long been the two main source regions.

11. This opinion was expressed by several agricultural employers. One of them, who regularly hires Andalucians for the season, indicated that some of them want to work simply for the number of days that qualify them for unemployment benefit. If he hires Andalucians on this basis, he has to keep finding new workers as the season progresses.

12. The high degree of casualisation in the labour market should not be forgotten. As noted in the Introduction, Spain has the highest incidence of temporary

employment in its labour force in the OECD (see the annual reports of the Organisation for Economic Co-operation and Development, *Employment outlook*).

13. Even if they also do unskilled tasks, these workers have been considered 'skilled workers' in Table 4.2. I agree with Beechey (1988) that skills have at least as much to do with ideological or social constructions as with complex, technical competences. Aware of this point, a skilled job is here taken to be one that requires a special knowledge, either through training, experience or qualification, for its fulfilment, irrespective of the (negative) social value that may be attached to it. For instance, in farming, there are skilled jobs like a foreman or a tractor driver. In the case of construction, all worker categories, except labourer, are considered skilled.

14. He is the only employee of a small family-based farm that specialises in vegetable production. The skilled tasks are undertaken by members of the family.

15. This source of information (*Estatísticas Demográficas* of the Portuguese *Instituto Nacional de Estatística*) does not disaggregate the profession of foreigners by region of residence. However, the low number of non-Portuguese labourers in the agricultural sector (in one of the EU countries with the highest percentage of its working population in this sector points to the low impact of foreigners in all regions.

16. The whole Peninsula is centred on an elevated plateau - the *Meseta*. Three out of the five long peninsular rivers cross both states. The rivers Tagus and Douro flow from inland Spain into the Atlantic Ocean at Lisbon and Porto, respectively. The Guadiana river, in the southwestern part of the Peninsula, is a physical border between Spain and Portugal at many points of its trajectory. The other two large fluvial basins are the Ebro, in the Peninsula northeast, and the Guadalquivir, in the south.

17. The *Reconquista* [a gradual process of expulsion of the Moors from the Iberian Peninsula by the different Peninsular kingdoms across eight centuries], which brought about the distribution of the extensive conquered lands to clerical and knights' orders, is the origin of many *latifundia* [big estates] in both the Portuguese Alentejo and in the regions of Castilla-La Mancha, Extremadura and Andalucía in Spain. A more recent shared experience is rule by dictatorship (Salazar and Caetano in Portugal and Franco in Spain), both of which ended in the mid-1970s. Both of these dictatorships implemented a policy of subsidising farm commodity prices, in order to 'protect' their social base, which was deeply rooted in rural small holdings (Baptista, 1993a; Barciela López, 1986) . Yet this policy mainly benefited the big landowners who employed workers rather than owner occupiers (Barciela López, 1986; Cruz-Villalón, 1987; Avillez et al., 1988; Baptista, 1994).

18. Portugal has one of the world's largest industries for tomato processing for export (Eccles and Fuller, 1970; Naylon, 1981). This production is largely under contract with multinational food firms that were previously located in Italy and Spain (Avillez et al. 1988).

19. Even if this occurs to a lesser extent, Spain also exhibits a deficit in its farm trade. The reason for this lies in the volume of imported processed food products (Salmon, 1995).
20. The *Programa Específico do Desenvolvimento da Agricultura Portuguesa* established that Portugal was eligible to receive, during a 10 year period, 700 million ECU subsidies, initially reimbursing 50 per cent of the country's outlays for structural improvement measures. These included upgrading crop and livestock quality, improvement of processing and marketing, and incentives for augmenting landholdings and to help ageing farmers retire (Eisfeld, 1989).
21. Official figures show that the average annual emigration in the period 1950-59 was 27,582. For the period 1960-69, 67,677 emigrants left the country annually and 101,099 for 1970-75 (Anido and Freire, 1978).
22. The unemployment rate goes up in the off-peak tourism season, from October to March. In 1994, it was 7.5 per cent for the first trimestre and 7.4 per cent for the fourth trimestre. The Portuguese average does not fluctuacte so much across the year as the Algarve rate. The importance of tourism for the economy of Algarve is the main reason for its greater fluctuation

5 The Construction Sector: Building an Immigrant Niche in Portugal

By contrast with farming, Chapter 5 will show that construction provides jobs for immigrants in both Portugal and Spain.[1] Even so, there are substantial differences between the two countries. The most obvious is that African workers in construction are not as numerous in Spain as in Portugal. Even a glimpse at construction sites in the region of Lisbon or Algarve gives the idea that African-born immigrants comprise a significant element in the sector's workforce. Employment of Africans from the (ex-) Portuguese colonies in construction can be traced back to the late 1960s in Portugal (Carreira, 1982; Saint-Maurice and Pires, 1989; Saint-Maurice, 1995). At that time, Africans from the colonies moved to within Portuguese borders. Yet the independence of the colonies did not stop the inflow of Africans into the sector. The longer tradition of African workers in construction in Portugal than in Spain may be one reason for divergences on immigrant employment patterns across the border. Linked to this, an aim of this chapter is to examine reasons for substantial cross-border differences in African employment in construction.

A second aim focuses on better understanding of how this sector, which has different monthly and annual cycles to agriculture, creates dissimilar opportunities for African employment. For farming, immigrants worked in an unstable environment, with few permanent contracts. In this regard, the considerable number of African males in construction that was found in the Portuguese survey provides the analysis with varying contexts for immigrant employment. These workers came into the country in successive stages spread over a number of decades. Compared with Spanish agriculture, they have not faced a temporally consistent employment situation, as both the economy and legislative provisions have changed over time. But if Africans are found to be in a precarious work situation in construction, regardless of when they came to the country, this will provide support for the segmentation thesis on immigration work; assuming that any precariousness is not universal to the sector or more broadly to the whole economy. What will give an indication of whether this is the case is worker substitution. In the case of Spanish farming, substitution occurred because local workers deserted farm activities. A question for this chapter is whether the same process has occurred in Portuguese construction. As well Chapter 5 explores whether this also takes place in Spanish construction, given the smaller numbers of Africans who find work in it (compared to Portugal).

This chapter is organised into three main sections. In the first one, the results of the Portuguese and Spanish surveys are compared in order to reach a conclusion on contrasting patterns of African employment. The second focuses on Portuguese construction. Here, two representative case studies of an old immigrant who had worked in the sector for all his employment history in Portugal and of a young construction worker, are used to illustrate main trends in the sector in the Atlantic country. The final section examines the build-up of an African employment niche in Portugal.

Construction, the Main Male African Employer

The construction industry is a large employer in both Portugal and Spain. Specifically, it gave employment to 8.2 per cent of the Portuguese labour force in 1993, and to 9.2 per cent of Spanish workers in the same year. These percentage figures are the highest in the EU (Table 5.1). Similarly, for both countries, the contribution of construction to Gross Value Added is amongst the highest of the EU (Table 5.1).

Construction is not only a large employer, but gives employment to many immigrant workers in both Portugal and Spain. For the latter, work permit data shows that the industry accounted for 8.8 per cent of the legal non-EU workers in 1996 (Comisión Interministerial de Extranjería, 1997). This percentage is only slightly lower than the national share of construction employment (9.2 per cent in 1993; Table 5.1). As with agriculture, non-EU nationals are concentrated in a few Spanish provinces, with immigrant employment recorded principally in metropolitan centres (Madrid and Barcelona) and tourism areas (Girona and the Balearic Islands). These four provinces accounted for 74.3 per cent of the total number employed in this sector in 1996 (Comisión Interministerial de Extranjería, 1997).

For Portugal, the importance of the industry for non-EU workers cannot be gauged from published residence permit data, as construction workers are aggregated with manufacturing workers in official statistics.[2]

As well, the Foreigners and Borders' Service [*Serviço de Estrangeiros e Fronteiras*] does not break down the occupation of non-Portuguese

Table 5.1   The Iberian construction industry in the EU context

	Employment		Firms by number of employees			GVA* 1993
	% all workers		<20	20-99	100 and more	% national
Austria	1993	7.9	1994	9.5	35.0	55.5	no data
Belgium	1992	6.5	1994	6.2	53.9	39.6	5.5
Denmark	1994	6.4	1992	50.1	24.9	25.0	5.3
Finland	1994	5.5	1994	59.5	17.5	23.0	no data
France	1994	6.5	1991	42.1	25.8	26.4	5.4
Germany	1994	7.1	1994	28.3	38.9	32.9	5.6
Greece	1992	6.7	no data			6.6
Ireland	1991	7.1	no data			5.0
Italy	1994	8.2	no data			5.8
Luxembourg	no data		1994	27.5	40.8	31.8	7.6
Netherlands	1994	5.9	1994	36.6	36.6	26.3	5.4
Portugal	1993	8.2	1994	44.9	27.2	26.7	7.0
Spain	1993	9.2	1992	68.1	12.6	19.3	8.0
Sweden	1994	5.6	1993	38.0	15.6	46.4	no data
UK	no data		1994	37.7	22.5	39.8	5.9

* The proportion of construction in the national Gross Value Added has been calculated from GVA figures at market prices.

Sources: For the percentage of construction workers in the labour force and the size of construction firms, United Nations (1997). For GVA data, Eurostat (1997a).

nationals by region of residence. Fortunately, the Census provides an alternative (as yet unpublished) information source. From unpublished 1981 Census data, França (1992) showed that 60 per cent of male nationals of Cape Verde were employed in construction. Likewise, using the 1981 Census for the distribution of the foreign population by activity, alongside residence permit data, Esteves (1991) estimated that 56 per cent of the foreign population from the ex-colonies of Portugal were employed in construction in 1988.[3] Yet the survey that the Association of Construction Employers [*Associação de Empresas de Construção e Obras Públicas*] carries out annually amongst firms with more than 100 employees indicates that PALOP nationals accounted for only 4.1 per cent of employees in 1995 (Associação de Empresas de Construção e Obras Públicas, 1997). However, this figure presents a partial image of the reality of the sector, because, according to unpublished data provided by the Ministry of Employment and Social Security, firms with more than 100 workers only constituted 1.1 per cent of the total number of firms and less than 30 per cent of workers in Portuguese construction in 1995 (see also Table 5.1).

Adding support to the idea that construction is a key immigrant employer in Portugal, my survey found that 18 out of 69 interviewed African workers were employed in this industry at the time of their interview (Table 4.4). Even more notable, construction employment was the domain of male immigrants, for all of these 18 were men. It follows that more than 50 per cent of the interviewed male African workforce had a construction job. Furthermore, more than half of interviewed African employees in construction (10 out of 16)[4] said that African-born immigrants constituted more than half the workers on their construction site. In Girona, although 21 out of 151 interviewees worked in construction (Table 4.1), the sector is not as dominant. To support this point, the survey only found one person out of the 21 who was employed in a firm where immigrants made up more than 50 per cent of employees. This contrasting pattern is not surprising, given differences in wages in the sector across the border. Whereas wages in construction were above the Spanish average in 1993 (Banco Bilbao Vizcaya, 1997),[5] the wages that Portuguese construction firms offered in 1993 were 89 per cent of the average for the country (Ministério do Emprego e da Segurança Social, 1994). This helps put in context why the sector is more attractive for Spanish workers than for Portuguese ones.

Not only is construction a major immigrant employer in Portugal, but it is also a major port of entry into Portuguese labour markets. Specifically, 23 out of the 69 African-origin workers had their first employment in the industry (Table 4.4). If the focus is exclusively on males, the importance of the sector for first employment is even more marked, for 23 out of the 37 men interviewed had their first job in construction. In the Girona survey, the role of construction as a source of first employment is less notable. The industry appears more open to immigrant first employment than manufacturing, but has far fewer entering it than farming (Table 4.1). Furthermore, construction provides jobs for the whole of the employment trajectory of African-born workers in Portugal. Thus 10 out of the 18 on construction jobs had never worked in another sector in Portugal. For Spain, the survey points to a quite different picture. Here only one of the 21 who worked in construction when interviewed had spent the whole of his time in the labour force in the sector. However, 62 out of the 151 interviewed Africans in Spain declared that they had worked in construction at some point while in the country. Data for Spain point to a high intersectoral mobility pattern, with immigrants being hired in periods of high employment in construction. By contrast, African-born immigrants find jobs in the sector throughout their labour force participation in Portugal.

Table 5.2   Type of job and hired status of interviewed construction workers in Iberia

	Portugal	Spain
Kind of job		
Skilled [a]	14	1
Unskilled [b]	4	20
Hired status		
No contract	14	3
Temporary	1	14
Permanent	1	4
Self-employed	2	
Total	18	21

Notes:
a)   Unskilled jobs refer to labourers.
b)   Skilled jobs refer to bricklayers, carpenters, locksmiths, plasterers, etc.
Source: Interview surveys.

This stable demand for immigrant employment is not accompanied by permanent jobs in Portuguese construction. Indeed, for the bulk of Africans in construction (14 out of the 16 employees), not having a contract was the rule, rather than the exception (Table 5.2). This is not a new trend in the industry, as eight out of the 14 workers without contracts had never been legally hired in construction. Yet, for an additional six workers, the trend was from permanent or temporary contracts toward no contract work.

From a broader perspective, data from the Portuguese Employment Survey [*Enquérito ao Emprego*] show a low number of permanent contracts for PALOP male nationals. To be specific, the percentage of permanent contracts is substantially lower for PALOP nationals than for all workers. Furthermore, permanent contracts are 15 per cent lower for

African males than for their female counterparts. Even if data are not broken down by economic sector, the weight of construction work in African male employment (as seen in my survey results) points to the significance of work in this sector in accounting for differences in contractual relationships by sex and nationality (Instituto Nacional de Estatística, 1996e).

No-contract employment relations are directly in line with the spread of casualisation in construction, accompanied by the growth of subcontracting in Portuguese construction (Pinto and Queiroz, 1996). The increase in subcontracting, which represents a strategy of passing economic risk on to smaller companies and construction workers, has been a general trend in the industry in Europe (Rainbird and Syben, 1991). Yet subcontracting is not necessarily synonymous with irregularity. For Spain, subcontracting passed from 11 per cent of turnover in the industry in 1970 to 20 per cent in 1989 (excluding self-employed workers; Carreras Yáñez, 1992). This share of subcontracting in total business in the industry has hardly changed over the 1990s, with 19 per cent of construction works being done by subcontractors in 1996 (Ministerio de Fomento, 1997). Yet the Girona survey shows that only three out of the 21 interviewed Africans were not working with a contract.

Associated with an increase in subcontracting in Portuguese construction, there has been a trend toward smaller firms in the sector. In 1980, Portugal had 14,009 firms in the industry. They employed 221,000 people. By 1991, the number of employees had grown slightly (247,780), but the number of firms had doubled to 31,406 (United Nations, 1997). It is in the smaller firms that immigrants are more likely to find employment. To be specific, 12 out of 16 employees who were interviewed for this research in Portugal worked for companies with less than 20 workers. This same pattern is observed in Spain, for 17 out of the 20[6] worked for firms with less than 20 employees. Significantly, just one person in Portugal (and nobody in Spain) worked for a company with more than 50 employees. Yet being employed in a small construction firm does not mean casual work, as the Spanish survey shows (albeit this was more the norm in Portugal).

So far we have seen that the small size of firms and the increase in subcontracting (that is, the structure and the evolution of the sector) are common characteristics in construction in both countries. Yet the outcome for immigrant hired status is quite different. A deeper look at no-contract work in Portuguese construction shows that amongst the 14 non-contracted workers, the survey identified five so-called 'self-employed' workers. These were self-employed workers for social security purposes,[7] but they were really employees of a subcontractor (i.e. they were not employed for a specific task, but worked on a more 'permanent' basis for one employer).

This is in line with the irregular practices described by Rodrigues (1992) in her analysis of Portuguese labour markets over the 1980s, as well as with a general growth of 'self-employment' in the construction industry (563.6 per cent for 1974-1989; Pinto and Queiroz, 1996). By contrast, only two 'real' self-employed workers were found in my survey (i.e. they did not work for an employer, but dealt directly with clients for specific jobs). Whether legal or irregular, it is clear that the growth in self-employment is a characteristic of Portuguese construction. This increase has also been observed in the British construction industry, where 24.7 per cent of workers were in self-employment in 1970 and 47.9 per cent in 1986 (Rainbird, 1991). In Spain, the increase in self-employment is less noticeable. Quoting Labour Force Survey data [*Encuesta de Población Activa, EPA*], Carreras Yáñez (1992) showed that self-employment in construction in 1977 was 15 per cent of total employment. This percentage had grown to 29 per cent by 1985, but had fallen back to 21 per cent by 1990. My survey in Girona did not identify any self-employed African in the construction sector.

In construction, self-employment is more common amongst skilled workers (see, for instance, Rainbird, 1991). Interviews with employers in Girona support this idea. The bulk of the firms that I contacted in Girona had a permanent staff of labourers and bricklayers, with other skilled workers in self-employment, who were hired temporarily for specific work (e.g. carpenters, plasterers). Set in this context, the Girona survey shows that 20 out of 21 construction workers did unskilled jobs. By contrast, the majority of African-born immigrants were occupied in skilled work in Portugal. Some interviewees indicated that it is common practice for subcontractors to specialise in a skilled task (e.g. carpenters), with firms sometimes supervising the activities of an array of subcontractors. Interviews with construction employers showed how fragmented the building process was in Portugal, with a large share of the permanent employees of some firms being comprised exclusively of administrative and technical staff.

From the employees' point of view, many African immigrants in Portugal stated that they preferred non-contracted forms of labour.[8] They argued that wages were higher either in the informal economy or as 'self-employed' workers. In reality, net wages are higher, as taxes are not deducted, but gross wages in Portuguese construction are not. Moreover, some interviewed workers declared that they could choose whether to be hired or not, with the non-contract option being selected by the majority of them. According to construction employers, the growth in casualisation started at the beginning of the 1980s, with African-born workers voluntarily leaving firms, in some cases to set up their own subcontractor firm or at least to work on an informal basis. Even if net wages are higher in the informal economy, it may look contradictory that workers voluntarily move toward casual patterns of employment. In this sense, many African interviewees stated that jobs were easy to find in construction. This suggests that there are labour shortages in the industry. These shortages were also pointed out by employers, who argued that the Lisbon area in particular had experienced a construction boom due to large building and infrastructure projects (see also Expresso, 1996). Set in this context, illegal recruitment of Angolans to meet labour shortages in construction has been reported in the media (Jolliffe, 1990), alongside irregularities in the hiring policies of construction firms (Carvalho, 1997).[9]

The key to the process of casualisation and informality is the (poor) role of the Portuguese state in controlling the industry (Rodrigues, 1984; Ferreira, 1988). Illustrating this pattern, an employer told me that many public works (e.g. roads) that are contracted to large construction firms are subcontracted to many small firms. This practice, which is against the law (Pinto and Queiroz, 1996), highlights that the state is not able to control their 'own' works. As interviews with employers indicated, and some employment histories confirm, the move toward casualisation was more acute at the end of the 1970s and beginning of the 1980s. Indeed, for 1981, Lobo (1985), comparing statistics from the Ministry of Labour and the Portuguese Institute of Statistics, estimated that almost half of the workers in construction were in the informal economy (i.e. they were either non-hired employees or irregular self-employed workers). In the period 1981-1986, the housing sector was de-regularised, with a reduction of public housing and decisive support for the private housing sector through low-interest credits for buying houses (Ferreira, 1988). A similar pattern was found in Britain over the 1970s and 1980s, when the de-regulation of the sector expanded self-employment and casualisation, alongside the proliferation of small firms and subcontracting (Ball, 1978; Ball, 1988; Evans, 1991). Yet the tighter regulation of the sector in Germany (e.g. forbidding subcontractor chains) demonstrates that the path toward greater (or lesser) casualisation is linked to state control (Koch, 1991). Had there been more rigorous control by the Portuguese state, the fragmentation of the construction industry, and the consequent increase in subcontracting and casualisation, would have been less pronounced.

Whatever the personal choice of workers or not, casualisation and informality in the Portuguese industry is growing. The picture for the Spanish construction industry is different, as the majority of the 21 interviewed Africans were hired on a temporary basis. Although the path toward non-contracted labour is not seen in Spain, the overwhelmingly temporary basis of immigrant employment in this country points to a different kind of casualisation in the industry. In short, although the industry presents similar employer characteristics (small-sized firms) and contract trends (growth in subcontracting), African employment reveals contrasting traits in Portugal and Spain. The main points of difference are fivefold:

- Immigrant over-representation in Portuguese construction is not observed in the Spanish industry. This over-representation of Africans in Portuguese construction relates to a long tradition of immigrant employment in the industry. In the late 1960s, immigrants filled labour shortages that were occasioned by earlier waves of Portuguese emigration to Europe and the colonial wars (Carreira, 1982; Saint-Maurice and Pires, 1989; Saint-Maurice, 1995).
- Whereas intersectoral mobility is slight in Portugal, this mobility is normal in the industry of its neighbour country. This points to a more stable demand for immigrant labour in construction in Portugal, as well as to African employment fluctuating with the state of the construction industry in Spain.
- African-born workers are a more skilled labour force in Portuguese construction than in Spain. Africans in Portuguese construction are not only found in unskilled jobs, but in all work categories (Table 5.2).
- Even if the sector exhibits common trends, casualisation in the construction sector occurs in different ways in the two Iberian states. In Spain, temporarily-contracted immigrant labourers shift jobs to other sectors (as high intersectoral mobility demonstrates). This is not a characteristic of immigrant employment, but a general trend in a sector that guarantees few permanent jobs (see, for instance, Tamames, 1985). In Portugal, construction offers abundant jobs on an irregular or informal basis. Yet this more stable demand has not seen a corresponding rise in contracted employment. Again, this is a characteristic of the sector as a whole, and not just of immigrant employment (see, for instance, Pinto and Queiroz, 1996).
- The long employment histories of many African-born workers in Portuguese construction, plus immigrant views on non-contracted labour, points to immigrants being agents in the casualisation process of the Portuguese industry. Yet, even if Africans may be happy with the move toward casual work, since it implies less taxation (and, consequently, higher wages), the key element in understanding increases in casualisation is the role of the state (as demonstrated by Ball, 1988, for Britain; or Koch, 1991, for Germany). De-regulation of Portuguese construction, alongside the poor control of the state over the sector, has had a decisive impact on the growth in subcontracting and

casualisation in this industry (Rodrigues, 1984; Ferreira, 1988; Pinto and Queiroz, 1996).

The Construction Industry through the Life Cycle of two 'Portuguese' Workers

Processes of subcontracting and casualisation in Portuguese construction have occurred in an industry with high African employment. Here the example of an 'old immigrant' (who came into the country in the mid-1970s) shows how the evolution of construction has had an impact on individuals. New entries in the 1990s were in a sector completely different from those who started work in the 1970s and early 1980s. The employment trajectory of a young construction worker is used here to contrast the experience of a more established worker with a recent entrant. This second case study demonstrates that untrained young Africans are in a worse position in the labour market than their more established counterparts. Yet labour outcomes are similar in both cases, regardless of dissimilar labour histories in the industry.

Mr. Moraes was born in what is now the Republic of Cape Verde in 1959.[10] He defined his family as poor (in 1985 an estimated 42 per cent of the Cape Verdean population lived below the official poverty line of \$170 per year; Reynolds, 1990). When he was in primary school, he started work as a carpenter's assistant with his father. In the early 1970s, he moved to Algarve with his father and one brother. Their migration is not exceptional. In the end of the 1960s and early 1970s, Cape Verdean workers moved in large numbers to Portugal, especially to the Lisbon area and Algarve, to fill labour shortages that Portuguese emigration had left in manufacturing and construction (Carreira, 1982; Saint-Maurice and Pires, 1989; Saint-Maurice, 1995). Mr. Moraes lived in the factory where his father worked for two years. In the first year of his stay in Portugal, he finished his last year of primary school. In the second year he started work as a labourer in the construction of a hotel in Quarteira (Algarve). To illustrate the working and living conditions of these workers in the mid-1970s, a spokesman of the Lisbon Construction Workers' Union described the general picture as regards Cape Verdean workers in the following way:

> The Cape Verdean is subjected to exploitation [...]. They live in barracks built only for housing coloured workers, whereas it would be much better if whites and non-whites occupied the same type of accommodation. The employer class plays on this, having been made aware, especially after the 25 of April [day of the Carnation Revolution], of the risks that might be incurred if the two were closer to one another and could exchange views

easily. As a typical example of [...] exploitation [...] when they want to go home they usually give notice that they want their accounts regulated before leaving and meantime book a place on the plane or boat. However, when they are ready to leave and go to see their employer, he replies that he does not have the money and cannot pay them. (quoted by Carreira, 1982, p. 93-4)

At the end of 1974, the family decided to move back to Cape Verde. Yet, within a short period, Mr. Moraes decided to return to Algarve on his own. Shortly after returning to Portugal, he started living in a shanty town of Algarve. Shanty towns spread in Portugal in the years after the independence of the African colonies, when thousands of *retornados* (Portuguese-born return migrants from the colonies), alongside many refugees, moved to Portugal (Lewis and Williams, 1985; Dubois, 1994). These population inflows emphasised the incapacity of the Portuguese construction sector (and the Government) to provide housing for the population (for the deficits of the housing sector in Portugal, see Cardoso, 1983; Salgueiro, 1985; Cardoso and Perista, 1994). In fact, despite the booming construction industry which was mainly oriented toward new accommodation (e.g. Algarve's accommodation sector offered 6,905 beds in 1970, but by 1988 this number had risen to 55,139; Silva and Silva, 1991), shanty towns are now part of the 'landscape' of the majority of Algarve coastal municipalities. During his time living in the shanty town, Mr. Moraes started cohabitating with a female partner. His partner is a Portuguese national, from the Azores. He married her in 1996. Although he could obtain Portuguese nationality, as he has spent a long time living in the country,[11] he has no intention of applying for it. He argued that his life would not change at all. They have two sons.

As soon as he returned from Cape Verde, he started work for a large construction firm, first as a labourer, later as a carpenter. He had a permanent contract for 15 years. This point is relevant as it fits a general pattern for African workers, of skilled work being obtained after experience has been gained in the Portuguese construction industry. Thus my survey found that 12 out of the 14 skilled workers learned their skills in Portuguese construction, with a further two gaining their construction skills in their countries of origin. In 1990, Mr. Moraes quit his permanent job in a large firm for a non-contracted job with a subcontractor. The reason for this move was the higher wages that were offered by the subcontractor. After two years, he accepted another job under the same working conditions (no contract, no social security), with a different subcontractor. This last subcontractor had four African-origin employees. Speaking for himself, Mr. Moraes reckoned that it was not difficult to find construction jobs in Algarve.

This pattern contrasts with that of Mr. Lopes, who was born in São Tomé in the mid-1960s.[12] In 1972, all the family moved from São Tomé to Portugal. After the independence of the colonies in 1975, Mr. Lopes (and his family) took Cape Verdean nationality (his parents were from the islands originally), although he has never visited the Cape Verde islands in his life. Since 1972, the family has always lived in Setúbal because his father's job is in that city.

Mr. Lopes did four years of compulsory schooling [*4. classe*] and started work in the construction sector when he was sixteen. Since then, he has had just one year with a regular contract with a firm. For the other 15 years in construction, he had worked without a contract, despite frequent employment shifts from one subcontractor to another. Yet some subcontractors obliged him to pay his social contribution as a 'self-employed' worker (albeit he was employed), if he wanted to obtain the job. In this way, and according to Mr. Lopes, the employer tried to avoid legal problems which may arise in case of job casualties. As Mr. Moraes, he learned the profession of carpenter after two years of being in the industry as a construction labourer. Even if he lived in Setúbal, he was interviewed in Algarve. He was in this southern region, living in a relative's home, in search of employment in construction.

He has had an irregular employment trajectory, which has worked against the possibility of him becoming a Portuguese citizen, as he cannot demonstrate continuous legal work in the country for six years. Indeed, his five-year residence permit had expired when he was interviewed, as he could not demonstrate the soundness of his financial resources (e.g. a contracted work) to renew it. A lawyer was helping Mr. Lopes to sort out his legal situation. His situation is not exceptional, as four out of the 14 interviewed employees in construction were illegal residents at the time of their interview. These four make up more than half of those (seven) who were found in my survey without a residence permit (Table 3.7). This suggests that illegal residence is substantial amongst construction workers. The unstable legal situation of Mr. Lopes hampered his mobility, since he argued that if he had Portuguese nationality he would leave Portugal for France, as his sister did. He knew that legal non-EU nationals could not work outside the country in which they have legal residence.

These two examples show the same labour market outcome. That is, no work contract with subcontractors and intrasectoral mobility. This is the rule for the bulk of those employed in the sector. The difference between these two cases lies in their contrasting personal circumstances. In the first case, Mr. Moraes moved voluntarily from formal to informal work, for higher wages in the informal economy, and this did not cause any legal complication. Indeed, he believed that jobs in construction were easily available for him. By contrast, Mr. Lopes had not chosen irregular work and this caused legal complications, alongside mobility restrictions (as he wanted to leave the country). Furthermore, this less experienced young worker found problems when obtaining jobs in the construction sector.

Conclusion

First openings for Africans in Portuguese construction started in the late 1960s owing to labour shortages in the industry due to large-scale Portuguese emigration into Central and Northern Europe (Carreira, 1982; Saint-Maurice and Pires, 1989; Saint-Maurice, 1995). The independence of the African colonies has not stopped the inflow into construction, with the sector currently being the main male African employer (Esteves; 1991; França, 1992; Machado, 1997). Nowadays, the sector gives jobs to African-origin employees, to the self-employed, and, as employers told me, even to a few African subcontractors (albeit none of this last group was identified in my survey). All this points to an African niche in the construction sector.

As for Spanish farming, the creation of an immigrant niche in Portuguese construction lies in the unattractiveness of the sector for non-immigrants. This lack of attractiveness comes from low wages and high casualisation in construction. Wages in Portuguese construction are clearly below the average for the economy (Ministério do Emprego e da Segurança Social, 1994). This is even more remarkable when compared with Spain, where construction wages are above the average (Banco Bilbao Vizcaya, 1997). Not surprisingly, due to differentials in wages, some construction workers expressed their desire to work in construction elsewhere in Europe (as Mr. Lopes stated). This point on further emigration is developed in Chapter 8. The second reason for the unattractiveness of construction for Portuguese workers lies in its high casualisation (Lobo, 1985; Rodrigues, 1992; Pinto and Queiroz, 1996). In the spread of casualisation, which has been accompanied by the fragmentation of large firms into smaller units, the de-regularisation of the housing sector has been a key element (Ferreira, 1988). Similarly, the de-regularisation of British construction brought about growth in casualisation (Ball, 1978; Ball, 1988; Evans, 1991). As seen for Germany, more rigorous control by the state can result in less irregularities in the construction industry (Koch, 1991). Low wages and high casualisation render the sector unattractive for non-immigrants. Like Spanish farming, African workers are found in construction because Portuguese-born white workers do not accept the working conditions in the sector. This suggests that there is scarce competition between immigrants and other workers in construction.

Of course, it is a matter of debate whether lack of competition exists in Spanish construction, as this offers higher wages than the average. Not surprisingly, and contrary to what is observed for farming, construction is not a main immigrant port of entry. Unlike Portugal, the sector does not give employment to Africans for all their employment histories in Spain, but offers work on an irregular, fixed-term, contracted basis. The reasons for African employment in Spanish construction need further explanation. More than the unattractiveness of the sector as a whole, possible explanations may come from locational effects associated with different employment structures which can lead to labour shortages in construction. Chapter 7 examines the match between labour supply and labour demand in different economic sectors in the light of such differences in local economic mix.

For Portugal, although labour shortages caused by the lack of attractiveness of construction jobs looks to be the main reason for 'promoting' Africans into skilled work, the survey nonetheless found that the majority of interviewed Africans did have skilled jobs (e.g. carpenters, plasterers). As the example of Mr. Moraes denotes, skills are gained through experience in Portuguese construction. Even if this is not associated with stable employment (which is not sought by some interviewees), this adds support to human capital principles in the sense that more professional jobs are obtained through labour experience in the sector and longer stays in host societies. Yet the nature of construction work in Portugal is clearly secondary (i.e. non-contracted, unstable, fixed-term jobs). Experienced workers do not believe that this is a problem, as they dispose of their skills, experience and labour market knowledge to change jobs easily. Yet, for new entrants (as Mr. Lopes), who lack such experience and information, no access to hired work may put their legal situation in the country at risk.

Construction is the main male African employer in Portugal. So is accommodation services and restaurants for immigrant women. Yet, as for construction, Africans are found in greater numbers in accommodation services and restaurants in Algarve than in Girona. As explained in the next chapter, one decisive element in understanding different labour outcomes in these industries is the contrasting gender composition of African inflows.

Notes

1. The discussion on immigrants in Iberian construction is further developed in Mendoza (2000).
2. Official statistics show that three out of four employed African workers had a job in either construction or manufacturing in 1996. By contrast, these industries only gave

employment to about 20 per cent of European nationals and 23 per cent of Brazilians (Instituto Nacional de Estatística, 1997a).

3. The Portuguese *Instituto Nacional de Estatística* informed me that it was not possible to break down 1991 Census data on foreigners by branch of economic activity.

4. Two immigrants were self-employed (see Table 5.2).

5. The average wage in construction was 3,283 thousand pta. in Spain in 1993. This figure was 3,148 thousand pta. for the whole economy (Banco Bilbao Vizcaya, 1997).

6. One person did not reply to this question in the Girona survey.

7. This practice, known as *recibos verdes* [green receipts, called after the colour of the form], is not illegal. What is illegal is that employers pass responsibility for the payment of social security contributions onto employees. In May 1996, the Portuguese Government was preparing a law to restrict the use of this practice (and consequently was seeking to foster new contracts). This law was intended to clarify the status of a self-employed worker [*trabalhador independente*] (Garrido and Vicente, 1996). By September 1997, this law had not been debated in the Portuguese Parliament.

8. Out of 21 interviews, only one construction worker in Spain expressed similar views to his Portuguese counterparts.

9. Carvalho (1997) denounced the lack of control over construction employers who were building the International Exposition for Lisbon 1998. The example is quite relevant as the state fails even to oversee construction work that is financed by public money. According to this media source, irregularities are found in the lack of a contracted status for many employees and in safety regulations that are not followed on building sites.

10. The island Republic of Cape Verde lies about 500 km. west of Dakar (Senegal) in the north Atlantic Ocean. Comprising 10 islands, Cape Verde became an independent republic on 5 July 1975. Its estimated population was 350,000 inhabitants at mid-1987. Praia, the main city and capital, had just under 50,000 inhabitants in the mid-1980s. It has been estimated that 600,000 Cape Verdeans live abroad. This figure is about twice the population of the islands. The remittances that these emigrants sent back covered 40 per cent of the Cape Verde trade deficit in 1979 (Reynolds, 1990).

11. Those married with a Portuguese national can apply for Portuguese nationality after three years of marriage, so Mr. Moraes could not naturalise through marriage at the time he was interviewed.

12. São Tomé is a plantation island where the eastern slopes and coastal flatlands are covered by large cocoa and coffee estates [*roças*]. São Tomé and Príncipe obtained independence from Portugal in 1975 (Pélissier, 1990).

6 African Employment in Tourist Activities: Immigrants in the Accommodation and Restaurant Industries

The previous chapters have showed that farming and construction were the main (male) African employers in Spain and Portugal, respectively. Yet these two sectors offer few openings for female Africans. In order to consider female immigrant involvement in Iberian labour markets, Chapter 6 analyses African employment in the accommodation and restaurant sector. As will be shown, women are over-represented in these industries in both Portugal and Spain. Yet it may be the case that, even if the sector is female-dominated, few openings exist for African female workers. Adding a further twist to the argument, accommodation services and restaurants may (also) give jobs to African men. A further consideration is that the gender composition of African immigrants in these industries may vary from Portugal to Spain, reflecting differences in African inflows into the two Iberian countries.

The scope of African employment in Spanish farming and Portuguese construction is directly related to the lack of attractiveness of these sectors for Iberian workers. Yet, at least for Spain, tourism-related activities are attractive to 'native' workers. Two decades ago, this was revealed by Greenwood (1976). He showed that young agricultural workers in the Basque country deserted farming for tourism-related activities, even for lower wages. Tourism represented the new values of a 'modern' urban lifestyle. Some opinions of farmers, which were reported in Chapter 4, point to this pattern holding today in Girona, where tourism competes for workers with farming in the summer, which is the peak season for both activities. As Spaniards are more prone to accept tourism-related work, this suggests that Africans do not fill labour shortages in the accommodation and restaurant sector left by Spanish workers. The reasons for the employment of Africans must be sought elsewhere. However, what is true for Spain may not fit Portugal.

Even if local or in-migrant Iberian nationals look forward to working in these industries, it may be the case that different groups of workers are oriented toward different segments of the labour market. However, even if all Africans are found in the secondary segment of labour markets (as seen for the bulk of Africans in Spanish farming), they are unlikely to be 'alone' in this segment in accommodation services and restaurants. If this is confirmed, the presence of immigrants in secondary labour markets could not be taken as an indicator of an unsatisfied labour demand (Pugliese, 1993).

Thus this chapter explores reasons for divergences (if any) in African employment. To do so, the first part of this chapter places these two industries in the broad perspective of the development of tourism industries in Portugal and Spain. Here, it is seen that demand for labour in accommodation services and restaurants largely varies according to business-type. The second part of the chapter concentrates on hiring practices and employers' views on African employment. It does so by focusing on three hotels in Girona and one in Algarve. The views of employers are then contrasted with the results of the African interview survey to build up a general picture of immigrant employment in accommodation services and restaurants. In the conclusion, the processes and actors that lie behind patterns of African employment are examined.

Regional Demand for Labour in the Accommodation and Restaurant Industries

Employment generation is the most important output which is derived from tourism inflows in both Portugal and Spain (Lewis and Williams, 1991; Valenzuela, 1991). The Spanish Tourist Board [*Instituto Español de Turismo*] has calculated that either directly or indirectly tourism was responsible for 11.2 per cent of total national employment in 1990 (González and Moral, 1996). Likewise, Valenzuela (1991) has estimated that tourism was directly responsible for the 1,234,000 jobs in Spain in 1994 (740,000 directly and 494,000 indirectly). If the number of direct and indirect jobs are put together, tourism is responsible for about one in 10 jobs in the country. For Portugal, official statistics give a lower share in total employment, with accommodation and restaurants providing 4.4 per cent of total employment in 1994 (Instituto Nacional de Estatística, 1995). The significance of the sector is greater than just employment, as indicated by estimates that tourism-related industries accounted for about 10 per cent of the Spanish Gross National Product in 1994 (Secretaría General de Turismo, 1996). For Portugal, the figure has been put at 6-7 per cent of the Portuguese GNP for 1991 (Corkill, 1993).

Disaggregating these numbers by industry, tourism inflows are directly responsible for employment generation in three main activities: (i) accommodation and restaurants; (ii) air passenger transport; and (iii) travel agencies and tour operators (World Tourist Organization, 1988). For accommodation services, international statistics consider a tourist to be a visitor who stays at least one night in the place visited (see, for instance, World Tourist Organization, 1985; Eurostat, 1997c). For restaurants, the employment impact is most clearly seen in tourism areas, as it is evident in the high tourism season when many more employees are taken on (or longer working hours are demanded of existing staff). Tourism is also indirectly responsible for the creation of employment in other services (e.g. garbage collection firms and retailing), and even in manufacturing (e.g. ceramics production for tourists in Girona, as pointed out by employers) or farming (due to increases in the consumption of fresh fruit and vegetables, see Hermans, 1981, for a case study of Cambrils, Tarragona).

Focusing on accommodation services and restaurants, in Spain these industries provided 872,805 jobs in 1993 (Banco Bilbao Vizcaya, 1997), which constituted 6.8 per cent of the total workforce (Table 6.1). Even more noteworthy, these industries created 69,254 jobs over the 1991-93 period, when jobs in the whole Spanish economy fell by 353,280 (Banco Bilbao Vizcaya, 1993; 1997). For Portugal, the role of the accommodation industry seems less dynamic, as there was a job decline of 7.5 per cent over the period 1992-96 (Comissão de Coordinação da Região do Algarve, 1993; Instituto Nacional de Estatística, 1997). Job losses went even deeper in Algarve, with the labour force passing from 13,022 in July 1992 to 11,891 in July 1996 (Comissão de Coordinação da Região do Algarve, 1993; Instituto Nacional de Estatística, 1997).

The fact that tourism activities are responsible for one out of 10 jobs in Spain is linked to the country ranking amongst the world's first in its number of tourist visitors. Indicative of the strength of the sector, visitor numbers rose from less than 1 million in 1950 to 52 million in 1992 (Albert-Piñole, 1993). In this development, the state has played a leading role. Not surprisingly given the scale of expansion, mass tourism was seen as a major source of foreign currency during the Franco dictatorship (Cals, 1974; Pi-Sunyer, 1996). In this regard, Pearce (1987) argued that the eagerness of the state to foster tourism was seen in the frequent devaluation of the peseta (1959, 1967, 1971, 1973, 1980-81), which was designed in part to maintain the competitiveness of the sector.[1] Mass tourism development which fitted the model of 1960s Fordist mass consumption

(Urry, 1990) thrived under the implicit support of the regime's economic policies (Cals, 1974; Pearce, 1989). By contrast, the state in Portugal[2] favoured attracting higher income visitors (Cavaco, 1980; Boniface and Cooper, 1994; Bote Gómez and Sinclair, 1996). As a indication of the different impact this strategy has had, the Spanish Costa del Sol has more bed capacity than the whole of Portugal (Lewis and Williams, 1991).

Table 6.1 The contribution of accommodation and restaurant industries to the economies of the Autonomous Communities

	Gross Value Added		Employment in accom. and restaurants			Hotel beds
	Million	%	Number	%	%	Number
	Pta.	GVA	of jobs	change	region	
	1993	1993	1993	1991-93	1993	1994
Andalucía	584,191	7.6	131,602	14.3	7.2	129,548
Aragón	106,378	5.3	21,631	4.9	5.1	17,973
Asturias	82,258	5.5	17,465	18.6	5.0	11,181
Balears	478,627	29.6	101,975	3.9	31.4	232,660
Canarias	315,768	13.6	69,926	4.0	14.7	98,448
Cantabria	50,194	6.7	10,789	14.1	6.4	10,306
Castilla-La Mancha	94,843	4.3	23,890	19.6	4.7	10,385
Castilla y León	184,998	5.0	45,822	24.4	5.5	20,064
Catalunya	710,094	6.1	138,773	5.5	6.2	172,062
Extremadura	57,102	4.9	15,262	21.8	5.2	7,197
Galicia	211,477	6.0	47,115	13.0	5.0	26,461
Madrid	610,707	5.9	112,073	5.2	6.0	39,158
Murcia	66,087	4.9	14,305	15.5	4.5	10,931
Navarra	44,367	4.8	9,238	4.7	5.0	4,394
País Vasco	155,819	4.4	31,020	10.7	4.6	11,638
Rioja (La)	18,806	3.9	3,974	3.1	3.9	2,749
Valencia	379,770	6.3	76,459	2.6	5.9	70,281
Ceuta & Melilla	6,460	3.5	1,486	-6.5	3.8	1,210
Spain	4,157,946	6.8	872,805	8.6	6.8	876,646

Sources: Banco Bilbao Vizcaya (1993; 1997). For the number of beds in hotels, Eurostat (1997c).

Yet the Portuguese strategy had its successes. An 85.5 per cent increase in international tourism income between 1980-1987 (the highest in the EU over this period; Lavery, 1993) is one measure of this, with the expansion of sun-sea-sand package holidays that assisted this growth being linked to state policies (Lewis and Williams, 1989; Edwards and Sampaio, 1993).

Not surprisingly given the emphasis placed on sun-sea-sand package holidays, hotel accommodation is highly concentrated on the Spanish coastal strip, with just five provinces (Alicante, the Balearic Islands, Barcelona, Girona and Málaga) accounting for one-half of Spain's recorded bed space (Pearce and Grimmeau, 1985). The same can be said for camp ground capacity, as two-thirds is located in four provinces (Barcelona, Castellón, Girona and Tarragona; Pearce, 1987). This concentration has resulted in an unequal impact of tourism on regional economies. As seen in Table 6.1, the accommodation and restaurant industries contributed 29.6 per cent of Gross Value Added in the Balearic Islands and 13.6 per cent in the Canary Islands in 1993. The contribution is less important in more diversified regions (like Andalucía, Catalunya or Valencia). At a provincial level, tourism is directly responsible for Girona and the Balearics occupying, respectively, first and second place amongst the Spanish provinces in terms of their per-capita income (Valenzuela, 1991). In terms of employment, accommodation services and restaurants accounted for 31.4 per cent of the total workforce of the Balearic Islands and 14.7 per cent in the Canary Islands in 1993, although such high values sharply contrast with other Spanish regions (Table 6.1). Nevertheless, regarding the evolution of employment in these industries by Autonomous Community, in recent years there has been important relative growth in inland areas that have traditionally been less popular tourist destinations (Castilla-La Mancha, Castilla y León, Extremadura; Table 6.1). Although with varying intensity, a rising trend in employment is observed across all 17 Autonomous Communities.

An unequal regional distribution of tourism incomes and employment is also observed in Portugal, where there is a heavy concentration in three locations – Lisbon and its surroundings, Algarve and Madeira (Edwards and Sampaio, 1993; Montanari, 1995). In fact, Algarve alone accounted for 32 per cent of international visitor nights in 1996 and had 40 per cent of total accommodation on offer (Instituto Nacional de Estatística, 1997). Furthermore, the three (coastal) municipalities [*concelhos*] of Albufeira, Loulé and Portimão accounted for three-quarters of total Algarve accommodation in 1994, with inland *concelhos* having a very limited capacity (Instituto Nacional de Estatística, 1995). Even if Algarve started by attracting (and still attracts) an up-market segment of the tourism market, as seen in the development of golf courses, tennis centres and riding stables (Lewis and Williams, 1991), the bulk of the expansion of tourism activities in the region has been produced by low-spending sun-sea-sand visitors (Lewis and Williams, 1989; Pimpão, 1991). Thus Algarve presents similar characteristics to the mass tourism that is observed in some Spanish regions in the 1990s. Indeed, Algarve is highly dependent on international tourist markets that are driven by tour operators (Vieira, 1997). The most important of these is the (low spend) UK market, which accounted for 32 per cent of all bed nights in 1996.[3] The second most important market is made up of German visitors, who represented a further 26 per cent of all bed nights (Instituto Nacional de Estatística, 1997).

The specialisation of the industry on sun-sea-sand tourism has brought about a remarkable seasonality. In Portugal, tourists arriving in this peak season increased over the 1970s and 1980s, passing from 44 per cent of international visitors in 1972 to 48 per cent in 1984 (Lewis and Williams, 1991). This increased seasonal peak has risen due to the development in Portugal, and especially in the Algarve, of a mass tourist, summer market (Lewis and Williams, 1991; Pimpão, 1991; Vieira, 1997). As another example of the seasonality of the Portuguese hotel industry, the occupancy rate of bed-places goes up from 25 per cent in January to 67 per cent in August (Eurostat, 1997c). In Spain, 43 per cent of international visitors arrived either in July or August in 1990 (Albert-Piñole, 1993). Thus the 81 per cent of the occupancy rate of hotel places in August is half in January (41 per cent in 1994; Eurostat, 1997c). Yet González and Moral (1996) observed that, although international tourism demand is still concentrated in summer, there are positive trends in Spanish tourism to decrease seasonality in the sector (e.g. the growth of permanent foreign residents in tourism areas, a rising trend in winter visits by elderly foreigners, and an increase in domestic visitors).[4]

Contrary to what is observed in other industries, this pattern of mass consumption has not led to the disappearance of small- and medium-sized businesses. Indeed, long before post-Fordism was widely talked about, Cals (1974: 148) forecast that mass tourism would not end the dominance of small- and medium-sized establishments in Iberia as these enterprises were better suited to addressing more personal, individual tastes. Certainly, for Spain, 59 per cent of hotels had less than 50 beds in 1991 and just 11 per cent had more than 200 places (Instituto Nacional de Estadística, 1993). Similarly, 67 per cent of Portuguese hotels had less than five employees in 1994 and only 11 per cent had 20 or more employees (Vieira, 1997).

Yet this pattern of mass consumption has led to control over the commercialisation process by foreign tour operators and travel agencies (Marchena Gómez and Vera Rebollo, 1995; Aguiló Pérez, 1996; Williams, 1996). This has significantly affected the accommodation on offer in coastal Mediterranean regions (Montanari, 1995). In the case of Algarve, while the more traditional hotel sector has stagnated since the 1970s, there has been a substantial rise in demand for apartments and self-catered holidays, which has mainly been associated with holiday packages offered by international tour-operators[5] (Silva and Silva, 1991). Yet foreign visitors (and tour operators) are not the only ones who have been responsible for the progressive abandonment of the traditional hotel industry, since domestic visitors have followed their foreign counterparts in preferring apartment and self-catered holidays (Matias, 1992). As a result, for Algarve, apartments[6] represented 47 per cent of hotel accommodation on offer in 1996 (Instituto Nacional de Estatística, 1997). If hotels which also offer apartments are added, the share of this type of accommodation soars to 69 per cent (Instituto Nacional de Estatística, 1997).[7] Illustrating the expansion of these establishments in Algarve over the 1980s, about 90 per cent of growth in the number of workers employed in the accommodation sector over the period 1980-92 was in apartments and hotels which offer self-catering holidays (Comissão de Coordinação da Região do Algarve, 1993).

Tourism in the more diversified regional economies of Iberia has proved to be less dependent on tour operators (Shaw and Williams, 1994). In the case of Catalunya, recent trends help explain the relatively autonomy of the sector from tour operators. First of all, domestic tourism increased in the 1980s and 1990s. As for Spain as a whole, the late 1980s crisis of the tourism industry, which saw remarkable reduction in expenditure by international tourists, was offset by growth in domestic tourist numbers (González and Moral, 1996). Secondly, the city of Barcelona is an increasingly popular destination for short-break holidays, while its residents (and visitors) constitute potential tourists for the whole of Catalunya. Aware of this fact, an association of small- and medium-sized hotel owners on the Costa Brava (Girona) have successfully launched a campaign to attract domestic visitors in the off-peak season. The offer this group has put together consists of themed holiday packages in spring and autumn (e.g. sailing or gastronomic week-ends; Klemm and Martín-Quirós, 1996). Thirdly, proximity to France (the French took 44 per cent of international bed nights in Catalunya in 1993; Generalitat de Catalunya, 1994), and low usage of tour operators by the French (Shaw and Williams, 1994), helps reduce the dependence of the Catalan industry on foreign companies.

Yet, there are coastal localities in Catalunya which specialise in tour operator holidays. Thus Cals and associates (1977) identified two distinctive tourist markets on the Girona Costa Brava. Those that were tour operator driven carried the hallmarks of mass tourism in several coastal localities (Roses, Blanes, Lloret de Mar; see the location on these towns on Figure 4.2). Contrasting with these, other localities were dominated by small-scale private tourism, whether domestic or international in origin (e.g. Cadaqués or L'Escala on the coast, and the inland municipalities of Figueres and Girona). Yet, in interview, the president of the Girona Hotel Federation [*Federació Provincial d'Hoteleria de Girona*] made clear that, even for mass tourism destinations, where a notable part of the accommodation is offered by large hotels or hotel chains, small- and medium-sized businesses still cover a significant part of demand. As an illustration, whereas in the mass-tourism oriented resort of Lloret de Mar 23,388 hotel places were offered by 91 establishments with 100 or more beds, the rest of the 6,993 hotel places were provided by 94 hotels of smaller size (Generalitat de Catalunya, 1994).

As will be shown, these trends are crucial to understanding regional demand for labour in the accommodation and restaurant industries. These trends can be summarised under three points:

- A major part of the development of tourism in Iberia has been linked to a relatively low-cost sun-sea-sand type tourism that is driven by demand for competitive prices. This element of the industry is concentrated in coastal areas. Not only is there concentration in space, but also in time. Quoting official data provided by the Spanish Tourism Board [*Instituto Español de Turismo*], Valenzuela (1991) calculated that employment falls by one-fifth in the low-season on the Costa del Sol and in the Balearics, and by 30 per cent in Alicante. For Portugal, there is a 30 per cent adjustment in employment between summer and winter in Algarve, a 7 per cent deviation in Lisbon, which has year-round cultural and business tourism, but only a 2 per cent shift in Madeira (Shaw and Williams, 1994).

- Even though there are some common trends for the whole of Iberia, different trends do exist across its regions. Algarve, the Balearic Islands and the Canary Islands[8] have a remarkably high reliance on international tour operators (and, effectively, on international tourists; see, for instance, Williams, 1996). Other regions (e.g. Andalucía, Catalunya) have more complex industries, with tour operators driving the development of tourism in some localities (e.g. Torremolinos, Lloret de Mar), but with others dominated by small-scale (domestic or international) tourism.

- The hotel industry is divided into two broad segments, with the first constituted of large hotels and hotel chains, and the second with an array of small- and medium-sized firms. The next section takes this point further. Here, four hotels are examined to outline differences in hiring policies, labour conditions and employers' attitudes toward African workers in different types of establishment.

Iberia: A Tale of Four Hotels

The first of the four hotel examples is situated in an inland locality in Girona. The hotel is open for the whole year and caters for both tourists and travellers, as it is situated on a crucial road linking Barcelona and France. By contrast, the second hotel relies exclusively on international tourists who are brought into the hotel through tour operators. The third case has similarities with the first one, in the sense that is situated in the same locality and its clients are similar. What makes this hotel different is that it has a large number of Moroccan employees. Finally, and different from the other three examples, the fourth establishment is situated in Algarve. This large hotel is open for the whole year and specialises in apartment and studio facilities.

Hotel A is situated in Figueres, a small city of 34,573 inhabitants (1991), that lies in northern Girona, near the French border. The city has always been a commercial centre for surrounding agrarian municipalities. According to the 1991 Census, 62 per cent of its working population was occupied in tertiary activities (Institut d'Estadística de Catalunya, 1993). The city had nine hotels and 19 pensions in 1997. These employed 879 people (unpublished data provided by the Catalan Institute of Statistics [*Institut d'Estadística de Catalunya*]). Interviewed employers explained that the accommodation on offer in the city expanded in 1992 as a consequence of the Barcelona Olympic Games (Figueres was one of the cities in which Olympic events took place).

Hotel A is a three-star[9] family-owned property that started operations in the 1960s. The current manager explained that increasing competition in recent years had pushed the hotel to change furniture in its rooms and make improvements in the dining room, the bar and the reception. The hotel relies on both international and domestic visitors. Its manager informed me that the bulk of visitors are independent travellers. In summer, international visitors (especially the French) outnumber Spaniards. Although summer is the peak season, the establishment does not shut in winter. This is a trend common to all the hotels and pensions of the city. In winter, occupancy is much lower and is mainly comprised of domestic visitors. The hotel does not have any regular contracts with tour operators. Only when coastal hotels are full, do tour operators bring clients to the hotel.[10]

In the peak summer months the hotel hires two extra temporary workers to add to the normal complement of 14 permanent staff. These two workers are hired via private employment firms that specialise in temporary work. Staff on permanent contracts are distributed as follows: one manager, three receptionists, four kithen staff (one of them, chef), two waiters, one person in charge of the laundry service, two cleaners and one maintenance person. Almost half of the staff have skilled jobs (chef, reception employees, manager and the person in charge of small repairs). The two extra workers in July and August are hired for cleaning rooms. The manager explained that more than eight hours a day are worked in the peak season, especially by the cleaning staff. Yet the firm compensates for these extra hours by allowing employees to clock up less working hours in winter. Just one foreigner is hired in Hotel A; a national from an EU country who does one of the shifts on reception. According to the manager, Africans are not hired because there is a good permanent staff. In the manager's words:

> Sometimes Africans come here to ask if work is available. But all of them are men who want to work in the kitchen. We already have permanent staff in the kitchen. We need two extra women for cleaning rooms and corridors in the summer. That's all.

Hotel B is a two-star hotel, with 55 rooms in coastal Lloret de Mar. As a reflection of the importance of tourism for this locality, accommodation alone offered 35 per cent of the jobs in town in 1991. For the same reason, the permanent population of 17,095 residents in 1991 (Institut d'Estadística de Catalunya, 1993) soars to an estimated 180,000 residents in summer (Lever, 1987). Hotel B is part of a chain of hotels and camp sites, scattered along the Costa Brava and in the province of Barcelona. The chain is Catalan-owned. Booking is centralised by the administration of the company. The chain also centralises the purchase of food and drinks, so better prices can be negotiated. Tour operators provide the bulk of Hotel B customers. According to its manager, tour operators contact the Hotel in September to negotiate prices for the next season.[11]

The hotel has not carried out any major renovation work in the last five years. One week before the hotel opens (it is normally closed from the beginning of October to the end of April), the manager decides if any minor work needs be done. No one is in charge of the surveillance of maintenance tasks in winter. According to its manager, this lack of investment is due to a guaranteed number of visitors in the peak season, who are attracted by the sun-sand-sea attractions of Lloret de Mar. Larger hotels than this one have longer seasons, as they can use the higher prices (and higher profits) generated in the peak season to compensate for lower prices in the off-peak season. Yet, according to the manager, even large hotels are closed by the end of October in Lloret de Mar.

Members of staff in the hotel vary in number from eight in July-August to six over the rest of the months that the hotel is open. The six are occupied on the following tasks: one manager (also in charge of reception), one waiter, three cleaners and one watchman. Apart from these six employees, two extra workers are hired for the reception and for cleaning in July-August. In reality, however, employees have to do other tasks, apart from those that are designed in their contracts. 'The staff are not enough when there is full occupancy'. The average working hours per day are 10 or even 12 hours. The majority of employees had been hired by the firm for many years. When extra workers are needed, jobs are advertised in public spaces on the streets. The manager explained that many people ask for jobs at the beginning of the season. 'I take note of their name and telephone number, just in case'. There were two foreigners employed by the firm in 1997. These were the manager and one of the cleaners, both of whom were French. During the 1996 season the hotel hired one Moroccan as a watchperson. There is no specific reason for not hiring Africans. 'They need a work permit though. What I cannot do is sort out the hassle of dealing with all the red tape'. According to the President of the Girona Hotel Federation [*Federació Provincial d'Hoteleria de Girona*], there is a strong tradition of in-migrant inflows from central and southern Spain to fill jobs in the larger hotels in Lloret de Mar. Although there are no official statistics on the number of seasonal in-migrant workers, Lever (1987) suggested that over 12,000 non-local residents seasonally move into the locality from other Spanish towns to work in tourism industries.

As for Hotel A, Hotel C is in Figueres. Both hotels have similar characteristics (the same category, with independent travellers constituting the bulk of the visitors, and they are both open for the whole year). As with the manager of Hotel A, the owner of Hotel C reckoned that competition had grown extraordinarily over the 1992-1997 period. As a result of this, the hotel had installed air conditioning and bathrooms in all 60 rooms in the hotel. The hotel also has a restaurant which does not just serve hotel clients, but has a large clientele of local residents. The restaurant specialises in Catalan cuisine and enjoys a good reputation in the northern Girona Empordà region. The restaurant is the main activity of the hotel in winter.

Increased competition in recent times has led to a reduction in the staff numbers (of seven people between 1992 and 1997). These seven employees all retired or left the firm, but have not been replaced. The owner complained about a lack of flexibility in the labour market and the high price of sacking workers, so he 'has' to wait for them to leave voluntarily or retire. In 1997, there were 30 people permanently employed in Hotel C over the whole year, with four of them working in the restaurant. In addition, there were five workers on temporary contracts (four workers were hired for cleaning in the summer season and one was employed as a kitchen assistant). A significant part of the staff are Moroccans (seven employees). Five are on temporary contracts and a further two on permanent contracts. Moroccans constitute all the temporarily-hired workers in the firm. Except for one worker who is in charge of the warehouse, these nationals do unskilled jobs and work with little responsibility (cleaners, kitchen assistants and laundry staff). Some of the work undertaken by the permanent (Spanish) staff who left the firm during the 1992-1997 period has been taken over by temporary (Moroccan) workers. Arguing the reasons for hiring Moroccans, the owner argued that 'if Spaniards carry out these unskilled tasks, they do so unwillingly [*a desgana*]'.

Four-star Hotel D is in Albufeira, a tourist-oriented municipality with 40 per cent of the total accommodation on offer in Algarve (Comissão de Coordinação da Região do Algarve, 1993). The hotel had 71 apartments, 94 studios and six rooms on offer in 1997. Similar to all the hotels of the locality, Hotel D is open for the whole year. This contrasts with the seasonal closure of pensions in Albufeira. Within this municipality, large establishments do offset lower takings in the low season with profits made during the summer. Close to full occupancy is reached from July to September, with the winter low season having an average of 60 per cent occupancy.

The manager explained that the clientele comes mainly through international tour operators. The hotel deals with a range of German, British and Dutch operators, so it has a diversified source of potential clients. The overall impression from interviews with employers in Algarve was that high quality hotels could choose the tour operator they wanted to work with. In the specific case of Hotel D, its manager described the tour operator operations as follows:

> They buy packages at lower prices and sell it to individual clients. Generally, the contracts have a deadline. If the apartments or studios are not occupied by this date, we are free to sell them again. This allows us to 'play' on prices and room availability. Yet the hotel has sometimes been overbooked. If this is the case, it is the hotel's responsibility and we are obliged to give a similar (or better) type of accommodation to clients in Albufeira and, occasionally, compensate them. Otherwise, the tour operator does so from our money.

Regarding the hotel staff, 54 workers were employed in August 1996. They were distributed across the following occupational bands as follows: three administration staff (accountant services are in Lisbon), six receptionists, six in the snack bar service area, six in the restaurant, three in the pub, one in the shop and two in the launtry (plus five in charge of maintenance and 22 cleaners). It is worth noting that more than 50 per cent of the employees in this hotel, which basically offers apartments and studios, are engaged in cleaning, whether rooms (22), clothes (two) or dishes (four between restaurant, bar and pub). All the cleaners were women. In terms of seasonality, the number of employees in the hotel went down by 17 between August and January, with the main share of the decrease coming from the cleaning staff. Here there were 12 less by January 1997. The majority of the 37 people who worked in the low season were permanently-hired staff, with three being on temporary contracts (all of them cleaning staff). Regarding the hotel's policy of hiring people, the manager said that:

> The law does not allow employers to hire workers for less than six months (except in extraordinary circumstances). On the other hand, employees do not accept contracts that are less than six months, since they would not be eligible for unemployment benefits.[12] Last year, we had real problems hiring a cleaner for the restaurant. Usually our staff list is enough. Otherwise, we put adverts in bars and, finally, we go to the Job Centre [*Centro de Emprego*]. We do not really trust the *Centro de Emprego* because everybody can get a job at the peak season, if they really want to. Unemployed workers at the peak season are bad workers.

The hotel had no foreigners on its staff at the moment of interview. Regarding its hiring policy, the manager said that 'even if our clientele is mainly non-Portuguese, we cannot hire a person who is not fluent in Portuguese'. Of course, this does not apply for PALOP nationals, for whom the only requirement is a valid residence permit. In his words, 'sorting out all the red tape for a non-legal resident is simply too complicated'.

Taken together, these four hotel examples highlight four particular points:

- Even if there are openings for immigrants in the hotel industry, African employment does not seem to be widespread in the sector. Only in the case of Hotel C was the number of Moroccans considerable. Neither Hotel A nor B had any hired African, but one and two EU nationals respectively were employed.
- Seasonality, which varies by location, hotel size and hotel category, affects employment opportunities. Algarve establishments need workers the whole year round, with the peak season being in the

summer. Yet the need for more workers in July and August is observed in all kind of establishments, whether they shut or not.

- Even if the majority of jobs in these hotels are unskilled (namely, cleaning and serving), the characteristics of jobs depend on the type of hotel. For instance, apart from the manager, Hotel C only needs unskilled workers (watchpeople, cleaners, waiters/waitresses). For Hotel D, one out of two workers do cleaning.
- Linked to this last point, cleaning, which constitutes a considerable share of the jobs in the industry, is mainly done by women. This was clear in all types of establishments in both Algarve and Girona.

Immigrant Employment in Accommodation and Restaurant Industries

This section contrasts the four previous points which were highlighted in the survey on employers with the results of the survey on African employees. By comparing manager/employer's views with those of employees, the aim is to build a more complete picture of immigrant employment in accommodation services and restaurants.

Accommodation Services and Restaurants as African Employers

For Spain, non-EU workers constituted 1.3 per cent of the total labour force in these industries in 1993.[13] By nationality, the analysis of Aragón Bombín and Chozas Pedrero (1993) on 1991-92 legalisation data showed that a wide range of nationalities are occupied in these industries (Dominicans, Peruvians, Filipinos and Chinese), with a marginal presence of Moroccans and an irrelevant number of other African nationals. This heavily contrasts with other West European countries. Thus, immigrants made up 38 per cent of total employment in the Swiss accommodation and restaurant sector, 24 per cent in West Germany and 18 per cent in Sweden in 1982-83 (Williams and Shaw, 1991). Likewise, King (1995), quoting data from Eurostat, demonstrated that foreigners are well represented in the tourist-related sectors in Switzerland and Luxembourg (above 30 per cent for those employed in hotels, catering and distribution), although much less so in the Netherlands and the UK (below 5 per cent of the work force), with France, Belgium and Germany occupying intermediate positions.

For Girona, the survey found that 20[14] out of the 151 Africans interviewed were working either in the accommodation industry or in restaurants at the moment of their interview. This constituted 13.2 per cent of the sample, which was a lower percentage than the representation of these activities in total employment in the province (16.6 per cent of jobs in

1993; Banco Bilbao Vizcaya, 1997). Furthermore, contrary to what is seen in agriculture, African workers are scattered across firms in the sector, with 13 out of the 19 African employees in accommodation services and restaurants being the only hired worker of African origin in their firm. Confirming this picture, the President of the Girona Hotel Federation [*Federació Provincial d'Hoteleria de Girona*] indicated that African employment in the industry was rare. The same source said that non-Spanish Europeans were more frequent than Africans in the hotel industry. Taking all the foreigners together, the President felt that less than 10 per cent of staff in this sector were non-Spanish.

Indicating that this employment picture might be more general for Spain, in a survey carried out on Moroccan workers in Mallorca, it was concluded that these nationals take hardly any jobs in tourism industries. When Moroccans did work in the sector, they held the most unskilled jobs (e.g. dishwashers). Specifically, out a sample of 242 interviewed Moroccans, it was found that just 5.4 per cent worked in hotels and restaurants. This contrasted with 46.7 per cent of the survey in construction, 27.7 per cent in personal services (e.g. gardeners) and 13.7 per cent in farming (Consell Insular de Mallorca, 1993). This distribution is of special relevance as the Balearic Islands have the highest percentage of workers occupied in accommodation and restaurants for any Autonomous Community (see Table 6.1). Likewise, a survey of seasonal employment in the provinces of Alicante, Almería, the Balearic Islands, Lleida, Murcia and Tarragona found only 12 foreign workers out of a sample of 245 who were engaged by hotels or restaurants. All of these workers were Europeans (Metra-Seis, 1995).

Three factors impinge on the relatively low African employment in the Girona survey, and, more generally, in Spain:

- First, local Spanish residents are increasingly occupying all kinds of jobs in the accommodation and restaurant sectors. According to the President of the Girona Hotel Federation [*Federació Provincial d'Hoteleria de Girona*], 'in the past, local residents occupied more skilled jobs (as managers or working in reception), but nowadays, they do all kinds of jobs, whether unskilled or skilled'. Along the same lines, an agricultural employer said that local Spanish women and young people (who were the traditional seasonal labour force on his holding in the peak-season) now prefer tourism-related jobs, as these offer higher wages than farming. Supporting this, wages in accommodation and restaurants in Spain were twice those offered in farming in 1993 (Banco Bilbao Vizcaya, 1997).

- Aware of the willingness of the Spanish to take jobs in these industries, and following allocations in the Spanish quota system, the Girona Office of the Ministry of Labour and Social Security [*Delegación Provincial del Ministerio de Trabajo y Seguridad Social*] is restrictive in allowing non-EU nationals into jobs in accommodation services and restaurants. The norm is that a first work permit is not issued to non-EU workers for employment in tourism, unless it is as a kitchen assistant, cleaner, gardener or watchperson. This is because current legislation establishes that initial work permits will not be granted if a Spanish, other EU or legal non-EU national is available for a job. So the offices of the Ministry of Labour and Social Security review applications in the light of provincial unemployment figures by sector. In the case of Girona, it is argued that there are many unemployed workers who are willing to do tourism-related jobs, apart from the above-mentioned tasks. Furthermore, for those who were not legalised in the 1991-92 campaign, job restrictions also apply for their first five years in the country, which is the time needed to secure a five-year work permit (see Chapter 3). For Girona, these restrictions are lifted after the third renewal of an up-to-one-year permit, which corresponds roughly to a period of legal residence of two and a half years in the country. To illustrate the significance of these legal barriers, a worker who gets an initial work permit (e. g.) for a farming job in Girona has to stick to this sector until the third renewal. These barriers condition the entry (and probably the permanence) of Africans into the accommodation and restaurant sector.
- Finally, the fieldwork revealed that employers were not inclined to hire Africans for skilled jobs. Sometimes they argued that Africans did not have the right skills or experience for the job (see Chapter 8 for an analysis of the characteristics of the African labour force), sometimes they would not hire Africans for jobs which required dealing directly with clients (e.g. receptionists or waiters) as they claimed that Africans were insufficient aware of Western manners, and sometimes because they said that their firms had a good permanent staff in charge of more skilled jobs. Whatever the reason, it is clear that these more skilled jobs are better-paid and that Spanish (or other EU) nationals are eager to take them.

For Algarve, the survey found that 13 out of 39 of African workers were employed in either accommodation services or restaurants.[15] Employment in the tourism sector was found to be predominantly the domain of female immigrants, for all 13 of the interviewed Africans in these industries were women. This represents half the interviewed female immigrants in the region. Furthermore, more of 40 per cent of my Algarve respondents declared that their main job in Portugal had been (or was) in these industries. In addition, the fact that staff in particular firms are mainly of African origin confirms the importance of the sector to this immigrant group. To be specific, five out of the 13 who were employed in tourism at the moment of their interview worked in hotels, camp grounds or restaurants in which African-born workers constituted more than half the employees; with further three saying that they were not the only African-born worker. These survey results point to accommodation establishments and restaurants being major African employers in Algarve.

Yet the evidence from the African survey differs from the situation reported for Hotel D, which had no African worker hired amongst its 56 employees in August 1996. But a closer look at the size of establishments in which Africans work helps explain this (Table 6.2), for PALOP immigrants are largely employed in hotels, pensions and, especially restaurants, with less that 25 employees (rather than in large tourist complexes, such as Hotel D). It is worth noting in this regard that large establishments tend to offer more secure jobs (as they do not shut in winter in Algarve) and better wages. In this sense, it is notable that 42.4 per cent of those employed in Portuguese accommodation establishments and restaurants with less that 10 employees earned the minimum wage in March 1992. This percentage contrasts with the 2.3 per cent of workers who earned the minimum wage in companies with 50-99 employees, or the 0.4 per cent for those firms with 100 or more workers (Ministério de Qualificação e Emprego, 1993).

The same is found for Girona where African immigrant employment is mainly found in small outlets (Table 6.2). By contrast, establishments with more than 25 employees only gave employment to three out of 20 interviewees. Interviews with trade unions and employers cast light on the small number of Africans who are employed in large hotels and big chains in Girona. According to these sources, trade unions are far more active in large-sized establishments. As a consequence, employers must stick to the work categories that are defined by the collective agreement for the sector.[16] In small businesses, as the fieldwork revealed, workers usually undertake many tasks, regardless of their written work category. It is in this latter type of establishment that a 'flexible' immigrant labour force is likely to be employed. Due to their unstable legal status, this workforce is also likely to be less demanding on employers over job descriptions and conditions (see Chapter 3).

Table 6.2   Present employment of interviewed Africans in the accommodation and restaurant industries in Algarve and Girona, by size and type of establishment

	Algarve	Girona
Size of the establishment		
Self-employed worker		1
Less than 10	7	8
From 10 to 25	4	8
More than 25	2	3
Type of establishment		
Restaurant	10	10
Accommodation	3	10
Total	13	20

* These figures include those out of work at their interview whose last job was in accommodation services and restaurants.

Source: Interview surveys.

A Cyclical Demand for Labour

The descriptions given on specific hotels also raise the issue of varying demand for labour, depending on the location, size and category of an establishment, with more workers needed in the peak summer season. The traditional source to match this seasonal demand has been (internal) in-migration (see, for instance, Cavaco, 1980, for Portugal; and Lever, 1987; Valenzuela, 1991; Salvà i Tomàs, 1991; Marchena Gómez and Vera Rebollo, 1995, for Spain). Yet interviewed employers, along with representatives of hotel and accommodation federations, point to these inflows as being less important nowadays. Probably the most important reason for this decrease is that some former, temporary in-migrants have become permanent residents. Thus, Salvà i Tomàs (1991) showed that the Balearics saw a growth of 78 per cent in population during the period 1950-86. This was accompanied by an increase in the tertiary sector from 27 per cent of the working population to 66 per cent. Likewise, the Girona population multiplied almost three times over the period 1960-1985 (Valenzuela, 1991). Although on a lesser scale, somewhat similar trends are observed in Portugal. Cavaco (1980) showed that demand for labour in coastal Algarve generated two in-migrant inflows, one from the villages of inland Algarve, which lie beyond the daily commuting distance of coastal centres, and the other from poorer villages elsewhere in Portugal. Furthermore, against the trend for the region, inland Algarve municipalities with little (sun-sea-sand) tourism appeal suffered notable population decreases in the period 1981-1991 (Instituto Nacional de Estatística, 1984; 1996c).

Focusing on Girona, not unexpectedly given the seasonality of tourism activities, the interview survey found only one worker (out of 19 employees) on a permanent contract (Table 6.3). Yet the hotel examples showed that there is demand for permanent labour all the year round in this industry. Even if certain establishments shut in winter, certain jobs are required for the whole year (e.g. those looking after infrastructure in hotels and camp sites, as well as restaurant workers). In this regard, the Girona survey identified seven out of 15 workers who were on temporary contracts (plus one with a permanent contract) who had worked for the same firm all

Table 6.3   Present employment of interviewed Africans in the accommodation and restaurant industries in Algarve and Girona, by hired status and length of time with the current employer

	Algarve	Girona
Hired status		
Self-employed worker		1
Permanent	1	1
Temporary	5	15
None	5	3
Worker is unsure	2	
Length of time with current employer		
6 months or less	5	10
6 months-1 year	3	1
More than 1 year	5	9
Total	13	20

* These figures include those out of work at their interview whose last job was in accommodation services and restaurants.

Source: Interview surveys.

the year round for more than one year. These workers did not have permanent contracts. This pattern was also observed for African employment in Spanish agriculture, where workers were occupied with different tasks during the agricultural cycle (harvesting, pruning, spraying, etc.; Chapter 4).

Despite the permanent character of some temporary-hired workers, the point is that few permanent contracts are offered to African-born employees in Girona. This provokes workers to consider shifting from the accommodation and restaurant sector to industries that offer more secure and less seasonal jobs. In this regard, only eight out of the 19 who worked in these industries in Girona at the moment of their interview stated that their first job in Spain had been in the sector. Furthermore, out of the 22 who declared that their main job in Spain had been in accommodation services or restaurants, only 11 had entered Spanish labour markets through a job in these industries. Out of these 22, 14 were in the accommodation and restaurant sector at the time of their interview. All these data show a noticeable intersectoral mobility from and into these industries in Spain. Losses from accommodation services and restaurants to other sectors or activities are offset by new employees from other sectors coming into accommodation and restaurants. This helps confirm the picture of few permanent jobs being available for Africans. It suggests also that African workers are happy to return to the sector when jobs are available (even if the job is temporary). This occurs for three main reasons:

- First, consider that accommodation and restaurants is the third sector examined in this book, with the same unstable pattern of employment observed in all three. This points to few permanent jobs being available for African workers in Spain, regardless of the sector of activity. Furthermore, the figure of 15.0 per cent for those without contracts in accommodation services and restaurants in my survey is lower than the 29.4 per cent for farming (Table 4.2) and similar to the 14.3 per cent in construction (Table 5.2). It follows that if Africans cannot change jobs in search of stability, then perhaps they can choose the best (available) paid jobs available to them.
- Even if accommodation establishments and restaurants offer wages below the Spanish average, these are twice than those offered in farming, which constitutes the main African employer in Spain (see the indicators of the Spanish economy by sector, branch of activity and province which are published biannually by the Banco Bilbao Vizcaya). More significantly, Aragón Bombín and Chozas Pedrero (1993), in a survey of legalised non-EU workers in the 1991-92 legalisation process, found that wages in hotels were higher than the average wage of those

who had their Spanish residence legalised (75,000 pta./month). Moreover, whereas wages are generally paid per worked hour (or piece rate) in farming, a monthly wage is guaranteed in the accommodation and restaurant industries. On top of wages, some businesses offer perks such as meals or free accommodation.

By contrast with Girona, the picture for African employment in the tourism industry in Algarve is more similar to the commonly described model of immigration into Southern European tourism activities, in which seasonal, irregular jobs dominate. The interview survey data points to a high degree of informality in the tourism industry, with five out of 13 African workers not having any contract (plus two who said they were unsure about their hired status) (Table 6.3). Furthermore, despite a lower seasonality of tourism activities in Algarve than in Girona, the number of permanent contracts in my survey is similarly miniscule (Table 6.3). This pattern is consistent with the portrait depicted by King (1995, p.184) who argued that '[...] it is precisely the tourism sector where the encounter between the black economy and immigrant workers is most sharply demonstrated'. In Algarve, this 'encounter' is most likely to occur in small establishments.

Despite substantial casualisation in these industries, low intersectoral mobility is observed in accommodation establishments and restaurants for Africans (as in Portuguese construction, Chapter 5). These industries retain more of their workers in Algarve than in Girona. Specifically, all 13 who had a job in accommodation or restaurants at the moment of their interview declared that their main job in Portugal, in terms of the number of years they had spent working, had been in these industries. Furthermore, seven out of the 13 whose last (or current) job was in these industries had entered Portuguese labour markets through a job in accommodation services or restaurants. This is consistent with the message that these industries are major African employers in Algarve.

African Employment and Job Skills

The interview surveys clearly show this trend. Effectively, 12 out of 13 had unskilled jobs in Algarve, as did 17 out of 19 employees in Girona.[17] No notable differences exist across the border regarding job skills. Immigrants in these industries tend to work as kitchen assistants, watchpeople, waiters/waitresses and cleaners in both areas. Generally, Africans are not employed in jobs that require higher qualifications (e.g. as receptionists or in administrative services). The survey identified just three (out of 33) African workers who carried out skilled activities (a hotel receptionist, a person who was responsible for the warehouse of a hotel and a skilled worker in hotel maintenance).

To put this in context, Williams and Shaw (1991) suggest that unskilled and semi-skilled work constitute 90 per cent of the jobs created by tourism in Spain. Yet, even if unskilled work is the norm, interviews with employers clearly indicate that the number of skilled workers depends upon the quality and the size of an establishment. For instance, an interview with the manager of a large first class camp site in Girona showed that 30 per cent of the 150 peak-season employees do skilled work (10 managers, 16 receptionists, five administrative employees, 10 hosts and hostesses, two trained lifeguards, three electricians). Yet, for small family-owned pensions, fieldwork revealed that members of the family do the administrative tasks, supervise activities and, if necessary, do unskilled tasks. Employees (if any) are required to do an interchangeable array of unskilled tasks. Primarily, when Africans are found in accommodation services and restaurants in Iberia, they are employed in small-sized establishments which require 'flexible' unskilled workers.

Cleaning Jobs and Female Workers

Employers made it clear that cleaning was a female job. Probably for this reason, statistics show that women are proportionally more numerous in these industries than in the whole economy. To be specific, whereas 46.0 per cent of workers in the Spanish hotel accommodation industry were women in 1991 (Instituto Nacional de Estadística, 1993), only 36.2 per cent were female in the whole workforce in 1996 (Instituto Nacional de Estadística, 1997b). In Portugal, whereas 53.0 per cent of the hotel accommodation industry was female (Instituto Nacional de Estatística, 1997), the percentage of women in the total workforce was 45.6 per cent in 1996 (Ministério para a Qualificação e o Emprego, 1997). More importantly for our purposes, women constituted about 60 per cent of the workers in apartments and self-catering hotels in Algarve in 1996 (Instituto Nacional de Estatística, 1997). In these establishments, as the example of Hotel D denotes, a substantial share of available jobs are for cleaning.

A similar job segmentation by sex has been noted by Breathnach and associates (1994) in their study of the Irish tourism sector. They found that the over-representation of women in accommodation services and restaurants was directly related to the number of female workers in cleaning. Likewise, Hennessy (1994) has shown that the occupation of the women in tourism-related activities in Looe (Cornwall) was mainly low-skilled (i.e. waitressing, cleaning and bar work), part-time and seasonal. From Greek official data, Leontidou (1994) argued that women maintain the 'housewife' role in hotel employment (i.e. cooking and cleaning), while men are gardeners and drivers, with waiters and administrative staff being more mixed (yet with a male majority).

A different point is how this employment structure affects immigrant women. Statistics clearly show that African women represent a small percentage of legal African workers in Spain (Figure 6.1). This contrasts with the situation of Latin-American nationals, for whom women had 60 per cent of the number of work permits in 1996.

Figure 6.1   The share of women in the total number of work permits in Spain, 1989-1996

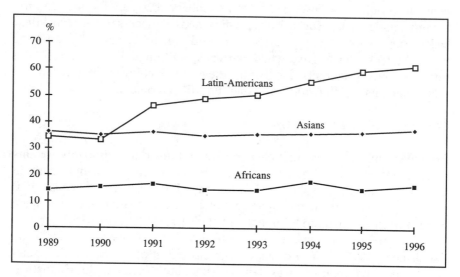

* EU nationals have not needed a work permit since 1992 (for Luxembourg nationals, since 1993).

Source: Ministerio de Trabajo y Seguridad Social (annual).

Even if Spanish work permit statistics display only part of the picture (for instance, the trade union CCOO reported that about 80 per cent of female immigrants in Catalunya work without a contract; Secretaria de la Dona de CCOO, 1994), my Girona survey only found 10 female workers out of 151 interviewed Africans.[18] This low number of African female workers is, first of all, a reflection of male-dominated immigration from African countries into Spain. In 1993, the gender ratio in Spain was close to one African woman for three men in the country (see Eurostat, 1995, for the gender composition of non-Spanish residents in the EU by country).[19] In other words, the low number of African female immigrants in paid work is primarily a result of their small total number compared to their male counterparts.

Furthermore, even if this trend is changing fast, African women generally follow their husbands to Spain (Solé, 1994; Ribas Mateos, 1996; see also Table 6.4 which shows that six out of the 10 interviewed women went to Spain because of their partner). Since farming is a major activity for African males, a large part of African married women end up living in agricultural municipalities in Girona. This does not help further female immigrant involvement in labour markets because few labour openings are offered to African women in these type of localities. While there is plenty of work for African male labourers, employers argued that there is no reason for hiring a woman for (hard) farming activities.[20] As an example, according to a social worker in an agricultural town, none of the eight married Moroccan women or two women from Senegambia who lived in town had paid work. It seems that if African women in agricultural localities want to work, they need to commute to service localities where there are plenty of jobs in accommodation establishments and restaurants. This does not help further female immigrant work in Girona. As a male Moroccan, who was resident in the agricultural town of Sant Pere Pescador, noted:

> My wife has been offered a job in a pizzeria in Empúria Brava [a neighbouring tourist town], but her working time would be not compatible with mine, so I cannot take her to work. Besides, her Spanish is rather poor and our children are quite young. I'd rather she stayed at home.

Focusing on the 10 women who were interviewed in Girona, Table 6.4 displays information on both current job in Iberia, last job in country of origin, as well as current legal status and year of arrival in Spain. Here it is seen that seven out of the 10 interviewed females did cleaning, either in an accommodation establishment or on a personal basis.[21] Supporting this idea, an interviewed Moroccan expressed his views with the following words:

> My wife works as a cleaner in a rest home. Women find work quicker than men, cleaning factories, houses, restaurants. There are also old people who need help. They would not hire a man [*No van a contratar a un hombre*]. Women get jobs quickly, although they do not speak the language.

The second job for which women seem to be better prepared is as a kitchen assistant (see Table 6.4). But in this case immigrant women are in competition with men. As made clear in interviews, whereas immigrant men in Girona would not accept a job as a cleaner, they were willing to take jobs as a kitchen assistant (see also the example of Hotel A). Indeed, out of 20 Africans involved in work in accommodation services and restaurants, 15 were men. Significantly, none of these 15 did a cleaning job. They worked in kitchens or did other jobs in accommodation services (e.g. watchpeople).

Table 6.4   Interviewed African women in paid work in Girona

No.	Year	Channel *	Current legal status	Current labour status	Last or current job in Iberia	Branch of activity
37	1991	c	Work and residence permit	Hired employee	Cleaner	Hotel
46	1986	a	Residence permit	Non-hired employee	Cleaner	Domestic services
68	1985	a	Work and residence permit	Unemployed	Unskilled worker	Manufact.
79	1987	a	Residence permit	Non-hired employee	Kitchen assistant	Restaurant
101	1987	a	Residence permit	Non-hired employee	Cleaner	Domestic services
105	1972	b	Spanish national	Self-employed	Boarding house owner	Hotel
110	1987	a	Work and residence permit	Hired employee	Cleaner	Cleaner firm
111	1992	b	Work and residence permit	Hired employee	Kitchen assistant	Restaurant
129	1992	b	EU family residence card	Non-hired employee	Cleaner	Domestic services
148	1980	a	Work and residence permit	Hired employee	Cleaner	Hotel

* Immigration channels:
   a)   Family reunion.
   b)   A girl friend lived in Girona.
   c)   An aunt lived in Girona.

Source: Girona interview survey.

By contrast, for Portugal, the survey did not find any African-born man in the accommodation and restaurant sector which appears to be the domain for immigrant women (Table 6.5). Amongst these 13 female workers, the survey identified cleaners, as well as kitchen assistants; but not watchpeople.

Table 6.5 Current job of interviewed Africans in Portugal, by economic sector and sex

	Women	Men	Total
Primary		1	1
Manufacturing	4	7	11
Construction		18	18
Accommodation and restaurants	13		13
Other services	15	11	26
Total	32	37	69

Source: Portuguese interview survey.

The involvement of female immigrant workers in the Portuguese accommodation and restaurant sector is directly related to the level of wages in these industries, with overall wages in 1993 being 83 per cent of the national average (Ministério do Emprego e da Segurança Social, 1994). This is true for both sexes. Yet it is far more notable for women, with wages for females in accommodation services and restaurants being almost half the average salary for males in Portugal (Figure 6.2). In other words, if jobs are available in a better-paid sector (e.g. construction for African males), there is no reason for workers, whether immigrants or not, to take up work in accommodation services or restaurants. If we add to this picture the fact that Africans work in small establishments (noting that these establishments offer even lower wages), it is not surprising that some labour shortages arise in this type of business. This was pointed out by several interviewed employers. It is these labour shortages that provide a niche that is partially occupied by African-born women.

Although this pattern cannot be confirmed by official statistics,[22] evidence from both surveys suggest that the involvement of African women in Portuguese labour markets is higher than in Spain. This is related not only to more labour market opportunities for African women in Portugal, but also to dissimilarities in the African population in both countries. Put simply, alongside demands for labour in these industries, the employment of African women in the accommodation and restaurant sector reflects the different gender composition of African inflows in Portugal and Spain, as well as dissimilar approaches to female paid work in the African communities in each of these countries. This is an issue that will be examined in depth in Chapter 8.

Figure 6.2   Average monthly wage (in thousand of escudos) in the accommodation and restaurant industries, and in the Portuguese economy by sex, 1988-1993

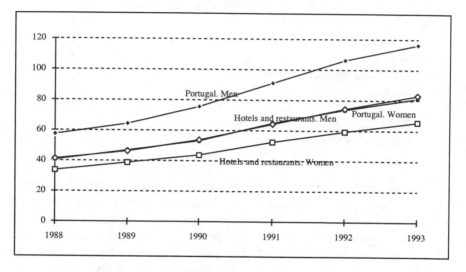

Source: Ministério do Emprego e da Segurança Social (1994)

Conclusion

A key point concerning the lack of competition between African and other workers in Spanish farming and Portuguese construction was the unattractiveness of these sectors for local Iberian workers. Here analysis of the accommodation and restaurant industries also points to low competition between Africans and other employees. However, this is not due to all businesses in these industries being unattractive for Iberian workers, but because labour segmentation in these industries delimits uneven opportunity structures which present (some) job openings for Africans. Throughout this chapter it has been seen that employment in accommodation services and restaurants is segmented:

- By type of job, with Africans mainly found in unskilled temporary work. This is partly due to the sector being characterised by high seasonality and a considerable proportion of unskilled activities. Even workers in more 'permanent' jobs are found in seasonal contract situations.

- By type of firm, with small establishments providing the bulk of jobs for African workers in both Portugal and Spain. For the former, wages in small establishments are below the average for the sector, with the sector itself offering wages considerably below the average for the whole economy. For Spain, collective agreement procedures appear to be applied less strictly in small accommodation establishments and restaurants. Both lower wages and more 'flexible' practices in applying labour procedures help create openings for the entry of Africans in small-sized establishments.

- By sex, different from the previous two points, segmentation reveals contrasting trends in Portugal and Spain. For Portugal, African men are not found in accommodation services and restaurants. This is because available jobs for Africans in these industries offer lower wages than men are able to secure elsewhere, particularly in construction. By contrast, African men are found in Spanish accommodation establishments and in restaurants. More important than differences by economic sector, the employment of women in Spanish labour markets is related to the availability of a specific type of job (namely, cleaning), which is not regarded by employers as being suitable for males, whatever their origin. Significantly, cleaning also constitutes the main job for African women in the Portuguese accommodation and restaurant industries.

This is not to say that Iberian workers are not found in unstable jobs in small firms. What it means is that Africans are overwhelmingly found in these jobs in the accommodation and restaurant sector. This labour outcome is directly related to the action of two main actors:

- The State, with Spanish rules clearly defining which jobs are available for non-EU workers in their initial work permits. These are allowed in three types of unskilled work (namely, serving, cleaning and surveillance) in accommodation services and restaurants. Even if legal restrictions on type of job are lifted as Africans stay longer, this is a considerable barrier to the entry of non-EU nationals into this sector. Significantly, however, this factor was not influential in Portugal.

- Employers, who made it clear in the fieldwork that they do not believe Africans are qualified for skilled work. Whether this responds to prejudice or not is discussed in Chapter 8, which analyses the type of skills of this labour force. At another level, employers and managers expressed their preference for women alone to do cleaning work.

This chapter has demonstrated that accommodation services and restaurants have some openings for African workers. Yet it has been seen that the Portuguese industries are more open to Africans than their Spanish counterparts. Perhaps the access for Africans in these industries in the more 'difficult' Spanish context (at least compared to Portugal) depend on local circumstances. For instance, the hotel industry in a municipality with a low unemployment rate may have problems finding kitchen assistants, waiters or cleaners (as seen for the Algarve hotel industry). The next chapter explores differences in African labour outcomes by type of municipality. The point to stress here is that patterns of African employment may respond to local circumstances (and not exclusively to demand for labour in a sector).

Notes

1. Several interviewed accommodation employers argued that the excellent 1997 tourist season was directly related to the weakness of the Spanish currency.
2. In contrast with Spain, Portugal was one of the countries that increased its investment in tourism promotion over the period 1979-84. In these years, the state spent between three and six million dollars annually on tourism promotion (World Tourism Organization, 1988).
3. The year 1996 was a bad one for British visitors to the Algarve, according to employers in the accommodation industry. They feel that the dependence of the region on British tourism is higher than this figure suggests. Some support for this view is the fact that UK visitors accounted for 51.6 per cent of all bed nights in 1985 (Lewis and Williams, 1989).
4. An interesting campaign to fight against seasonality has been launched by the Institute of Social Services [*Instituto de Servicios Sociales, INSERSO*]. This Institute promotes tourism programmes for pensioners in the off-peak season. Between October and April, those aged over 65 can travel and stay for 14 days in any one of a selected number of seaside resorts at low prices. In 1989-90, 13,000 pensioners made use of the campaign (Valenzuela, 1991).
5. In 1990, 90 per cent of British tourists in Portugal (the most important foreign nationality in terms of bed nights in Algarve) were channelled through tour operators (Shaw and Williams, 1994).
6. *Apartamentos turísticos* and *aldeamentos turísticos* on the classification of Portuguese accommodation establishments.
7. The rest of hotel accommodation in the region is mainly in hotels which offer a more traditional service (23.6 per cent), with pensions having 7.2 per cent of the total.

8. Insularity is mentioned as a problem that faces the expansion of domestic tourism (Pearce, 1987). In the case of Algarve, Portuguese nationals are amongst the least travelled in Europe. In 1990, a survey for the European Travel Monitor found that 49 per cent of the Portuguese population did not make any overnight trip at all away from home (compared with 25 per cent of Spaniards; Commission of the European Communities, 1993).

9. There are five categories of hotels (more stars means better quality). Hotels are classified by the administration of each Autonomous Community.

10. This happened in the summer of 1997. According to employers, this season was one of the best for the hotel sector in the Costa Brava, with hotels in this area being overbooked. In interview, the President of the Girona Hotel Federation [*Federació Provincial d'Hoteleria de Girona*] complained about the temporal concentration of holidays by Spaniards in the summer months. He believed that the staggering of holidays amongst Spaniards should be promoted so that overbooking in coastal resorts, which is thought to produce a bad image for the industry, would be mitigated.

11. The manager informed me that there were two kinds of deals with tour operators: (i) guaranteed contracts, where tour operators pay for rooms, even if they are not occupied; and (ii) normal contracts. Under the former, prices are kept down, as rooms can be filled if the tour operator does not use them. Under the latter, prices are negotiated per night and bed, separately.

12. To be eligible for unemployment benefits in Portugal, it is necessary to have worked one year and a half in the last two years.

13. There were 872,805 employees in accommodation services and restaurants in Spain in 1993 (Banco Bilbao Vizcaya, 1997). The number of non-EU nationals in these industries was 11,250 (Comisión Interministerial de Extranjería, 1994).

14. Nineteen employees and an owner of an unofficial boarding house which mainly accommodated Moroccan nationals.

15. None of the 30 African-born workers who were interviewed in the Peninsula of Setúbal were employed in accommodation services or restaurants.

16. In the case of hotels, the collective agreeeement is signed by hotel trade unions and employers' organisations in a province. The 1996 agreement accepted a degree of labour mobility inside a firm, so work categories are now 'allowed' to be somewhat blurred. For the President of the Girona Hotel Federation [*Federació Provincial d'Hoteleria de Girona*]: 'This is definitely good for the industry. Before, we were forced to employ more people than we really needed to cover all the jobs in all the seasons. Now, at the low season, we can reduce staff by using workers in a flexible way. I personally hope that this new measure is applied correctly. Obviously, the kitchen chef should not peel potatoes'.

17. Managers, receptionists, kitchen chefs, maintenance workers have been considered to be 'skilled workers' in accommodation services and restaurants. Waiters/waitresses, cleaning staff, watchpeople, kitchen assistants have been classified as 'unskilled workers' here.

18. Solé and Herrera (1991) found a smaller percentage of women in their research on foreign labour immigration from developing countries in Catalunya. For their study, out of 228 immigrants, female workers constituted 6 per cent.

19. Paradoxically, the main publications of the Spanish Institute of Statistics [*Instituto Nacional de Estadística*] (namely, *España: Anuario Estadístico* and *Boletín Mensual de Estadística*) only disaggregate the number of foreigners by nationality and province of residence (and not by sex). The published statistics of the Foreigners' Inter-Ministerial Commission [*Comisión Interministerial de Extranjería*] (*Anuario Estadístico de Extranjería*) broke down the number of residence permit holders by sex until 1992. The statistics of the Ministry of Labour and Social Security do disaggregate the number of work permit holders by sex (amongst other variables).

20. This is not to say that women do not play an active role in Girona agriculture. In the fieldwork, it was clear that local women are in charge of farms just as men are. As well, daughters and sons who do other activities (e.g. students) help the family in the harvest. Furthermore, non-employed women have been a traditional source of labourers in the picking season. For more information about women in Spanish farming, see García-Ramon et al (1995). Another relevant consideration on women in farming revolves around male emigration. This has stimulated the incorporation of women into agriculture in sending countries, as demonstrated by Arizpe and Aranda (1986) for northern Mexico or Brettell (1986) for northern Portugal.

21. This includes the owner of an unofficial boarding house. Amongst other tasks, she is in charge of cleaning and feeding the Moroccans who live in the house.

22. Published statistics do not break down the number of non-Portuguese workers by sex and branch of activity. Yet the Foreigners and Borders' Service provide the number of foreign residents by nationality, as well as the number of new entrants every year by country of origin, disaggregated by sex.

7 The Role of the 'Locality' in African Employment Patterns

Previous chapters have investigated reasons for the employment of African workers in Iberian farming, construction, accommodation services and restaurants. They have concluded that Africans are mainly found in secondary labour markets. Yet, even if this trend is common for the three previously analysed activity sectors, the employment of African workers in Iberia is uneven. For instance, even in Girona farming, where Africans constitute the bulk of seasonal workers, some medium- to large-sized firms keep hiring in-migrants from Andalucía (instead of employing Africans; see Chapter 4). The reason for this was linked to firm characteristics (large firms need to secure a number of workers for the whole season), but also depended on local circumstances (some small municipalities do not have an African resident population to match the demand for seasonal workers). This chapter takes up an implicit issue in this last point by exploring whether geography matters in determining patterns of African employment in Iberian labour markets. To do so, the chapter analyses African involvement in labour markets by type of municipality. The key point here is that differences in African employment may result from the characteristics of places (and not exclusively from the character of an economic sector).

The matching process between labour supply and demand (and consequently competition for jobs) is produced at the local level (Massey, 1979; Peck, 1989). Thus it may occur that unemployment at a national level is compatible with labour shortages in certain 'economic places' (i.e. for certain economic sectors in particular places). This has already been demonstrated for Portuguese construction and Spanish farming. Yet these shortages were linked to internal changes in the sector (e.g. the move toward more intensive farming techniques for Spain). Perhaps, for other sectors, labour shortages depend on local circumstances (more than the sector as a whole). To explore this possibility, this chapter compares African employment patterns in diverse economic activities in different local economic structures.

Owing to striking differences in local employment structures between Girona, Algarve and Setúbal (e.g. no agricultural towns with African workers were identified in Portugal, see the Methodological

Appendix), this chapter compares African employment in municipalities with dissimilar labour market characteristics in Portugal and Spain separately (rather than undertaking a cross-border analysis of municipalities with similar economic bases). In the first part of this chapter, patterns of African employment are compared in the three main local settings in Girona: agricultural, service and manufacturing-based towns.

African Employment in Girona's Municipalities

The 151 Africans who were interviewed in Girona lived (and worked) in municipalities with contrasting economic bases. In brief, the municipalities in which fieldwork was undertaken can be classified into four types, based on the characteristics of their employment structure (as identified through 1991 Census data at the municipal level, which was provided by the Catalan Institute of Statistics – *Institut d'Estadística de Catalunya*). Here the main characteristics of these municipal types are presented (for more information about specific places, see the Methodological Appendix):

- Agricultural municipalities. Here farming provides at least a quarter of total employment. This contrasts with a figure of 5.9 per cent for the whole labour force in the province of Girona, and a figure of 3.4 per cent for Catalunya, who worked in farming in 1991.
- Manufacturing-based municipalities. The proportion of the workforce in this sector is well above the provincial or Catalan averages. The range of values recorded for places classed in this group is lowest in La Bisbal d'Empordà (39.2 per cent) and highest in Breda (62.1 per cent).
- Municipalities that are heavily reliant on tourism. The tertiary sector here accounted for more than 50 per cent of the workforce. Tourism also has an indirect effect on construction activities, which was associated with proportionally more jobs in this sector in these towns than in the province (12.4 per cent in 1991) or Catalunya (8.2 per cent).
- Medium-sized municipalities with more-diversified, service-oriented economies (Figueres, 34,573 inhabitants and Blanes, 25,663). Here, a combination of tourism and the provision of commercial activities for surrounding areas puts the bulk of jobs in services (61.9 per cent in the case of Figueres). Manufacturing covers about a quarter of the working population in these municipalities. The primary sector has insignificant weight in employment figures.

This four-fold classification reflects the well-diversified economic base of the province. Yet what was unexpected was that Africans were found to live (and work) in all four municipal types. In this regard, Table 7.1 shows the employment sector for the current (or last) job of those interviewed by the municipal-type of the place of residence. This table shows that there is a correlation between the sector of activity in which Africans work and the type of municipality in which they live. Specifically, 18 out of 34 Africans who lived in a town dominated by farming worked in this sector, just as 33 of those who lived in places dominated by tourism activities worked in the tertiary sector (out of 58). These data suggest that Africans 'fit' the local employment structure; in other words, Africans are where jobs are, regardless of the sector.

Table 7.1   Sectors of economic activity of interviewed Africans in Girona, by municipal-type of residence

Economic sector	Type of municipality				
			Services		
	Agricult.	Manufact.	Tourism	Diversified	Total
Farming	18	3	10	7	38
Forestry	1	1	4	3	9
Construction	6	4	5	6	21
Manufactures	2	15	6	2	25
Services	7	6	33	12	58
Total	34	29	58	30	151

Source: Girona interview survey.

Immigrants are mainly found in the sector which gives more jobs to the workforce as a whole. This occurs in all type of municipalities. This is not to say that Africans are over-represented in the dominant economic activity of a locality. A relatively high presence of immigrant workers might be found for one sector, across all local economic settings, because of general labour shortages in this particular sector (so more than a 'locality effect' is involved). In this regard, Table 7.2 compares the proportion of Africans by economic sector and locality-type with the percentage of the total workforce.

Comparing African labour outcomes with patterns of employment for the workforce as a whole, it is observed that in farming, the presence of Africans is considerably higher than the weight of the sector in the whole workforce. This applies for all four municipal types. For agricultural 'towns', farming gave employment to 31.3 per cent of the 1991 Census population, but provided jobs to 52.9 per cent of African workers who declared that they lived in one of these towns. Yet over-representation in agriculture is even more remarkable in other types of municipality. Thus the proportion of Africans in farming is twice the rate for the whole workforce in manufacturing-dominated places, seven times the rate in tourism-oriented towns and 10 times higher in 'other services' municipalities. This confirms the picture of African employment in farming being general in Girona, regardless of the economic base of the municipality of residence.

Table 7.2 Employment by economic sector, municipal-type of residence and origin of workers in Girona (%)

	Type of municipality									
Economic sector	Agriculture		Manufact.		Services				Girona	
					Tourism		Diversified			
	Africa	All origins	Africa	All origins	Africa	All origins	Africa	All origins	Africa	All origins
Farming	52.9	31.3	10.3	4.9	17.2	2.4	23.3	2.2	31.8	5.9
Construct.	17.6	10.9	13.8	11.0	8.6	19.3	20.0	12.5	13.9	12.4
Manufact.	5.9	17.3	51.7	48.9	10.3	15.0	6.7	25.4	15.2	31.3
Services	20.6	39.9	20.7	35.1	56.9	60.7	40.0	59.1	39.1	49.7

Notes:
a) Columns do not sum 100 per cent, since other primary sector activities rather than farming are not presented in the Table.
b) The Census is the only official source which provides data on the structure of the employed population by municipality. The category 'all workers' corresponds to the 1991 Census employed population for the Girona municipalities in which the fieldwork was carried out.

Source: For Africans, Girona interview survey. For all workers, 1991 unpublished Census data, provided by the *Institut d'Estadística de Catalunya. Institut* published data by economic sector (Institut d'Estadística de Catalunya, 1993). Yet published statistics do not disaggregate farming from other primary sector activities by municipality.

For construction, Africans are over-represented in all types of municipality, except in the tourism-dominated ones. This is unexpected, owing to the significance of construction in this municipal type (Table 7.2). A key official in the Construction Employers' Association [*Unió d'Empresaris de la Construcció de la Província de Girona*] cast light on this. He argued that the firms which built the large accommodation and housing projects have found their activities threatened by the end of a period of rapid expansion in tourism activities and second homes construction along the coastal strip. This has led to down-sizing and companies have struggled (relatively) to secure new contracts. As a result, new workers are less likely to find employment in the construction sector in tourism-dominated areas than in other towns. By contrast, as will be shown in a later section, small building firms in agricultural municipalities have a 'loyal' clientele. This has allowed them to resist cyclical changes in the construction market better, despite their smaller (and theoretically more vulnerable) size.

By contrast, for manufacturing and service industries, Africans are well-represented only in the dominant sector of a municipality. For instance, whereas Africans working in the manufacturing sector made up 15 per cent of my survey, this percentage was higher than 50 per cent in centres that specialised in manufacturing. This suggests that a 'locality effect' may be in place for both service-centred and manufacturing towns.

Places of Work and Places of Residence: Africans as Commuters

Immigrants are mainly found in the sector which gives more jobs to the workforce as a whole. This occurs in all types of municipality. However, 45 per cent of Africans did not work in the dominant sector (or sectors)[1] of the municipality in which they lived (Table 7.1). Yet Africans, as with other workers, may commute to work. This is to say that the characteristics of a place of residence may differ from a municipality of work. Taking this into account, Table 7.3 shows the economic sector of interviewed Africans by municipality of work. In this table, employees that cannot be associated with a permanent employment site (e.g. maintenance firm workers) have been classified in a separate category.[2] This table reinforces the idea that Africans 'fit' the local employment structure, since there is a clear correlation between the dominant sector in the workplace and African employment in it. To be specific, whereas the proportion of workers in farming was 'only' 52.9 per cent of those who lived in an agricultural town, the proportion was 63.4 per cent for those who worked in an farming-dominated municipality.

Yet those who work in the manufacturing or construction sectors have a similar presence when comparisons are made by place of work and place of residence. This is to say that the 25 manufacturing workers live and work in the same municipality. So do the 21 who were employed in construction. In other words, there is no commuting associated with either manufacturing or construction. This denotes that manufacturing and construction firms which give employment to Africans have a 'local' flavour. In the case of manufacturing, Vázquez-Barquero (1992) has noted that a quarter of manufacturing employment in Girona was in family-owned businesses. These firms associate strongly with specific towns. This idea is further developed in other sections of this chapter. The point to stress here is that some economic activities have a labour force catchment area that is larger than others (at least in terms of African employment).

Table 7.3 Sectors of economic activity of interviewed Africans in Girona, by municipal-type of workplace

Economic sector	*Type of municipality*		*Services*		No permanent location	Total
	Agriculture	Manufact.	Tourism	Diversified		
Farming	26	3	8	1		38
Forestry	3	1	4		1	9
Construct.	6	4	5	6		21
Manufact.	2	15	6	2		25
Services	4	3	35	10	6	58
Total	41	26	58	19	7	151

Source: Girona interview survey.

Linked to this last idea, service activities and, especially farming, attract workers to municipalities in which tourism and farming dominate the economy. Focusing on farming centres, 34 African workers lived in such places (Table 7.1), but 41 worked in one of them (Table 7.3). More important for our purposes, 26 workers were employed in farming in an agricultural centre, but only 18 of them lived in an agricultural-dominated place. Of special relevance to understanding this pattern is the number of Africans who lived in a diversified municipality (yet with little provision of farming jobs) and commuted to an agricultural centre. This is the case for six out of the 30 interviewees who had their residence in these service towns.

Exploring this last point further, half of the 10 interviewed Africans who lived in Figueres (a service-dominated, well-diversified town) commuted to farming work in surrounding agricultural municipalities. Black Africans in Figueres mainly live in the Marca de l'Ham quarter. This neighbourhood was built in the 1960s, as a result of new demands for housing occasioned by in-migration from other parts of Spain. Marca de l'Ham is a working class area that lies on the outskirts of Figueres. Its blocks of apartments contrast with surrounding houses and fields. The bad reputation of the area affects the price of housing, which is lower than in central Figueres. According to a social worker in the local branch of a Catholic organisation, relatively low house prices (plus an abundance of flats as some former residents leave on retiring or experiencing upward professional mobility) were the main reason why the first Black Africans moved into the area. Nowadays, the Black African community of the town lives exclusively in La Marca de l'Ham. Moroccans, who are the first foreign nationality in Figures, are more dispersed. Yet there is a concentration of these nationals in the old town, which is an area of poor housing. Another example of immigrant residences being in bad housing areas is the old red light district of the city of Barcelona, el Raval. This area has seen considerable growth in immigrant communities from different origins since the mid-1980s. These three examples illustrate that immigrants are concentrated in housing in 'marginal' areas. As a social worker pointed out '[...] nobody sees Africans as consumers – but they are. The most clear example is the housing market. They rent flats – sometimes unacceptable flats for locals (let alone for tourists)'.

The example of La Marca de l'Ham highlights that immigrant residential choices are not necessarily linked to work circumstances. Crucial to understanding these residential patterns are the social networks which channel information about housing to new immigrants. Indicative of this, the Africans who live in the *barri* are from the foula ethnic group (and not from sarajhoule or mandinga groups which are present in other municipalities of Girona). The foula ethnic group is organised in an association which holds its meetings in the Marca de l'Ham local (Catholic) church. The idea that residential patterns of Africans are partly conditioned by previously immigrant decisions has been demonstrated extensively in the literature. For instance, Rex and Moore (1967) in their classic study of the Birmingham's immigrant communities or Byron (1993) in more recent research on the Nevisian community in Leicester have shown that residential 'choices' for immigrants are restricted by information on housing markets provided by previous immigrants (plus discrimination in housing access).

The point to stress from this section is that farming has an area of influence which goes beyond the limits of agriculturally-based municipalities. In the next section, it will be shown that commuting from service to farming areas which is observed for Africans is not seen for other workers.

Agricultural Municipalities: Flexible African Workers in Intertwined Economies

The fact that Africans commute to agriculturally-dominated areas is not surprising owing to low unemployment in these places. Figure 7.1 shows that the higher the percentage of people in farming, the lower the unemployment rate. This is even more striking if data on unemployed workers are analysed by branch of economic activity. For Girona, in July 1994, just 197 unemployed people in the province were registered as previously having been employed in farming (Generalitat de Catalunya, 1995). This constitutes less than 1.2 per cent of total unemployment, whereas agriculture employed 5.9 per cent of Girona's active working population, according to the 1991 Census (Institut d'Estadística de Catalunya, 1993). These figures confirm, once again, the existence of labour shortages in farming, and point to a lack of competition for jobs in the sector, as well as pointing to the 'rationale' behind African commuting.

Unlike Africans, despite labour shortages in farming and high unemployment, Catalan urban residents are not prepared to move to rural areas to work as agricultural labourers. As a matter of fact, at least since the 1960s, population dynamics in Girona (as in the rest of Spain) have been in the opposite direction (García Barbancho, 1975; Cardelús and Pascual de Sans, 1979; Nadal, 1984). Indeed, the population growth that occurred in service-oriented coastal municipalities after the 1960s was not followed by inland rural municipalities. As a result, the population of rural Girona has diminished, in a context in which substantial increases have been recorded in tourism-oriented municipalities (Valenzuela, 1991). This pattern of population decline in rural municipalities was challenged somewhat by the arrival of new African residents in the 1980s. To illustrate this point, the population dynamics of the main agricultural municipality in my survey is examined. Sant Pere Pescador had 27.9 per cent of its working population employed in farming in 1991 (unpublished 1991 Census data, provided by the *Institut d'Estadística de Catalunya*). Its population has changed little over most of the century, with 1,058 inhabitants in 1900 and 1,045 in 1981 (Cals, 1987). This 'stability' has existed, despite massive population increases in neighbouring tourism municipalities (e.g. in 1981 population of Roses was three times larger than in 1900). Yet since 1981, Sant Pere Pescador has seen considerable growth in its population due to an inflow of new African residents, with the town's population growing by 35 per cent over the period 1981-1995. Thus, in July 1995, 243 foreign nationals (amongst them, 120 Moroccans, 59 Gambians and 17 from other African nationalities) were registered amongst the 1,412 residents (unpublished data provided by the Town Council of Sant Pere Pescador). In other words, new

Figure 7.1 Unemployment rate by share of workforce in farming* in Girona municipalities, 1991

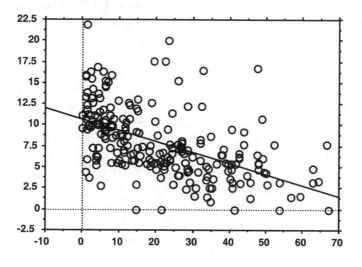

x axis: % of the labour force in farming by municipality; y axis: unemployment rate.

* The Catalan Institute of Statistics has published 1991 Census data by municipality and economic sector (Institut d'Estadística de Catalunya, 1993), with farming being aggregated with other primary sector activities.

Source: Unpublished 1991 Census data, provided by the *Institut d'Estadística de Catalunya*.

immigrant inflows not only help farming run, but also inject new life into otherwise stagnant agricultural communities. Unfortunately, this positive benefit is barely recognised (if at all) by the residents of (conservative) rural Girona. In this regard, according to key informants in the area, the change of mayor in Sant Pere Pescador in 1995 was partly a consequence of exploiting anti-immigration feelings in the election campaign (e.g. by saying that too much money had been channelled toward the town's immigrant association).

Yet the employment of Africans in farming is not only restricted to agricultural municipalities, but affects all the places in my survey. To be specific, 12 out of 38 Africans in farming worked in a municipality in which this sector was not dominant (Table 7.4). Even so, African employment in farming may reveal distinctive trends in agricultural municipalities than in others. For instance, it may be that, as jobs are available in other sectors, labour shortages are more acute in non-agrarian municipalities. Thus employers may be 'pushed' to secure their employees by hiring them permanently. In fact, the picture in Girona is the opposite. In this regard, Table 7.4 shows the contract pattern and type of job (unskilled vs. skilled) for farm employees by municipal-type. It is clear that a more skilled pattern of agricultural employment exists in places where this sector plays a leading role in the local economy. As seen in Chapter 4, the more skilled workers are more likely to secure permanent employment. A more precarious and predominantly less skilled pattern of employment is found in non-agricultural municipalities. To be specific, half of those in non-agricultural municipalities worked with no contract, compared with less than a quarter in agricultural municipalities. The tendency for unemployment to be lower in agricultural municipalities, alongside the general picture of labour shortages in Girona farming, seemingly has a positive effect in creating more secure patterns of employment for African workers in agriculturally-based municipalities. This has to be put in the context of a declining demographic trend for many agricultural places, which is directly related to the lack of attractiveness of farming activities; and, from a broader perspective, of 'rural' life.

Table 7.4 Interviewed farm workers in Girona, by type of job and municipal-type of workplace

	Agricultural municipalities	Other municipalities	Total
Farming, unskilled	18	12	30
Farming, skilled	8		8
No contract	5	6	11
Temporary	17	5	22
Permanent	4	1	5
Total	26	12	38

Source: Girona interview survey.

Fieldwork also revealed that farming interacts with other economic sectors at a local level. Directly, several agricultural employers had other businesses (e.g. their own shop in town or properties that are rented to either tourists or to temporary or permanent residents), apart from working their land. Indirectly, agriculture also has multiplier effects for construction, as properties need to be maintained. In this regard, interviews with small construction employers pointed out that their work closely follows economic cycles in agriculture (and tourism). As a construction employer explained:

> The peak season is just before the tourist season. Everybody wants to finish off something. The lowest activity peak is summer. It is the highest season for both tourist activities and agriculture, so employers are not doing repairs on their properties.

Small construction businesses are deeply rooted in specific municipalities. As several construction employers in agricultural municipalities pointed out, rarely do farmers, restaurant employers or the town council offer minor work contracts to construction firms from outside the town. A 'We're from town, we know each other' opinion captures prevailing sentiments amongst construction employers. Close associations between clients and firms have positive consequences for the survival of these small businesses. This occurs in an increasingly competitive sector, as many larger firms from coastal locations are now more actively seeking contracts for activities in small places that were the traditional 'reserve' of small- and medium-sized firms (e.g. small repairs or municipal public works). The main comparative advantage of small- and medium-sized firms is price, since larger companies do the work quicker. As explained by a construction employer in an agricultural municipality: '[...] we cannot ask the prices of Girona, let alone Barcelona. Our major advantage point is precisely our [lower] prices, not the time of finishing the job nor better quality'. African workers are found in these small construction businesses (see Chapter 5), which are more likely to be based in agrarian places.

The embeddness of construction in the local fabric has implications for African employment. Thus, some interviewed Africans said that they are asked regularly to do various tasks on the employer's lands or properties, apart from the farming tasks that are written in their contracts. As an illustration, the first interviewed African for this project started work in Sant Pere Pescador as a temporary non-hired agricultural labourer. After two years of working with the same employer (and legalising his residence), he was undertaking minor works on his employer's properties in town in the off-peak season (e.g. painting), in order to make these dwellings suitable for renting. This work was undertaken alongside his usual agricultural tasks. In the same direction, construction employers explained that, when they are working for farmers, agricultural employers sometimes offer their (African) workforce as employees on construction sites. In a construction employer's words, '[...] sometimes agricultural employers or other clients tell us that an African who is working for them will help us as an assistant. They save money [as the work can be done in less time, the work is less costly] and it makes no difference to us [*a nosaltres tant ens és*]'. These examples help us understand the survival (and dynamism) of farming in the area. As well, these examples complete the picture of an African labour force that is 'used' interchangeably between jobs (as depicted in the analysis of agriculture in Chapter 4). In this case, however, Africans do not simply take on different tasks inside one economic sector, but undertake dissimilar tasks in different economic sectors. In the municipal setting, African workers smooth the interaction between employers and businesses by providing an adaptable workforce.

To summarise the previous points concerning agricultural municipalities:

- The specifics of a municipality do not provide the main reason for the employment of Africans in farming. Immigrants are over-represented in this sector in the four municipal types of the Girona survey. Labour shortages in agriculture are related to the sector being unattractive for local and in-migrant Spanish workers (see Chapter 4), and not to specific local conditions. Yet municipal location does help explain differences in contractual relations of employment, with a less precarious pattern of employment in agricultural municipalities. This is due to labour shortages being more acute in low unemployment agricultural places.

- Construction firms in agricultural settings are small in size and deeply embedded in local networks. Relations between construction employers and other employers are largely based on contacts and mutual trust. This provides construction employers in agricultural centres with a secure, regular base of work throughout the year. Agricultural employers additionally often own businesses in more than one branch of economic activity. In this context, some Africans who are employed as agricultural workers occasionally do construction work following their employer's requirements. In other words, Africans constitute a flexible labour force across tasks and sectors.

Municipalities with High Service Employment

By contrast with agricultural municipalities, although the relationship is not linear, it generally holds that the greater the importance of services for the local economy, the larger the number of people out of work. This prompts the idea that service-oriented municipalities should have fewer labour openings for immigrants.

Figure 7.2 Unemployment rate by share of workforce in services in Girona municipalities, 1991

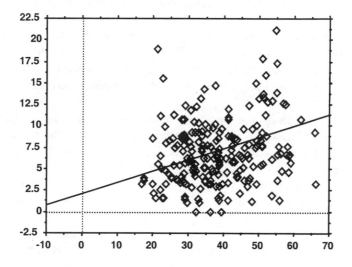

x axis: % of the labour force in services by municipality; y axis: unemployment rate.

Source: Institut d'Estadística de Catalunya (1993).

This adds an important insight to this analysis, as it provides one reason why non-immigrants may accept jobs in service centres. Regardless of the social status of the job in these places, unemployment in these centres tends to be high. Illustrating the impact of this, the President of the Blanes Hotel Association [*Associació d'Hoteleria de Blanes*] explained that:

> [...] there are no foreigners in Blanes hotels because there are no jobs for them. The town has the highest unemployment rate of the province. There are many unemployed workers in the locality who take on unskilled jobs. For skilled jobs, the Association has an agreement with the Department of Labour of the Catalan Government [*Departament de Treball de la Generalitat de Catalunya*], so we organise courses for would-be hotel workers. These workers complement their education with training in hotels.

However, as seen in Chapter 6, accommodation establishments and restaurants did provide some employment for Africans. Even if this does not occur in Blanes, Africans do find jobs in the accommodation and restaurant sector in other service centres. In this regard, African employees, employers and key informants made it clear that there were openings for Africans in Figueres hotels and restaurants. To highlight the relevance of local circumstances for African labour outcomes, the reasons for divergent African employment in these two places are discussed. Differences in African employment do not lie in the economic diversification of the town, since both fall in the same category of medium-sized places with a diversified economy. The reasons for the divergence have to be found elsewhere.

A first reason is the unemployment rate. According to the 1991 Census, whereas Blanes had a 21.1 per cent unemployed, the Figueres rate was half this. Several factors explain this. For one, as the President of the Blanes Hotel Association [*Associació d'Hoteleria de Blanes*] told me, the artificial fibre factory of the town, which employed about 3,000 employees in the 1960s, reduced its staff to a third by the mid-1990s. To put this data in context, Blanes had 11,197 people either working or in search of work in 1991 (Institut d'Estadística de Catalunya, 1993). Second, unlike Blanes, Figueres hotels do not shut in winter (see the examples of Hotel A and C in Chapter 6). This is because inland Figueres attracts many off-peak visitors due to its cultural activities (e.g. the Salvador Dalí Museum), and to the natural beauties of the region (e.g. Figueres is situated between the coast and the Pyrenees; see Figure 4.2). Its good location between the coast and the mountains is reinforced by the main road that links Barcelona and France crossing near Figueres, so many travellers overnight there. By contrast, Blanes hotels rely on a sun-sea-sand package, with hotels closing from October to April. These two factors explain the higher unemployment of Blanes. They also explain why there are very few openings for Africans in the Blanes hotel industry.

Complementary to this, a second reason for the divergent employment pattern in accommodation services and restaurants in Blanes and Figueres lies in the characteristics of African communities in each place. In the case of Figueres, there is a well-established Moroccan community. According to key informants in the town, some of these Moroccans came to the town in the 1960s. At that time, as the labour trajectories of immigrants who have been living in Spain for 20 years or more indicate, construction was the main port of entry into Spanish labour markets. Yet, as construction experienced drastic job losses in the period 1975-1985 (Espina, 1990; Salmon, 1995), many workers transferred to other sectors. In the case of Figueres, hotels offered some openings for

Moroccans. For instance, Mr. Hassam started work in the construction sector in Spain in 1973 ('there was plenty of work in construction at that time'). After doing several jobs of short length in this sector, he entered one of the Figueres hotels in 1975 ('there had been other Moroccans working in the hotel before me'). Since then Mr. Hassam has been employed continuously in the hotel. In 1986, his wife and children came to Figueres. This is a trend for the Moroccan community in Figueres, as the Figueres population register shows that women were one third of legal residents from this country in 1995 (unpublished data provided by the Department of Statistics of the Council of Figueres). Since employers prefer women for cleaning (Chapter 6), the gender composition amongst Moroccans eased the entry of these nationals in the hotel industry. This was the case for Ms. Hammila who is a young female worker in a Figueres hotel. She was brought to Spain by her father, with the rest of her family, in 1980. Ms. Hammila finished her compulsory schooling in Figueres and started work right afterwards. When interviewed, she was working in a hotel with a one-year contract. She explained to me that there were five employees who worked the whole year round (three Moroccans and two Spanish). 'In the summer, two Spanish [from Granada, Andalucía] come from the season'. By contrast, the African community in Blanes dates from the 1980s, as Black Africans headed north from Barcelona's intensive agriculture (Gozálvez Pérez, 1995). This population arrived in Blanes when unemployment was already high due to manufacturing re-structuring. Furthermore, according to social workers, the African population in Blanes is constituted largely of single men, who are highly mobile and are mainly employed in farming in surrounding rural municipalities. Labour outcome differences by nationality (and origin) are further developed in the next chapter. Here the point has been raised to note divergences in labour outcomes by municipality which are linked to the characteristics of immigrants.

Although these two towns illustrate contrasting patterns of African employment in the accommodation industry, when Africans are employed in the sector, the jobs they hold predominantly tend to be unskilled and temporary. To be specific, in Chapter 6 it was revealed that only two out of the 19 interviewed African employees in Girona who worked in accommodation establishments or restaurants did a skilled job (and only one out of 19 had a permanent contract; Table 6.3). Regardless of the municipality of work, the pattern of African employment is clear. However, what is true for accommodation services and restaurants may not hold for other service industries.

In this regard, the survey identified 11 workers in private garbage collection companies. It became clear during my fieldwork that these companies largely employ Moroccans in northern Girona, with this nationality representing half of the labour force in such firms in some municipalities. More relevant for our purposes, half of the interviewed African workers had permanent contracts with these garbage collection companies. These two traits – the high proportion of Africans and the permanent character of employment – require explanation which relates to the character of the subsector. The collection of garbage and the street cleaning service in northern Girona is basically done by one large firm. I was informed by employees of this firm that the company uses decentralised administration and relies strongly on its local foremen. The 'fragmentation' of production into successive local-based units has been seen by the company as the most appropriate means of responding to the rather unstable demand for cleaning in tourism places (e.g. a concert may provoke a change in work shifts). When foremen are Moroccan, they recruit 'their' employees from amongst members of their own community. A counterbalance reported by the staff is that they have to endure what they describe as abusive practices by Moroccan foremen over employees of their own nationality. Control over the labour force by foremen is high. Moroccans are sometimes forced to do unpaid jobs or accept work-times that Spaniards refuse. Thus, although foremen act locally, the municipality itself is not really relevant to creating a niche in cleaning firms for Africans. The substitution of local Spanish workers by immigrants originates in the hiring practices of the large firm, alongside the fact that cleaning tasks are considered low-status by many Spanish workers. Yet cleaning is not rejected in places where the service is provided by municipally-owned firms, such as the city of Barcelona. The privatisation of this service appears to be a key factor in the entry of immigrants into this kind of work. But the point to stress is not ownership, but the emergence of 'irregular' practices in certain service agencies in this industry. Illustrating this point, for the Lancaster economy, Murgatroyd and Urry (1984: 121) identified:

> [...] some distinctive factors which affect the labour process within service work. First, labour-power has to be expended more closely to where the consumer demands it, and has implications for the spatial structuring of such industry [...] There is also some degree of control maintained by many service workers over the nature of their work [...] In the service sector, capital (and the state) tend to economize on labour costs, not principally through direct increases in productivity (though this of course happens) but rather through the employment of sectors of the labour force which can be employed at less than the average wage for white males.

These two examples highlight the role of local circumstances in patterns of African employment in two ways:

- For accommodation, more than general labour shortages, openings for Africans are related to local circumstances. This is consistent with the positive relationship that is found between unemployment rates and service activities in Girona. As well, it is consistent with the message which has been put forward in other chapters regarding the attractiveness of accommodation jobs for 'native' workers.

- For garbage collection companies, the dynamics of particular service agents (rather than the specifics of a place) provide a more solid foundation for explaining African employment patterns. Yet labour for this service is organised at a local level. In this way, (Moroccan) foremen match demand for cleaning services in a specific place with the availability of (African) workers.

Manufacturing-Based Municipalities: Skill Shortages at Local Level

By contrast with both service-oriented and agricultural towns, there is neither a positive nor a negative relationship between unemployment and the relative weight of manufacturing in Girona municipal employment structures (Figure 7.3). Thus the local unemployment rate does not give insight into competition between Africans and other workers in Girona manufacturing.

Turning to the interview survey, only in centres of notable manufacturing activities is African employment in the sector close to the rate for the whole of the local labour force. To be specific, more than half of the Africans who worked in manufacturing-based municipalities had a job in this sector (Table 7.3). This contrasts with the employment of Africans in manufacturing in other municipal types, which remains at under 15 per cent of those interviewed. Even if African employment in the sector is only remarkable in manufacturing-based centres, the proportion of Africans in the manufacturing sector is a noteworthy figure, given the Government's restrictions on non-EU foreigners in the manufacturing sector (the quota system does not allocate jobs for m Table 3.2). In line with legal restrictions, manufacturing rarely gives first employment to Africans (as farming does), but it does at later stages in their employment trajectory in Spain. Thus, whereas just six out of the 151 interviewed African workers in Girona found their first (non-contracted) manufacturing workers; employment in Spain in the manufacturing sector, this figure rises to 25 for current jobs (Table 4.1). Adding to the sense that African employment in manufacturing is low, 14 out of 25 worked in manufacturing were the only African employed in their firm. A further seven said that there were more Africans in the firm, but they did not constitute 50 per cent of the employees.[3] The exception is the three who declared that they worked in industries in which Africans were the bulk of the employees; one in a timber yard, another in a mill and a third in a ceramic firm. This low African involvement in Girona manufacturing is not surprising given the wages in the sector are well above the average in Catalunya (for the whole economy, the average wage was 16,581 ECU per year in 1993, manufacturing offered an average of 18,040 ECU per year; Eurostat, 1997a).

Figure 7.3 Unemployment rate by share of workforce in manufacturing in Girona municipalities, 1991

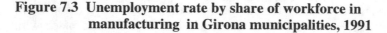
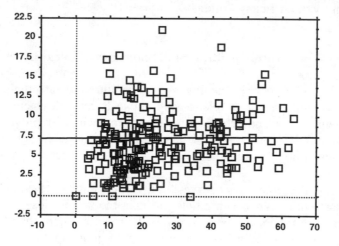

x axis: % of the labour force in manufacturing by municipality; y: axis unemployment rate.

Source: Institut d'Estadística de Catalunya (1993).

Yet manufacturing is far from homogeneous. As seen for service industries in the previous section, differences in African labour outcomes by municipality may vary according to branch of activity. In this regard, reflecting the diversity of manufacturing industries, Table 7.5 shows the type of work undertaken by Africans in manufacturing by industrial sector.

Here, it is seen that Africans work in a considerable number of manufacturing industries, from ceramics to metallurgical firms.

The diversity of the industries that employ Africans can be classified in two main groups: those which offer unskilled jobs to African workers (ceramic firms, agro-industries, timber yards and plastic and polyester firms) and those in which Africans did skilled jobs (metallurgical industries and carpentry workshops). For the first group, jobs in these industries tend to have slight attraction to Catalan workers because of their hard working conditions (i.e. ceramics, and plastic and polyester firms) or because they are regarded as low status occupations (i.e. agro-industries, timber yards). These two factors have created some openings for immigrants. Capturing the point that ceramics is not an attractive industry for 'native' workers, a social worker stated that '[...] labour conditions in the ceramic industries are tough. The town's people avoid them [*la gent d'aquí fuig*]'.

Table 7.5 Interviewed manufacturing workers in Girona, by type of job and branch of activity

	Total	Skilled jobs	Permanent jobs
Ceramic and marble firms	6	1	
Agro industries	5		1
Timber yards	4		1
Plastic and polyester firms	4		
Metallurgical industries	3	2	1
Carpentry	3	2	
Total	25	5	3

Source: Girona interview survey.

As an illustration of this, Africans are employed in the two main ceramic municipalities in Girona - La Bisbal d'Empordà and Breda - although these two specialise in different segments of the industry. Giving a clearer idea of differences in production specialisation in La Bisbal d'Empordà and Breda, a ceramics employer explained that:

> [...] in La Bisbal, ceramics are more manual [*artesanal*] than in Breda. We produce for the tourism market or export to retailers in France. Nowadays, retailers from southern France just come round and load up their lorries. In Breda, everything is more mechanised and production is also cheaper. It is a more market-oriented production.

As for agro-industries, African employment is restricted to parts of the industrial process that are less desirable for non-immigrants. Specifically, my survey found that Africans were employed exclusively in mills and abattoirs. Similarly, the Gabinet d'Estudis Socials (1995) study on immigration into the manufacturing-based Osona area, in the province of Barcelona, revealed that immigrants worked in abattoirs in meat industries (and not on production lines). The need for workers was acute in the 1980s due to the expansion of these industries in the region, with worker numbers rising by 222.7 per cent over the period 1964-87. This increase contrasts with a decline of 17.0 per cent in the labour force for manufacturing industries as a whole in Osona (Gabinet d'Estudis Socials, 1995).

A different case is the employment of immigrants in metallurgical industries and carpentry workshops. Reasons for African employment in skilled work in these industries cannot be traced to their unattractiveness. In this regard, an employer of a metallic door firm that gave work to 10 non-EU workers (out of 100 employees) offered an insight on African employment:

> There are no good welders or painters in La Bisbal. We used to go to the employment offices of the city of Girona to hire them [La Bisbal has its own employment office]. But as soon as they find another job closer to their home town, they leave. Our main competitor is in Barcelona. They do not have problems hiring skilled workers. There are plenty of them in the Metropolitan Area of Barcelona. The immigrant population has been of great help in the expansion of our firm. Our staff has grown from 40 in 1990 to almost 100 in 1997, as we are increasingly selling in international markets. In the beginning immigrants who came in search of work were poorly prepared. But nowadays there are good trained workers. Furthermore, they live in town. In our firm, we have Moroccans, Filipinos and one Gambian.

The scarcity of skills at the local level looks to be a key element in the entry of non-EU nationals in this firm. This is further demonstrated by the employment of skilled workers in carpentry. An employer in this sector similarly argued that there was a lack of good professionals amongst the Catalan population. To broaden this point, a study of the Osona's labour market (Cambra Oficial de Comerç, Indústria i Navegació de Barcelona, 1989) showed that the employment offices of the region had problems finding skilled workers for job vacancies. The study concluded that those who were registered as job seekers did not have the skills that the region's construction, metal-related industries and textiles needed.

However, African employment in manufacturing is not necessarily growing (as seen for Girona farming). In the case of manufacturing-based Arbúcies, it has been declining. The African population did make its presence felt in manufacturing in the second half of the 1980s, when, in common with the general trend for Spanish manufacturing, jobs expanded (Espina, 1990; Salmon, 1995). According to interviewed employers, in the period 1986-1990, as part of this growth, Africans enter the manufacturing local workforce. Yet, by 1995, African employment in Arbúcies was largely gone. The main argument that employers put forward for this was the lack of skills of Africans, as well as their poor discipline. As one employer explained:

> No. We do not have immigrants. They are poorly prepared. We used to have in the past, but we had a lot of problems. They were an undisciplined workforce. I'm not the only case, you can ask other firms around and you'll get the same answer. Employers in Arbúcies do not hire Africans any more. If we need workers, and they are not available locally, we hire them through a temporary work agency which is located in the city of Girona [only 30 minutes away by freeway]. The agency specialises in metal workers. The new motorway makes commuting easier for workers.

Crucial to understanding the move toward 'native' workers is the new road facilities that link this otherwise isolated municipality [Arbúcies] with Girona.[4] This shows that Catalan workers are eager to commute to do manufacturing work. The reason for this commuting has been pointed out before, as manufacturing firms offer good wages. But, even if wages are attractive in La Bisbal d'Empodà, some substitution of Catalans by immigrants has taken place in metallic-related firms. One reason is road links. Paradoxically, La Bisbal d'Empordà is closer to Girona than Arbúcies in terms of geographical distance, but the road that links La Bisbal d'Empordà with the city of Girona is the connection from Barcelona-France to popular Costa Brava resorts (see Figure 4.2). In addition, the road goes through many municipalities in the area. This makes the journey to work cumbersome. As I well know, in summer, the trip from La Bisbal to Girona may take up to one hour. By contrast, the freeway from Girona to Arbúcies is a modern elevated road which avoids the mountains and the towns of the region. Also influencing employer decisions to hire immigrants in La Bisbal d'Empordà is the fact that, as one employer told me, '[...] immigrants come round in search of work'. If employers are happy with immigrant skills, they do not have to bother to announce job vacancies. From the previous examples, it follows that the pattern of African employment in skilled manufacturing work depends largely on local circumstances.

Yet, although the pattern of African labour outcomes in manufacturing varies by municipality, the point is that there are labour shortages in the sector. Some of these labour shortages are met by immigrants (as seen in La Bisbal d'Empordà) and other by non-immigrants (as shown for Arbúcies). The reasons for these labour shortages depend on the type of firm. For agro-industries or ceramics, some labour shortages are produced for unskilled work, owing to rejection of jobs in these firms by Spaniards. For skilled work, labour shortages originate in a scarcity of Spanish professionals for certain activities in specific localities.

African Employment in Portuguese *Concelhos*

By contrast with Girona, only one type of locality, those which specialise in tourism industries, was identified in Algarve. For this reason, another region in Portugal - the Península of Setúbal - was analysed. In this way, a broader base for evaluating African labour outcomes in Portugal was provided. Even if there has been decline in recent decades, economic specialisation in the Setúbal Península has largely been based on manufacturing. Today, as in so many manufacturing regions, services take the lead in providing jobs in Setúbal. In these two regions, 69 interviews were carried out – 39 in five Algarve *concelhos* and a further 30 in two municipalities in the Península of Setúbal. These interviews are classified by branch of activity and type of municipality of residence in Table 7.6.

Table 7.6 Sectors of economic activity of interviewed Africans in Portugal, by municipal-type of residence

	Algarve[a]	Setúbal[b]	Total
Primary sector	1		1
Construction	6	12	18
Manufacturing	4	7	11
Accommodation and restaurants	13		13
Other services	15	11	26
Total	39	30	69

Notes:
a)   The Algarve municipalities correspond to tourism-oriented places.
b)   The Setúbal *concelhos* are basically manufacturing centres.

Source: Portuguese interview survey.

As for Girona, Africans are mainly employed in the dominant sectors of economic activity in tourism-oriented Algarve. Thus, construction, accommodation services and restaurants gave employment to almost half of those who were interviewed (Table 7.6). With 'other services', these sectors accounted for 35 of the 39 interviewed Africans. The dominant sector for Africans in Setúbal is construction, which employed 40 per cent of the sample, with manufacturing giving employment to a further 25 per cent. All this suggests that Africans 'fit' local employment structures.

Table 7.7 Employment by economic sector, municipal-type of residence and origin of workers in Portugal (%)

Economic sector	Type of locality					
	Tourism localities			Manufacturing localities		
	Africa	All origins		Africa	All origins	Pen.
		Municip*	Algarve		Municip*	Setúbal
Primary	2.6	10.8	13.5		1.9	4.0
Construction	15.4	12.6	14.2	40.0	9.2	9.5
Manufactures	10.3	7.7	7.8	23.3	25.6	24.6
Hotels/restaurants	33.3	16.4	15.8		5.3	5.0
Other services	38.5	52.5	48.6	36.7	58.0	56.9

* Municipalities where fieldwork took place (see Appendix 1 for information on the specific *concelhos*)

Sources: For Africans, Portuguese interview survey; for the other data, Instituto Nacional de Estadística (1996c)

However there are substantial differences between the employment of the immigrants who were interviewed and the sectoral picture for the whole employed population. In this regard, Table 7.7 compares both structures. The first trend to outline is the small number of African workers who worked in the primary sector. Crucial to this trend is the fact that farming is neither a main port of entry nor an employer of African workers in Portugal (Chapter 4). However, the primary sector (including fisheries) provided 13.5 per cent of the Algarve employment in 1991 (Table 7.7). Indeed there were 8,698 fishermen in Algarve in 1993, which was 25.2 per cent of the Portuguese figure (Instituto Nacional de Estatística, 1995). Yet, showing these operations are on a small scale (as pointed out by the President of the Fisherman's Trade Union [*Sindicato de Pescadores do Algarve*]) and are likely to come under pressure to re-structure their operations (as noted by a social worker of one of the main fishing ports of the region, Olhão), Algarve boats only contributed 12.0 per cent of total fishing output of the country (Instituto Nacional de Estatística, 1995). Neither farming nor fisheries are nowadays important African employers. Yet the fishery sector was in the past. In my fieldwork, three men declared that they come from fishermen families. They worked in the fisheries in Africa and this was one reason why they moved to Algarve. As the fisheries no longer provide a solid economic basis, two of them transferred to other sectors.

Second, for construction, Table 7.7 shows substantial differences between the pattern of employment of Africans and of the workforce as a whole in manufacturing centres. Thus, the 40.0 per cent of the Africans found in construction in Setúbal is noteworthy when compared with less than 10 per cent of total workers in this sector in the municipalities of my fieldwork as well as in the Península as a whole. Even if over-representation of Africans in construction is less acute in Algarve, the sector gave employment to 15.4 per cent of those interviewed. The reasons for this over-representation were analysed in Chapter 5. The key point there was that the Africans filled jobs that were left by Portuguese emigration to Europe in the late 1960s and continued to occupy these jobs on account of their relatively low pay. Interviewed construction workers report that labour shortages still affect both Metropolitan Lisbon and Algarve. This is to say that the key factor in the entry (and continuance) of African workers in construction is not the locality, but the sector.

Third, for accommodation services and restaurants, these industries give employment to 20.6 per cent of the labour force of the Algarve's municipalities in which the fieldwork took place. But the presence of Africans is even more remarkable than this already high percentage. Noting the relevance of local employment structures, the survey did not identify any worker in accommodation services or restaurants in Setúbal.

Finally, manufacturing accounted for the current or last employment of 10.3 per cent of those interviewed in Algarve, and almost a quarter of Africans interviewed in Setúbal (Table 7.7). Unlike accommodation services, Africans are over-represented in this sector in both regions. Whereas African-born workers were found in the Algarve's fish-processing industries, these workers were mainly employed in electronical companies and metal-related firms. Reasons for manufacturing employment are worth examining in detail.

African Employment in Portuguese Manufacturing: the 'Locality'
Approach

Focusing in Setúbal, the presence of Africans in manufacturing is close to the share for the sector in the workforce of Portugal. However, the significance of the sector for African employment is higher than this figure suggests. If we add those who had their main job in manufacturing (yet were out of the sector at the time of their interview), the sector was responsible for the last, current or main job of almost a third of those who were interviewed in the Península. The main characteristics of these 11 workers are summarised in Table 7.8 which shows the current situation of workers, alongside their experience in manufacturing. Out of the 11, four were engaged in work in the sector, three were unemployed workers whose last job was in manufacturing and a further four had left manufacturing after being employed in it for at least 10 years. That seven workers out of the 11 had left the sector is a good illustration of the degree of re-structuring that has been occurring in heavy industries in Setúbal.

As an illustration, 46 Mr. Nunes (interview 193; Table 7.8) had worked for the state-owned steel company Siderurgia Nacional[5] for 21 years after he arrived from Cape Verde in 1973. According to Mr. Nunes, '[...] at that time, it was easy to join the firm. My brother was already working there'. During the time he worked for the company, he was promoted to quality controller, and then to management. As the company was reducing staff numbers, he reached an agreement with the firm to quit his job at 44. With his redundancy money, he set up his own import-export business. The other six workers who left manufacturing were less lucky, with three out of work and the other three now engaged in construction.

By contrast with the previous example of declining employment in heavy industries, employment in electronics companies has expanded. For the whole of Portugal, the number of workers in this industry in 1996 was 17.6 per cent higher than the 1992 figure (Associação Nacional de Industriais de Material Eléctrico e Electrónico, 1997). According to the President of the Electrical and Electronics Employers' Association [*Associação Nacional de Industriais de Material Eléctrico e Electrónico*], firms mainly employ low-paid female unskilled labour. This pattern of employment in electronics firms has been reported already in the literature (see, for instance, Green, 1983; Hancock, 1983; Scott, 1992). One interviewed worker in such a firm is 24-year-old Ms. Menezes. This young woman arrived in Portugal in 1990 where part of her family had been living in Seixal (Peninsula of Setúbal). Her first jobs in Portugal were as a kitchen assistant. At the moment of her interview, she was working in an assembly line of an electronic components firm in Seixal. According to her,

Table 7.8 Current labour market situation and experience of manufacturing workers in the Península de Setúbal

No	Current situation in labour market	Experience in the manufacturing sector in Setúbal
193	Self-employer worker	Skilled job, then, clerical work for Siderurgia Nacional for 21 years
194	Unemployed *	Skilled manual worker for Siderurgia Nacional for 17 years
197	Construction skilled worker	Unskilled manual work for Siderurgia Nacional for 13 years
202	Welder in a metallurgical firm	He has worked for the same metallurgical firm for 23 years
206	Locksmith in a construction firm	Skilled manual work in a metallurgical firm for 18 years
210	Construction unskilled worker	Skilled manual work in a metallurgical firm for 10 years
211	Unemployed *	Short contracts for unskilled and skilled work in metallurgical firms
213	Line-assembly work in electronics company	Her current job is her first job in manufacturing.
214	Line-assembly work in electronics company	She has been working in the same electronics firm for five years
218	Quality controller in a metallurgical firm	Skilled manual worker (15 years) and manager (5) in two firms
219	Unemployed *	Unskilled manual worker for Siderurgia Nacional for 20 years

* Unemployed workers have been classified as manufacturing workers in Table 7.6, owing that their last job was in this sector.

Source: Portuguese interview survey.

'[...] getting the job was not difficult. I knew they hired women, so I went there and applied for a job'. She renewed her contract monthly and her wage was 66,000 escudos in 1996 (the average wage of women in manufacturing in 1993 was 70,900 escudos in 1993; Ministério do Emprego e da Segurança Social, 1994). According to Ms. Menezes, on the assembly line in her company, only women were employees, with many of them of African-origin. For Ms. Menezes, women were preferred because, '[...] perhaps we have better aptitudes for the job than men [*os homens se calhar não têm tanto jeito para fazer este tipo de trabalho*]'. More than origin, they argue, the real discriminating element when hiring employees in these firms is gender ('I knew they hired women'). In other words, African women find work in these industries as much as other working women who are ready to accept low wages. In this regard, Table 7.9 highlights a general trend in the expansion of female employment in Portugal over the period 1981-1993. This has been accompanied by a relative reduction in wages in manufacturing.

These examples of specific worker experiences are indicative of labour market trends in Setúbal. First, the long employment histories of African (male) workers in manufacturing, that have ended up with job loss, or a transfer of activity into construction, reflect the end of heavy manufacturing dominance in Setúbal (as observed in other Western European regions; see, for instance, Howell et al, 1988, for an analysis of the world crisis in the steel industry). Secondly, the shorter employment trajectories of African (female) workers in manufacturing show the changing base of manufacturing in Setúbal. The key point here is that the main reason for transnational electronics industries coming in the Península is not local factors but lies in national circumstances (mainly the low price of the workforce in Portugal, with wages being ever lower for women; Branco and Melo, 1992; Brassloff, 1993; International Monetary Fund, 1995).

Table 7.9 Wages by sex in selected branches of activity in Portugal

	Percentage in relation to national average wage				Women in industry (%)	
	All workers		Women			
	1988	1993	1988	1993	1981	1993
Primary sector	71.5	68.5	67.8	67.9	51.1	51.7
Manufacturing	90.5	89.9	86.9	84.9	35.3	42.0
Construction	83.2	89.0	103.6	106.5	1.9	4.4
Retail, restaurant & accomm.	97.3	98.0	95.6	95.1	41.4	42.8
Bank, insurance & other services	162.2	150.6	183.1	173.2	33.8	39.5
Average wage	100.0	100.0	100.0	100.0	39.4	44.5

Sources: Ministério do Emprego e da Segurança Social (1994). For the percentage of female workers in 1981, Instituto Nacional de Estatística (1983b).

As for Algarve, the survey identified four Africans who were employed in the fish-processing industry. As told by an official of the

Fishermen's Trade Union [*Sindicato dos Pescadores*], and confirmed by a social worker in Olhão,[6] employment in fish-processing industries has shrunk, following the crisis of fisheries in the region. Yet there still are few large firms in the region.[7] For instance, Ms. Mendonça (interview 169) worked for a firm with 130 workers. She informed me that her wage was 59,000 escudos a month in 1996 (compared with the average wage in manufacturing 70,900 in 1993; Ministério do Emprego e da Segurança Social, 1994). Ms. Mendonça told me that working overtime was normal practice, with 275 escudos (about one pound at the current exchange rate) being paid per hour. She also said that the bulk of the workers in the production line were female; with a substantial part of them being of African origin.

Certainly, there is a 'local effect' in Portuguese manufacturing. African employment in Algarve is observed in an industry whose origin lies in the fishing tradition of certain municipalities (e.g. Olhão). Electronics companies are not that geographically determined. For instance, the Setúbal *distrito* only produced 16 per cent of the Portuguese electronics output in 1995 (Braga, for instance, in northern Portugal had 18 per cent of the final production in the same year; Associação Nacional dos Industriais de Material Eléctrico e Electrónico, 1997). Furthermore, there is a crucial common trend in these two industries - they are labour-intensive with women being in the majority on production lines; many of them are of African origin. More than origin or race, the discriminatory element for employers when hiring a worker is their sex.

Conclusion

African labour outcomes in Portuguese manufacturing are a consequence of sectoral dynamics which, in turn, are conditioned by international and national trends. Comparing Algarve and Setúbal, differences exist in the type of industry, but not in the type of jobs which are offered to female (immigrant) workers. Rather than origin, the previous examples of the electronical companies and fish-processing firms suggest that there is a segmentation by sex in Portuguese manufacturing, with labour-intensive firms offering low-paid jobs for female workers. This is in line what Berger and Piore (1980) stated about the dual nature of labour markets being linked to type of firm. These researchers have argued that capital-intensive firms are more likely to be associated with more regular production and more stable demand for their products than labour-intensive firms. This second group of industries generally provides employment in secondary labour markets (Berger and Piore, 1980).

By contrast, for Girona, the municipal-level characteristics do have importance in explaining African employment patterns. Yet the precise role of such local-level influences do vary by sector and industry. Thus, for farming, there are no noteworthy differences in African employment, with over-representation of African workers observed in all kind of municipalities. This confirms the trend observed in Chapter 4, with labour demands in intensive family-based agriculture holding the key to understanding increased African involvement. Where inter-municipal differences are recorded is in skills used and patterns of hired work. To be specific, African workers are more likely to undertake skilled work and have a permanent contract in agricultural centres that in other municipalities. It follows that there is a 'locality effect' in place. Local circumstances help improve African employment prospects in a sector that is still characterised by a high degree of seasonality and casualisation (see Chapter 4).

Construction also looks to be a sector that is open to inter-local variations. Employment in Girona construction is heavily segmented between type of firm and by type of place. For example, no large firms were found in the agricultural towns that were examined during my fieldwork. The small firms of rural Girona operate in a framework of tight connections between the construction sector and the rest of the rural economy. Indeed, the survival of certain small firms in construction appears to be linked to a particular idea of the local community that is held in rural towns. For Africans, these connections at a local level result in African farm labourers doing construction tasks at agricultural wages. Local Spaniards would be much more reluctant than Africans to accept construction work under these circumstances.

For both service and manufacturing industries in Girona, openings for Africans are mainly located in municipalities that have a strong service sector or manufacturing base, respectively. Yet, whereas these openings are for unskilled labour in services, some of openings in manufacturing are of a skilled nature (e.g. carpenters, welders). This points to there being some labour shortages in manufacturing, not only for (undesirable) unskilled jobs (as demonstrated by employment in ceramics or agro-industries), but also for some skilled ones. This last fact is directly related to a lack of skilled manual Spanish workers for several occupations (as shown by Gabinet d'Estudis Socials, 1995; Abril et al., 1998). So far we have not analysed if these professionals have worked in the same profession throughout their labour employment in Spain (or if they have been forced to do unskilled jobs in adverse circumstances). If they secure a stable job in their field (or if can change jobs inside the borders of their profession), this will indicate that these workers are employed in the primary labour market. This issue is developed in the next chapter. The point here is that skilled labour shortages do not appear throughout Catalunya (e.g. according to interviewed employers, the main advantage of Barcelona-based competitors was their greater availability of skilled workers). Thus, if a pattern of upward mobility is confirmed for this group of skilled workers in manufacturing, local factors will be a key element that helps break the barrier between the primary and secondary segments of the labour market.

Finally, comparisons between municipalities with the same economic base (yet with contrasting African employment patterns) shows that inter-local variation occurs for two further reasons:

- The characteristics of the local African population. The example of Blanes and Figueres indicates that the well-established Moroccan community in Figueres has gained access to hotel jobs. By contrast, a more recent Black African community in Blanes has restricted access to jobs in the accommodation sector. Here differences in hotel labour outcomes are linked to year of arrival and gender composition in these two groups. In the next chapter, African patterns of employment by nationality are explored deeper. In this analysis, the occupational and educational endowments of workers will be taken into account to find reasons for divergences in labour outcome by nationality or origin.

- Contrasting patterns of geographical mobility for Africans and other workers. Spanish workers are reluctant to move to places permanently in order to find jobs (as pointed out by several employers in La Bisbal for manufacturing). Yet it seems that Spaniards are more ready to commute to work (as seen for Arbúcies). This contrasts with Africans, who appear to be willing to live where jobs are (as seen in the high correlation between places of work and residence, with the notable exception of those living in the diversified municipalities of my survey). Without doubt, a greater propensity to change residence (or commute) is a competitive advantage for workers in labour markets. This is explored in detail for African workers in Iberian labour markets in Chapter 8.

Notes

1. For tourism centres, both services and construction have been considered the main economic sectors of municipalities. For other municipal-types, the dominant sector is farming, manufacturing and services, respectively.
2. Construction firms may work in more than one locality. Yet, as will be seen later, many of these firms are family-owned locally-based companies with their businesses limited to specific places.

3. It is remarkable that no Europeans, other than Spanish nationals, were found in any of the manufacturing firms in which Africans worked. This is different from accommodation industries in which European nationals were found in a greater proportion than Africans.

4. The Girona Metropolitan Area (which includes the municipalities of Girona and Salt) had a working population of 36,832 people and an unemployed population of 3,749 which constituted 9.2 per cent of the total workforce in 1991. Manufacturing gave jobs to 28.1 per cent of those working in 1991. This percentage is similar to the average for the province (Institut Català d'Estadística, 1993).

5. Siderurgia Nacional, Portugal's only steel producer, was set up in the mid-1950s as a joint company and nationalised in 1975. When Portugal joined the European Union in 1986, it was given four years to re-structure and transform it from a state-supported company to one without permanent subsidies. This affected employment, which passed from 5,900 workers in 1986 to 3,200 in 1993 (Moinou, 1995). This is only one example of the loss of manufacturing jobs in the region. For the period 1981-85, it has been calculated that 11,031 manufacturing jobs were lost in the Península (Torres, 1996).

6. According to the Fishermen's Trade Union, Olhão, Portimão and Vila Real de Santo António are the main fishing ports in the region.

7. Showing the tradition for eating fish-processed food, Portuguese restaurants usually offer fish paté (as well as butter or cheese) with bread before serving the main course. Spanish restaurants do not have this practice.

8 African Employment in Iberian Labour Markets: The Supply Side

In previous chapters the demand for African labour has been discussed extensively. This has been done from both a sectoral and a 'locality' perspective. Yet labour market outcomes depend not only on the demand for labour, but also on the characteristics of the labour force. An indication of the importance of these characteristics was shown in Chapter 7 when differences in African employment in service and manufacturing centres were linked to the attributes of immigrants. This is a key point for theorists, who argue that the characteristics of workers - their nationality being one such attribute - as well as their capacity to 'adapt' to the society they come to, explain differences in immigrant income. Although segmentation theory has brought forward important criticisms of neo-classical ideas, recent theoretical developments in this tradition have incorporated the qualities of the workforce, although these were systematically neglected by early scholars working in this tradition of labour market analysis (Morrison, 1990). Notably in this regard, a recent issue of International Migration Review (volume 31, winter 1997) saw several scholars arguing that human capital theory principles are valid for understanding immigrant incorporation in host labour markets. Yet, '[...] the underlying concepts, frameworks, and theoretical propositions need to be reexamined and tested against contemporary research findings' (DeWind and Kasinitz, 1997: 1108). This notion provides the base for Chapter 8 which seeks to explore how far human capital ideas help us understand African labour market incorporation. To do this, the first part of the chapter is devoted to an analysis of the attributes of workers, alongside examining their training in Iberia. Consideration is paid to oral language skills, since a large amount of human capital research points to correspondence between fluency in a language and labour market outcomes (e.g. Reimers, 1985; Hirschman and Wong, 1990; Chiswick, 1991; Zimmermann, 1994). The focus here is to see if this is relevant to the incorporation and upward mobility of Africans in Iberian labour markets.

For neo-classical approaches, the education and training of the labour force are key elements in understanding patterns of change in work (e.g. Johnson and Salt, 1990). According to these approaches, skilled and professional workers are more likely than unskilled ones to move between jobs (and consequently change residence), since the latter may be replaced more easily than the former (Flowerdew and Salt, 1979). For neo-classical researchers, there is a connection between education, training and labour market outcomes; as there is between workers' occupational and educational endowments and job turnover. However, for dual labour market theorists, these connections are denied for workers in segmented labour markets. Indeed, in a context of fixed-term contracts (as seen in other chapters), patterns of change in work seem to be substantially affected by labour market conditions (more than being the result of worker choice). Thus the second part of this chapter examines the characteristics of African job turnover in Iberia, and explores the relevance of skills to it.

Crucial in deciding a change of job is information about work availability. There is an extensive literature which indicates that immigrant social networks are a key element through which information about jobs is channelled (Grieco, 1987; Tilly, 1990; Portes and Sensenbrenner, 1993; Portes, 1994). Networks reduce the risks and uncertainties of migration into a new country, especially in the current context of tight immigration policies and a recent history of economic recession in the EU. Yet there are more 'conventional' ways of obtaining information about jobs (e.g. employment agencies). The point is that access to information on jobs, if this is limited to immigrant networks, may channel workers into specific jobs (or occupations). Taking this in mind, this chapter compares the role of immigrant networks with more official channels that Africans may use to obtain employment. This comparison is undertaken by exploring differences by country of destination (Portugal or Spain), of origin (Moroccans, West Africans or Africans from ex-Portuguese colonies) and the sex of immigrants. Comparing the usage that immigrants make of networks by nationality has been neglected by the literature (Böcker, 1995), so have comparisons by sex (Boyd, 1989; Sassen, 1995). Yet the different usage of networks by host country, nationality or sex may be vital for understanding dissimilarities in African employment.

Immigrant Skills: Do They Make a Difference?

In previous chapters, the labour market outcomes of Africans have not been disaggregated by nationality. However, nationality (or origin) is a key variable in human capital theory, since workers from the same origin may face a common situation in their attempts to adapt to the labour markets of destination countries (e.g. similarities of educational background, language, etc.). Amongst other reasons, this occurs because there are groups of immigrants that are more eager to 'adapt' to a society of destination (as shown, for instance, by Borjas, 1982, for the Cuban community in the USA). Providing some insight on the prospects of this, Table 8.1 breaks down labour outcomes by nationality. The main conclusion from this table is that there are no remarkable differences in the jobs that Moroccans, West Africans or Africans from the ex-Portuguese colonies (PALOP) undertake in Iberia. Specifically, 85.1 per cent of interviewed Moroccans, 82.8 per cent of the West Africans and 58.0 per cent of those from the ex-Portuguese colonies, undertake unskilled work in Iberia. In other words, whatever their origin, unskilled jobs[1] constituted the bulk of the work that Africans secure in the Peninsula.

Where differences by nationality do arise is when African employment is examined by economic sector (Table 8.2). Thus, West Africans are rarely employed in service industries compared with either Moroccans or PALOP Africans. To be specific, services gave employment to almost half of interviewed Moroccans in Spain and more than half the Africans from the ex-colonies in Portugal (yet only to 23.4 per cent of West Africans). Contrasting with this trend, and focusing in Spain, farming is more popular for West Africans than for Moroccans, with the sector providing jobs to almost half the former group, but less than a quarter of the latter. So, even if descriptions of job skills are similar, there are differences in access to better-paid service jobs (better-paid compared to farm work at least). The main advantage that service work has over agriculture is that workers in service industries get a guaranteed monthly wage (see Chapter 4, for more information about farming; and Chapter 6 for accommodation services and restaurants). However, West Africans are not only working in farming in Girona. Table 8.2 reveals that manufacturing, a sector which also provides good monthly incomes, gives proportionally more employment for West Africans than for Moroccans. However, out of the 11 Moroccans who were in manufacturing, four did skilled work, whereas only one West African, amongst 14 in the sector, was in the same position. Thus, even if work is mainly of an unskilled variety for Africans in Spain, there are differences in access to service sector jobs and more skilled jobs in manufacturing between Moroccans and those from West Africa.

Table 8.1 Current employment[a] of interviewed Africans in Iberia, by nationality group and type of job

	Skills at Iberian labour markets				
	Unskilled Manual	Skilled Manual	Professional clerical work	Self-empl. workers	Total
Moroccans[b]	74	10	2	1	87
West Africans[b]	53	8		3	64
PALOP countries[c]	40	20	5	4	69
Total	166	39	7	8	220

Notes:
a) Those out of work at their interview have been classified in this table according to their last job.
b) All Moroccans and West Africans were interviewed in Spain. West Africans refers to nationals from Gambia and Senegal (plus one interviewed from Mali).
c) For Portugal, all interviewed Africans were originally from the ex-Portuguese colonies (PALOP).

Source: Interview surveys.

Table 8.2 Current employment of interviewed Africans in Iberia, by nationality group, economic sector and sex

	Moroccans		West Africans		PALOP countries	
Economic sector	Women	Men	Women	Men	Women	Men
Primary		20		27		1
Construction		13		8		18
Manufacturing	1	10		14	4	7
Services	8	35	1	14	28	11
Total	9	78	1	63	32	37

Source: Interview surveys.

Formal Education and Labour Outcomes in Girona

These better prospects in labour outcomes for Moroccans could be a product of longer periods of formal education amongst the Maghreb population, as compared to West Africans. In this regard, Table 8.3, shows the level of formal education of African workers by type of job in Iberia.[2] More than half of the interviewees who came from West African countries had never followed any formal education programme. By contrast, a third of Moroccans had done at least a course at secondary school. However, there is not necessarily a direct relation between the skills required to do a specific job and formal levels of education. A clear example of this is the fact that four out of the eight West Africans who had a skilled job at the time of their interview had not followed a formal programme of education (Table 8.3). If we focus on those who were interviewed in Spain with at least a secondary school diploma, we find that almost 80 per cent of these workers were in unskilled jobs. Furthermore, the access of Moroccans to service jobs is not related to their years of schooling, since the percentage of those in services who had not finished primary school hardly differs from the figure for the whole of the interviewed Moroccan population. It follows that there is no positive correlation between level of formal education and labour market outcomes. This is true for Moroccans and West Africans.

To understand the lack of relation between years in formal education and patterns of incorporation into Girona labour markets, Table 8.4 shows the skills employed by Africans in Iberian labour markets. This table reveals that a third of interviewed skilled workers were in farming. As stated in Chapter 4, skilled tasks in farming are 'reserved' for workers who are employed the whole year round. These are flexible workers who do unskilled, semi-skilled and skilled tasks along the agricultural cycle. The suitability of these workers for farming tasks does not come from their rural background. Even if six out the seven skilled farm employees did work in agriculture in their countries of origin (Table 8.4), interviewed Africans stressed the sharp differences that exist between Girona's and African agriculture. An often quoted example of this is that trees are not pruned in West African farming. From their interviews, it was clear that the specific skills used by African workers in Girona (e.g. driving a tractor, working as a foreman and, in the case of West Africans, pruning trees) have mainly been learned after leaving their home country. The suitability of these workers for agricultural employment came from other factors. As an agricultural employer declared: 'Africans are good workers, and are used to the hard working conditions of farming. Africans have got a good physical endurance, so they put up well with hard agricultural tasks'. In other words, their 'skills' come from their physical condition and their aptitude for the work. Table 8.4 also reveals that some of these workers regularly do tasks in construction (interviews 1 and 41). Furthermore, as seen in Chapter 7, employers in the construction sector indicated that farmers sometimes provide their firms with workers from amongst their African agricultural labour force. In short, in Girona labour markets the two main skills of agricultural skilled workers are physical endurance and job flexibility.

Table 8.3   Current employment[a] of interviewed Africans in Iberia, by nationality group, type of job and level of formal education

	No studies	Primary unfinished	Primary completed	Second educat.	Higher education	Total
Moroccans[b]						
Unskilled manual	14	17	20	21	2	74
Skilled manual	3	2	2	3		10
Professional				1	1	2
Self-employed	1					1
Total	18	19	22	25	3	87
West Africans[b]						
Unskilled manual	33	13	5	3		53
Skilled manual	4	1	1	2		8
Self-employed	2					2
Total	39	14	6	5		64
PALOP countries[c]						
Unskilled manual	10	19	6	3	1	40
Skilled manual	1	10	6	4		20
Self-employed		2	1	1		4
Clerical/profess.				2	3	5
Total	11	31	13	10	4	69

Notes:
a)   Those out of work at their interview have been classified in this table according to their last job skills.
b)   All Moroccans and West Africans were interviewed in Spain. West Africans refers to nationals from Gambia and Senegal (plus one interviewed from Mali).
c)   For Portugal, all interviewed Africans were originally from the ex-Portuguese colonies (PALOP).

Source: Interview surveys.

Table 8.4   Interviewed skilled and professional African workers in Girona, by type of job and the last job held in country of origin

N.	Economic sector	Job description	Last job country of origin	Country origin
1	Farming	Flexible worker in farming and construction	Market-oriented agriculture	Morocco
5	Services	Qualified halal butcher	Street hawker	Morocco
7	Farming	Foreman (Flexible worker)	Subsistence agriculture	Senegal
15	Farming	Foreman (Flexible worker)	Subsistence agriculture	Senegal
36	Manufact.	Carpenter	Carpenter	Morocco
41	Farming	Flexible worker in farming and construction	Subsistence agriculture	Morocco
54	Farming	Flexible worker in farming	Market-oriented agriculture	Senegal
58	Services	Hotel receptionist	Draughtsman	Morocco
61	Construct.	Bricklayer	Subsistence agriculture	Morocco
63	Manufact.	Skilled marble worker	Carpenter	Morocco
82	Construct.	Bricklayer	Subsistence agriculture	Morocco
83	Services	Hotel manager	Unskilled, manufacturing	Morocco
87	Manufact.	Locksmith	Blacksmith	Morocco
89	Farming	Flexible worker in farming	Street hawker	Gambia
94	Services	Teacher of Spanish to Moroccan children	No work in origin country	Morocco
104	Construct.	Bricklayer	Subsistence agriculture	Gambia
107	Manufact.	Furniture restorer	Painter. Flat decorator	Morocco
108	Manufact.	Welder	Clerical job in manufact.	Senegal
124	Services	African clothes tailor	Tailor	Senegal
133	Farming	Flexible worker in farming	Market-oriented agriculture	Mali

Source: Girona interview survey.

Table 8.4 also shows that there are 10 African skilled workers in manufacturing and service industries. Out of the 10, three were engaged in skilled jobs that primarily serviced local African communities (an African clothes tailor, a teacher of the Spanish language for Moroccan children, a butcher in a halal shop). A further five were in jobs in short supply at a local level (as seen in Chapter 7). Only in two cases is it possible to support the notion that there is competition for jobs between Africans and other workers (interviews 58 and 83), since these two workers are in highly-appreciated tourism-related jobs. For the bulk of skilled workers in manufacturing and services, their jobs were either previously non-existent (e.g. halal butcher, tailor of African clothes) or in short supply locally (e.g. carpenters, welders). It follows that Africans in skilled work are generally in slots in Girona labour markets for which there are no available Spanish workers.

Formal Education and Labour Outcomes in Portugal

By contrast with Spain, there is a slight tendency for more qualified jobs to go to those with higher levels of formal education in Portugal. For instance, six out of the 14 who had at least secondary school diplomas were involved in professional or clerical jobs (Table 8.3).[3] Of the remainder, four were in skilled manual work and a further four were engaged in unskilled work. However, out of the four unskilled workers with at least secondary education, there were two young women who were mainly occupied with studying, so unskilled work was a way to support their studies (and not a final labour outcome; interviews 188 and 221; Table 8.5). A further case of unskilled work was a Mozambican national who was a restaurant cleaner (yet a teacher in her country of origin; interview 189; Table 8.5). She was pursuing higher education, as she felt that she could get a better job through it.

The same Mozambican national outlines a relevant trend in Portuguese immigration. She said that the Portuguese state did not recognise her diploma as a teacher in a primary school. This diploma was issued by the Portuguese administration in Mozambique. The reason for the denial was that she arrived in Portugal in 1988 when the ad-hoc board for assessing PALOP qualifications [*Quadro Geral de Adidos*], which was created in 1975, had disappeared. Through the Quadro, the Portuguese state had accepted diplomas and certificates issued during the Portuguese administration in Africa up to the mid-1980s (Pires et al., 1987; Rocha-Trindade, 1995). The termination of this board put a halt to the 'easy' transference of 'African' qualifications into the Portuguese system.

206 Labour Immigration in Southern Europe

The previous 'easy' transference of qualifications is highlighted by Ms. Cardoso (interview 174, Table 8.5). She was a nurse in the Luanda Hospital (the Angolan capital). When the civil war started, she and her husband decided to move to Portugal. They lived in a hotel which was paid for by the IARN [*Instituto de Apoio aos Refugiados Nacionais,* an ad-hoc board which was created to deal with the refugee crisis, see also Lewis and Williams, 1985] from February 1976 to January 1977. In this time, she applied for the acceptance of her nurse diploma and her marriage (this was crucial to apply for the Portuguese nationality, as her family was not originally from Portugal, but her husband's was). In November 1976, she started work in the Faro Hospital as a fixed-term employee, although the equivalence decision had not arrived ('I needed to work'). When the Quadro finally accepted her diplomas in mid-1977, she became a permanent employee in the Faro Hospital.

Table 8.5 Profile of interviewed Africans with at least a secondary school diploma in Portugal

No	Nationality	Year immig.	Current job Sector	Job description	Sex	Job country origin
162	Guinea-Bissau	1986	Services	Clerical job	F	Teacher
163	Portuguese	1976	Services	Clerical job	F	No job
174	Portuguese	1974	Services	Nurse	F	No job
175	Portuguese	1976	Services	Nurse	F	Nurse
179	Portuguese	1982	Services	Nurse	F	Nurse
186	Angola	1992	Services	Hotel cleaner	F	Researcher
188	Angola	1980	Services	School cleaner	F	No job
189	Mozambique	1988	Services	Restaur. cleaner	F	Teacher
193	Portuguese	1973	Services	Self-employed	M	Teacher
194	Cape Verde	1969	Manuf.	Skilled worker	M	Foreman
202	Portuguese	1973	Manuf.	Welder	M	Sales assist.
206	Cape Verde	1973	Constr.	Locksmith	M	Unskilled manuf.
218	Portuguese	1975	Manuf	Quality control	M	Skilled manuf.
221	Cape Verde	1975	Services	Door-to-door seller	F	No job

Source: Portuguese interview survey.

This case contrasts with another nurse (interview 179). Ms. Funes finished her course in 1977 in Angola. The certificate she obtained was issued by the Angolan Government. This was not automatically accepted in Portugal in 1982, when she arrived in Portugal. For this reason, Ms. Funes had to follow a one-year course before starting work as a nurse in the country. This highlights that, under certain conditions, the Portuguese state has accepted diplomas issued in African countries. When acceptance of certificates or diplomas is granted, professionals from other countries can work in Portugal (see Chapter 3). This is not the case for Spain. Since the 1985 Foreigners' Act, non-EU nationals have few chances of working legally in a professional or clerical job. This was not the case until 1985. In fact, in the 1960s and 1970s, many professionals, mainly from South America, worked as doctors and psychologists in Spain (Recolons, 1998).

Britain provides a comparable example with the Portuguese situation. In 1984 Brown found that West Indian women were over-represented in nursing (quoted by Harzing, 1995). More recently, figures from the General Medical Council revealed that the number of foreign doctors who registered to work in the UK was 5,500 in 1997,[4] more than 60 per cent of the total for that year and twice the number of 10 years before (quoted by Burke, 1998). Further evidence is provided by Buchan and associates (1992) who revealed that health care occupations account for 4 per cent of the total number of work permits in Britain in 1991. About three-quarters of this percentage goes to nursing. The main reason for the weight of foreign labour in nursing is low wages in this profession (Buchan et al., 1992).

Nurses may be an isolated case or this might apply to a broader range of professions, where there are labour shortages (in the Portuguese low unemployment context). The example of Britain, another low unemployment economy in the EU context (yet with an immigration policy that is far more restrictive than the Portuguese, see Marie, 1996), also points to labour shortages in health professions resulting in easier access to work for immigrants. A similar pattern is seen in the employment of Ms. Soares (interview 162) in public administration. She finished secondary school in Guinea Bissau in 1986. Through a co-operation programme between Guinea and Portugal (for specific details of the conditions and types of grants of Portuguese institutions, see França, 1992), she went to Lisbon at the end of secondary school. After a failed course in Lisbon University, she found her current job in Faro. Ms. Soares has been successively contracted for specific jobs as a 'self-employed' worker (even if she has regular working times) for five years. She told me that in her office there were about 30 people in the same hired situation as hers.[5] This case highlights that, through 'co-operation' programmes, Africans can first study, and later work, in Portugal. As the President of the Guinea-Bissau Association [*Associação de Solidaridade Guineense*] said in interview,

'[...] the Africans that you can see at universities came to Portugal through co-operation exchanges with their countries of origin. They are not second generation'. However, whether through acceptance of African diplomas or through special programmes, the evidence shows that there are few openings for African immigrants in professional or clerical jobs.

By contrast with the previous situation, the Portuguese survey found a remarkable proportion of unskilled workers. This is directly related to Africans having low levels of schooling. To be specific, 29 out of the 40 unskilled workers who were interviewed had not finished primary education. These data suggest that unskilled labour outcomes in Portugal are mainly occasioned by low levels of formal education. This situation is similar to that found by Zimmermann (1994), who showed that the slight wage progression of Turkish workers in West Germany was due to (low) levels of education and job skills. Likewise, for immigrant women in the USA, Schoeni (1998) argued that disparities in completed years of schooling explains a substantial share of differences in labour market outcomes between Latin Americans and other immigrants.

The idea that Africans possess few years of formal schooling is supported by census data. In this regard, Esteves (1991) showed that Africans from the (PALOP) ex-colonies had the lowest formal educational levels amongst foreigners who lived in Portugal in 1981. To be specific, 80 per cent of Africans from the PALOP countries had a maximum of four year of schooling [*quarta classe*]. More recently, the presidents of both the Guinea-Bissau and the Cape Verde associations told me that education was a priority for their associations. As an illustration, the President of the Guinea-Bissau Association [*Associação de Solidaridade Guineense*] concluded that:

> [...] we've got training courses for young people because the bulk of African youngsters do not finish their nine years of compulsory schooling. Almost none of them reaches university [...] The educational situation of Africans in Portugal is a serious problem.

As a summary of the material on differences by nationality,

- There are no fundamental differences by nationality between Africans regarding the type of job they do in Iberia. Whatever their origin, African-born workers are over-represented in unskilled tasks. Yet minor differences by nationality are observed. For Spain, Moroccans have better access to service jobs and do proportionally more skilled manufacturing work than West Africans. Comparing Africans in Portugal and Spain, it seems that workers who have followed at least secondary school courses from PALOP countries are more likely to find a professional or clerical job than Africans of similar educational standing in Spain. In good part this is linked to the operation (and enforcement) of the Spanish quota system.

- There is no relation between years of formal education and labour market outcomes in Spain. More than 80 per cent of Moroccans with at least secondary school diplomas do an unskilled job in Girona. Furthermore, more than half of the West Africans in skilled work had not obtained a primary school certificate. This is related to the nature of the skilled tasks that are available for Africans in Spain, which are restricted to those manual occupations in short supply locally or to servicing African communities. A similar conclusion was reached from the survey research of Ramírez Goicoechea (1996). He found that the key element in understanding African skilled work in Spain was local labour market need (and not African formal education or skills).

- By contrast, levels of formal education help explain differences in African labour market outcomes in Portugal. There is a positive relation between more years in formal education and better labour market prospects. The low professional profile of Africans in my survey is associated with low levels of formal education amongst interviewees. This is a general trend for former immigrants (as seen by 1981 Census data), second generation Africans (as stated by immigrant associations) and recent immigrants (as demonstrated by statistics on the level of schooling of new legal residents).

Job Progression and Oral Skills

The previous analysis focused on the level of formal education of African workers at the time of their interview. It did not take into account the 'investment' of Africans in education in a host country. Yet a quarter of those who were interviewed in Portugal had taken a course in the mainstream education system in the country. This seems to contradict the generally low level of formal education which was found in my survey. Yet this 25 per cent includes immigrants who arrived at a school age and followed compulsory schooling in Portugal. Furthermore, whatever the years of education or the country in which the course took place, those who had not finished primary school represent 60 per cent of respondents in my survey. In the case of those who have secondary school diplomas (Table 8.5), the survey found interviewees who followed their whole education in their country of origin, a second group who started their education in Africa and continued it in Portugal, others who were 'forced' to continue their education in Portugal so that their qualifications were accepted, and a further small group of persons who arrived in the country as children and pursued all their education in Portugal. The survey did not observe substantial differences by the place where education took place. The message to put across in this regard is that there is a slight tendency for those with more years of schooling to be in skilled or professional work, irrespective of where their education took place. To confirm this, three out of the four who had at least secondary school diploma and were employed in unskilled work, were studying at the point of their interview. It follows that they believe that 'investment' in education was worthwhile. However, apart from these three people, other interviewees showed no interest in pursuing an education programme. This suggests that there is polarisation in the African population, with the majority not associating upward job mobility with education, and a minority holding the opposite idea.

Rather than formal education, Girona's Africans are more likely to do a language course, if they follow any education programme. Specifically, out of 151 interviewees, 31 declared that they were studying at their interview. Out of these 31, 23 were engaged in a course to improve their oral or written Spanish or Catalan, four attended classes in the mainstream education system[6] and six were on training courses organised by employment offices or trade unions.[7] These data denote the relevance of language courses for African workers, and implicitly show that language is felt to be a barrier for work progression in Girona labour markets. Further supporting the relevance of these courses is the fact that a third of those interviewed had attended a language course at some point of their stay in Spain. Fluency in the language(s) of a destination society is not unreasonably regarded as vital for most economic activity, except for specific jobs (e.g. as an employee in an 'ethnic' shop, for high-skilled jobs in a transnational corporation, or for unskilled manual tasks). In this regard, there is a huge literature on the impact of a (lack of) knowledge of the English language on immigrant wages in the USA (see, for instance, Reimers, 1985; Hirschman and Wong, 1990; Chiswick, 1991). This research generally stresses the importance of English fluency in accounting for differential wages between immigrants.

In this regard, Table 8.6 displays the level of oral language competence by nationality, from the interviews conducted in Girona.[8] There is no attempt to quantify precisely language skills here (such as using an IELTS or TOEFL test). However, using broad categories it was not difficult to allocate interviewees to bands of language competence. This is used here for illustrative purposes, with only general trends considered. It is accepted that other sources were not available to verify the categorisation used, although when a second person was present at the interview, the language assessment was checked. As an indicator of broad trends, the results are considered to have validity. Table 8.6 shows that half of the West Africans (and a third of Moroccans) were categorised as having a poor level of oral Spanish or Catalan (categories 'poor' and 'insufficient').

Contrary to what is observed in the USA, a comparison of these categories with job taken in Girona shows that good oral Spanish (or Catalan) is not associated with more skilled work. For West Africans, the four interviewees who were regarded as having a very good level of Spanish were employed in unskilled tasks in agriculture and services. Similarly, 11 out of the 14 Moroccans with very good oral skills were involved in unskilled work. By contrast, four West Africans who were felt to have a poor knowledge of Catalan (or Spanish) were in skilled manual work (as a welder, a carpenter, a flexible worker in agriculture and a tailor). Thus, even if oral Spanish (or Catalan) is good, Africans do not seem to secure skilled work, and if they are in skilled manual work this does not generally require a good oral knowledge of these languages.

Table 8.6   Level of oral language of interviewed Africans in Girona, by nationality group

| | Level of oral language | | | | |
	Very good[a]	Good[b]	OK[c]	Insufficient[d]	Total
Moroccans	14	43	22	8	87
West Africans	4	26	29	5	64
Total	18	69	51	13	151

Notes:
a)   Good use of tenses (e.g. subjunctive) and a fluent speaker.
b)   Good use of verbs, but incorrect use of tenses, although a (reasonably) fluent speaker.
c)   Incorrect use of verbs (e.g. Yo habla, I speaks) and not a fluent speaker. Communication in Spanish/Catalan is possible.
d)   Communication in Spanish/Catalan is not possible. Interviews conducted in another language.

Source: Girona interview survey.

This analysis of the oral skills of Africans in Girona confirms the message that has been put across so far. Labour market outcomes in Spain do not differ according to immigrant human capital endowments. Neither are they due to Spanish (or Catalan) proficiency. Rather evidence confirms that Africans in Spain are placed in secondary labour markets, regardless of their origin, years of formal education or oral skills.

Immigrant Networks and Mobility Patterns within Iberia

More than education, an element which seems crucial for African employment is their tendency to move residence in search of work, not simply between countries, but also within a country of destination. The fact that immigrants are more likely to change places of residence than others for work reasons has been demonstrated in the literature (e.g. Morrison, 1971; Bailey, 1988). In the case of Spain, changes of residence within the country have decreased enormously since the mid-1970s (and when this takes place, it generally involves short distances; Olano, 1990; Blanco Gutiérrez, 1993; Bentolila, 1997). It follows that if Africans are ready to change residence within Iberia, they enjoy a comparative advantage in its labour markets.

Theoretically, we can expect different types of workers to produce different types of labour migration. According to neo-classical approaches, internal labour migration is expected to be less important for unskilled than for skilled and professional workers (Flowerdew and Salt, 1979; Johnson and Salt, 1990). However, the seven skilled agricultural workers of my survey were not a mobile workforce. They have been working for the same farmer for many years. As a result, these workers have been 'promoted' into skilled and supervisory tasks after on-the-job training. Furthermore, they are likely to be permanent employees (at least in the sense of working all year round). Skilled workers in farming are considered to be more than employees. Employers and employees alike described them as members of the farm 'community' (see Chapter 4). Other skilled workers in the survey (e.g. those in jobs aimed at African communities; interviews 5, 94 and 124, Table 8.4) also showed no interest in moving jobs, nor had they undertaken home relocations in Spain in the past. Only the employment stories of four skilled workers (namely; one carpenter, one locksmith, one marble skilled worker, and one bricklayer)[9] show that these workers move 'freely' within the narrow confines of their profession. As an illustration, Mr. Harishi (interview 36; Table 8.4) had worked in four carpentry workshops in the province of Girona over the period 1991-95. He declared that: 'I have never been out of work in Spain. Carpentry is a small world. Everybody knows each other'. He moved jobs in order to accept better work offers. All this depicts a fragmented picture of job mobility for skilled workers, with mobility associated to promotion for a limited number of professionals and professions (and under certain personal circumstances).[10]

By contrast with skilled workers, the survey identified a regular pattern of unskilled worker job mobility. For one, there is a pattern of temporary farmer work following different agricultural campaigns across Spain. Working on several harvests during a single year was something the bulk of the interviewed Africans who had been employed in Spanish farming had done in the past. Yet, as seen in Chapter 4, Africans tend to transfer into other employment sectors or to more 'permanent' jobs in farming the longer they reside in Spain. However, the need for more workers in the picking season (plus the fact that harvests do not occur in the same month across Spain) stimulates movement in search of work during an 'elongated' harvest time. Quantifying the weight of these 'cyclical' workers in the total number of farm workers is not easy, since some Africans transfer to other economic sectors in the same area when they are unemployed (rather than moving residence). An indication of the relevance of this movement comes from the number of employees who were without a contract or had temporary work at the point they were interviewed. Effectively, half the farm employees in my survey had to find another job when harvest time was over.[11] One of these workers is Mr. Fashira, who was hired as a temporary worker in the apple campaign in Girona when interviewed. He had worked in Barcelona's strawberry sector, in vegetable collection in Girona, in the peach and apple campaigns in Lleida and in cherry collection in Zaragoza. Other researchers have pointed to this pattern of regular labour migration within Spain (Colectivo IOÉ, 1994; Santana Afonso, 1994; Ramírez Goicoechea, 1996). As an example, Colectivo IOÉ (1994) identified a substantial group of temporary African agricultural workers who move around Spain in search of work. These researchers mentioned the following production activities as important immigrant farm employers: the strawberry campaign in Huelva; fruit collection in Lleida and Girona; the orange campaign in Valencia and Murcia; and asparagus and potato collection in La Rioja. This 'cyclical' movement does not originate with worker skills, but arises from the needs of sectors that are short of workers in different parts of Spain. In other words, at least for farming, unskilled African workers are more likely to move jobs than skilled ones in Spain.

For Portugal, job turnover is widespread amongst all type of workers in construction. The employment trajectories of the bulk of construction workers show substantial job changes. These changes do not imply job downgrading, since they occur within the limits of their occupation for skilled workers. As an illustration, skilled worker Mr. Sines (interview 158) started work in construction in 1972, when he arrived in Portugal. He has worked as a bricklayer for five firms ('I only work for firms'). As the bulk of the skilled workers of my survey, he learned his profession in the firm. In 1994, he quit a permanent job for non-hired work. The reason for this was higher wages as a 'self-employed worker' ('They pay more. They offered me an "ordinary" contract, but I turned it down'; see also the example of Mr. Moraes in Chapter 5). In his interview, he declared that it was not difficult to obtain jobs in construction in Algarve. In his case, job changes are motivated by the search for better wages. In other words, job turnover is not the result of the end of a contract, but arises from the search for better personal prospects. However, this does not hold true for all construction workers. The example of Mr. Peres (interview 161) shows that work changes in Portuguese construction are also motivated by cyclical switches in the demand for workers in a sector which is dominated by high casualisation and precariousness. He arrived in Algarve in 1989, when he started work as an unskilled non-contracted worker. Later he found a more stable job in a firm. In the five years he was with the firm, Mr. Peres learned a profession [*armador de ferro*]. As the firm reduced its staff dramatically, he was made redundant. At his interview, he was working without a contract for a subcontractor. A similar unstable labour position was held by Mr. Grosso (interview 185). Since he arrived in Portugal in 1985, he has worked in Lisbon for three years for one firm and for five subcontractors in different Algarve coastal municipalities over seven years. Unlike Mr. Peres, Mr. Grosso, who has always been an unskilled worker, has never had a contract. Through the 1992-93 legalisation process, he obtained legal residence, but he lost it as he had no access to regular, contracted work. That construction work and illegal residence goes hand-in-hand is demonstrated by the fact that all four men who had illegal residence in my survey were construction workers (Table 3.7). Three of these four were unskilled workers. From the previous examples, it follows that skills are gained through experience in construction (see also Chapter 5). Only for experienced (skilled) construction workers are changes of workplace inclined to be voluntary. In other cases, as for workers in accommodation services and restaurants, high job turnover responds to switches in the business cycle.

Changes of workplace are not generally associated with long distance movements. For Spain, the majority of Africans had had their longest period of Spanish employment in one job in the province of Girona. Specifically, 128 out of 151 interviewed had their longest held job in this province. Only three out of these 151 had their longest held Spanish job out of Catalunya. Furthermore, only 12 per cent of the survey had been employed out of Catalunya at any point in their employment history.[12] Similar to the position in Girona, the geographical location of a current job is likely to be the same as for the longest held job for African-born workers in Portugal. For instance, 36 out of 39 who were interviewed in Algarve had their longest held employment in the region.

The trend is for job turnover in Iberia to be accompanied by restricted geographical mobility. For the regions studied here, this is due to two main factors. The first is a high level of unskilled job availability (and also skilled work in Portuguese construction). For Girona, high rates of inter-sectoral mobility between farming, construction and, to a lesser extent, accommodation establishments and restaurants, indicate that jobs are available in many economic sectors. The transfer of workers between sectors is eased by the low skill requirements of the jobs Africans take. As an example of this, Mr. Seim's first job in Spain was on a Girona camp site. Here he helped dismantle its infrastructure before it closed for winter. After this work, which only lasted a few days, he cleared out a forest for its private owner for six months. Through friends, who already were working there, he then found a job in farming. At the beginning, he was only in charge of cattle. When interviewed, he mainly worked in the farmer's mill. This person had worked in farming, forestry, accommodation and manufacturing in the 10 years he had lived in Girona. But all these jobs have something in common - they are unskilled. For Portugal, inter-sectoral mobility is less noticeable (see Chapter 5 for construction; Chapter 6 for accommodation establishments and restaurants). The trend is for workers to move within one economic sector – accommodation services and restaurants for women and construction for men. The reasons for this have been explained elsewhere (see Chapter 5 for construction; and Chapter 6 for accommodation services and restaurants). The point has been raised here to show that high availability of unskilled work in Algarve accommodation services and restaurants (as well as abundant number of jobs in the construction sector in the region) reduces inter-sectoral and inter-regional mobility.

A second reason for immigrants not moving long distances when changing jobs is that the majority of African workers see Iberia as their final destination (Table 8.7). It means that the current place of residence for the bulk of African workers in Iberia is not considered to be provisional. So, if a change of residence is needed, it will bring about similar personal disruptions for these workers as for Iberians. In this regard, 60 per cent of interviewed Moroccans, as well as half of West Africans, said that they would like to stay permanently in Spain. For Portugal, even if a majority of Africans showed an interest in staying in the country, a third expressed a willingness to move out of Portugal, with a further 26 per cent undecided on this issue. Linked to the views of those living in Spain, Africans either bring their families to live with them or create new ones. To be specific, almost 40 per cent of the Africans who were interviewed in Spain (and 56.2 per cent of those in a partner relationship) lived with their 'spouse' in the country. For Portugal, reflecting the older character of the African inflows, 84.6 per cent of interviewed African-born workers with a partner lived with their partner at the time of their interview. Out of eight who said that they were not living with their 'spouse', two were in Africa, three partners were elsewhere in Portugal, and the remaining three lived in France.

Table 8.7   Would you like to stay in Iberia in the future? (%)

	Moroccans[a]	West Africans[a]	PALOP countries[b]
Yes	59.8	51.6	42.0
No	20.7	20.3	31.9
It depends	17.2	26.5	26.1
No answer	2.3	1.6	
Total	100.0	100.0	100.0

Notes:
a)   All Moroccans and West Africans were interviewed in Spain. West Africans refers to nationals from Gambia and Senegal (plus one interviewed from Mali).
b)   For Portugal, all interviewed Africans were originally from the ex-Portuguese colonies (PALOP).

Source: Interview surveys.

Even if the bulk of Africans expressed their intention to stay in Iberia, the number of African-born workers who would move out of Portugal is high. Despite long years of residence (see Table 3.8 for year of arrival of Africans in Portugal; Table 3.4 for Spain), these immigrants are more likely to want to move out of Portugal than their counterparts in Spain. Reasons for this lie in (low) wages in Portugal (compared to the rest of the EU) and the existence of a well-established immigrant network with other European countries (for the Cape Verde community in France, see Lesourd, 1988).[13] In other words, higher wages can be obtained for the same (unskilled) job, with the risk of emigration being cushioned by immigrant networks. This not only applies for immigrants, but for all Portuguese workers. Nationals from this country constitute the only potential emigrant nationality group in the EU, according to Simon (1991). In this regard, researchers have shown that Portuguese and Cape Verde nationals in Spain are concentrated in the same geographical areas and economic sectors (López Trigal and Prieto Sarro, 1993). The prospect of (further) emigration might even have been intensified by the development of the Single European Market. Certainly, there is evidence that legally-resident (non-EU) immigrants, along with young people and certain categories of skilled workers, are the most mobile international migrants within the Union (Simon, 1991; Kastoryano, 1994).[14] Yet, even if

Moroccans are a well-established community in France,[15] the intention of these nationals to stay in Spain is higher than for Cape Verdeans in Portugal.

Table 8.8 Profile of potential emigrants from Iberia

	Spain			Portugal		
	Potential leavers		All interview.	Potential leavers		All interview.
	N.	%	%	N.	%	%
Male	31	100.0	93.4	12	54.5	53.6
Good oral Spanish or Catalan	21	67.7	57.6			
Portuguese nationality[a]				7	31.8	46.4
Year of arrival in 1986 and after	21	67.7	62.9	7	31.8	24.6
Urban origin	17	54.8	35.8	4	18.2	40.6
30 years and less in 1995	16	51.6	38.4	8	36.4	20.3
Secondary and higher education	13	41.9	21.8	4	18.2	20.3
Single	12	38.7	29.8	7	31.8	31.9
Skilled workers[b]	7	22.6	15.5	8	36.4	38.5

Notes:
a)   Only three Moroccans with a EU passport were interviewed in Girona.
b)   Self-employed workers excluded.

Source: Interview surveys.

To cast further light on the divergent intention of stay by nationality and country of residence, Table 8.8 shows the characteristics of those who expressed the view that they would like to leave Iberia. Here differences between Portugal and Spain are relevant. For Girona, the potential emigrant has dissimilar characteristics from the rest of the sample. The potential leaver is more likely to be a single male, to be more educated, of urban-origin, young and with a satisfactory level of Spanish (or/and Catalan). The reasons expressed for wishing to leave Girona amongst the more educated was their limited access to professional jobs in Spain. By contrast, from the Portuguese survey, there were no clear characteristics for those who would like to leave the country in terms of sex, marital status, education or job skills. The lack of any clear distinguished educational or job skill feature for potential emigrants is related to general considerations about better economic prospects in other EU countries. This applies for all types of workers. However, the survey shows that those who arrived in Portugal before 1986, as well as those who have naturalised, are less willing to move out of the borders of the country. This occurs even if these workers do not have any restraint on working or living elsewhere in Europe. As examined in Chapter 3, Portuguese nationality is compulsory for permanent employment in public administration (e.g. hospitals, municipality-owned firms, state-owned industries) or for public housing. So those who have naturalised tend to be older than the general survey and are more likely to have permanent employment (Table 3.11). Securing permanent employment (plus long stays in Portugal) looks to be a deterrent to further emigration.

To summarise the main points of the section,

- Evidence from Girona does not show that skilled African workers are a mobile workforce. This is related to the type of skills that are 'available' for these workers in Girona labour markets (agricultural skilled workers, jobs aimed at Africans). Only in a few cases are professions in short supply. By contrast, the need for more labourers during the peak season stimulates a 'cyclical' movement of unskilled workers in search of work (see also Colectivo IOÉ, 1994; Santana Afonso, 1994; Ramírez Goicoechea, 1996).

- For Portugal, the high job turnover of Africans in construction, accommodation services and restaurants is largely motivated by employment instability and the precariousness of work in these industries. This applies to unskilled and some skilled (construction) workers. For other skilled workers in construction, job changes are made in response to the availability of better-paid jobs. The key element to understanding this contrasting situation amongst skilled workers is experience in the sector, with young entrants sharing the generally more precarious, less advantageous situation of unskilled workers in general. For this latter group, changes in work are basically a response to labour market conditions.

- Those who declared that they would like to leave their host country have distinctive characteristics in Portugal and Spain. The more educated profile of would-be emigrants in Spain, compared with the rest of the survey, emphasizes the limited access that Africans with more years of formal education have for professional work in the country. By contrast, the lack of a distinct set of educational and occupational characteristics for those who wish to leave Portugal points to other reasons for emigration. Amongst them, wage differentials between Portugal and other EU countries look to be a decisive element. Finally, rather than favouring emigration, naturalised immigrants are less likely to want to cross the Portuguese border for better-paid jobs elsewhere. This is because those who are naturalised are in a more stable situation in labour markets, as well as having lived in the country for substantially longer.

Immigrant Networks and Job Search Strategies

The literature suggests that central to a change of job is the role immigrant networks play in providing information about job availability (as demonstrated by Grieco, 1987; Tilly, 1990; Portes and Sensenbrenner, 1993; Portes, 1994). In this sense, Table 8.9 confirms the relevance of family-and-friend networks for interviewed Africans in Iberia. Significantly, almost half of the Moroccans, West Africans and workers from ex-Portuguese Africa mentioned relatives or acquaintances as the way they found their present job. Likewise, the survey research of Gabinet d'Estudis Socials (1995) on immigrants from developing countries in Catalunya found that 82 out of 176 had obtained jobs through family and friends from their home country. Statistics further support the vital role of immigrant networks in understanding patterns of employment in Spain. In this regard, data on residence by nationality reveals a high concentration of nationalities in certain provinces, while work permit data reveals that specific occupations are 'preferred' by certain nationalities of immigrants (the Spanish Institute of Statistics [*Instituto Nacional de Estadística*] provides figures on the number of foreigners who are living legally in Spain by nationality and province annually;[16] for work permit data, the Ministry of Labour and Social Security has published a detailed account of foreign workers annually since 1986).[17] As an illustration, half of the 4,401 Gambians who were living in Spain in 1996 resided in Girona (Comisión Interministerial de Extranjería, 1997). As seen previously in this chapter, West Africans had few years of formal education (Table 8.3), and their Spanish was generally poor (Table 8.6). At least for their first job, help, advice and support from relatives or friends who are already living in the country is critical to understanding why workers from inland rural Gambia1[18] with a poor knowledge of European languages[19] are working in rural municipalities in northern Catalunya.

Whereas there are no substantial differences between Africans in their use of different channels for obtaining employment in Girona, there are important differences for Africans in Portugal and Spain. To be specific, a third of African-born workers relied on more conventional channels (e.g. newspapers, adverts on the street, employment agencies, getting registered in the firm as a job seeker) to obtain a job in Portugal. These channels were barely used by Africans of any nationality in Girona. As a Portuguese hotel manager explained to me:

[...] the PALOP immigrants use the same channels as the Portuguese. Either they fill a form at the reception, reply to our adverts or are contacted through the Employment Centre [*Centro de Emprego*], just as with Portuguese workers.

Table 8.9   Channel used for interviewed African workers[a] to obtain current job in Iberia, by nationality group

	Moroccans[b]	West Africans[b]	PALOP countries[c]	Total
Friends and family	40	30	31	101
'Asking' [d]	30	22	4	56
Employers' initiative [e]	5	4	2	11
Conventional channels [f]	6	3	27	36
No answer	5	3	1	9
Total	86	62	65	213

Notes:
a)   Self-employed workers excluded.
b)   All Moroccans and West Africans were interviewed in Spain. West Africans refers to nationals from Gambia and Senegal (plus one interviewed from Mali).
c)   For Portugal, all interviewed Africans were originally from the ex-Portuguese colonies (PALOP).
d)   Employees go round workplaces checking if job vacancies are available.
e)   Employers ask employed Africans if they know somebody who may be interested in a job. In other cases, employers go round bars or places where Africans gather.
f)   Employment agencies, adverts in public places, and registration with firms as job seekers.

Source: Interview surveys.

The reason for divergence in the use of more conventional ways of obtaining information on employment lies in the peculiarities of Portuguese labour markets and the characteristics of Africans in this country. Effectively, low unemployment rates and low wages in the Portuguese economy make it difficult for employers to get employees for the least desirable jobs. In this sense, accommodation establishments made it clear that it was hard to find workers at the mid-peak season. Set in this context, for the least desirable and worse-paid jobs (such as cleaning or assembly line work), potential employees do not need the selective information that family or friends provide in order to know where to find work; companies are active in advertising openings that they need to fill. The second reason for divergence in the use of 'official' channels comes from the characteristics of African-born workers in Portugal. They are fluent in the Portuguese language (even if it is not their first language).[20] Furthermore, because of previous colonisation, many are used to the country's work procedures and habits.[21] The general point is that immigrants with language or cultural ties with the country they move to find it easier to use mainstream job hunting methods.

A second difference between Africans in the Portuguese and Spanish surveys is the number who declared that they had found their job by 'asking'. This practice is much more common in Girona than in Portugal. What is meant by 'asking' is that Africans go round workplaces checking if job vacancies are available. If employees are needed, the job seeker starts working as soon as possible. In my survey, a third of Africans in Girona replied that they had obtained their current employment in this way (Table 8.9). A point to stress is that this way of looking for a job shows a general knowledge of job locations. As well, it is a reflection of the high Spanish unemployment context. The fact that employees go to workplaces is seen by employers as a sign of the eagerness of Africans to work. By contrast, the use of more conventional channels (e.g. public adverts on the street, employment agencies) denotes an active role by employers, which is more likely to occur (in Girona) for skilled work, where there are labour shortages.

What should also be examined are gender differences in the use of networks and other job seeking channels. In the literature, gender differences have been pointed out as crucial to understanding dissimilarities in labour outcomes by sex (see, for instance, Grasmuck and Pessar, 1991; Hanson and Pratt, 1991; Sassen, 1995). The general argument is that women's labour market outcomes are more dependent on family and friend networks than those of men. This is seen to be an outcome of a more restricted job search methods by women, which puts them in a worse position in labour markets. Despite the logic of this argument, my Portuguese survey does not show remarkable differences by sex in immigrant job searches. Table 8.10 shows that the main channels for Africans getting a job in Portugal are family and friends, followed by conventional channels. This holds true for both women and for men. Perhaps the main reason for this is the plentiful job availability in Portugal, which eases immigrant access to mainstream channels for getting jobs (even for those who are considered to be in a disadvantageous position in labour markets, such as immigrant women). For Girona, even if the 10 interviewed women (out of 151 African workers) make the comparison with Portugal difficult, it is appropriate to note that six out of 10 women found their job through family and friends. This represents a percentage higher than the 45.8 per cent of the men who declared that they relied on these networks to obtain current employment, but on so small a sample this cannot be considered to be 'significantly' different.

Table 8.10   Channel used for interviewed African workers to obtain current job in Portugal, by sex

	Women	Men
Family and friends	15	16
'Asking'	1	3
Employer's initiative	2	
Conventional channels	13	14
No answer		1
Total	31	34

Notes:
a)   Self-employed workers are excluded.
b)   See notes on Table 8.9 for the definition of the categories used on this table.

Source: Portuguese interview survey.

When analysed by worker skills, more skilled employees in Portugal are more inclined to have used conventional channels. This is the case for the five professional women in the sample (interviews 162, 163, 174, 175 and 179; Table 8.5). For men, skilled workers are also more likely to rely on mainstream channels than other workers. To be specific, out of the 14 who declared that they had used a 'conventional' way of getting their job, five were unskilled employees, with the other nine engaged in skilled work. Even if this refers mainly to men, for Spain, strategies for finding jobs vary between workers depending on type of job. To be specific, whereas 20 per cent of skilled and professional workers use mainstream channels, less than 5 per cent of unskilled workers obtained a job through these ways.

In short:

• By country of residence, Portuguese Africans are more likely to use more conventional means of finding a job than Spanish Africans (e.g. newspapers, employment agencies). This is because of greater job availability, as a consequence of lower unemployment, and on account of the characteristics of African-born workers (e.g. they are generally fluent Portuguese speakers). These two factors positively affect the access of Africans to mainstream ways of finding a job in Portugal.

• By nationality, there are no substantial differences in job acquisition methods for Africans in Spain. Family and acquaintance networks helped half of Moroccans and West Africans (as well as PALOP nationals in Portugal) find their current job. The reliance of Girona workers on 'asking', which was not significantly used in Portugal, looks to be the result of the scarcity of jobs in the Spanish economy.

- By sex, the Portuguese sample shows that, contrary to dominant ideas in the immigrant network literature, women and men make similar use of channels for finding employment. A progression to more conventional channels is nonetheless observed for skilled or professional workers, regardless of their sex. Both the abundant number of jobs and the characteristics of Africans again have a positive impact on opening job searches to mainstream ways of obtaining jobs (even for immigrant women who are generally considered to be placed in a disadvantageous position in labour markets).

Conclusion

The main conclusion of this chapter is that, whereas human capital postulates do not explain African labour outcomes in Spain, they give a partial explanation to African involvement in Portuguese labour markets. A similar conclusion was reached by Cazorla and associates (1979), when analysing return migration from Central and Northern Europe to Algarve and Andalucía. Cazorla and associates (1979) found that neo-classical postulates partially explained labour outcomes of return immigrants in Algarve (e.g. some of them could invest or apply their capital and skills when returning). By contrast, return migrants to the surveyed Andalucian areas found a more rigid labour market, dominated by high, structural unemployment. The acquired (human) capital of Andalucian returnees was not found to be invested in economic activities. The bulk of these former emigrants went back to their old situation of labourers.

Focusing on my survey results in Spain, the three indicators which have been examined in this chapter point to segmentation theory holding the key to the explanation of African labour outcomes. For one, there is no relation between levels of formal education and patterns of employment for Africans. This is the reason why educated Africans look more likely to move out of Spain. Second, job turnover is associated with precariousness and casualisation. The number of Africans in fixed-term contracts, which has been seen in previous chapters, confirms this. Only in a few cases (and because these professions are in short supply in the country), is upward labour mobility (or better wages) associated with changes in work. Evidence from the survey also shows that the group which is more likely to move in search of work in Spain is unskilled harvest workers. Third, to find a job, Africans rely on either family and friends or their own initiative ('by asking'). The use of mainstream job hunting was not noteworthy for workers in my survey. These three trends confirm that Spanish labour markets are segmented by race.

By contrast, the evidence for Portugal supports some human capital theory postulates. First, there is progression between type of job and level of education. Yet this is because of the current situation of Portuguese immigration. This is highly conditioned by low unemployment (Modesto et al., 1992; Brassloff, 1993; International Monetary Fund, 1995), and by recent links with previous colonies. In this regard, until mid-1980s, an ad-hoc board examined the diplomas which were issued in Portuguese Africa to grant acceptance for their holders to work in Portugal. Nowadays, co-operation programmes ease the inflow of African students into Portugal (see, for instance, França, 1992; Rocha-Trindade, 1995). Some stay in the country as workers. This helps confirm human capital principles only in the narrow confines of current political and economic circumstances. Second, job turnover is sometimes associated with better professional prospects. In the case of skilled construction workers, some employment trajectories show that Africans move following (perceived) better incomes, even if this implies non-hired relations with employers. Yet this occurs in a context of ready job availability (and it is restricted to those workers with many years of experience). Finally, the access of Africans to mainstream job hunting is more widespread in Portugal than in Spain. Even if skilled and professional workers are more likely to use mainstream channels, these are also used by unskilled workers. The reason for this is again the characteristics of Portuguese labour markets, with employers finding difficulty in obtaining unskilled workers in the peak season for certain activities (as seen for accommodation services and restaurants in Algarve).

Education levels, job turnover, and the use of social networks for job acquisition, denote considerable differences between Portugal and Spain, with the former confirming some postulates of human capital theorists. By contrast, evidence from Spain shows that Africans are situated in the secondary segment of the labour market, irrespective of these considerations.

Notes

1. A skilled job is here taken to be one that requires a special knowledge, either through training, experience or qualification, for its fulfilment, irrespective or the (negative) social value that may be attached to it. For instance, in farming, there are skilled jobs like a foreman or a tractor driver. In the case of construction, all worker categories, except labourer, are considered skilled.

2. The questionnaire asked about years of study, kind of courses taken and the place where a course was undertaken (see questionnaire on Appendix 2).

3. Thirteen employees and one self-employed worker in charge of an import-export business.

4. The figure does not include 6,600 overseas doctors with a limited period of registration, which allows them to train in Britain (Burke, 1998).

5. This irregular (yet not illegal) practice is called *recibos verdes* ['green receipts', named after the colour of the relevant employment form]. This has been explained before in Chapter 5.

6. Two of these four cases were young Moroccans who were temporarily employed in restaurants for the peak season. They were brought into the country by their families and 'normally' entered the mainstream education system. A third was following an adult course to obtain the primary school diploma [*graduado escolar*] and a further one who worked as a halal butcher was pursuing higher education at the University of Girona. A further four Africans had obtained the *graduado*. These four were not studying at the time of their interview and were employed in unskilled work (two in accommodation, one in manufacturing and the fourth in a garbage collection company). Three out of these four entered the mainstream education system as children, since they were brought to Spain by their families. The fourth passed examinations to obtain the primary school diploma, after attending an adult course.

7. These figures do not sum to 31 because two workers were engaged in two courses.

8. Most interviews lasted up to an hour. In this time, it was possible to evaluate the level of comprehensive and usage of Spanish (the language of 130 interviews) or Catalan (which was chosen by eight interviewees). A further 13 interviews were conducted in either another language (English or French) or were conducted in Spanish with the help of an (unofficial) translator. As I am not a Portuguese native speaker, I could not assess the level of Portuguese competence with sufficient conviction from the interviews. As a consequence, this analysis is limited to Girona.

9. This bricklayer said that it was easy for him to change jobs within construction as a skilled worker. By contrast, the other two interviewed bricklayers expressed concern about difficulties in getting a skilled job. They believed that they could easily go back to unskilled work in construction, when their present contract expired.

10. Four skilled workers in manufacturing or services in my survey (one furniture repairer, one welder and two professional workers in hotels) showed no intention of changing jobs. Two out of these four saw their job as their final stop in their Spanish employment story. A third case is a person who wanted to legalise his residence, before deciding on any move.

11. Out of 38 on farm jobs, 11 were non-contracted workers, and another eight had temporary jobs. This last figure does not include 10 temporary jobs who have been working with the same employer for more than one year. Four who regularly moved back to their country of origin at the end of the season are also excluded (see Table 4.3).

12. Nine in farming, four in construction and six in services.

13. Many of those interviewed had family in France (or, to a lesser extent, Spain). Cape Verde has even considered joining the group of Francophone countries (see for instance Moura, 1996, who reports the visit of President Jorge Sampaio to Cape Verde). According to this media source, the President of the Republic stated that the *lusofonia* [the Association of Portuguese-speaking countries] was out of discussion because Portugal was not competing with France in Africa.

14. See Chapter 5 for the example of a Cape Verdean construction worker who would like to go to France for work. He has stayed in Portugal because his Cape Verdean nationality and his Portuguese residence permit do not allow him to work in France.

15. There were 572,652 Moroccan nationals in France in 1990 (Hargreaves, 1995). To outline the significance of this figure, the number of Moroccans in France is higher than the figure for all foreign nationalities in Spain (538,984 in 1996; Comisión Interministerial de Extranjería, 1997), and three times the number of foreign residents in Portugal (172,912 in 1996; Instituto Nacional de Estatística, 1997a).

16. See the annual series on *España: Anuario Estadístico* and *Boletín Mensual de Estadística* (see Appendix 1 for more information about Spanish official publications on immigration).

17. Statistics are given on the number of permits which have been granted annually. These data include renewed permits, so the exact number of new entrants in Spanish labour markets cannot be deduced from these statistics. Since 1989, the statistics have also given the stock of work permit holders at the end of the year, so new entrants can be deduced from the two stock figures.

18. Thirty-five out of the 38 Gambians interviewed had rural backgrounds.

19. Four out of 38 Gambians declared that they could speak English, 11 said that they had some knowledge of the language. The remaining 23 could not speak any English. The Gambia obtained independence from the UK in 1965.

20. Twenty out of 69 interviewed African-born workers said that Portuguese was their mother tongue.

21. As an example, it was clear throughout the fieldwork that African immigrants turn to the Portuguese Foreigners and Borders' Service easily [*Serviço de Estrangeiros e Fronteiras*]. In Girona, immigrants have more trust in NGOs or lawyers than in the Foreigners' Office [*Oficina de Extranjeros*].

9 Conclusion

Southern Europe is increasingly attracting new labour immigrants from less developed countries. Even if literature is nowadays paying more attention to this trend, research on Southern Europe immigration have mainly focused on statistical accounts, with few theoretical insights. Proposing a more theoretical perspective, a main objective of the book is to asses the validity of neo-classical and structuralist ideas on immigrant labour market incorporation. In previous chapters this has been done through the analysis of the incorporation of African-born workers in three economic sectors (i.e. farming, construction and tourist activities) in Portugal and Spain. Examined evidence comes from extensive fieldwork in both countries which was collected using a common methodology (see Appendix 1). In the conclusion the common trends of the previous partial sectoral analysis are contrasted and examined at the light of two main theoretical lines of labour economics.

In the three examined economic sectors, evidence from Girona suggests that Spanish labour markets are segmented by race. My surveys of African workers and their (potential) employers found that Africans mainly secure work in secondary labour markets in Girona. Certainly the majority of interviewees did unskilled work (84.3 per cent of employees in my survey), were employed in jobs that were associated with inferior social status (e.g. agricultural labourers, cleaners) and had fixed-term jobs that were not part of the promotion ladder of their firm (only 15 per cent of the survey's employees had secured a permanent contract). These labour outcomes bear little relation to the educational endowments of Africans (e.g. 80 per cent of Moroccans with at least secondary school diplomas had an unskilled job). Were my respondents Spanish (or other EU) citizens, we would expect them to have had higher status work and (even in these times of 'flexible' work arrangements) more job security than Africans possess. This confirms Piore's (1979, p.17) postulates on the incorporation of immigrants into host labour markets. Using his words,

> [...] the jobs [that immigrants hold] tend to be unskilled, generally but not always low paying, and to carry or connote inferior social status; they often involve hard or unpleasant working conditions and considerable insecurity;

they seldom offer chances of advancement toward better paying, more attractive job opportunities.

Throughout this book, it has been seen that two elements combine to produce this segmented outcome in Spain:

- The state puts African nationals in a fragile legal situation. For one, restrictions on geographical and occupational mobility apply for the first three years of residence in the country. This conditions entry (and stay) in labour markets in general, and in manufacturing and service industries in particular (with the exception of specific unskilled tasks). Additionally, according to the procedures in place during my fieldwork, Africans (except from Equatorial Guinea) had to renew their annual work permit at least five times in order to secure a five-year work permit. In a context of fixed-term contracts, this means that Africans needed to secure a work contract in order to renew their residential status. As both the media (e.g. Pérez Oliva, 1995; Fuente, 1998) and the scientific literature have reported (e.g. Izquierdo Escribano, 1991; Colectivo IOÉ, 1992; Santos, 1993a), the passage from legality to illegality is not unusual amongst Spanish immigrants. This produces a situation that is consistent with Portes's (1981) strictures about immigrant legal status tending to be of a tenuous nature, ranging from illegality to temporary stays.
- Employers select (or reject) employees according to their race or origin. Farmers prefer Africans because they believe that they are used to hard agricultural work (even if the farming system of their origin country is very different from Girona's intensive agriculture). By contrast, accommodation employers would not hire an African person for a reception job because they are held to be a poorly educated workforce (even if a percentage of Africans in my survey were young workers who had completed secondary school courses). Although not the only consideration when hiring workers, employers did discriminate between potential recruits according to their race, nationality or origin. This is in line with what Reich and associates (1973) and Gordon (1989) have argued about employers' recruitment practices. For employers, then, immigrants are not simply workers who are endowed with different skills and familiarity with a language, but are used in qualitatively different ways from 'native' employees (Piore, 1979).

Obviously, Africans are not the only workers who are found in secondary labour markets. This is an especially relevant point in the context of the high unemployment and substantial element of casualisation in Spanish labour markets (see, for instance, Centro de Investigaciones Sociológicas, 1986; Recio, 1986; Miguélez Lobo, 1989). Competition can be expected for jobs even in the secondary segment of labour markets between 'natives' and Africans. As Pugliese (1993: 514) has noted, '[...] the presence of an immigrant labour force cannot be taken as an indicator of an unsatisfied labour demand, even in the secondary labour market'. However, evidence from Girona demonstrates that a key element behind the emergence of African labour market niches is the lack of attractiveness of jobs for non-immigrants. This has provoked an unsatisfied labour demand, which has come to be met by African workers. Whether through family support mechanisms or state support, potential 'native' workers do not feel that they 'must' accept jobs of this kind. This process has been shown for farming (Chapter 4), for certain branches of manufacturing (e.g. agro-industries, Chapter 7), and for specific occupations elsewhere (e.g. cleaning, Chapter 6).

The rejection of farming tasks by 'native' workers is a key element in understanding the scope of African employment in Spanish agriculture. The existence of African workers in this sector only became noticeable in the early 1980s in Barcelona and Almería (Giménez Romero, 1992; Ramírez, 1993). From these first 'enclaves' of African employment, African workers have come to be found in a wide array of provinces along the Mediterranean coast, in the Ebro Valley and in a few southern inland provinces (Figure 4.1). This 'expansion' has been stopped in areas where there is a ready availability of Spanish labourers and few other job openings (e.g. Cruces Roldán and Martín Díaz, 1997, on the Cádiz example), where there is an abundance of family workers and small-sized holdings dominate the farm landscape (for Galicia; see Colino Sueiras, 1984; Calcedo Ordóñez, 1996) and where Portuguese inflows meet the harvest demand for labourers (for Castilla-León, see López Trigal and Prieto Sarro, 1993; López Trigal, 1996; for Badajoz, Iríbal and Gil, 1998). This confirms that Africans are most likely to be found in places where labour shortages exist in farming (for Valencia, Avellá Reus, 1991; for Lleida, Balcells, 1991; for Almería, Roquero, 1996). Key to the 'expansion' of African invovement in agriculture has been knowledge of where demand for seasonal labour is needed, as some immigrants move to follow work in different Spanish farming cycles (see also Colectivo IOÉ, 1994; Santana Afonso, 1994; Ramírez Goicoechea, 1996). The process of expansion of an African niche in intensive production then flows due to the spread of knowledge of farm openings for Africans. This job knowledge is mainly channelled through immigrant networks (almost half of the Girona survey found their jobs through friends and relatives, Table 8.9). As a consequence, we find that, as the geography of African involvement in Spanish farming has spread, geographical concentrations of single (or multiple) African nationalities have emerged. In Girona the hallmark of this concentration is the presence of workers from The Gambia.

For other jobs and sectors, the unattractiveness of work (and consequently lack of competition for jobs) is more arguable. This is the case for construction and for skilled jobs in manufacturing. The 'locality' here is the key element for understanding African patterns of employment. For construction, the presence of Africans is related to the character of construction firms in agricultural municipalities. In this type of centre, the transference of African labour power from farming to unskilled construction work sometimes took place under the same employer's business. The embeddedness of (small) construction firms in the fabric of agricultural places not only eased 'job mobility' amongst Africans, but was also decisive for the survival of these (generally) small-sized businesses. For manufacturing, African employment in skilled jobs directly related to labour shortages. According to interviewed employers (and as reported in other empirical research; see Gabinet d'Estudis Socials, 1995), shortages have arisen for skilled work (e.g. welders, painters). This is not to say that there is a general lack of welders or painters in Spain. Rather there are shortages of these professions in certain municipalities (as seen in Chapter 7). The reason why Spanish workers do not change residence (or commute long distances) to fill these shortages lies in the low labour mobility of Spanish workers (as shown by much research; Olano, 1990; Bentolila, 1992; Romero González and Albertos Puebla, 1996; Bentolila, 1997), alongside active immigrant job search methods (one-third said that they went to the firm or farm to ask about job vacancies; Table 8.9). This suggests that the composition of the African labour force in manufacturing depends on local circumstances. Local factors also explain the uneven distribution of African employment in the hotel industry, as well as differences in patterns of African employment in medium- to large-sized farms. This is in line with what Massey (1979) and Peck (1989) have argued about the composition of labour markets, which they see as depending largely on local employment structures. A more arguable point is that local circumstances help break the barrier between the primary and secondary segments of labour markets for African workers. Due to the high-level of employment instability amongst these nationals, and the small number of African skilled manufacturing workers (and those that hold such jobs are mainly on temporary contracts), it is difficult to conclude that a 'locality effect' in general eases access to the primary segment of the economy (at least for Africans). Even so, in Spain the access of Africans to skilled work is conditioned by local employment structures.

By contrast, segmentation by race is not general across all economic sectors in Portugal. In fact, there is a slight progression in African labour market outcomes in Portugal based on human capital endowments (Table 8.3). Seen through this interpretive lens, the unskilled pattern of African employment in Portuguese labour markets (which applied for 66.7 per cent of my survey; Table 8.3) is related to low levels of schooling. This is consistent with human capital theoretical postulates which see a close connection between workers' investment in education and labour market outcomes (Sjaastad, 1962; Becker, 1964). However, the link between years of formal education and labour market outcomes occurs in a (perhaps conjunctural) favourable political and economic situation. The Portuguese state recognised the diplomas that were issued under its African administrations until the early 1980s (Lewis and Williams, 1985; Pires et al., 1987). Nowadays, through co-operation programmes with the ex-colonies, there is a possibility for African students to pursue further education in Portugal (França, 1992; Rocha-Trindade, 1995). For some, this is the first step toward permanent immigration. This possibility is eased because, while Portuguese immigration policy is restrictive, as in the rest of the EU countries, once a visa is granted, gaining legal residence in the country is a less complicated process than in other EU countries (Marie, 1996). Whether this is a direct consequence of recent historical links and of low unemployment (which consequently may change), remains an open question. The point to stress here is that, unlike Spain, the state does not 'push' Africans into secondary labour markets. Set against this, it must be noted that it is likely that the labour market conditions of non-PALOP immigrants would be more restricted (e.g. less chance that their qualifications are recognised), and newer immigrants are confronted with a less welcoming labour market situation (albeit much of this has to do with changes in the private sector, rather than state policy).

Even given this, segmentation postulates remain valid in a Portuguese setting. In this regard, 27 women (out of 32 interviewees) were engaged in unskilled jobs (with only four having permanent contracts). Yet the main reason for employers hiring women was not their race, but their sex. In this regard, key informants, employers and African employees stated that farms, manufacturing firms, accommodation establishments and restaurants prefer to hire female workers for some tasks: women for the harvest season in Algarve; women for the production line in electronical companies or fish-processing firms; and women for cleaning hotels and restaurants. This is not to say that female workers were preferred for all jobs in these sectors. On the contrary, employers viewed their labour force in a highly segmented way, with some jobs 'designated' for women and others open to men. Of course, not all women are in unskilled work.

Through snowball sampling, the Portuguese survey found five African-born women who were employed in professional or clerical jobs, although this was just five amongst 32 interviewed females. Most commonly, it seems, women must accept (hard) labour conditions and (low) wages which are dominant in the activities that employers have 'allocated' to them. In this environment, women without labour prospects, other than unskilled, low-paid work, are found in the secondary segment of labour markets. Putting this in context, more than half of the 27 female, non-professional workers had not finished primary school. This divided employment structure is consistent with Baganha's (1998) message on current Portuguese immigration. This analyst argues that the Portuguese economy at present generates opportunities for the economic incorporation of immigrants both at the bottom and at the top of the occupational ladder.

For men, the Portuguese survey also points to a divided employment situation. For one, more experienced, skilled workers in construction felt they had 'freedom' to change their job in order to secure better prospects and wages (this was certainly not a characteristic of secondary labour markets). However, younger, less experienced, unskilled workers had more difficulty obtaining jobs. This difficulty increased the chances of a loss of legal residential status, and hampered access to this status for others. Yet, irrespective of interviewee opinions, construction in Portugal offers few (permanent) contracts (14 out of the 16 construction workers had no contract; Table 5.2) and is characterised by a high degree of casualisation (Lobo, 1985; Rodrigues, 1992; Pinto and Queiroz, 1996). It follows that, even if some elements of primary labour markets are present for certain workers (such as wage progression associated with job turnover, and the acquisition of skills through experience), the nature of construction work in Portugal is dominated by secondary labour market features (i.e. non-contracted, unstable, fixed-term jobs). If there is a change in the good prospects that Portuguese construction has seen in recent years (due to the large infrastructure projects of the state, e.g. the 1998 Lisbon Expo, the new bridge over the River Tagus), the labour situation of African (or non-African) workers in the industry may become (even) more vulnerable.

Whoever you ask in Portugal (government officials, university researchers or 'ordinary' people), all answers point to construction as the main economic sector for African males. Even a glimpse at the Expo site in Lisbon confirms this. Africans started to be employed in Portuguese construction in the late 1960s due to labour shortages in the industry that were occasioned by large-scale Portuguese emigration into Central and Northern Europe (Carreira, 1982; Saint-Maurice and Pires, 1989; Saint-Maurice, 1995). Inflows into the sector did not stop after the independence of the African colonies, with the sector currently being the main male

African employer (Esteves; 1991; França, 1992; Machado, 1997). Crucial to this trend is the unattractiveness of the sector for Portuguese workers, owing to the precarious pattern of employment in the sector (as the previous examples of African employment indicate) and because wages are lower than the average for the whole economy (Ministério do Emprego e da Segurança Social, 1994). It would be reasonable to presume that a critical factor in the process of consolidation of an immigrant niche is the action of social networks (Tilly, 1990; Portes, 1994; Waldinger, 1994).

In fact, differences in the usage of social networks are revealed in this book. Even if Africans in Portugal and Spain rely strongly on family-and-friend networks, Africans in Portugal are more likely to use 'conventional' methods of job search than their Spanish counterparts. This has been explained in terms of differences in economic circumstances, as well as in the characteristics of African residents, in these countries. Yet no major differences in African patterns of employment are observed in terms of access to skilled work on one side or the other of the border. In other words, the different usage of social networks leads to the same (unskilled) labour outcome. This evidence does not add support to the idea that social networks help break the barrier between the primary and the secondary segments of labour markets (as seen in the ethnic enclave literature, Wilson and Portes, 1980; Bailey and Waldinger, 1991; Portes and Bach, 1985). But the cross-border comparison also does not support the view that access to mainstream job hunting channels substantially changes immigrant labour outcomes (as held by Reimers, 1985; Hirschman and Wong, 1990; Chiswick, 1991). According to these latter analysts, immigrant networks channel immigrants into 'slots' in host labour markets which hamper further job progression. It is true that a majority of African workers are in unwanted labour market 'slots' in Iberian labour markets. But the role of immigrant networks in shaping this pattern looks to be limited. Immigrant networks are the main information source on the availability of jobs for Africans in both Portugal and Spain. But these 'available' jobs are delimited by the state (for Spain), by employers and by 'native' workers (for both Portugal and Spain), as well as by the human capital endowments of African workers (for Portugal). More than a cause of labour outcomes, the use of social networks seems to be a consequence of the segmented nature of labour markets (with, for instance, skilled and professional workers being more likely to use mainstream job hunting methods), combined with the particular opportunity structures that arise from the peculiarities of national economic circumstances. In the high-unemployment Spanish context, it is probable that word-of-mouth also ranks high amongst the job hunting methods used by 'native' workers. In low-unemployment Portugal, the scarcity of workers for certain jobs leads employers to announce job vacancies (so conventional methods are broadly used amongst African workers). But, whatever the economic conjuncture and the usage of social networks, immigrant networks cannot be seen as a decisive element in shaping (either positively or negatively) immigrant labour outcomes in Portugal or Spain.

Contrary to what has been argued in the literature (e.g. Hanson and Pratt, 1991; Sassen, 1995), no basic differences are observed in the usage of social networks by men and women in Portugal. The proportion of female workers is almost half my Portuguese sample, but less than 10 per cent of the Spanish one. It is not my survey that is unusual in noting this dissimilarity, as other questionnaire surveys (see Solé and Herrera, 1991; Gozálvez Pérez, 1995) and official data (see Figure 6.1) show that this is roughly the share of women in the African labour force in Spain. Despite low numbers, the literature points toward a broader involvement of women from African countries (particularly, Morocco) in the Spanish domestic sector (Sánchez Martín, 1992; Ribas Mateos, 1996). The demand for immigrant workers for domestic sector activities occurs in parallel with greater involvement of 'native' workers in paid work (Solé, 1994; Chell, 1997). Yet, for Portugal, the survey found that the employment of African women was not restricted to the domestic sector. There are some openings for female (immigrant) workers in accommodation services and restaurants, and in manufacturing. The Portuguese experience might give insight on future developments in female labour immigration in Spain, especially if social ties between North Africa and Spain strengthen. Although for manufacturing this might be arguable, due to the particularities of the sector in Portugal (Branco and Melo, 1992; Courakis and Roque, 1992), for Spanish accommodation services and restaurants, the involvement of female immigrants may well increase in the future. For one, employers prefer women for cleaning, which constitutes many jobs in accommodation services and restaurants. Secondly, alongside geographical proximity to Morocco, economic crisis in this Maghreb country has hit urban dwellers hard (Colectivo IOÉ, 1994), which could expand the female immigrant presence in Spanish labour markets. This prospect arises because, as Moroccans stressed in their interviews, there is a more 'liberal' approach toward women being in paid work in urban centres in that country.

The previous discussion has focused on workers. Nothing has been said about self-employment amongst the African communities. On this there are two main conclusions from my survey. The first is the low involvement of Africans in self-employment on both sides of the border (about 5 per cent of the Portuguese survey and less than 3 per cent of the Spanish). This contradicts evidence gathered for the USA by Bailey (1987) who argued that almost all every foreign-born group are over-represented amongst small business owners. Yet my Portuguese survey results show a share of African self-employment which is similar to that in official statistics (see Instituto Nacional de Estatística, annual). However, for Spain, 1991-92 legalisation data (the 1985-86 data are not significant, since registering as a self-employed worker was a frequent way for employees who could not prove pre-contract arrangements to obtain legal residence; Izquierdo Escribano, 1991) show that 10 per cent of those who 'legalised' were engaged in self-employed activities (Ministerio de Trabajo y Seguridad Social, 1993). Even if there are discrepancies about the truthfulness of this figure (see Aragón Bombín, 1993 and Santos, 1993a, for contrasting opinions), the character of African employment in Girona may have conditioned the low level of self-employment in the survey. In other words, ethnic entrepreneurship may be more notable in other parts of Spain. In this regard, in cities (rather than in the Girona rural areas or medium-sized towns) ethnic businesses would appear to be more likely to expand. This is not only because immigrant communities are larger in cities, but also because city services have catchment areas that go beyond the limits of the municipality (and sometimes beyond the state's borders, as seen in the creation of 'transnational' ethnic businesses across EU countries, e.g. Tarrius, 1996; Beltrán Antolín, 1997). Apart from relatively low numbers in self-employment, the survey also points to these activities having an irregular character in Iberia. The most clear example of this is the Portuguese construction sector, where self-employment is often used to avoid taxation. This is in line with the diffuse border between self-employment and the informal economy that some analysts have found difficult to trace (Moulier Boutang, 1992; Palidda, 1992; Costes, 1994; King and Konjhodzic, 1995).

This book has examined hypotheses from two main theoretical lines in labour economics. As far as I know, no research has evaluated the postulates of either neo-classical or segmentation theories in the field of international immigration into Iberia. At the same time, as Portes (1997) has noted, cross-border comparisons are a neglected issue in studies of international (labour) migration. In this regard, this book has highlighted differences (and similarities) in two proximate geographical (and political) settings. It has concluded that segmentation theory explains African labour outcomes in Spain, but only gives partial explanation to the same phenomenon in Portugal. This key difference is largely explained by current political circumstances (e.g. recent historical links between Portugal and former African colonies) and present-day economic conditions (e.g. low unemployment), both of which ease (or, at least, do not hamper) the transference of those with medium- to high-education diplomas into primary sector jobs in Portugal. Were these circumstances to change, even these Africans may face more restricted access to jobs in Portuguese labour markets (as seen in Spain).

Appendix 1: Methodology

In order to assemble the data necessary to provide a detailed account of the incorporation of African workers in Iberian labour markets, work had to be undertaken using different information fields. Specifically, the research involved a compilation of official statistical data, as well as a review of the literature on immigration into the Iberian Peninsula. Official data were used to delimit the areas of study of the fieldwork and the economic sectors which were focused on when examining African employment in Iberia. The fieldwork was phased in three stages:

- July-December 1995. Fieldwork in Girona. In all, 20 key informants (i.e. social workers, presidents of immigrant associations, members of non-governmental organisations, and government officials) were contacted and 151 Africans were interviewed.
- January-June 1996. Fieldwork in Algarve and Setúbal. A total of 15 key informants and 69 African-born workers were interviewed.
- July-October 1997. Employer survey in Girona, Algarve and Setúbal. In all, 32 interviews were conducted with employers in Girona and 20 in Portugal.

Official Statistical Data

Official statistical data on foreign residents in Spain came from four basic sources:

- Residence permits. This information is compiled by the Ministry of Interior and published by different public bodies. The oldest source to trace back the number of foreigners in Spain is the *España: Anuario Estadístico* of the Institute of Statistics [*Instituto Nacional de Estadística, INE*]. Since the mid-1980s, the INE has also pusblished the monthly *Boletín Mensual de Estadística*. These two sources are not specifically aimed at identifying immigration levels, but do give basic information on legal foreign residents and workers, by nationality and province of residence. Probably the most exhaustive source for immigration data are the *Anuario de Migraciones* of the General Directorate for Migration [*Dirección General de Migraciones*][1] and the *Anuario de Extranjería* which is published by the Foreigners' Inter-

Ministerial Commission [*Comisión Interministerial de Extranjería*]. These two sources give extensive information on foreign residents and workers, non-Spanish students, naturalisations, as well as data on asylum seekers and refugees. In the case of the *Anuario de Migraciones*, data on Spanish emigration, the legalisation campaigns and the quota systems are also compiled.

*   Work permits. Apart from the above publications which give some tables based on work permits, the main source on foreign workers in Spain is the annual compilation of statistics of the Ministry of Labour and Social Security (from 1996, the Ministry of Labour and Social Affairs). This Ministry has published the *Estadística de Permisos de Trabajo a Extranjeros* annually since 1986. This gives information about the permits that are granted by sex, age, nationality, type of permit, province of residence and economic sector. Yet this is not inflow data (which would give an indication of the number of new legal foreign entrants in Spanish labour markets annually), because renewals and new permits are not distinguished. However, since 1989 the Ministry has also provided information on the total number of permits at the end of each year which are broken down by the above-mentioned variables. This is an exhaustive source of information on the incorporation of non-EU workers (since 1986, EU nationals have not needed a work permit for self-employed activities; from 1992 most EU nationals - and from 1993 all EU nationals - have not needed for work in Spain). On request, the Ministry sent me more detailed tables on foreign workers for the four Catalan provinces by economic sector and profession. Through the analysis of work permit data, it became clear that, despite the relevance of tourism activities in Girona, the proportion of non-EU nationals in services was lower that in other provinces (e.g. Barcelona or Tarragona).

*   Census. A population census is carried out every 10 years by the Spanish INE, with the collaboration of the Institutes of Statistics of the Autonomous Communities, who may add questions to the main questionnaire aimed at their own Communities. The Institutes of Statistics publish accounts on their respective population. In the case of the Catalan Institute of Statistics [*Institut d'Estadística de Catalunya*], 1991 Census data are also available on floppy disk. My request for census data, which is free for researchers and public institutions, was channelled through the Social Science Library of the Universitat Autònoma de Barcelona. Data were provided me by municipality for Catalunya. Crosschecking the number of foreigners in

Table A1.1 Labour market indicators of the fieldwork municipalities in Girona

	Total population	Unempl rate	Working population Agricult.	Primary	Const.	Manuf	Services
Agricultural municipalities							
L'Armentera	743	3.4	28.5	28.5	10.7	19.6	41.3
Borrassà	476	4.1	26.9	27.4	9.7	18.8	44.1
Fortià	502	3.5	26.8	26.8	17.3	21.4	34.5
La Pera	381	8.2	23.8	23.8	9.5	33.9	32.7
S. Pere Pescador	1,199	7.8	27.9	30.4	10.1	8.7	50.7
La Tallada	284	2.5	47.9	47.9	6.3	17.6	28.2
Torroella de Fluv.	297	7.0	56.8	56.8	3.8	8.3	31.1
Ventalló	521	5.0	44.8	44.8	9.5	9.0	36.7
Surveyed munic.	4,403	6.0	31.3	31.9	10.9	17.3	39.9
Manufacturing municipalities							
Arbúcies	4,550	4.6	5.1	5.2	7.8	55.3	31.7
Bisbal d'Empordà	7,778	7.2	2.8	2.9	15.9	39.2	42.0
Breda	3,221	8.5	3.5	3.5	8.8	62.1	25.6
S Hilari de Sacalm	4,704	7.5	4.4	4.4	7.5	61.8	26.3
Sta. Coloma de F.	8,239	7.4	7.4	7.5	11.2	42.6	38.7
Surveyed municip.	28,492	7.0	4.9	5.0	11.0	48.9	35.1
Tourism municipalities							
Cadaqués	1,810	6.6	1.8	3.1	26.0	15.4	55.4
Castelló Empúries	3,637	12.5	11.7	11.7	13.5	17.4	57.5
L'Escala	5,178	13.9	2.8	6.6	18.9	19.5	55.0
Llançà	3,495	12.7	2.0	8.8	22.6	11.8	56.8
Lloret de Mar	15,018	25.2	0.8	1.1	10.8	9.2	78.8
Palafrugell	17,417	13.8	2.4	2.8	24.3	21.7	51.3
Roses	10,303	17.3	1.5	10.4	24.1	10.4	55.1
Surveyed municip.	56,858	17.5	2.4	5.0	19.3	15.0	60.7
Diversified service municipalities							
Blanes	25,663	21.1	2.3	4.4	14.3	26.6	54.7
Figueres	34,573	10.7	2.1	2.2	11.3	24.6	61.9
Surveyed municip.	60,236	15.1	2.2	3.1	12.5	25.4	59.1
Girona	509,628	10.7	5.9	6.7	31.3	12.4	49.7
Catalunya	6,059,494	14.2	3.4	3.7	36.2	8.2	51.9

Source: 1991 Census data provided by the Institut d'Estadística de Catalunya.

the 1991 Census by nationality and municipality of residence, it became clear that Africans lived in municipalities which had distinctive economic specialisations in the province of Girona. According to the main economic indicators identified through 1991 Census, these municipalities were classified into four categories – those with high agricultural employment, manufacturing centres, tourism-oriented centres and places with diversified economies. To make this classification, first agricultural places were selected. These municipalities stand out as having shares of their labour force in farming as high as four times the average for the province. The weight of manufacturing in a centre delimited a second municipal-type in this classification. Thus, those municipalities with their labour force being as much as three times the average of the province fall within the category of manufacturing places. As well the share of labour force in manufacturing was the decisive element to separate tourism-oriented municipalities from more diversified service places. Thus, manufacturing provides jobs to twice the Girona average of 12.4 per cent in the more diversified service municipalities; and less than twice in the tourism-oriented ones. Methodologically, this fourfold classification was used as the base for the fieldwork. Table A1.1 shows the main demographic and economic indicators of the specific municipalities where the fieldwork was carried out.

- Municipal Population Registers [*Padrón Municipal de Habitantes*].[2] Registers have basic information (e.g. sex, age, address, nationality) that is used by municipalities for different purposes (e.g. municipal taxes, elections). The INE compiles the data that are provided by municipalities and publishes its annual report *Migraciones*, which gives an account of internal migration. Every five years, municipalities, with the INE and the Institutes of Statistics of the Autonomous Communities, update their Registers. In the development of my fieldwork, some municipalities gave me addresses of foreigners living in their towns that were drawn from these Registers. But, in the majority of cases, officials argued that providing such information was against the law. Even in these cases, indications of the neighbourhoods in town where I would find African immigrants were given to me.

By contrast with this variety of official sources, official Portuguese data offer more limited insights on legal immigrants (and far less on ethnic minorities). The basic sources of information here are:

- Residence permits. The Portuguese Institute of Statistics [*Instituto Nacional de Estatística, INE*] publishes data that the Foreigners and

Borders' Service [*Serviço de Estrangeiros e Fronteiras*] collects from residence permits. The main publication of the Portuguese INE on immigration is *Estatísticas Demográficas*. This offers a table on foreign residents by nationality[3] and *distrito* of residence. From 1986, for the whole of Portugal, the number of foreigners by nationality has also been broken down by sex, age and group of professions (e.g. manufacturing and construction workers are put together in this classification). From 1990, employers have been disaggregated from employees by nationality for Portugal. From 1992, data on new permits has also been offered, by nationality, sex and age.

Table A1.2 Labour market indicators of the fieldwork municipalities in Algarve and Setúbal

	Total Population	Working population Primary	Constr.	Manuf.	Accom.	Other services
Albufeira	20,949	6.7	12.8	3.9	35.3	41.3
Faro	50,761	10.1	9.9	7.6	7.8	64.6
Loulé	45,585	12.6	15.6	8.1	17.2	46.5
Olhão	36,812	19.1	13.1	12.2	6.1	49.5
Portimão	38,833	5.1	12.7	6.0	24.1	52.1
Surveyed munic.	156,128	10.8	12.6	7.7	16.4	52.5
Algarve	341,404	13.5	14.2	7.8	15.8	48.7
Seixal	116,912	0.5	9.4	25.2	4.9	60.0
Setúbal	103,634	3.8	9.0	26.0	5.8	55.5
Surveyed munic.	220,546	1.9	9.2	25.6	5.3	58.0
Pen. Setúbal	640,493	4.0	9.5	24.6	5.0	56.9

Source: Instituto Nacional de Estatística (1996c). Data on accommodation and restaurant employment provided by the Portuguese Institute of Statistics [*Instituto Nacional de Estatística*].

• Census.[4] Updated every 10 years, the census gives limited information on foreign residents. This basically consists of the number of foreigners by nationality, age, sex and municipality of residence. For ethnic minorities, the Portuguese Census does not ask questions concerning race. On request, the Portuguese INE disaggregates further information from this source. Yet I was informed that 1991 Census data on foreigners could not be broken down by occupation or economic sector.[5] Through the 1991 Census, two main types of municipalities were identified - tourism-dominated Algarve *concelhos* and manufacturing-oriented Setúbal municipalities.

The main constraint on any survey research in the field of immigration is lack of precision in official statistics. The census gives an indication of where immigrants live (as they voluntarily fill in an official form), as well as which activities immigrants are employed in. The statistics that are provided by Ministries are more reliable about the volume of legal immigration. Yet these data are only disaggregated by province (for Spain) or *distrito* (for Portugal). In the case of Spain, the Girona office of the Ministry of Labour and Social Security gave me unpublished work permit data by municipality. Yet these data were not broken down by nationality, sector of activity or sex of legal immigrants. It follows that it was not possible to define an interview survey population using official statistical criteria. Taking the division of municipalities according to their economic specialisation as a framework for interviews, snowballing was the method used to identify African workers in the fieldwork.

Immigrant Interview Survey

First, key informants (i.e. presidents of immigrant associations, social workers and government officials) were contacted in Girona. The intention of these interviews was to gain an overview of the operation of local labour markets, and to provide a broad perspective on the role of immigrant workers within it. Local-based immigrant associations in Girona (e.g. Sant Pere Pescador's Associació 'Al-Jamaa', La Bisbal-based Asdiqa, and GRAMC, which organises itself into local assemblies) were the most common starting point for gaining access to individuals. On some occasions, following official municipal indications about where Africans lived, I approached immigrants in public spaces or at their homes. Through snowballing, 151 interviews with Africans were carried out in four types of municipality. This sample gives ample indications of the variety (or the similarity) of African labour outcomes in the province.

The strategy which was proved successful in Girona did not work as well in Algarve. One reason was that immigrant associations are heavily centralised in Lisbon and its surroundings. For instance, the Cape Verde Association in Lisbon [*Associação Cabo Verdiana*] tried to open a regional office in Algarve unsuccessfully. Faro's Angola House [*Casa de Angola*] was closed at the time of my fieldwork. For Algarve, municipal officials and social workers provided information about the areas where Africans lived, and on certain occasions addresses. This could have biased my survey, as the municipal sources mainly have information on social service users or shanty town dwellers. Aware of this, I contacted the Faro Hospital and the regional administration [*Comissão de Coordinação da Região do Algarve*] to broader my Portuguese sample. In this way, a small number of professional workers were interviewed. For Setúbal, through the Cape Verde Association of Seixal [*Associação Cabo Verdiana do Seixal*], 30 individuals were interviewed in the region.

Interviews were carried out through a questionnaire (Appendix 2). This questionnaire focused on:

- The employment histories of immigrants. This constitutes a substantial part of the questionnaire, which combines intentionally broad, open questions about worker's employment history, with more specific questions on first and current employment.[6]
- Education. Questions were asked about formal education in countries of origin, as well as any educational or vocational courses that the interviewee had taken in the host country. Additional information on language proficiency was asked (and was evaluated from interviews in Catalan or Spanish).
- Family circumstances. Here interviewees were asked about their marital status, as well as details about their spouse's work. Additional information about type of accommodation was also gathered. Those who had a family in their country of origin were asked about their views on family reunion.
- Legal status. This covered type of residential status in Iberia, the way interviewees had obtained their legal status/naturalisation, and difficulties in obtaining/renewing permits. Aware of the suspicion that this issue might raise, these questions were asked at almost the end of interviews, when both the interviewer and the interviewee were more relaxed.
- Intentions of stay. A broad, open question on her/his intention of stay in the host country closed the questionnaire.

Employer Interview Survey

The immigrant interview survey gave a clear guide on the economic sectors and the professions of Africans in the areas of study. In Girona, for example, Africans were found to be willing to work in any economic sector, as revealed by their frequent changes in employment. But, to understand the mosaic of dissimilar rates of involvement across economic sectors, alongside the divergent attributes of immigrants who gain employment in specific sectors, investigation of employer attitudes and expectations about labour force requirements was necessary. Employer interviews focused on the opportunities and restraints that they face in hiring labour and retaining workers, with particular attention to the manner in which immigrant workers are capable (or not) of meeting employer labour needs. The intention was to identify if there were inadequacies in labour supply that employers feel compel them to hire immigrant workers. This included employer evaluations of the advantages of immigrants over their own nationals in the labour market. A critical question was why employers in the same sector have dissimilar views and practices toward the employment of immigrants (not simply in general terms but also in comparing firms that do employ immigrants with those that do not). Attention was given to the manner in which immigrants gain employment (i.e. the mechanisms through which they come to the attention of employers as potential employees). Interviews with immigrant workers had already provided some insight on this issue, but a more comprehensive view was obtained through the identification of employers' strategies for attracting the appropriate skills and other labour requirements they need.

The employer survey centred on the main African economic activities in Iberia, according to previous results. For Girona, these sectors were farming, construction, the accommodation industries, as well as ceramics and metallurgical firms. For Algarve, the selected sector were construction and accommodation industries; and, for Setúbal, construction and manufacturing. The previous division of municipalities according to their economic structure was also the base for the employer survey. Thus eight economic centres (two for each of municipal-type), two Algarve *concelhos* and a further two in Setúbal. Not all economic sectors above were studied in all types of municipality. For instance, the few manufacturing firms in tourism-dominated centres had already been identified as offering no work for Africans, so manufacturing firms were not approached there.

First, a mail questionnaire survey (Appendix 3) was sent to 100 employers in Girona, 50 employers in Algarve, and 50 in Setúbal. The questionnaire was translated into Catalan, Spanish and Portuguese. The aim of this survey was to provide quantitative information on employer attitudes and employment practices. Despite a second mailing and follow-up telephone calls, this questionnaire had a poor response rate. In all, just 10 questionnaires were completed from Girona; six from Algarve and one from Setúbal. Even when questionnaires were completed, in many cases information was missing, especially for questions on financial matters.

The small number of replies that were received from the mail questionnaire meant that another approach had to be used to gather information. This resulted in a more qualitative approach being adopted. First, this was done through contact with employer associations. Associations provided the first list of potential employers to contact. The telephone directory also gave employers' names, addresses and telephone numbers. Finally, the 151 interviews with Africans in Girona, as well as the 69 in Portugal, gave me specific indications of firms that employed immigrants. In all, 32 interviews were conducted with employers in Girona and 20 in Portugal. The sample of selected companies includes firms which hire immigrants, as well as companies which do not. Approaching employers in Girona was easier than in Algarve or Setúbal. This seemed to be because of the family-based structure of the bulk of Girona firms, which made it simpler to contact the person with responsibility for hiring workers. In larger manufacturing or accommodation firms in Portugal, there was more reluctance to speak 'on behalf of the company'.

The questionnaire that was sent to employers with little success was used for interviews with employers. Yet, rather than emphasising the quantitative parts of the questionnaire, interviews were organised around the general issues of the questionnaire (e.g. seasonality of businesses, recruitment practices, competition and EU economic integration). Only for information concerning staff members, was a more numerical approach adopted (specifically, the staff numbers by professional category type, contract type, sex and origin were asked).

Data Coding and Analysis

After the fieldwork, immigrant interviews were coded. The statistical package that I used to code and process the data from the African interview survey was SPSSx. Due to the characteristics of the immigrant questionnaire, a substantial number of interviews provided the research with 'extra' information on opinions and beliefs about the current (labour) situation in host countries, as well as background information about origin countries. Analysis was also undertaken through qualitative techniques (e.g. by using quotations that reflect common views amongst a considerable number of respondants or that explain the logic for their views). The same qualitative technique was used for the employer survey.

A first set of results from the immigrant survey was sent to the European Commission in October 1995. This constituted the final report of my Human Capital and Mobility fellowship (proposal no. ERB4001GT931634). A second report, which incorporated some employer survey results, was produced at the end of my second European Union fellowship in March 1998 (proposal no. ERB4001GT956581). The final product of these two projects is this book.

Notes

1. The General Directorate for Migration [*Dirección General de Migraciones*] was the former Spanish Institute of Emigration [*Instituto Español de Emigración*]. Under this latter name, it published the *Agenda del Instituto Español de Emigración*. The *Dirección General de Migraciones* was at first part of the Ministry of Labour and Social Security, and later of the Ministry of Social Affairs. With the Conservative Party victory in the 1996 elections, the Ministry of Social Affairs merged with the Ministry of Labour and Social Security into the Ministry of Labour and Social Affairs. In order not to complicate the messages given to the reader in this book unnecessarily, the *Anuario de Migraciones* has been quoted under *Dirección General de Migraciones* (instead of under the successive Ministries of which the General Directorate has formed part).
2. New residents should register in the municipality they have moved into. If the resident is Spanish, he/she also should de-register from the municipality that he/she is leaving. Both processes are done by filling a specific form - the *Documento de Altas y Bajas Padronales.*
3. Before 1974, there are no data on Africans, as they were Portuguese nationals. From 1974 to 1983, all African nationalities are aggregated into one category. For 1984 and 1985, Cape Verde nationals are separated from other African nationals. From 1986, all the African ex-colonies are distinguished in this statistical source.
4. Portuguese municipalities do not have Population Registers. *Concelhos* create ad-hoc registers for specific purposes (e.g. elections or the re-housing of dwellers of shanty towns).
5. The Portuguese Employment Survey [*Inquérito ao Emprego*] asks about worker nationality. Information on foreigners is not published, but is available on request. Equally, the Spanish Employment Survey [*Encuesta de Población Activa*] enquiries about worker nationality. The published statistics, from this source, give the number of foreign workers by economic sector, occupation and group of nationalities (i.e. EU nationals, other Europeans, Latin Americans and others) annually for the whole of Spain.
6. Some questions were intentionally repeated. For instance, immigrants were asked about changes of residence, and, later on, about their employment histories. When interviewees described the jobs that they have taken, I could mention the places where they had lived and linked to their work history. In this way, information was double-checked. This approach also helped create more rapport with the person I was interviewing.

Appendix 2: Immigrant Interview Questionnaire

Interview number
Municipality, day and time of interview

1. Sex
    Male ☐   Female ☐

2. Current nationality (or nationalities), and nationality at birth (in case he/she naturalised).

3. Marital status.
Single ☐   Married ☐   Other (please, specify) ☐

4. Year and place of birth.

5. Year of arrival in host country.

6. What is your first language?

7. Please, indicate which language(s) you can speak fluently.

8. What is your employment situation now? (employed, self-employed, unemployed looking for a job, unemployed not looking for a job, retired, handicapped, houseperson).

CHANGES OF RESIDENCE

9. Please indicate which countries and municipalities you have lived in, the years (approximately) you lived there, and the reasons for any change of residence.

Years   Municipality and country of residence   Reason change residence

EDUCATION IN ORIGIN COUNTRY

10. Please, specify the level of formal education that you have reached, indicating the number of years of schooling and the diplomas you have obtained.
(If it does not become clear from the answer, ask if the interviewee can read and write her/his first language.)

EDUCATION IN HOST COUNTRY
11. Specify the educational or vocational training courses that you have undertaken in the host country (formal education, training courses, language courses, etc.), the years and the place where the course took place.

EMPLOYMENT HISTORY
12. Please could you give details of the jobs that you have done?

Town   Job description   Years start/end Reason change work

EMPLOYMENT HISTORY

13. First employment in the host country- Please, tell which was your first job in Portugal/Spain, where, when it was, and how did you obtain this job.

14. Current employment - Please, what is (was) your current job (or last, if the employee is out of employment at her/his interview), where did you work, when did you start (and finish) work there, and how did you obtain this job.

15. How many people work in your current firm? Are you the only African in it? If not, how many Africans are employed in your firm? Do (other) foreigners work for the firm?

16. Working condition of current (or last) job
Working hours per week
Working times
Wage
Paid holidays?
Type of contract
Length of contract

17. If Africans and other workers do the same type of work, do you believe that their wages are the same as yours?

18. Trade unions - Do you know if trade unions are active in your employment sector?
          Yes   No
If the answer is positive, ask if he/she is member of a trade union.

19. Do you think trade union policies have an effect on immigrant workers?

FAMILY CIRCUMSTANCES

20. How many people are you living with, and what is their relationship to you (if any)?

21. What type of housing do you have? (e.g. room, flat, shanty).

22. Have you got a partner?
    Yes   ☐   No   ☐   (Go to question 28).

23. Nationality (nationalities) of your partner (is he/she naturalised?).

24. Are you currently living with her/him?
    Yes   ☐   No   ☐
In case of negative answer, where is he/she living?

25. Please, describe the job of your partner.

26. <u>In case the partner is out of work in the host country</u>, is he/she looking for a job? If the answer is negative, state the reasons.

27. <u>In case the partner is in the origin country</u>, would you like your family come to Portugal/Spain? Whatever the answer, specify the reasons why he/she wants (or does not want) her/his family in the host country.

LEGAL STATUS

28. (If the interviewee has not naturalised) Do you have legal residence in this country? What type of residence permit do you have now? When did you obtain legal residence in the country? How many times have you renewed the permit?.

29. (If the interviewee has naturalised) When did you obtain the nationality? On what grounds did you obtain nationality (e.g. marriage, years of legal residence)? What was your work/residential status before naturalising?

30. Have you lost your legal status in the host country in the past?

    Yes   ☐   No   ☐

If so, specificy the reasons.

31. Did you have help when legalising your work/residential status in the host country?

    Yes   ☐   No   ☐

If so, specify which organisation that helped you and what type of help was given.

INTENTION OF STAY

32. Would you like to stay in Portugal/Spain in the next five years?

    Yes   ☐   No   ☐

Whatever the answer, please, give your reasons.

Notes and comments
Language of interview:

Level of the language (only for interviews in Catalan/Spanish):

Appendix 3: Employer Interview Questionnaire

Locality   Date

Firm name

Position of the person who answers the questionnaire in this firm

1. Is your business open the whole year?

               Yes   No

If not, over what time period did the firm close in 1996?

2. Does your company subcontract any service (e.g. cleaning)?

             Yes   No

If yes, which services?

3. Is there any time period when extra workers are needed (e.g. apple season in September in the agricultural sector; July-August in the tourist sector)?

             Yes   No

Time period   Number of extra employees   Tasks to be done

_____   _____

_____   _____

_____   _____

_____   _____

_____   _____

4. What were the average working hours of each employee per day in your company in the busiest and the least busy months of the last year? (If the number of hours did not change through the year, please fill in the column "Busiest month", leaving the column "Least busy month" blank.)

	Busiest month	Least busy month
Average working hours/week	%	%

5. How many people did your company employ in the busiest and the least busy months of last year? (if the number of employees did not change through the year, please fill in the column "Busiest month", leaving the column "Least busy month" blank).

	Busiest month	Least busy month
Name the month		
Males		
Females		
Full-time workers		
Part-time workers		
Administrative workers		
Skilled workers		
Unskilled workers		
Family members		
Those on permanent contracts		
Those on temporary contracts		

Administrative staff: employees in charge of management and administration (e.g. secretaries, managers, accountants).
Skilled workers: employees in charge of supervision and control (e.g. quality controller, foremen); employees with technical skills (e.g. carpenters, bricklayers, electricians, mechanics, receptionists, skilled manufacturing workers, drivers).
Unskilled workers: employees in charge of unskilled tasks (e.g. kitchen assistants, watchpeople, cleaning men/women, waiters/waitresses, line production workers, labourers).

6. What percentage of the skilled workers employed by your company in the busiest and the least busy months of 1996 had any kind of technical qualification (e.g. college training)?(if the number of skilled workers did not change through the year, please fill in the column "Busiest month", leaving the column "Least busy month" blank)

	Busiest month	Least busy month
Qualified skilled workers	%	%

7. In what year did the present owner take control of this business?

8. How has your firm changed over the period 1992-1997? Please, state the percentage of change either positive (please, use the symbol plus, "+") or negative (please use the symbol minus, "-") for the following enterprise indicators (e.g. if costs have decreased by 25 per cent over the period 1992-1997, please write - 25%). If the present owner took control of this business after 1992, please state the change from that moment until 1997.

                                    Change 1992-1997

Costs   % _____
Labour costs   % _____
Other costs   % _____
Labour productivity   % _____
Profits   % _____

9. Do you consider that your firm is facing stronger competition now that in 1992 (or from the year you took up your business)?

                Yes   No
If yes, could explain the reasons for this increase in competition?

10. Has your firm undertaken any changes in its activities since 1992? (e.g. product diversification, new marketing strategies). If the present owner took up the business after 1992, please state the changes from that moment until 1997.

Yes   No

If yes, please state these changes

11. Has the number of people employed or working in your company changed over the period 1992-1997? Please, indicate the number for July 1992 and July 1997. If the present owner took up the business after 1992, please state the number in July at that year and in 1997.

	July 1992	July 1997
Total number of employees		
Average hours worked per employee		
Family members		
Those on permanent contracts		
Those on temporary contracts		
Those working full-time		
Those working part-time		

12. In the busiest month of 1996, what were the nationalities of your employees? Please indicate the number of employees by nationality and sex, full-time or working-time status, professional category and hired status.

	Spanish	Other EU	Africans	Others
Males				
Females				
Full-time workers				
Part-time workers				
Administrative workers				
Skilled workers				
Unskilled workers				
Family members				
Those on permanent contracts				
Those on temporary contracts				

Administrative staff: employees in charge of management and administration (e.g. secretaries, managers, accountants).
Skilled workers: employees in charge of supervision and control (e.g. quality controller, foremen); employees with technical skills (e.g. carpenters, bricklayers, electricians, mechanics, receptionists, skilled manufacturing workers, drivers).
Unskilled workers: employees in charge of unskilled tasks (e.g. kitchen assistants, watchpeople, cleaning men/women, waiters/waitresses, line production workers, labourers).

13. If you employ African immigrants, would you indicate the reasons (tick the following statements as very important reasons, important reasons or irrelevant).

	Very important	Important	Irrelevant
Shortage of adequate qualified employees			
Shortage of seasonal employees			
Shortage of employees all year round			
Locals do not want to work in these tasks			
Africans are better prepared to do these jobs			
Africans are flexible workers			
Africans do the same job in less time			
Other reasons (please, state them)			

14. If you do not employ African immigrants, would you indicate the reasons why (tick the following statements as very important, important or irrelevant).

	Very import.	Important	Irrelevant
I have a long established good staff			
I do not employ extra seasonal workers			
Africans are poorly qualified workers			
Extra administrative problems			
Extra problems due to cultural differences			
Africans are not flexible workers			
Africans work less hard			
Other reasons (please, state them)			

15. Could you tick the recruitment practices used by your firm when hiring <u>seasonal</u> workers?

___ Seasonal workers know me and the same workers come to me each season

___ Seasonal workers ask me if there are jobs available

___ I ask my employees if they know somebody willing to work for me

___ Employment offices (e.g. Spanish INEM)

___ Adverts in the local press, on public sites, etc.

Other channels (please, state them)

16. Could you tick the recruitment practices used by your firm when hiring skilled workers?

___ They learn their skills in the firm

___ Skilled workers ask me if there are jobs available

___ I ask my employees if they know somebody willing to work for me

___ Employment offices (e.g. Spanish INEM)

___ Adverts in the local press, on public sites, etc.

Other channels (please, state them).

Please, use this space for any comment you wish to make.
Thanks for replying to this questionnaire.

Bibliography

Abellán, C., Felgueroso, F. and Lorence, J. (1997), 'La Negociación Colectiva en España: Una Reforma Pendiente', *Papeles de Economía Española*, vol. 72, pp. 250-60.

Abril, P., Castellet, R., Montenegro, S., Moreno, C. and Salas, I. (1998), *Inmigración Africana y Formación Continua en Cataluña*, Institut per al Desenvolupament de la Formació Ocupacional/Unió General de Treballadors (UGT), Barcelona.

Aguiló Pérez, E. (1996), 'Evolución y Expectativas de la Actividad Turística', in A. Pedreño Muñoz (ed.), *Introducción a la Economía del Turismo en España*, Civitas, Madrid, pp. 45-68.

Albert-Piñolé, I. (1993), 'Tourism in Spain', in W. Pompl and P. Lavery (eds), *Tourism in Europe: Structures and Developments*, Cab International, Oxon, pp. 242-61.

Aldrich, H., Jones, T.P. and McEvoy, D. (1984), 'Ethnic Advantage and Minority Business Development', in R. Ward and R. Jenkins (eds), *Ethnic Communities in Business: Strategies for Economic Survival*, Cambridge University Press, Cambridge, 189-210.

Álvarez Rodríguez, A. (1996), *Guía de la Nacionalidad Española*, Ministerio de Trabajo y Asuntos Sociales, Madrid.

André, I.A. (1991), 'The Employment of Women in Portugal', *Iberian Studies*, vol. 20, pp. 28-41.

Anido, N. and Freire, R. (1978), *L'Émigration Portugaise: Présent et Avenir*, Presses Universitaires de France, Paris.

Apap, J. (1997), 'Citizenship Rights and Migration Policies: The Case of Maghrebi Migrants in Italy and Spain', in R.L. King and R. Black (eds), *Southern Europe and the New Immigrations*, Sussex Academic Press, Brighton, 138-57.

Appleyard, R.T. (1991), *International Migration: Challenge for the Nineties*, International Organization for Migration, Genève.

Aprell Lasagabaster, C. (1994), *Régimen Administrativo de los Extranjeros en España: Ciudadanos Comunitarios y Nacionales de Terceros Estados*, Universidad de Málaga/Marcial Pons, Madrid.

Aragón Bombín, R. and Chozas Pedrero, J. (1993), *La Regularización de Inmigrantes durante 1991-1992*, Ministerio de Trabajo y Seguridad Social (Informes y Estudios. Serie General, 4), Madrid.

Arizpe, L. and Aranda, J. (1986), 'Women Workers in the Strawberry Agribusiness in Mexico', in E. Leacock and H. I. Safa (eds), *Women's Work: Development and the Division of Labor and Gender*, Bergin & Garcey Publishers, Massachusetts, pp. 174-93.

Arnalte, E. and Cena, F. (1993), 'La Agricultura y la Política Agraria en España durante el Período de Transición Democrática', *Agricultura y Sociedad*, vol. 68-69, pp. 289-312.

Ashton, D., Maguire, M. and Spilsbury, M. (1990), *Restructuring the Labour Market: the Implications for Youth*, Macmillan Press, Basingstoke.

Associação de Empresas de Construção e Obras Públicas (1997), *Relatório AECOPS da Construção 1996*, Associação de Empresas de Construção e Obras Públicas, Lisbon.

Associação Nacional dos Industriais de Material Elétrico e Electrónico (1997), *Monografia da Indústria Eléctrica e Electrónica Portuguesa 1992-96*, Associação Nacional dos Industriais de Material Eléctrico e Electrónico, Lisbon.

Atkinson, J. (1987), 'Flexibility or Fragmentation?: The United Kigdom Labour Market in the Eighties', *Labour and Society*, vol. 12, pp. 87-105.

Avellá Reus, L. (ed.) (1991), *Necesidades de Mano de Obra en la Recogida de Naranja en la Comunidad Valenciana: Estudio de la Inmigración Magrebí y Condiciones de Trabajo en el Sector*, Unpublished report for the Dirección General de Migraciones, Madrid.

Avillez, F. (1993), 'Portuguese Agriculture and the Common Agricultural Policy', in J. de S. Lopes (ed.), *Portugal and EC Membership Evaluated*, Pinter, London, pp. 30-56.

Avillez, F. and Langworthy, M. (1987), 'Intensive Agriculture in the Vale do Tejo', in S.R. Pearson, F. Avillez, J.W. Bentley, T. J. Finan, R. Fox, T. Josling, M. Langworthy, E. Monke and S. Tangermann (eds.), *Portuguese Agriculture in Transition*, Cornell University Press, Ithaca, pp. 107-23.

Avillez, F., Finan, T. and Josling, T. (1988), *Trade, Exchange Rates and Agricultural Pricing Policy in Portugal*, The World Bank, Washington.

Bacalhau, M. (1984), 'Regional Distribution of Portuguese Emigration according to Socio-Economic Context', in T.C. Bruneau, V.P. da Rosa and A. Macleod (eds), *Portugal in Development: Emigration, Industrialization, the European Community*, University of Ottawa Press, Ottawa, pp. 53-63.

Bach, R.L. and Schraml, L.A. (1982), 'Migration, Crisis and Theoretical Conflict', *International Migration Review*, vol. 16, pp. 320-41.

Baganha, M.L. (1998), 'Immigrant Involvement in the Informal Economy: The Portuguese Case', *Journal of Ethnic and Migration Studies*, vol. 24, pp. 367-85.

Bailey, A.J. (1988), 'Getting on your Bike: What Differences does a Migration History Make?', *Tijdschrift voor Economishe en Sociale Geografie*, vol. 80, pp. 312-17.

Bailey, T.R. (1987), *Immigrant and Native Workers: Contrasts and Competition*, Westview Press, Boulder.

Bailey, T.R. and Waldinger, R. (1991), 'Primary, Secondary and Enclave Labor Markets: A Training Systems Approach', *American Sociological Review*, vol. 56, pp. 432-45.

Baker, G.L. (1976), 'The Invisible Workers: Labor Organization on American Farms', in R. Merrill (ed.), *Radical Agriculture*, Harper & Row, New York, pp. 143-67.

Balcells, A. (ed.) (1991), *Moviments Migratoris a Lleida i Comarca: Problemàtica Sòcio-laboral a la Campanya Fruitera*, Ajuntament de Lleida, Lleida.

Ball, M. (1978), 'British Housing Policy and the House Building Industry', *Capital and Class*, vol. 4, pp. 78-99.

Ball, M. (1988), *Rebuilding Construction: Economic Change and the British Construction Industry*, Routledge, London.

Ballard, R. and Ballard, C. (1977), 'The Sikhs: The Development of South Asian Settlement in Britain' in J.L. Watson (ed.) *Between Two Cultures*, Blackwell, Oxford, pp. 21-56.

Ballbé, M. and Pich, E. (1994), *Dictamen sobre la Adecuación al Ordenamiento Jurídico Vigente de las Propuestas que Formula Cáritas para la Reforma del Reglamento de Extranjería*, Unpublished report for Cáritas, Barcelona.

Banco Bilbao Vizcaya (biannual), *Renta Nacional de España y su Distribución Provincial*, Banco Bilbao Vizcaya, Bilbao.

Baptista, A.M. and Moniz, F. (1985), *Migrações Internas: Algumas Observações a partir dos Fluxos Inter-regionais no Período 1973-1981*, IACEP/NEUR, Lisbon.

Baptista, F.O. (1993a), *A Política Agrária do Estado Novo*, Afrontamento, Oporto.

Baptista, F.O. (1993b), 'La Agricultura Portuguesa ante la Nueva PAC', in *Agriculturas y Políticas Agrarias en el Sur de Europa*, Ministerio de Agricultura, Pesca y Alimentación, Madrid, pp. 383-90.

Baptista, F.O. (1994), 'A Agricultura e a Questão da Terra: Do Estado Novo à Comunidade Europeia', *Análise Social*, vol. 29, pp. 907-21.

Baptista, F.O. (1995), 'Agriculture, Rural Society and the Land Question in Portugal', *Sociologia Ruralis*, vol. 35, pp. 309-21.

Barciela López, C. (1986), 'Los Costes del Franquismo en el Sector Agrario: La Ruptura del Proceso de Transformaciones', in R. Garrabou, C. Barciela and J.I. Jiménez Blanco (eds), *Historia Agraria de la España Contemporánea: el Fin de la Agricultura Tradicional (1940-1960)*, Crítica, Barcelona, pp. 383-454.

Barron, R.D. and Norris, G.M. (1976), 'Sexual Divisions and the Dual Labour Market', in D.L. Barker and S. Allen (eds.), *Dependence and Exploitation in Work and Marriage*, Longman, London, pp. 47-69.

Bauer, T. and Zimmermann, K. (1994), 'Modelling International Migration: Economic and Econometric Issues', in *Causes of International Migration: Proceedings of a Workshop*, Office for Official Publications of the European Communities, Luxembourg, pp. 95-115.

Becker, G.S. (1964), *Human Capital: A Theoretical and Empirical Analysis, with Special Reference to Education*, University of Chicago, Chicago.

Beechey, V. (1988), 'Rethinking the Definition of Work: Gender and Work', in J. Jenson, E. Hagen and C. Reddy (eds), *Feminization of the Labour Force: Paradoxes and Promises*, Polity Press, Cambridge, pp. 45-62.

Beltrán Antolín, J. (1997), 'Immigrés Chinois en Espagne ou Citoyens Européens?', *Revue Européenne des Migrations Internationales*, vol. 13, pp. 63-79.

Bentley, J.W. (1992), *Today There Is No Misery: The Ethnography of Farming in Northwest Portugal*, The University of Arizona Press, Tucson.

Bentolila, S. (1992), 'Migració i Ajust Laboral a les Regions Espanyoles', *Nota d'Economia*, vol. 43, pp. 85-99.

Bentolila, S. (1997), 'La Inmovilidad del Trabajo en las Regiones Españolas', *Papeles de Economía*, vol. 72, pp. 168-76.

Bentolila, S. and Dolado, J.J. (1994), 'Labour Flexibility and Wages: Lessons from Spain', *Economic Policy*, vol. 18, pp. 55-99.

Berger, S. and Piore, M.J. (1980), *Dualism and Discontinuity in Industrial Societies*, Cambridge University Press, Cambridge.

Berges, M.T. (1993), 'La Inmigración Filipina', in C. Giménez Romero (ed.) *Inmigrantes Extranjeros en Madrid: Estudios Monográficos de Colectivos Inmigrantes*, Comunidad de Madrid, Madrid, pp. 561-619.

Berlan, J.-P. (1986), 'Agriculture et Migrations', *Revue Européenne des Migrations Internationales*, vol. 2, pp. 9-32.

Berlan, J.-P. (1987), 'La Agricultura y el Mercado de Trabajo: ¿Una California para Europa?', *Agricultura y Sociedad*, vol. 42, pp. 233-45.

Bielby, W.T. and Bielby, D.D. (1992), 'I Will Follow Him: Family Ties, Gender Role Beliefs, and Reluctance to Relocate for a Better Job', *American Journal of Sociology*, vol. 97, pp. 1241-67.

Bilbao, A. (1990), 'La Lógica del Estado del Bienestar y la Lógica de su Crítica: Keynes y Misses', *Papers: Revista de Sociologia*, vol. 34, pp. 13-29.

Black, R. (1992), *Crisis and Change in Rural Europe: Agricultural Development in the Portuguese Mountains*, Avebury, Aldershot.

Black, R. (1994), 'Asylum Policy and the Marginalization of Refugees in Greece', in W.T.S. Gould and A.M. Findlay (eds), *Population Migration and the Changing World Order*, John Wiley & Sons, Chichester, pp. 145-60.

Blanchard, O. and Jimeno, J.J. (1995), 'Structural Unemployment: Spain versus Portugal', *American Economic Review*, vol. 85, pp. 212-8.

Blanco Fernández de Valderrama, C. (1993), 'The New Hosts: The Case of Spain', *International Migration Review*, vol. 27, pp. 169-81.

Blanco Gutiérrez, M.A. (1993), 'Hacia una Restructuración de las Migraciones Interregionales en España', *Estudios Geográficos*, vol. 210, pp. 51-74.

Blanes, A., Gil, F. and Pérez, J. (1996), *Población y Actividad en España: Evolución y Perspectivas*, Caja de Ahorros y Pensiones de Barcelona, Barcelona.

Böcker, A. (1995), 'Migration Networks: Turkish Migration to Western Europe', in *Causes of International Migration: Proceedings of a Workshop,* Office for Official Publications of the European Communities, Luxembourg, pp. 151-71.

Böhning, W.R. (1972), *The Migration of Workers in the United Kingdom and the European Community*, Oxford University Press, Oxford.

Böhning, W.R. (1981), 'Elements of a Theory of International Economic Migration to Industrial Nation States', in M.M. Kritz, C.B. Keely and S.M. Tomasi (eds),

Global Trends in Migration: Theory and Research on International Population Movements, Center for Migration Studies, New York, pp. 28-43.

Boissevain, J. (1984), 'Small Entrepreneurs in Contemporary Europe', in R. Ward and R. Jenkins (eds) *Ethnic Communities in Business: Strategies for Economic Survival*, Cambridge University Press, Cambridge, pp. 20-38.

Bonacich, E. (1973), 'A Theory of Middleman Minorities', *American Sociological Review*, vol. 38, pp. 583-94.

Boniface, B.G. and Cooper, C. (1994), *The Geography of Travel & Tourism*, Butterworth Heinemann, Oxford.

Borjas, G.J. (1982), 'The Earnings of Male Hispanic Immigrants in the United States', *Industrial and Labor Relations Review*, vol. 35, pp. 343-53.

Borjas, G.J. (1985), 'Assimilation, Changes in Cohort Quality, and the Earnings of Immigrants', *Journal of Labor Economics*, vol. 3, pp. 463-89.

Borjas, G.J. (1987), 'Immigrants, Minorities, and Labor Market Competition', *Industrial and Labor Relations Review*, vol. 40, pp. 382-92.

Borjas, G.J. (1989), 'Economic Theory and International Migration', *International Migration Review*, vol. 23, pp. 457-85.

Borooah, V.K. and Hart, M. (1995), 'Labour Market Outcomes and Economic Exclusion', *Regional Studies*, vol. 29, pp. 433-8.

Bote Gómez, V. and Sinclair, M.T. (1996), 'Tourism Demand and Supply', in M. Barke, J. Towner and M.T. Newton (eds), *Tourism in Spain: Critical Issues*, CAB International, Oxon, pp. 65-88.

Boyd, M. (1989), 'Family and Personal Networks in International Migration: Recent Development and New Agendas', *International Migration Review*, vol. 23, pp. 638-70.

Branco, F. and Mello, A.S. (1992), 'Why Are Wages in Portugal Lower than Elsewhere in the EEC?', in J.F. do Amaral, D. Lucena and A.S. Mello (eds) *The Portuguese Economy towards 1992*, Kluwer Academic Press, Boston, pp. 131-52.

Brandes, S. (1976), 'The Impact of Emigration of a Castilian Mountain Village', in J.B. Aceves and W.A. Douglass (eds), *The Changing Faces of Rural Spain*, John Wiley & Sons, New York, pp. 1-16.

Brassloff, W. (1993), 'Employment and Unemployment in Spain and Portugal', *Journal of the Association for Contemporary Iberian Studies*, vol. 6, pp. 2-24.

Breathnach, P., Henry, M., Drea, S. and O'Flaherty, M. (1994), 'Gender in Irish Tourism Employment', in V. Kinnaird and D. Hall (eds), *Tourism: a Gender Analysis*, John Wiley & Sons, Chichester, pp. 52-73.

Brettell, C. (1986), *Men who Migrate, Women who Wait: Population and History in a Portuguese Parish*, Princeton University Press, Princeton.

Buchan, J., Seccombe, I. and Bull, J. (1992), *The International Mobility of Nurses: A UK Perspective*, Institute of Manpower Studies (Report 230), University of Sussex, Brighton.

Burchell, B and Rubery, J. (1994), 'Divided Women: Labour Market Segmentation and Gender Segregation', in A. MacEwen-Scott (ed.), *Gender Segregation and Social Change*, Oxford University Press, Oxford, pp. 80-120.

Burke, J. (1998), 'Foreign Doctors Flood into Britain', *The Sunday Times*, 25 January 1998.

Byron, M. (1993), *The Housing Question: Caribbean Migrants and the British Housing Market*, School of Geography (Research paper 49), University of Oxford, Oxford.

Byron, M. (1994), *Post-War Caribbean Migration to Britain: the Unfinished Cycle*, Avebury, Aldershot.

Cabré, A. (1999), *El Sistema Català de Reproducció*, Proa/Institut Català de la Mediterrània, Barcelona.

Cabré, A. (1992), 'El Futur de les Migracions Estrangeres a Catalunya: Apunts per a una Perspectiva escolar', *Papers de Demografia*, vol. 63.

Cachón Rodríguez, L. (1995), 'Marco Institucional de la Discriminación y Tipos de Inmigrantes en el Mercado de Trabajo en España', *Revista Española de Investigaciones Sociológicas*, vol. 69, pp. 105-24.

Calcedo Ordóñez, V. (1996), 'Disparidades Regionales en la Agricultura Española', *Papeles de Economía Española*, vol. 67, pp. 110-33.

Cals, J. (1974), *Turismo y Política Turística en España: Una Aproximación*, Ariel, Barcelona.

Cals, J. (ed.) (1987), *L'Alt Empordà: Recursos i Estructura Econòmica*, Caixa d'Estalvis de Catalunya, Barcelona.

Cals, J., Esteban, J. and Teixidor, C. (1977), 'Les Processus d'Urbanisation Touristique sur la Costa Brava', *Revue Géographique des Pyrénées et du Sud-Ouest*, vol. 48, pp. 199-208.

Cambra Oficial de Comerç, Indústria i Navegació de Barcelona (1989), *Estudio Sòcio-econòmic de la Indústria a la Comarca d'Osona*, Delegació comarcal d'Osona de la Cambra Oficial de Comerç, Indústria i Navegació de Barcelona, Barcelona.

Campani, G. (1989), 'Du Tiers-Monde à l'Italie: Une Nouvelle Immigration Féminine', *Revue Européenne des Migrations Internationales*, vol. 5, pp. 29-49.

Campus, A. and Perrone, L. (1990), 'Senegalesi e Marocchini: Inserimento nel Mercato del Lavoro e Progetti Migratori a Confronto', *Studi Emigrazione/Études Migrations*, vol. 27, pp. 191-220.

Cardelús, J. and Pascual de Sans, À. (1979), *Movimientos Migratorios y Organización Social*, Península, Barcelona.

Cardoso, A.S. (1983), *The Illegal Housing Sector in Portugal: Bairros Clandestinos*, University of Reading (Geographical Paper, 78), Reading.

Cardoso, A.S. and Perista, H. (1994), 'A Cidade Esquecida: Pobreza em Bairros Degradados de Lisboa', *Sociologia: Problemas e Práticas*, vol. 15, pp. 99-111.

Carita, C. and Rosendo, V.N. (1993), 'Associativismo Cabo-Verdiano em Portugal: Estudo de Caso da Associação Cabo-Verdiana em Lisboa', *Sociologia: Problemas e Práticas*, vol. 13, pp. 135-52.

Carliner, G. (1980), 'Wages, Earnings and Hours of First, Second, and Third Generation American Males', *Economic Inquiry*, vol. 18, pp. 87-102.

Carreira, A. (1982), *The People of the Cape Verde Islands: Exploitation and Emigration*, C. Hurst & Company, London.

Carreras Yáñez, J.L. (1992), 'Perspectivas de la Construcción en la Década de los 90', *Papeles de Economía Española*, vol. 50, pp. 210-37.

Carrière, J.-P. (1989), *Les Transformations Agraires au Portugal: Crise, Réformes et Financement de l'Agriculture*, Economica, Paris.

Carvalho, M. (1997), 'O Verão Quente da Construção', *O Público*, 10 September 1997.

Castells, M. (1979), *City, Class and Power*, Saint Martin's Press, New York.

Castells, M. (1989), *The Informational City: Information Technology, Restructuring and the Urban-Regional Process*, Blackwell, Oxford.

Castillo Castillo, J. (1980), *La Emigración Española en la Encrucijada: Estudio Empírico de la Emigración de Retorno*, Centro de Investigaciones Sociológicas, Madrid.

Castillo, S. and Duce, R. (1997), 'El Paro Juvenil en Europa', *Papeles de Economía Española*, vol. 72, pp. 106-21.

Castles, S. and Kosack, G. (1973), *Immigrant Workers and Class Structure in Western Europe*, Oxford University Press, London.

Castles, S. and Miller, M.J. (1993), *The Age of Migration: International Population Movements in the Modern World*, Macmillan, Basingstoke.

Castles, S., Booth, H. and Wallace, T. (1987), *Here for Good: Western Europe's New Ethnic Minorities*, Pluto Press, London.

Catani, M. and Palidda, S. (1989), 'Devenir Français: Pourquoi Certain Jeunes Étrangers y Rénoncent?', *Revue Européenne des Migrations Internationales*, vol. 5, pp. 89-106.

Cater, J. (1984), 'Acquiring Premises: A Case Study of Asians in Bradford', in R. Ward and R. Jenkins (eds), *Ethnic Communities in Business: Strategies for Economic Survival*, Cambridge University Press, Cambridge, pp. 211-28.

Cavaco, C. (1980), *Turismo e Demografia no Algarve*, Progresso Social e Democracia, Lisbon.

Cavaco, C. (1981), 'Alguns Aspectos das Estructuras Agrárias de Portugal Continental', in *I Coloquio Ibérico de Geografía*, Ediciones Universitarias de Salamanca, Salamanca, pp. 117-29.

Cavaco, C. (1993), 'A Place in the Sun: Return Migration and Rural Change in Portugal', in R.L. King (ed.), *Mass Migration in Europe: the Legacy and the Future*, Belhaven, London, pp. 174-91.

Cazorla Pérez, J. (1989), *Retorno al Sur*, Siglo XXI/Oficina de Coordenación Asistencia a Emigrantes Retornados, Madrid.

Cazorla, J., Gregory, D.D. and Neto, J.P. (1979), 'El Retorno de los Emigrantes al Sur de Iberia', *Papers: Revista de Sociologia*, vol. 11, pp. 65-80.

Centro de Investigaciones Sociológicas (1986), *Condiciones de Vida y Trabajo en España*, Ministerio de Economía y Hacienda, Madrid.

Chant, S. (1992), 'Conclusion: Towards a Framework for the Analysis of Gender-Selective Migration', in S. Chant (ed.), *Gender and Migration in Developing Countries*, Belhaven Press, London, pp. 197-206.

Checa, F. (1995), 'Oportunidades Socioeconómicas en el Proceso Migratorio de los Inmigrantes Africanos en Almería', *Agricultura y Sociedad*, vol. 77, pp. 41-82.

Chell, V. (1997), 'Gender-Selective Migration: Somalian and Filipina Women in Rome', in R.L. King and R. Black (eds), *Southern Europe and the New Immigrations*, Sussex Academic Press, Brighton, pp. 75-92.

Chislett, W. (1997), *Portugal: Investment and Growth*, Euromoney publications, London.

Chiswick, B.R. (1978), 'The Effect of Americanization on the Earnings of Foreign-Born Men', *Journal of Political Economy*, vol. 86, pp. 897-922.

Chiswick, B.R. (1991), 'Speaking, Reading and Earnings among Low-Skilled Immigrants', *Journal of Labor Economics*, vol. 9, pp. 149-70.

Cia, B. and Piñol, À. (1994), 'Yo, Argelino: Inmigrantes Magrebíes Dicen Ser de Argelia para Evitar la Expulsión de España', *El País*, Catalan Edition, 8 March 1994.

Civitas (1994), *Legislación sobre Extranjeros*, Civitas, Madrid.

Closa, C. (1992), 'The Concept of Citizenship in the Treaty of European Union', *Common Market Law Review*, vol. 29, pp. 1137-69.

Colectivo IOÉ (1987), *Los Inmigrantes en España*, Cáritas Española (Documentación Social, 66), Madrid.

Colectivo IOÉ (1992), *Los Trabajadores Extranjeros en España*, Unpublished report for the Instituto Sindical de Estudios, Madrid.

Colectivo IOÉ (1994), *Marroquins a Catalunya*, Institut Català d'Estudis Mediterranis, Barcelona.

Coleman, D.A. (1992), 'Does Europe Need Immigrants?: Population and Work Force Projection', *International Migration Review*, vol. 26, pp. 413-61.

Coleman, D.A. (1995), 'Immigration Policy in Great Britain', in F Heckmann and W. Bosswick (eds), *Migration Policies: a Comparative Perspective*, Enke, Berlin, pp. 113-36.

Colino Sueiras, J. (1984), *La Integración de la Agricultura Gallega en el Capitalismo: el Horizonte de la CEE*, Instituto de Estudios Agrarios, Pesqueros y Alimentarios, Madrid.

Comisión Interministerial de Extranjería (annual), *Anuario Estadístico de Extranjería*, Comisión Interministerial de Extranjería, Madrid.

Comissão de Coordenação da Região do Algarve (1993), *Plano Regional de Turismo no Algarve: Capacidade de Alojamento Hoteleiro e Pessoal ao Serviço na Hoteleria,* Comissão de Coordenação da Região do Algarve, Faro.

Commission of the European Communities (undated), *Migration and Labour Mobility in the European Community*, Commission of the European Communities, Luxembourg.

Commission of the European Communities (1991), *Economic Paper: Portugal*, Commission of the European Communities, Directorate General for Economic and Financial Affairs, Brussels.

Commission of the European Communities (1993), *The Evolution in Holiday Travel Facilities and in the Flow of Tourism inside and outside the European Community: Main Report,* Office for Official Publications of the European Communities, Luxembourg.

Cónim, C. and Carrilho, M.J. (1989), *Situação Demográfica e Perspectivas de Evolução: Portugal 1960-2000*, Instituto de Estudos para o Desenvolvimento, Lisbon.

Consell Insular de Mallorca (1993), *Estudi sobre la Població d'Origen Magribí a Mallorca*, Consell Insular de Mallorca, Palma de Mallorca.

Convey, A. and Kupiszewski, M. (1996), 'Migration and Policy in the European Union', in P. Rees, J. Stillwell, A. Convey and M. Kupiszewski (eds), *Population Migration in the European Union*, John Wiley & Sons, Chichester, pp. 311-29.

Cook, E. and Hill, B. (1994), *Economic Aspects of Cereal Production in the EC*, Office for Official Publications of the European Communities, Luxembourg.

Corkill, D. (1993), *The Portuguese Economy since 1974*, Edinburgh University Press, Edinburgh.

Cornelius, W.A. (1994), 'Spain: The Uneasy Transition from Labor Exporter to Labor Importer', in W.A. Cornelius, P.L. Martin and J.F. Hollifield (eds), *Controlling Immigration: a Global Perspective*, Stanford University Press, Stanford, pp. 331-69.

Costa, H.A. (1994), 'A Construção do Pacto Social em Portugal', *Revista Crítica de Ciências Sociais*, vol. 39, pp. 119-46.

Costa-Lascoux, J. (1989), 'L'Europe des Politiques Migratoires: France, Italie, Pays-Bas, RFA', *Revue Européenne des Migrations Internationales*, vol. 5, pp. 161-77.

Costa-Pau, M. (1995), 'Crece un 34% el Número de Inmigrantes Ilegales Expulsados en el Área de Girona', *El País*, Catalan Edition, 7 December 1995.

Costes, L. (1994), *L'Étranger sous Terre: Commerçants et Vendeurs à la Sauvette du Métro Parisien*, L'Harmattan, Paris.

Courakis, A.S. and Roque, F.M. (1992), 'Portuguese Pattern of Trade in Manufactures', in J.F. do Amaral, D. Lucena and A.S. Mello (eds), *Portuguese Economy towards 1992*, Kluwer Academic Publishers, Boston, pp. 233-55.

Cózar, M.E. (1996), 'La Inmigración de Origen Marroquí en Almería', in Taller de Estudios Internacionales Mediterráneos (ed.), *Atlas de la Inmigración Magrebí en España*, Universidad Autónoma de Madrid, Madrid, pp. 115-17.

Cruces Roldán, C. and Martín Díaz, E. (1997), 'Intensificación Agraria y Transformaciones Socioculturales en Andalucía Occidental: Análisis Comparado de la Costa Noreste de Cádiz y el Condado Litoral de Huelva', *Sociología del Trabajo*, vol. 30, pp. 43-69.

Cruz-Villalón, J. (1987), 'Political and Economic Change in Spanish Agriculture 1950-1985', *Antipode*, vol. 19, pp. 119-33.

Cruz, J. (1993), 'El Futuro de las Agriculturas del Sur de Europa', in *Agriculturas y Políticas Agrarias en el Sur de Europa*, Ministerio de Agricultura, Pesca y Alimentación, Madrid, pp. 517-37.

Cutileiro, J. (1971), *A Portuguese Rural Society*, Oxford University Press, Oxford.

Cyrus, N. (1994), 'Flexible Work for Fragmented Labour Markets: The Significance of the New Labour Migration Regime in the Federal Republic of Germany', *Migration*, vol. 26, pp. 97-124.

Daveau, S. (1995), *Portugal Geográfico*, João Sá da Costa, Lisbon.

DeFreitas, G. (1991), *Inequality at Work: Hispanics in the U.S. Labor Force*, Oxford University Press, Oxford.

DeWind, J. and Kasinitz, P. (1997), 'Everything Old Is New Again?: Processes and Theories of Immigrant Incorporation', *International Migration Review*, vol. 31, pp. 1096-111.

Dirección General de Migraciones (annual), *Anuario de Migraciones*, Dirección General de Migraciones, Madrid.

Dirección General de Migraciones (1997a), *Informe: Contingente 1997*, Unpublished report for the Dirección General de Migraciones, Madrid.

Doeringer, P. B. and Piore, M. J. (1971), *Internal Labor Markets and Manpower Analysis*, Lexington Books, Lexington.

Drain, M. (1994), 'L'Agriculture Portugaise: Évolution et Perspectives', *Peuples Méditerranéens*, vol. 66, pp. 103-20.

Dubois, C. (1994), 'L'Épineux Dossier des Retornados', in J.-L. Miège and C. Dubois (eds), *L'Europe Retrouvée: Les Migrations de la Décolonisation*, L'Harmattan, Paris, pp. 213-46.

Dunbar, T. and Kravitz, L. (1976), *Hard Travelling: Migrant Farm Workers in America*, Ballinger, Cambridge.

Eaton, M. (1996), 'Residents Étrangers et Immigrés en Situation Irrégulière au Portugal', *Revue Européenne des Migrations Internationales*, vol. 12, pp. 203-12.

Eccles, J. and Fuller, G. W. (1970), 'Tomato Production in Portugal Promoted by the Heinz Company', in A. H. Bunting (ed.), *Change in Agriculture*, Duckworth, London, pp. 257-62.

Edwards, J. and Sampaio, F. (1993), 'Tourism in Portugal', in W. Pompl and P. Lavery (eds), *Tourism in Europe: Structures and Developments*, CAB International, Oxfordshire, pp. 262-84.

Eisfeld, R. (1989), 'Portugal in the European Community 1986-1988: The Impact of the First Half of the Transition Period', *Iberian Studies*, vol. 18, pp. 156-65.

El País (1995), 'El Ayuntamiento de El Prat se Declara a Favor del Derecho de Voto para los Inmigrantes', *El País*, Catalan Edition, 13 October 1995.

Enciso Rodríguez, J. P. and Sabaté, P. (1995), 'Dinámica Ocupacional de la Mano de Obra no Asalariada en las Explotaciones Agrarias Españolas', *Agricultura y Sociedad*, vol. 76, pp. 245-64.

Escuin Palop, V. (1991), *Régimen Jurídico de la Entrada y Permanencia de Extranjeros en España*, Centro de Estudios Constitucionales, Madrid.

Espina, A. (1990), *Empleo, Democracia y Relaciones Industriales en España*, Ministerio de Trabajo y Seguridad Social, Madrid.

Esteves, M. C. (ed.) (1991), *Portugal, País de Imigração*, Instituto de Estudos para o Desenvolvimento, Lisbon.

Etxezarreta, M. (1992), 'Transformation of the Labour System of Work Processes in a Rapidly Modernising Agriculture: The Evolving Case of Spain', in T. Marsden, P. Lowe and S. Whatmore (eds), *Labour and Locality,* David Fulton, London, pp. 44-67.

Etxezarreta, M. and Viladomiu, L. (1989), 'The Restructuring of Spanish Agriculture, and Spain's Accession to the EEC', in D. Goodman and M.

Redclift (eds), *The International Farm Crisis*, Macmillan, Basingstoke, pp. 156-82.

European Parliament (1996a), *Briefing on Asylum and Immigration Policy*, European Parliament, Task Force on the 'Intergovernmental Conference', Luxembourg.

European Parliament (1996b), *Briefing on the Intergovernmental Conference and the Schengen Convention*, European Parliament. Task Force on the 'Intergovernmental Conference', Luxembourg.

Eurostat (1995), *Migration Statistics 1995*, Office for Official Publications of the European Communities, Luxembourg.

Eurostat (1996), *Eurostat, Yearbook'96: a Statistical Eye on Europe 1985-1995*, Office for Official Publications of the European Communities, Luxembourg.

Eurostat (1997a), *Regions: Statistical Yearbook 1996*, Office for Official Publications of the European Communities, Luxembourg.

Eurostat (1997b), *Total Income of Agricultural Households: 1996 Report*, Office for Official Publications of the European Communities, Luxembourg.

Eurostat (1997c), *Tourism: Annual Statistics 1994*, Office for Official Publications of the European Communities, Luxembourg.

Eurostat (1998), *Data for Short-Term Economic Analysis*, Office for Official Publications of the European Communities, Luxembourg.

Evans, S. (1991), 'The State and Construction Performance in Britain', in H. Rainbird and G. Syben (eds), *Restructuring a Traditional Industry: Construction Employment and Skills in Europe*, Berg, New York, pp. 25-41.

Expresso (1996), 'Construção e Obras Públicas: Ordenados Aumentaram 6,1% em 95', *Expresso*, 13 April 1996.

Fawcett, J.T. (1989), 'Networks, Linkages and Migration Systems', *International Migration Review*, vol. 23, pp. 671-80.

Ferrão, J. (1987), 'Social Structures, Labour Markets and Spatial Configurations in Modern Portugal', *Antipode*, vol. 19, pp. 99-118.

Ferreira, A.F. (1988), 'Política(s) de Habitação em Portugal', *Sociedade e Território*, vol. 6, pp. 54-62.

Ferreira, A.C. (1994a), 'O Estado e a Resolução dos Conflitos de Trabalho', *Revista Crítica de Ciências Sociais*, vol. 39, pp. 89-117.

Ferreira, M.E. (1994b), 'Relações entre Portugal e África de Língua Portuguesa: Comércio, Investimento e Dívida (1973-1994)', *Análise Social*, vol. 29, pp. 1071-1121.

Ferrer Regales, M. and Calvo Miranda, J.J. (1987), 'The Recent Evolution of Regional Growth in Spain', *Iberian Studies*, vol. 16, pp. 20-34.

Fielding, A. (1993), 'Mass Migration and Economic Restructuring', in R.L. King (ed.), *Mass Migration in Europe: The Legacy and the Future*, Belhaven Press, London, pp. 7-18.

Flowerdew, R. and Salt, J. (1979), 'Migrations between Labour Markets in Great Britain', *Regional Studies*, vol. 13, pp. 211-31.

Fontana, J. and Nadal, J. (1976), 'Spain, 1914-1970', in C.M. Cipolla (ed.), *The Fontana Economic History of Europe: Contemporary Economies,* Collins/Fontana Books, Glasgow, pp. 460-529.

Fox, R. (1987), 'Extensive Farming in the Alentejo', in S.R. Pearson, F. Avillez, J.W. Bentley, T.J. Finan, R. Fox, T. Josling, M. Langworthy, E. Monke and S. Tangermann (eds), *Portuguese Agriculture in Transition*, Cornell University Press, Ithaca, pp. 85-106.

França, L. de (1992), *A Comunidade Cabo Verdiana em Portugal*, Instituto de Estudos para o Desenvolvimento, Lisbon.

Freeman, G.P. (1979), *Immigrant Labor and Racial Conflict in Industrial Societies: the French and British Experience 1945-1975*, Princeton University Press, Princeton.

Freeman, G.P. (1995), 'Modes of Immigration Politics in Liberal Democratic States', *International Migration Review*, vol. 29, pp. 881-902.

Fuente, I. (1998), 'El Cupo de los Sueños', *El País*, European Edition, 21 June 1998.

Fuentes, M.A., Cansino, M. and Echevarría, L. (1988), 'Inmigrantes Africanos en Lérida', *Población*, vol. 1, pp. 29-35.

Gabinet d'Estudis Socials (1995), *Entre el Sud i el Nord: Els Treballadors Estrangers a Catalunya*, Generalitat de Catalunya, Barcelona.

Galaz, J.A. (1993), 'La Inmigración Portuguesa en España', *Polígonos*, vol. 3, pp. 159-62.

Gale, S. (1973), 'Explanation Theory and Models of Migration', *Economic Geography*, vol. 49, pp. 257-74.

García Barbancho, A. (1975), *Las Migraciones Interiores Españolas en 1961-1970*, Instituto de Estudios Económicos, Madrid.

García Lizana, A. and Alcudia, P. (1990), 'The Evolution of the Spanish and Portuguese Economies and Labour Markets since the 1970s', *Iberian Studies*, vol. 19, pp. 84-94.

García-Ramon, M.D. (1985), 'Agricultural Change in an Industrializing Area: The Case of Tarragona', in R. Hudson and J. Lewis (eds), *Uneven Development in Southern Europe: Studies of Accumulation, Class, Migration and the State*, Methuen, London, pp. 140-54.

García-Ramon, M.D., Cruz Villalón, J., Salamaña Segura, I. and Villarino Pérez, M. (1995), *Mujer y Agricultura en España: Género, Trabajo y Contexto Regional*, Oikos-Tau, Barcelona.

Garmendía, J.A. (ed.) (1981), *La Emigración Española en la Encrucijada: Marco General de la Emigración de Retorno*, Consejo Superior de Investigaciones Científicas, Madrid.

Garrido, H. and Vicente, I. (1996), 'Restrições aos Recibos Verdes Vão Aumentar Contratos a Prazo', *Expresso*, 25 May 1996.

Generalitat de Catalunya (1994), *La Temporada Turística a Catalunya 1993*, Generalitat de Catalunya, Departament de Comerç, Consum i Turisme, Barcelona.

Generalitat de Catalunya (1995), *Atur Registrat a Catalunya*, Generalitat de Catalunya. Departament de Treball, Barcelona.

Giles, A.K. (1964), *Economic Aspects of Cereal Production*, Department of Agricultural Economics and Management, (Miscellaneous Studies 37), University of Reading, Reading.

Gimble, D.E. (1991), 'Institutionalist Labor Market Theory and the Veblenian Dichotomy', *Journal of Economic Issues*, vol. 25, pp. 625-48.

Giménez Romero, C. (1992), 'Trabajadores Extranjeros en la Agricultura Española: Enclaves e Implicaciones', *Estudios Regionales*, vol. 31, pp. 127-47.

Giner, S. and Sevilla, E. (1979), 'From Despotism to Parliamentarism: Class Domination and Political Order in the Spanish State', *Iberian Studies*, vol. 8, pp. 69-83.

Goldfarb, R.L. (1981), *Migrant Farm Workers: a Caste in Despair,* Iona State University Press, Ames.

González, P. and Moral, P. (1996), 'Analysis of Tourism Trends in Spain', *Annals of Tourism Research*, vol. 23, pp. 739-54.

Gordon, I. (1989), 'The Role of International Migration in the Changing European Labour Market', in I. Gordon and A.P. Thirlwall (eds), *European Factor Mobility: Trends and Consequences*, Macmillan, Basingstoke, pp. 13-29.

Gordon, I. (1995), 'Migration in a Segmented Labour Market', *Transactions of the Institute of British Geographers*, vol. 20, pp. 139-55.

Gozálvez Pérez, V. (1990), 'El Reciente Incremento de la Población Extranjera en España y su Incidencia Laboral', *Investigaciones Geográficas*, vol. 8, pp. 7-36.

Gozálvez Pérez, V. (ed.) (1995), *Inmigrantes Marroquíes y Senegaleses en la España Mediterránea*, Generalitat Valenciana, Valencia.

Graham, H. (1990), 'Money and Migration in Modern Portugal: An Economist's View', in D. Higgs (ed.), *Portuguese Migration in Global Perspective*, The Multicultural History Society of Toronto, Toronto, pp. 81-96.

Granovetter, M. (1985), 'Economic Action and Social Structure: The Problem of Embeddedness', *American Journal of Sociology*, vol. 91, pp. 481-510.

Grasmuck, S. and Pessar, P.R. (1991), *Between Two Islands: Dominican International Migration*, University of California Press, Berkeley.

Green, S.S. (1983), 'Silicon Valley's Women Work: A Theoretical Analysis of Sex-Segregation in the Electronical Industry Labor Market', in J. Nash and M.P. Fernández-Kelly (eds), *Women, Men, and the International Division of Labor*, State University of New York Press, Albany, pp. 273-331.

Greenwood, D.J. (1976), *Unrewarding Wealth: The Commercialization and Collapse of Agriculture in a Spanish Basque Town*, Cambridge University Press, Cambridge.

Greenwood, M.J. (1975), 'Research on Internal Migration in the United States: A Survey', *The Journal of Economic Literature*, vol. 13, pp. 397-433.

Grieco, M. (1987), *Keeping it in the Family: Social Networks and Employment Chance*, Tavistock, London.

Grossman, J.B. (1982), 'The Substitutability of Natives and Immigrants in Production', *Review of Economics and Statistics*, vol. 64, pp. 596-603.

Guibentif, P. (1996), 'Le Portugal Face à l'Immigration', *Revue Européenne des Migrations Internationales,* vol. 12, pp. 121-39.

Gurack, D.T. and Caces, F. (1992), 'Migration Networks and the Shaping of Migration Systems', in M.M. Kritz, L.L Lim and H. Zlotnik (eds), *International Migration Systems: a Global Approach*, Clarendon Press, Oxford, pp. 150-76.

Hadjimichalis, C. (1987), *Uneven Development and Regionalism: State, Territory and Class in Southern Europe,* Croom Helm, London.

Hammar, T. (1990), *Democracy and the Nation State: Aliens, Denizens and Citizens in a World of International Migration,* Avebury, Aldershot.

Hancock, M. (1983), 'Transnational Production and Women Workers', in A. Phizacklea (ed.), *One Way Ticket: Migration and Female Labour,* Routledge and Kegan Paul, London, pp. 131-45.

Hanson, S. and Pratt, G. (1991), 'Job Search and the Occupational Segregration of Women', *Annals of the Association of American Geographers,* vol. 81, pp. 229-53.

Hargreaves, A.C. (1995), *Immigration, 'Race' and Ethnicity in Contemporary France,* Routledge, London.

Harris, J.R. and Todaro, M.P. (1970), 'Migration, Unemployment and Development: A Two-Sector Analysis', *American Economic Review,* vol. 60, pp. 142-62.

Harzing, A.K. (1995), 'The Labour-Market Position of Women from Ethnic Minorities: A Comparison of Four European Countries', in A. van Doorne-Huiskes, J. Hoof and E. Roelofs (eds), *Women and the European Labour Markets,* Paul Chapman, London, pp. 53-71.

Haughton, G., Johnson, S., Murphy, L. and Thomas, K. (1993), *Local Geographies of Unemployment: Long-Term Unemployment in Areas of Local Deprivation,* Avebury, Aldershot.

Hendershott, A.B. (1995), *Moving for Work: the Sociology of Relocating in the 1990s,* University Press of America, Lanham.

Hennessy, J. (1994), 'Female Employment in Tourism Development in South-West England', in V. Kinnaird and D. Hall (eds), *Tourism: A Gender Analysis,* John Wiley & Sons, Chichester, pp. 35-51.

Hermans, D. (1981), 'The Encounter of Agriculture and Tourism: A Catalan Case', *Annals of Tourism Research,* vol. 8, pp. 463-79.

Hirschman, C. and Wong, M.G. (1990), 'Socioeconomic Gains of Asian Americans: Blacks and Hispanics 1960-1976', *American Journal of Sociology,* vol. 90, pp. 584-607.

Hirshleifer, J. (1970), *Investment, Interest and Capital,* Prentice-Hall, Englewood Cliffs.

Hoggart, K. and Mendoza, C. (1999) 'African Immigrant Workers in Spanish Agriculture', *Sociologia Ruralis,* vol. 39, pp. 538-62.

Hollifield, J.F. (1990), 'Migrants ou Citoyens: La Politique de l'Immigration en France et aux États-Unis', *Revue Européenne des Migrations Internationales,* vol. 6, pp. 151-83.

Hollifield, J.F. (1992), *Immigrants, Markets, and States: The Political Economy of Postwar Europe,* Harvard University Press, London.

Howell, T.R., Noellert, W.A., Kreier, J.G. and Wolff, A.W. (1988), *Steel and the State: Government Intervention and Steel's Structural Crisis,* Westview Press, Boulder.

Huang, F.Y. (1997), *Asian and Hispanic Immigrant Women in the Work Force: Implications of the United States Immigration Policies since 1965*, Garland Publishing, New York.

Hudson, R. and Lewis, J.R. (1984), 'Capital Accumulation: The Industrialization of Southern Europe', in A. Williams (ed.), *Southern Europe Transformed: Political and Economic Change in Greece, Italy, Portugal and Spain*, Harper & Row Publishers, London, pp. 179-207.

Hudson, R. and Lewis, J.R. (eds) (1985a), *Uneven Development in Southern Europe: Studies of Accumulation, Class, Migration and the State*, Methuen, London.

Hudson, R. and Lewis, J.R. (1985b), 'Recent Economic, Social and Political Changes in Southern Europe', in R. Hudson and J. Lewis (eds), *Uneven Development in Southern Europe: Studies of Accumulation, Class, Migration and the State*, Methuen, London, pp. 1-53.

Hunt, J. C. (1992), 'The Impact of the 1962 Repatriates from Algeria on the French Labor Market', *Industrial and Labor Relations Review*, vol. 43, pp. 556-72.

Huntoon, L. (1998), 'Immigration to Spain: Implications for a Unified European Union Immigration Policy', *International Migration Review*, vol. 32, pp. 423-50.

Illeris, S. (1989), *Services and Regions in Europe*, Avebury, Aldershot.

Institut d'Estadística de Catalunya (1993), *Estadística Comarcal i Municipal 1992*, Institut d'Estadística de Catalunya, Barcelona.

Institut d'Estadística de Catalunya (1997), *Anuari Estadístic de Catalunya 1996,* Institut d'Estadística de Catalunya, Barcelona.

Instituto de Apoio as Pequenas e Médias Empresas e ao Investimento (1991), *Estructura Empresarial do Distrito de Setúbal*, Instituto de Apoio as Pequenas e Médias Empresas e ao Investimento, Lisbon.

Instituto Nacional de Estadística (annual a), *España: Anuario Estadístico*, INE, Madrid.

Instituto Nacional de Estadística (quarterly b), *Encuesta de Población Activa (EPA)*, INE, Madrid.

Instituto Nacional de Estadística (monthly c), *Boletín Mensual de Estadística*, INE, Madrid.

Instituto Nacional de Estadística (1984), *Censo Agrario de España 1982*, INE, Madrid.

Instituto Nacional de Estadística (1985), *Censo de Población de 1981*, INE, Madrid.

Instituto Nacional de Estadística (1991), *Censo Agrario 1989*, INE, Madrid.

Instituto Nacional de Estadística (1993), *Encuesta sobre la Estructura de los Establecimientos Hoteleros 1991*, INE, Madrid.

Instituto Nacional de Estadística (1995), *Censo de Población de 1991*, INE, Madrid.

Instituto Nacional de Estatística (annual a), *Estatísticas Demográficas*, INE, Lisbon.

Instituto Nacional de Estatística (quarterly b), *Estatísticas do Emprego*, INE, Lisbon.

Instituto Nacional de Estatística (1984), *XII Recensamento Geral da População: Resultados Definitivos 1981*, INE, Lisbon.
Instituto Nacional de Estatística (1995), *Anuário Estatístico: Região Algarve 1994*, INE, Évora.
Instituto Nacional de Estatística (1996c), *Censos 91: Resultados Definitivos. Portugal*, INE, Lisbon.
Instituto Nacional de Estatística (1996d), *Estimativas de População Residente em 1994*, INE, Lisbon.
Instituto Nacional de Estatística (1996e), *Inquérito à Estructura das Explorações Agrícolas 1995*, INE, Lisbon.
Instituto Nacional de Estatística (1997), *Estatísticas do Turismo 1996*, INE, Lisbon.
International Monetary Fund (1995), *Portugal: Recent Economic Development*, International Monetary Fund, Washington.
Iosifides, T. (1997), 'Immigrants in the Athens Labour Market: A Comparative Study of Albanians, Egyptians and Filipinos', in R.L. King and R. Black (eds), *Southern Europe and the New Immigrations*, Sussex Academic Press, Brighton, pp. 26-50.
Iríbar, A. and Gil, A. (1998), 'Niños a Destajo en los Campos de Badajoz', *El País*, European Edition, 16 August 1998.
Izquierdo Escribano, A. (1991), 'La Inmigración Ilegal en España: Análisis de la Operación Extraordinaria de Regularización 1985-86', *Economía y Sociología del Trabajo*, vol. 11, pp. 19-31.
Izquierdo Escribano, A. (1992), *La Inmigración en España 1980-1990*, Ministerio de Trabajo y Seguridad Social (Informes. Serie general 17), Madrid.
Jabardo Velasco, M. (1993), 'Inmigrantes Magrebíes en la Agricultura: La Vega Baja del Segura (Orihuela)', in B. López García (ed.), *Inmigración Magrebí en España: El Retorno de los Moriscos*, Mapfre, Madrid, pp. 267-89.
Jenkins, R. (1985), 'Black Workers in the Labour Market: The Price of Recession', in B. Roberts, R. Finnegan and D. Gallie (eds), *New Approaches to Economic Life: Economic Restructuring, Unemployment and the Social Division of Labour*, Manchester United Press, Manchester. pp. 167-83.
Jimeno, J. and Toharia, L. (1994), *Unemployment and Labour Market Flexibility: Spain*, International Labour Office, Geneva.
Johnson, J.H. and Salt, J. (1990), 'Labour Migration: The General Context', in J.H. Johnson and J. Salt (eds), *Labour Migration: The Internal Geographical Mobility of Labour in the Developed World*, David Fulton Publishers, London, pp. 1-13.
Jolliffe, J. (1990), 'Angolans Work as Portugal's 'Slaves'', *The Guardian*, 20 January 1990.
Josling, T. and Tangermann, S. (1987), 'Commodity Policies', in S.R. Pearson, F. Avillez, J. W. Bentley, T. J. Finan, R. Fox, T. Josling, M. Langworthy, E. Monke and S. Tangermann (eds), *Portuguese Agriculture in Transition*, Cornell University Press, Ithaca, pp. 141-66.

Kastoryano, R. (1989), 'L'État et les Immigrés: France, Allemagne, Grande-Bretagne et États Unis', *Revue Européenne des Migrations Internationales*, vol. 5, pp. 9-20.

Kastoryano, R. (1994), 'Mobilisations des Migrants en Europe: Du National au Transnational', *Revue Européenne des Migrations Internationales*, vol. 10, pp. 169-81.

Kindleberger, C. (1967), *Europe's Postwar Growth: the Role of Labor Supply*, Harvard University Press, Cambridge.

King, R.L. (1984), 'Population Mobility: Emigration, Return Migration and Internal Migration', in A. Williams (ed.), *Southern Europe Transformed: Political and Economic Change in Greece, Italy, Portugal and Spain*, Harper & Row, London, pp. 145-78.

King, R.L. (1993), 'Recent Immigration to Italy: Character, Causes and Consequences', *GeoJournal*, vol. 30, pp. 283-92.

King, R.L. (1995), 'Tourism, Labour and International Migration', in A. Montanari and A. M. Williams (eds), *European Tourism: Regions, Spaces and Restructuring*, John Wiley & Sons, Chichester, pp. 177-90.

King, R.L. (1996), 'Migration and Development in the Mediterranean region', *Geography*, vol. 81, pp. 3-14.

King, R.L. and Konjhodzic, I. (1995), *Labour, Employment and Migration in Southern Europe*, University of Sussex (Research Paper 19), Brighton.

King, R.L. and Rybaczuk, K. (1993), 'Southern Europe and the International Division of Labour: From Emigration to Immigration', in R.L. King (ed.), *The New Geography of European Migration*, Belhaven, London, pp. 175-206.

King, R.L., Fielding, A. and Black, R. (1997), 'The International Migration Turnaround in Southern Europe', in R.L. King and R. Black (eds), *Southern Europe and the New Immigrations*, Sussex Academic Press, Brighton, pp. 1-25.

Klemm, M.S. and Martín-Quirós, M.A. (1996), 'Changing the Balance of Power: Tour Operators and Tourism Suppliers in the Spanish Tourist Industry', in L.C. Harrison and W. Husbands (eds), *Practicing Responsible Tourism: International Case Studies in Tourism Planning, Policy and Development*, John Wiley & Sons, New York, pp. 126-44.

Knignts, M. (1997), 'Migrants as Networkers: The Economics of Bangladeshi Migration to Rome', in R.L. King and R. Black (eds), *Southern Europe and the New Immigrations*, Sussex Academic Press, Brighton, pp. 113-37.

Koch, J. (1991), 'The Completion of the Internal Market and its Impact on the Building Sector in Europe', in H. Rainbird and G. Syben (eds), *Restructuring a Traditional Industry: Construction Employment and Skills in Europe*, Berg, New York, pp. 263-82.

Ladbury, S. (1984), 'Choice, Chance or no Alternative?: Turkish Cypriots in Business in London', in R. Ward and R. Jenkins (eds), *Ethnic Communities in Business: Strategies for Economic Survival*, Cambridge University Press, Cambridge, pp. 105-24.

Lains, P. (1994), 'O Estado e a Industrialização em Portugal, 1945-1990', *Análise Social*, vol. 29, pp. 923-58.

Lardíes-Bosque, R. (1997), 'Restructuración Económica y Turismo: La Nueva Versión de los Movimientos Migratorios en los Países de la Unión Europea', *Geographicalia*, vol. 35, pp. 149-75.

Lavery, P. (1993), 'A Single European Market for the Tourism Industry', in W. Pompl and P. Lavery (eds), *Tourism in Europe: Structures and Developments*, CAB International, Oxfordshire, pp. 80-98.

Lebon, A. (1979), 'Feminisation de la Main d'Œuvre Étrangere', *Hommes et Migrations*, vol. 963, pp. 27-33.

Lee, E. (1966), 'A Theory of Migration', *Demography*, vol. 3, pp. 47-57.

Leeds, E. (1980), 'Solutions to Dislocations in the Case of Portugal: Emigration vs. Mobilization', *Iberian Studies*, vol. 9, pp. 69-80.

Leontidou, L. (1994), 'Gender Dimensions of Tourism in Greece: Employment, Subcultures and Restructuring', in V. Kinnaird and D. Hall (eds), *Tourism: A Gender Analysis*, John Wiley & Sons, Chichester, pp. 74-105.

Lesourd, M. (1988), 'L'Émigration Internationale des Cap-Verdiens: Importance et Enjeux pour un Petit État Insulaire Sahélien', *Études Sahéliennes*, vol. 30, pp. 85-105.

Lever, A. (1987), 'Spanish Tourism Migrants: The Case of Lloret de Mar', *Annals of Tourism Research*, vol. 14, pp. 449-70.

Lewis, J. and Williams, A.M. (1985), 'Portugal's Retornados: Reintegration or Rejection?', *Iberian Studies*, vol. 14, pp. 11-23.

Lewis, J. and Williams, A.M. (1986), 'Factories, Farms and Families: The Impact of Industrial Growth in Rural Central Portugal', *Sociologia Ruralis*, vol. 26, pp. 320-44.

Lewis, J. and Williams, A.M. (1987), 'Productive Decentralisation or Indigenous Growth?: Small Manufacturing Enterprises and Regional Development in Central Portugal', *Regional Studies*, vol. 21, pp. 343-61.

Lewis, J. and Williams, A.M. (1989), 'A Secret No More: Europe Discovers the Algarve', *Geography*, vol. 74, pp. 156-8.

Lewis, J. and Williams, A.M. (1991), 'Portugal: Market Segmentation and Regional Specialisation', in A.M. Williams and G. Shaw (eds), *Tourism and Economic Development*, Belhaven Press, London, pp. 107-29.

Lianos, T.P., Sarris, A.H. and Katseli, L.T. (1996), 'Illegal Immigration and Local Labour Markets: The Case of Northern Greece', *International Migration*, vol. 34, pp. 449-84.

Lieberman, S. (1995), *Growth and Crisis in the Spanish Economy: 1940-93*, Routledge, London.

Light, I. and Bonacich, E. (1988), *Immigrant Enterpreneurs: Koreans in Los Angeles 1965-1982*, University of California, Berkeley.

Lirola Delgado, I. (1993), 'Spanish Viewpoints and Problems with the Schengen Convention, Free Movement of Persons and Aliens Law', in H.G. Schermers, C. Flinterman, A.E. Kellermann, J.C. Van Haersolte and G.-W. Van de Meent (eds), *Free Movement of Persons in Europe: Legal Problems and Experiences*, Martinus Nijhoff, Dordrecht, pp. 216-26.

Lobo, I. (1985), 'Estructura Social e Productive e Propensão à Subterraneidade no Portugal de Hoje', *Análise Social*, vol. 21, pp. 527-62.

Long, J.E. (1980), 'The Effect of Americanization on Earnings: Some Evidence for Women', *Journal of Political Economy*, vol. 88, pp. 620-9.

Lopes, J. da S. (1996a), *A Economia Portuguesa desde 1960*, Gradiva, Lisbon.

Lopes, I. (1996b), 'CGTP Troca Salários por Emprego', *Expresso*, 1 June 1996.

López Trigal, L. (1996), 'La Migration Portugaise en Espagne', *Révue Européenne des Migrations Internationales*, vol. 12, pp. 109-19.

López Trigal, L. and Prieto Sarro, I. (1993), 'Portugueses y Caboverdianos en España', *Estudios Geográficos*, vol. 210, pp. 75-96.

Loveridge, R. and Mok, A.L. (1979), *Theories of Labour Market Segmentation: A Critique*, Martinus Nijhoff, The Hague.

Machado, F.L. (1992), 'Etnicidade em Portugal: Contrastes e Politização', *Sociologia: Problemas e Práticas*, vol. 12, pp. 123-36.

Machado, F.L. (1997), 'Contornos e Especificidades da Imigração em Portugal', *Sociologia: Problemas e Práticas,* vol. 24, pp. 9-44.

Machado, F.L. and Perista, H. (1997), 'Femmes Immigrées au Portugal', *Migrations Société*, vol. 52, pp. 91-103.

Malheiros, J. (1997), 'Indians in Lisbon: Ethnic Entrepreneurship and the Migration Process', in R.L. King and R. Black (eds), *Southern Europe and the New Immigrations*, Sussex Academic Press, Brighton, pp. 93-112.

Ma Mung, E. and Simon, G. (1990), *Commerçants Maghrébins et Asiatiques en France: Agglomération Parisienne et Villes de l'Est*. Masson, Paris.

Maravall, J.M. (1993), 'Politics and Policy: Economic Reforms in Southern Europe', in L.C. Pereira, J.M. Maravall and C. Przeworski (eds), *Economic Reforms in New Democracies: A Social-Democratic Approach*, Cambridge University Press, Cambridge, pp. 77-131.

Marchena Gómez, M.J. and Vera Rebollo, F. (1995), 'Coastal Areas: Processes, Typologies and Prospects', in A. Montanari and A.M. Williams (eds), *European Tourism: Regions, Spaces and Restructuring*, John Wiley & Sons, Chichester, pp. 111-26.

Marie, C.V. (1995), *The EC Member States and Immigration in 1993: Closed Borders, Stringent Attitudes*, Office for Official Publications of the European Communities, Luxembourg.

Marie, C.V. (1996), 'L'Union Européenne face aux Déplacements de Populations: Logiques d'État face aux Droits des Personnes', *Revue Européenne des Migrations Internationales,* vol. 12, pp. 169-209.

Marsden, T., Lowe, P. and Whatmore, S. (1992), 'Labour and Locality: Emerging Research Issues', in T. Marsden, P. Lowe and S. Whatmore (eds), *Labour and Locality: Uneven Development and the Rural Labour Process*, David Fulton Publishers, London, pp. 1-18.

Marshall, J.N. (1988), *Services and Uneven Development*, Oxford University Press, Oxford.

Martín, C. (1997), 'El Mercado de Trabajo Español en Perspectiva Europea: Un Panorama', *Papeles de Economía Española*, vol. 72, pp. 2-20.

Martínez, M. (1995a), 'Cáritas Pide que los Inmigrantes Obtengan la Residencia Permanente a los Seis Años', *El País*, Catalan Edition, 17 February 1995.

Martínez, M. (1995b), 'Frente Común de los Municipios Catalanes en Defensa de los Inmigrantes', *El País*, Catalan Edition, 6 May 1995.

Martínez-Alier, J. (1986), '¿Labradores, Empresarios o Señoritos?', in R. Garrabou, C. Barciela and J.I. Jiménez Blanco (eds), *Historia Agraria de la España Contemporánea: El Fin de la Agricultural Tradicional (1940-1960)*, Crítica, Barcelona, pp. 534-66.

Martínez-Alier, J. and Roca Jusmet, J. (1988), 'Economía Política del Corporativisimo en el Estado Español: Del Franquismo al Posfranquismo', *Revista Española de Investigaciones Sociológicas*, vol. 41, pp. 25-62.

Martínez Veiga, U. (1989), *El Otro Desempleo: La Economía Sumergida*, Anthropos, Barcelona.

Martínez Veiga, U. (1997), *La Integración Social de los Inmigrantes Extranjeros en España*, Trotta/Fundación 1º de Mayo, Valladollid.

Marujo, A. and Rocha, J.M. (1996), 'A Última Oportunidade: Alto-Comisário para a Imigração e Minorias Étnicas Diz que Novo Processo de Legalização não Pode Deixar Ninguém de fora', *O Público*, 21 February 1996.

Massey, D. (1979), 'In What Sense a Regional Problem?', *Regional Studies*, vol. 13, pp. 233-43.

Massey, D.S. (1990), 'Social Structure, Household Strategies, and the Cumulative Causation of Migration', *Population Index*, vol. 56, pp. 3-26.

Massey, D.S. and García-España, F. (1987), 'The Social Process of International Migration', *Science*, vol. 237, pp. 733-8.

Massey, D.S., Alarcón, R., Durand, J. and González, H. (1987), *Return to Aztlan: the Social Process of International Migration from Western Mexico*, University of California Press, Berkeley.

Massey, D.S., Arango, J., Hugo, G., Kouaouci, A, Pellegrino, A. and Taylor, J.E. (1993), 'Theories of International Migration: A Review and Appraisal', *Population and Development Review*, vol. 19, pp. 431-66.

Matias, M.I. (1992), *A Indústria Hoteleira no Algarve: Aplicação da Metodologia dos Grupos Estratégicos*, Unpublished Master Thesis, Instituto Superior de Ciências do Trabalho e da Empresa, Lisbon.

Mendonsa, E.L. (1982), 'Benefits of Migration as a Personal Strategy in Nazaré, Portugal', *International Migration Review*, vol. 16, pp. 635-45.

Mendoza, C. (1994), *La Mobilitat dels Estrangers en les Empreses Transnacionals: Les Empreses Alemanyes de dos Sectors Econòmics a Catalunya*, Unpublished Master Thesis, Universitat Autònoma de Barcelona, Bellaterra.

Mendoza, C. (1997), 'Foreign Labour Immigration in High-Unemployment Spain', in R. King and R.L. Black (eds), *Southern Europe and the New Immigrations*, Sussex Academic Press, Brighton, pp. 51-74.

Mendoza, C. (2000) 'African Employment in Iberian Construction: A Cross-Border Analysis', *Journal of Ethnic and Migration Studies*, vol. 26, pp. 609-34.

Mendoza, C. (2001) 'The Role of the State in Influencing African Labour Outcomes in Spain and Portugal', *Geoforum*, vol. 32, 167-80.

Merigó, E. (1982), 'Spain', in A. Boltho (ed.), *The European Economy: Growth and Crisis*, Oxford University Press, Oxford, pp. 554-80.

Metra-Seis Consulting (1995), *Las Migraciones Laborales Interiores: Estudio de la Oferta de Empleo de Trabajos de Temporada en las Provincias de Almería, Alicante, Murcia, Baleares, Lérida y Tarragona*, Unpublished report for the Dirección General de Migraciones, Madrid.

Miguélez Lobo, F. (1989), 'El Trabajo Sumergido en España en la Perspectiva del Acta Única Europea', *Papers: Revista de Sociologia*, vol. 32, pp. 115-25.

Mingione, E. (1995), 'Labour Market Segmentation and Informal Work in Southern Europe', *European Urban and Regional Studies*, vol. 2, pp. 121-43.

Ministério da Administração Interna (1995a), *Nacionalidade por Naturalização e Estatuto de Igualdade*, Ministério da Administração Interna, Lisbon.

Ministério da Administração Interna (1995b), *Entrada e Permanência de Estrangeiros*, Ministério da Administração Interna, Lisbon.

Ministerio de Agricultura, Pesca y Alimentación (annual), *Anuario de Estadística Agraria,* Ministerio de Agricultura, Pesca y Alimentación, Madrid.

Ministerio de Fomento (1997), *Encuesta Coyuntural de la Industria de la Construcción 1996*, Ministerio de Fomento, Madrid.

Ministerio de Trabajo y Asuntos Sociales (1998), *Guía Laboral y de Asuntos Sociales 1997*, Ministerio de Trabajo y Asuntos Sociales, Madrid.

Ministerio de Trabajo y Seguridad Social (annual), *Estadística de Permisos de Trabajo a Extranjeros*, Ministerio de Trabajo y Seguridad Social, Madrid.

Ministerio del Interior (1994), *Informe sobre el Funcionamiento del Sistema de Expulsión de Extranjeros Previsto en la Ley Orgánica 7/1985*, Unpublished report for the Dirección General de Extranjería y Asilo del Ministerio del Interior, Madrid.

Ministério do Emprego e da Segurança Social (1994), *Enquadramento Estatístico dos Activos: Anuário de Estatísticas Sociais*, Ministério do Emprego e da Segurança Social, Lisbon.

Ministério para a Qualificação e o Emprego (monhtly), *Boletim Estatístico: Emprego, Formação, Trabalho,* Ministério para a Qualificação e o Emprego, Lisbon.

Modesto, L., Monteiro, M.L. and Neves, J.C. das (1992), 'Some Aspects of the Portuguese Labour Market, 1977-1988: Neutrality, Hysteresis and the Wage Gap', in J.F. do Amaral, D. Lucena and A.S. Mello (eds), *The Portuguese Economy towards 1992*, Kluwer Academic Press, Boston, pp. 153-74.

Moinou, S. (1995), *Privatization in the Iron and Steel Industry*, International Labour Organization, Geneva.

Montanari, A. (ed.) (1993), *Labour Market Structure and Development in Portugal, Spain, Italy, Greece and Turkey*, Edizioni   Scientifiche Italiane, Naples.

Montanari, A. (1995), 'The Mediterranean Region: Europe's Summer Leisure Space', in A. Montanari and A.M. Williams (eds), *European Tourism: Regions, Spaces and Restructuring*, John Wiley & Sons, Chichester, pp. 41-65.

Montanari, A. and Cortese, A. (1993), 'South to North Migration in a Mediterranean Perspective', in R.L. King (ed.), *Mass Migrations in Europe: The Legacy and the Future*, Belhaven Press, London, pp. 212-33.

Moreno Torregrosa, P. (1993), 'Argelinos y Marroquíes en Valencia: La Aportación Argelina a la Inmigración Magrebí en España', in B. López García (ed.), *Inmigración Magrebí en España: El Retorno de los Moriscos*, Mapfre, Madrid, pp. 241-66.

Morokvasic, M. (1984), 'Birds of Passage are also Women...', *International Migration Review*, vol. 28, pp. 886-907.

Morrison, P.A. (1971), 'Chronic Movers and the Future Redistribution of Population', *Demography*, vol. 8, pp. 171-84.

Morrison, P.S. (1990), 'Segmentation Theory Applied to Local, Regional and Spatial Labour Markets', *Progress in Human Geography*, vol. 14, pp. 488-528.

Moulier Boutang, Y. (1991), 'Dynamique des Migrations Internationales et Économie Souterraine: Comparaison Internationale et Perspectives Européennes', in S. Montagné-Villette (ed.), *Espaces et Travail Clandestins*, Masson, Paris, pp. 113-20.

Moura, M. (1996), 'A Lusofonia não se Negoceia', *O Público*, 15 May 1996.

Muñoz Pérez, F. and Izquierdo Escribano, A. (1989), 'L'Espagne, Pays d'Immigration', *Population*, vol. 2, pp. 257-89.

Murgatroyd, L. and Urry, J. (1984), 'The Re-Structuring of a Local Economy: The Case of Lancaster', in D. Massey and J. Allen (eds), *Geography Matters!*, Cambridge University Press, Cambridge, pp. 112-27.

Mylokenko, L., De Raymond, T. and Henry, P. (1987), *The Regional Impact of the Common Agricultural Policy in Spain and Portugal*, Commission of the European Communities, Luxembourg.

Nadal, J. (1984), *La Población Española (Siglos XVI a XX)*, Ariel, Barcelona.

Naredo, J.M. (1986), 'La Agricultura Española en el Desarrollo Económico', in R. Garrabou, C. Barciela and J.I. Jiménez Blanco (eds) *Historia Agraria de la España Contemporánea: El Fin de la Agricultural Tradicional (1940-1960)*, Crítica, Barcelona, pp. 455-98.

Naylon, J. (1981), 'Spain, Portugal and the EEC: A Troublesome Enlargement', *Bank of London and South America Review*, vol. 15, pp. 122-30.

Odé, A. (1996), *Migrant Workers in the Dutch Labour Market Today*, Thesis Publishers, Amsterdam.

Ogden, P. (1993), 'The Legacy of Migration: Some Evidence from France', in R.L. King (ed.), *Mass Migration in Europe: the Legacy and the Future*, Belhaven Press, London, pp. 101-17.

Olano, A. (1990), 'Las Migraciones Interiores en fase de Dispersión', *Revista de Economía y Sociología del Trabajo*, vol. 8-9, pp. 86-98.

O'Loughlin, J. (1986), 'Immigration to Western Europe, 1952-1982: A Time-Series Analysis of Movement to Sweden, France and Essen', *Enviroment and Planning A*, vol. 18, pp. 375-99.

Organisation for Economic Co-Operation and Development (annual a), *Employment Outlook*, OECD, Paris.

Organisation for Economic Co-Operation and Development (1995), *The OECD Jobs Study: Investment, Productivity and Employment*, OECD, Paris.

Organisation for Economic Co-Operation and Development (1997), *Labour Force Statistics 1976-1996*, OECD, Paris.

Ortiz, A. (1996), 'En la Aguja y el Pedal Eché la Hiel: Puerto Rican Women in the Garment Industry of New York City', in A. Ortiz (ed.), *Puerto Rican Women and Work: Bridges in Transnational Labour*, Temple University Press, Philadelphia, pp. 55-81.

Oso, L. and Catarino, C. (1997), 'Les Éffects de la Migration sur le Statut des Femmes: Les Cas des Dominicaines et des Marocaines à Madrid et des Cap-Verdiennes à Lisbonne', *Migrations Société*, vol. 52, pp. 115-30.

Palacio Morena, J.I. (1991), 'La Política de Empleo', in F. Miguélez and C. Prieto (eds), *Las Relaciones Laborales en España*, Siglo XXI, Madrid, pp. 307-29.

Palazón Ferrando, S. (1996), 'Latinoamericanos en España (1981-1994): Aproximación a un Fenómeno Migratorio Reciente', *Estudios Migratorios Latinoamericanos*, vol. 32, pp. 179-210.

Palidda, S. (1992), 'Le Développement des Activités Indépendantes des Immigrés en Europe et en France', *Revue Européenne des Migrations Internationales*, vol. 8, pp. 83-98.

Pascual de Sans, À. and Cardelús, J. (1990), *Migració i Història Personal: Investigació sobre la Mobilitat des de la Perspectiva del Retorn*, Universitat Autònoma de Barcelona, Bellaterra.

Payne, S.G. (1987), *The Franco Regime, 1936-1975*, The University of Wisconsin Press, Madison.

Pearce, D.G. (1987), *Tourism Today: a Geographical Analysis*, Longman, Harlow.

Pearce, D.G. (1989), *Tourist Development*, Longman, London.

Pearce, D.G. and Grimmeau, J.-P. (1985), 'The Spatial Structure of Tourist Accommodation and Hotel Demand in Spain', *Geoforum*, vol. 16, pp. 37-50.

Pearson, S.R. and Monke, E. (1987), 'Constraints on the Development of Portuguese agriculture', in S.R. Pearson, F. Avillez, J.W. Bentley, T. J. Finan, R. Fox, T. Josling, M. Langworthy, E. Monke and S. Tangermann (eds), *Portuguese Agriculture in Transition*, Cornell University Press, Ithaca, pp. 17-28.

Pearson, S.R., Avillez, F., Bentley, J.W., Finan, T.J., Fox, R., Josling G.T., Langworthy, M., Monke, E. and Tangermann, S. (eds) (1987), *Portuguese Agriculture in Transition*, Cornell University Press, Ithaca.

Peck, J.A. (1989), 'Reconceptualizing the Local Labour Market: Space, Segmentation and the State', *Progress in Human Geography*, vol. 13, pp. 42-61.

Peixoto, J. (1996), 'Recent Trends in Regional Migration and Urban Dynamics in Portugal', in P. Rees, J. Stillwell, A. Convey and M. Kupiszewski (eds), *Population Migration in the European Union*, John Wiley & Sons, Chichester, pp. 261-74.

Pélissier, R. (1990), 'São Tomé and Príncipe', in *Africa South of the Sahara 1990*, Europa Publications, London, pp. 828-32.

Pereira, A.M. (1992), 'Trade-off between Emigration and Remittances in the Portuguese Economy', in J.F. do Amaral, D. Lucena and A.S. Mello (eds), *The Portuguese Economy towards 1992*, Kluwer Academic Press, Boston, pp. 175-98.

Pérez Oliva, M. (1995), 'La Rueda de la Ilegalidad: La Mitad de los 105.000 Inmigrantes Legalizados en 1991 Vuelve a Estar en Situación Irregular', *El País*, Catalan Edition, 22 October 1995.

Pérez Yruela, M. (1990), 'La Sociedad Rural', in S. Giner (ed.), *España: Sociedad y Política*, Espasa-Calpe, Madrid, pp. 119-241.

Pérez Yruela, M. (1995), 'Spanish Rural Society in Transition', *Sociologia Ruralis*, vol. 35, pp. 276-96.

Peterson, W. (1958), 'A General Theory of Migration', *American Sociological Review*, vol. 23, pp. 256-66.

Petras, E.M. (1981), 'The Global Market in the Modern World-Economy', in M.M. Kritz, C.B. Keely and S.M. Tomasi (eds), *Global Trends in Migration: Theory and Research on International Population Movements*, Center for Migration Studies, New York, pp. 44-63.

Phizacklea, A. (ed.) (1983a), *One Way Ticket: Migration and Female Labour*, Routledge and Kegan Paul, London.

Phizacklea, A. (1983b), 'In the Front Line', in A. Phizacklea (ed.), *One Way Ticket: Migration and Female Labour*, Routledge and Kegan Paul, London, pp. 95-112.

Pimpão, A. (1991), 'Economia do Algarve: Preparar o Terceiro Milénio', *Sociedade e Território*, vol. 13, pp. 17-21.

Pinto, J.M. and Queiroz, M.C. (1996), 'Flexibilização da Producão, Mobilidade da Mão-de-Obra e Processos Identitários na Construção Civil', *Sociologia: Problemas e Práticas*, vol. 19, pp. 9-29.

Piore, M.J. (1975), 'Notes for a Theory of Labor Market Stratification', in R.C. Edwards, M. Reich and D.M. Gordon (eds), *Labor Market Segmentation*, D. C. Heath and company, Lexington, pp. 125-50.

Piore, M.J. (1979), *Birds of Passage: Migrant Labor and Industrial Societies*, Cambridge University Press, Cambridge.

Piore, M.J. (1986), 'Perspectives on Labor Market Flexibility', *Industrial Relations*, vol. 25, pp. 146-66.

Pires, R.P., Maranhão, M.J., Quintela, J.P., Moniz, F. and Pisco, M. (1987), *Os Retornados: um Estudo Sociográfico*, Instituto de Estudos para o Desenvolvimento, Lisbon.

Pi-Sunyer, O. (1996), 'Tourism in Catalonia', in M. Barke, J. Towner and M.T. Newton (eds), *Tourism in Spain: Critical Issues*, CAB International, Oxfordshire, pp. 231-64.

Plantenga, J. (1995), 'Labour Market, Participation of Women in the European Union', in A. van Doorne-Huiskes, J. Hoof and E. Roelofs (eds), *Women and the European Labour Markets*, Paul Chapman, London, pp. 1-14.

Poinard, M. (1994), 'Portugal 1974-1994', *Peuples Méditerranéens*, vol. 66, pp. 3-21.

Portes, A. (1981), 'Modes of Structural Incorporation and Present Theories of Labor Immigration', in M.M. Kritz, C.B. Keely and S.M. Tomasi (eds), *Global Trends in Migration: Theory and Research on International Population Movements*, Center for Migration Studies, New York, pp. 279-97.

Portes, A. (1994), 'Economic Sociology and the Sociology of Immigration: A Conceptual Overview', in A. Portes (ed.), *The Economic Sociology of Immigration: Essays on Networks, Ethnicity and Entrepreneurship*, Russell Sage Foundation, New York, pp. 1-41.

Portes, A. (1997), 'Immigration Theory for a New Century: Some Problems and Opportunities', *International Migration Review*, vol. 31, pp. 799-825.

Portes, A. and Bach, R. (1985), *Latin Journey*, University of California Press, Berkeley.

Portes, A. and Böröcz, J. (1989), 'Contemporary Immigration: Theoretical Perspectives on its Determinants and Modes of Incorporation', *International Migration Review*, vol. 23, pp. 606-30.

Portes, A. and Sensenbrenner, J. (1993), 'Embeddedness and Immigration: Notes on the Social Determinants of Economic Action', *American Journal of Sociology*, vol. 98, pp. 1320-50.

Portes, A. and Stepick, A. (1985), 'Unwelcome Immigrants: The Labor Market Experiences of 1980 (Mariel) Cuban and Haitian Refugees in South Florida', *American Sociological Review*, vol. 50, pp. 493-514.

Portes, A. and Walton, J. (1981), *Labor, Class and the International System*, Academic Press, New York.

Poulain, M. (1996), 'Migration Flows between the Countries of the European Union', in P. Rees, J. Stillwell, A. Convey and M. Kupiszewski (eds), *Population Migration in the European Union*, John Wiley & Sons, Chichester, pp. 51-65.

Pryor, R.J. (1981), 'Integrating International and Internal Migration Theories', in M.M. Kritz, C.B. Keely and S.M. Tomasi (eds), *Global Trends in Migration: Theory and Research on International Population Movements*, Center for Migration Studies, New York, pp. 110-29.

Pugliese, E. (1993), 'Restructuring of the Labour Market and the Role of Third World Migrations in Europe', *Environment and Planning D: Society and Space*, vol. 11, pp. 513-22.

Rainbird, H. (1991), 'Labour Force Fragmentation and Skills Supply in the British construction Industry', in H. Rainbird and G. Syben (eds), *Restructuring a Traditional Industry: Construction Employment and Skills in Europe*, Berg, New York, pp. 201-22.

Rainbird, H. and Syben, G. (1991), 'Introduction', in H. Rainbird and G. Syben (eds), *Restructuring a Traditional Industry: Construction Employment and Skills in Europe*, Berg, New York, pp. 1-21.

Ramírez, À. (1993), 'La Inmigración Magrebí en la Cataluña Agrícola: Marroquíes en el Litoral Catalán', in B. López (ed.), *Inmigración Magrebí en España: el Retorno de los Moriscos*, Mapfre, Madrid, pp. 225-39.

Ramírez Goicoechea, E. (1996), *Inmigrantes en España: Vidas y Experiencias*, Centro de Investigaciones Sociológicas/Siglo XXI, Madrid.

Ramos, R.M. (1976a), 'Nacionalidade e Descolonização: Algumas Reflexões a propósito do Decreto-Lei nº 308-A/75, de 24 de Junho (Continuação)', *Revista de Dereito e Economia*, vol. 2, pp. 331-62.

Ramos, R.M. (1976b), 'Nacionalidade e Descolonização: Algumas Reflexões a propósito do Decreto-Lei nº 308-A/75, de 24 de Junho', *Revista de Dereito e Economia*, vol. 1, pp. 121-51.

Ravenstein, E.G. (1889), 'The Laws of Migration', *Journal of the Royal Statistical Society*, vol. 52, pp. 214-301.

Recio, A. (1986), 'Economía Sumergida y Transformación de las Relaciones Laborales en España', *Papers: Revista de Sociologia*, vol. 27, pp. 131-54.

Recio, A. (1996), 'Mercado de Trabajo en España: Comentarios a la Reforma', in F. Laroca and A. Sánchez (eds), *Economía Crítica: Trabajo y Medio Ambiente*, Universitat de València, Valencia, pp. 93- 126.

Recolons, L. (1998), 'Migracions entre Catalunya i l'Estranger', in S. Giner (ed.), *La Societat Catalana*, Institut d'Estudis Catalans, Barcelona, pp. 243-71.

Reich, M., Gordon, D.M. and Edwards, R.C. (1973), 'A Theory of Labour Market Segmentation', *American Economic Association*, vol. 63, num. 2, pp. 359-65.

Reimers, C.W. (1985), 'A Comparative Analysis of the Wages of Hispanics, Blacks, and non-Hispanic Whites', in G. J. Borjas and M. Tienda (eds), *Hispanics in the US Economy*, Academic Press, Orlando, pp. 27-75.

Reis, M. and Nave, J.G. (1986), 'Emigrating Peasants and Returning Emigrants', *Sociologia Ruralis*, vol. 26, pp. 20-35.

Rex, J. and Moore, R. (1967), *Race, Community and Conflict: A Study of Sparkbrook,* Institute of Race Relations, Oxford University Press, London.

Reynolds, S. (1990), 'Cape Verde: Economy', in *Africa South of the Sahara 1990*, Europa Publications, London, pp. 339-40.

Rhoades, R.E. (1978), 'Intra-European Return Migration and Rural Development: Lessons from the Spanish Case', *Human Organization*, vol. 37, pp. 136-47.

Ribas Mateos, N. (1996), *La Heterogeneidad de la Integración Social: Una Aplicación a la Inmigración Extracomunitaria (Filipina, Gambiana y Marroquí) en Cataluña*, Unpublished PhD thesis, Universitat Autònoma de Barcelona, Bellaterra.

Robinson, V. (1984), 'Asians in Britain: A Study of Encapsulation and Marginality', in C.G. Clarke, D. Ley and C. Peach (eds), *Geography and Ethnic Pluralism*, Allen and Unwin, London, 231-57.

Roca Jusmet, J. (1993), *Pactos Sociales y Política de Rentas: el Debate Internacional y la Experiencia Española (1977-1988)*, Ministerio de Trabajo y Seguridad Social (Informes y estudios, serie general 2), Madrid.

Rocha-Trindade, M.B. (1995), *Sociologia das Migrações*, Universidade Aberta, Lisbon.

Rodrigues, C.M. (1984), 'Imperfeições ou Dualismo no Mercado de Habitação?: Urbanização Clandestina e Reprodução da Força de Trabalho em Portugal', *Sociedade e Território*, vol. 1, pp. 38-45.

Rodrigues, M.J. (1992), *O Sistema de Emprego em Portugal: Crise e Mutações*, Publicações Dom Quixote, Lisbon.

Rodríguez, C. and Torres, M. (1994), 'Los Municipios Catalanes Crean un 'Lobby' para Obtener Recursos con los que Integrar a los Inmigrantes Extranjeros', *El País*, Catalan Edition, 21 July 1994.

Romero, J. (1993), 'Problemas Estructurales de la Agricultura Española en el Contexto Comunitario', in *Agriculturas y Políticas Agrarias en el Sur de Europa*, Ministerio de Agricultura, Pesca y Alimentación, Madrid, pp. 415-38.

Romero González, J. and Albertos Puebla, J.M. (1996), 'Spain: Return to the South, Metropolitan Deconcentration and New Migration Flows', in P. Rees, J. Stillwell, A. Convey and M. Kupiszewski (eds), *Population Migration in the European Union,* John Wiley & Sons, Chichester, pp. 175-89.

Roquero, E. (1996), 'Asalariados Africanos Trabajando bajo Plástico', *Sociología del Trabajo*, vol. 28, pp. 3-23.

Roseira, M.J. (1977), 'Movimentos Migratórios dos Trabalhadores Rurais da Região de Portalegre', *Finisterra*, vol. 23, pp. 77-84.

Rubery, J., Smith, M., Colette, F. and Grimshaw, D. (1998), *Women and European Employment*, Routledge, London.

Saint-Maurice, A. (1995), 'Modes de Vie des Immigrants Cap-Verdiens Résidant au Portugal', *Espaces et Sociétés*, vol. 79, pp. 61-75.

Saint-Maurice, A. and Pires, R.P. (1989), 'Descolonização e Migrações: Os Imigrantes dos PALOP em Portugal', *Revista Internacional de Estudos Africanos*, vol. 10-11, pp. 203-26.

Salgueiro, T.B. (1985), 'A Habitação na Área Metropolitana de Lisboa', *Sociedade e Território*, vol. 3, pp. 54-66.

Salmon, K. (1995), *The Modern Spanish Economy: Transformation and Integration into Europe*, Printer, London.

Salvà i Tomàs, P.A. (1991), 'La Population des Îles Baléares pendant 40 Ans du Tourisme de Masse (1950-1989)', *Méditerranée*, vol. 72, pp. 7-14.

Sánchez Martín, M.E. (1992), *Nuestras Hermanas del Sur: la Inmigración Marroquí y el Servicio Doméstico en Madrid*, Unpublished report for the Dirección General de Migraciones, Madrid.

Sánchez, M., Rubio, J.L., Monago, J. and García, A. (1996), 'Marroquíes en Extremadura', in Taller de Estudios Internacionales Mediterráneos (ed.), *Atlas de la Inmigración Magrebí en España*, Universidad Autónoma de Madrid, Madrid, 154-58.

Sanchis, E. (1992), 'Mercado de Trabajo Juvenil y Políticas de Empleo', *Papers: Revista de Sociologia,* vol. 39, pp. 59-75.

San Juan de Mesonada, C. (1993), 'Agricultural Policy', in A. Almarcha Barbado (ed.), *Spain and EC Membership Evaluated*, Pinter, London, pp. 49-59.

Santana Afonso, A.I. (1994), *La Mano de Obra Marroquí en el Sector Agrícola*, Unpublished report for the Dirección General de Migraciones, Madrid.

Santos, L. (1993a), *De Nuevo sobre el Trabajador Extranjero y la Regularización de 1991: Reflexiones en torno al Estudio 'El Trabajador Extranjero y la Regularización de 1991' y sobre Política Migratoria*, Fundación Paulino Torras Domènech, Barcelona.

Santos, L. (1993b), 'Elementos Jurídicos de la Integración de los Extranjeros', in G. Tapinos (ed.), *Inmigración e Integración en Europa*, Fundación Paulino Torras Domènech, Barcelona, pp. 91-125.

Sapelli, G. (1995), *Southern Europe since 1945: Tradition and Modernity in Portugal, Spain, Italy, Greece and Turkey*, Longman, London.

Sassen-Koob, S. (1984), 'Notes on the Incorporation of Third World Women into Wage-Labor through Immigration and Off-Shore Production', *International Migration Review*, vol. 18, pp. 1144-67.

Sassen, S. (1995), 'Immigration and Local Labour Markets', in A. Portes (ed.), *The Economic Sociology of Immigration: Essays on Networks, Ethnicity and Entrepreneurship*, Russell Sage Foundation, New York, pp. 87-127.

Schermers, H.G., Flinterman, C., Kelermann, A.E., Haersolte, J.C. Van and Meent, G.-W. Van de (eds) (1993), *Free Movement of Persons in Europe: Legal Problems and Experiences*, Martinus Nijhoff, Dordrecht.

Schioppa, F.P. (ed.) (1991), *Mismatch and Labour Mobility*, Cambridge University Press, Cambridge.

Schmidt, C.M. (1994), 'Immigration Countries and Migration Research: The Case of Germany', in G. Steinmann and R.E. Ulrich (eds), *The Economic Consequences of Immigration to Germany*, Physica-Verlag, Berlin, pp. 1-20.

Schmitter Heisler, B. (1992), 'The Future of Immigrant Incorporation: Which Models? Which Concepts', *International Migration Review*, vol. 26, pp. 623-45.

Schoeni, R.F. (1998), 'Labour Market Outcomes of Immigrant Women in the United States: 1970 to 1990', *International Migration Review*, vol. 31, pp. 57-77.

Scott, A.J. (1992), 'Low Wage Workers in High-Technology Manufacturing Complex: The Southern California Electronical Assembly Industry', *Urban Studies*, vol. 29, pp. 1231-46.

Secretaría de la Dona de CCOO (1994), 'Mercat Laboral i Treball Domèstic', in *Les Dones Immigrades Desafien la seva Invisibilitat: I Jornades sobre les Dones Immigrades*, Ajuntament de Barcelona, Barcelona.

Secretaría General de Turismo (1996), *El Turismo en Cifras*, Secretaría General de Turismo, Madrid.

Shaw, G. and Williams, A.M. (1994), *Critical Issues in Tourism: A Geographical Perspective*, Blackwell, Oxford.

Silva, J. A. and Silva, J. V. da (1991), 'Algarve: Crescimento Turístico e Estructuração de um Espaço Regional', *Sociedade e Território*, vol. 13, pp. 22-32.

Silva, M., Amaro, R.R., Clausse, G., Cónim, C., Matos, M., Pisco, M. and Seruya, L.M. (1986), 'Return, Migration and Regional Development in Portugal', in E.S. Ferreira and G. Clausse (eds), *Closing the Migratory Cycle: the Case of Portugal*, Verlag Breitenbach Publishers, Saarbrücken, pp. 1-30.

Simon, G. (1991), 'Une Europe Communautaire de moins en moins Mobile?', *Revue Européenne des Migrations Internationales*, vol. 7, pp. 41-59.

Sjaastad, L.A. (1962), 'The Costs and Returns of Human Migration', *Journal of Political Economy*, vol. 70, pp. 80-93.

Solana, M. and Pascual de Sans, À. (1994), 'Els Residents Estrangers a Espanya', *Documents d'Anàlisi Geogràfica*, vol. 24, pp. 169-80.

Solé, C. (1988), *Catalunya: Societat Receptora d'Immigrants*, Institut d'Estudis Catalans, Barcelona.

Solé, C. (1994), *La Mujer Inmigrante,* Ministerio de Asuntos Sociales. Instituto de la Mujer, Madrid.

Solé, C. (1997), *Immigrants' Labour Irregularities*, Paper presented in the 'Migcities Conference', 29-31 May 1997, Warwick.

Solé, C. and Herrera, E. (1991), *Trabajadores Extranjeros en Cataluña: ¿Integración o Racismo?*, Centro de Investigaciones Sociológicas/ Siglo XXI, Madrid.

Soler, I. (1995), 'IC-EV Muestra su Apoyo a los Inmigrantes en su Busca del Voto de Sectores Juveniles', *El País*, Catalan Edition, 5 November 1995.

Sopemi (1995), *Tendances des Migrations Internationales: Rapport Annuel 1994*, OCDE, Paris.

Sopemi (1997), *Trends in International Migration: Annual Report 1996*, OECD, Paris.

Stark, O. (1991), *The Migration of Labor*, Blackwell Publishers, Cambridge.

Taller de Estudios Internacionales Mediterráneos (ed.) (1996), *Atlas de la Inmigración Magrebí en España*, Universidad Autónoma de Madrid, Madrid.

Tamames, R. (1985), *Estructura Económica de España*, Alianza Editorial, 16th Edition, Madrid.

Tarrius, A. (1996), 'La Réussite des Clandestins: Marocains et Réseaux Souterrains de Travail, de l'Agriculture au Commerce International', *Espaces et Sociétés*, vol. 87, pp. 13-35.

Tienda, M., Jensen, L. and Bach, R. (1984), 'Immigration, Gender and the Process of Occupational Change in the United States 1970-80', *International Migration Review*, vol. 18, pp. 1021-44.

Tilly, C. (1990), 'Transplanted Networks', in V. Yans-McLaughlin (ed.), *Immigration Reconsidered: History, Sociology and Politics*, Oxford University Press, New York, pp. 79-95.

Todaro, M.P. (1969), 'A Model of Labor Migration and Urban Development in Less Developed Countries', *American Economic Review*, vol. 59, pp. 138-48.

Toharia, L. (1997), 'El Sistema Español de Protección por Desempleo', *Papeles de Economía Española*, vol. 72, pp. 192-213.

Torres, A. (1996), *História de uma Crise: O Grito do Bispo de Setúbal*, Notícias, Lisbon.

Tout, D. (1990), 'The Horticulture Industry of Almería Province, Spain', *Geographical Journal*, vol. 156, pp. 304-12.

United Nations (1997), *Annual Bulletin of Housing for Europe and North America*, United Nations, Economic Commission for Europe (UNU/ECE), Geneva.

Unwin, T. (1985), 'Farmers' Perceptions of Agrarian Change in North-West Portugal', *Journal of Rural Studies*, vol. 1, pp. 339-57.

Urry, J. (1990), *The Tourist Gaze: Leisure and Travel in Contemporary Societies*, Sage, London.

Vale, M. (1991), 'Pequenas Empresas e Desenvolvimento Territorial: Estructuras Produtivas, Medidas de Apoio à Indústria e Intervenção dos Municipios', *Finisterra*, vol. 26, pp. 361-395.

Valenzuela, M. (1991), 'Spain: The Phenomenon of Mass Tourism', in A.M. Williams and G. Shaw (eds), *Tourism and Economic Development*, Belhaven Press, London, pp. 40-60.

Vázquez-Barquero, A. (1992), 'Local Development and the Regional State in Spain', in G. Garofoli (ed.), *Endogenous Development and Southern Europe*, Avebury, Aldershot, pp. 103-16.

Venturini, M. (1991), 'Immigration et Marché du Travail en Italie: Données Récentes', *Révue Européenne des Migrations Internationales*, vol. 7, pp. 97-114.

Vicente, J. de (1993), 'Los Inmigrantes Negroafricanos en la Comunidad Autónoma de Madrid', in C. Giménez Romero (ed.), *Inmigrantes Extranjeros en Madrid: Estudios Monográficos de Colectivos Inmigrantes*, Comunidad de Madrid, Madrid, pp. 251-336.

Vieira, J.M. (1997), *A Economia do Turismo em Portugal*, Publicações Dom Quixote, Lisbon.

Villaverde Castro, J. (1996), 'Interprovincial Inequalities in Spain 1955-91', *European Urban and Regional Studies*, vol. 3, pp. 339-46.

Viñals, J. and Jimeno, J.F. (1997), 'El Mercado de Trabajo Español y la Unión Económica y Monetaria Europea', *Papeles de Economía Española*, vol. 72, pp. 21-36.

Waldinger, R. (1993), 'Le Débat sur l'Enclave Ethnique: Revue Critique', *Révue Européenne des Migrations Internationales*, vol. 9, pp. 15-29.

Waldinger, R. (1994), 'The Making of an Immigrant Niche', *International Migration Review*, vol. 28, pp. 3-30.

Wallerstein, I. (1974), *The Modern World-System*, Academic Press, New York.

Warnes, A. (1991), 'Migration to and Seasonal Residence in Spain of Northern European Elderly People', *European Journal of Gerontology*, vol. 1, pp. 53-60.

Werbner, P. (1987), 'Enclave Economies and Family Firms: Pakistani Traders in a British City', in J. Eades (ed.), *Migrants, Workers and the Social Order*, Tavistock Publications, London, pp. 213-33.

White, P. (1993), 'Immigrants and the Social Geography of European cities', in R.L. King (ed.), *Mass Migration in Europe: the Legacy and the Future*, Belhaven Press, London, pp. 65-82.

Williams, A.M. (ed.) (1984), *Southern Europe Transformed: Political and Economic Change in Greece, Italy, Portugal and Spain*, Harper & Row, London.

Williams, A.M. (1996), 'Mass Tourism and International Tour Companies', in M. Barke, J. Towner and M.T. Newton (eds), *Tourism in Spain: Critical Issues*, CAB International, Oxfordshire, pp. 119-35.

Williams, A.M. and Shaw, G. (1991), 'Western European Tourism in Perspective', in A.M. Williams and G. Shaw (eds), *Tourism and Economic Development*, Belhaven Press, London, pp. 13-39.

Williams, A.M. and Shaw, G. (1994), 'Tourism: Opportunities, Challenges and Contradictions in the EC', in M. Blackswell and A.M. Williams (eds), *The European Challenge: Geography and Development in the European Community*, Oxford University Press, Oxford, pp. 301-20.

Williams, A.M., King, R.L. and Warnes, A.M. (1997), 'A Place in the Sun: International Retirement Migration from Northern to Southern Europe', *European Urban and Regional Studies*, vol. 4, pp. 115-34.

Wilson, T. and Portes, A. (1980), 'Immigrant Enclaves: An Analysis of the Labor Market Experiences of Cubans in Miami', *American Journal of Sociology*, vol. 86, pp. 295-319.

Winkelmann, R. and Zimmermann, K.F. (1993), 'Ageing, Migration and Labour Mobility', in P. Johnson and K.F. Zimmermann (eds), *Labour Markets in an Ageing Europe*, Cambridge University Press, Cambridge, pp. 255-83.

World Tourism Organization (1985), *Methodological Supplement to World Travel and Tourism Statistics*, World Tourism Organization, Madrid.

World Tourism Organization (1988), *Economic Review of World Tourism: Tourism in the Context of Economic Crisis and the Dominance of the Service Economy*, World Tourism Organization, Madrid.

Zimmermann, K.F. (1994), 'The Labour Market Impact of Immigration', in S. Spencer (ed.), *Immigration as an Economic Asset: the German Experience*, IPPR/Trentham Books, Stoke-on-Trent, pp. 39-64.

Index